THE LEFT AT WAR

NEW YORK UNIVERSITY PRESS
NEW YORK AND LONDON

THE
LEFT

MICHAEL BÉRUBÉ

AT
WAR

NEW YORK UNIVERSITY PRESS
New York and London
www.nyupress.org

Library of Congress Cataloging-in-Publication Data
Bérubé, Michael.
The Left at war / Michael Bérubé.
p. : cm. — (Cultural front)
Includes bibliographical references and index.
ISBN–13: 978–0–8147–9984–0 (cl : alk. paper)
ISBN–10: 0–8147–9984–1 (cl : alk. paper)
1. United States—Foreign relations—1989- 2. Radicalism—United States.
3. Politics and culture—United States. 4. Right and left (Political science)
I. Title.
JZ1480.B48 2009
335.020973—dc22   2009023971

New York University Press books are printed on acid-free paper, and their
binding materials are chosen for strength and durability. We strive to use
environmentally responsible suppliers and materials to the greatest extent
possible in publishing our books.

Manufactured in the United States of America

10 9 8 7 6 5 4 3 2 1

CONTENTS

ACKNOWLEDGMENTS

WRITING THIS BOOK has been a thoroughly collaborative enterprise for me. Chris Robinson, a brilliant assistant professor of political science at Clarkson University (and, like me, a lifelong fan of the New York Rangers), read the first complete draft of the book and offered a ten-page critique of everything I'd written to that point. Bruce Robbins, Cary Nelson, and Danny Postel read the second complete draft and gave me the confidence to start the third; Matt Burstein, assistant professor of philosophy at the University of Pittsburgh–Johnstown, generously offered to read the second draft as well, even though he was juggling four classes per semester. He too responded with a ten-page critique of everything I'd written; indeed, it was he who suggested the term "Manichean left," and I have taken the suggestion. Amanda Anderson and Eric Zinner read the third draft and let me know how to tweak the fourth into its current form; Ben Carrington read the Stuart Hall chapter and festooned the margins with incisive and instructive notes; Christopher Lane gave me invaluably stringent feedback on a talk I delivered just as I was mapping out the plan of the book; and Larry Grossberg read the Stuart Hall and cultural studies chapters with a characteristically keen eye.

I thank my audiences and interlocutors at the Fernand Braudel Center at Binghamton University; Rice University; the University of Delaware; the University of Michigan Global Ethnic Literatures Seminar; Northwestern University; the Colorado Center for Public Humanities at the University of Colorado–Denver and the Lab at Belmar; the University of Texas at Austin; the Center for Interpretive and Qualitative Research at Duquesne University; Washington University in St. Louis; the Institute for the Arts and Humanities at the University of North Carolina; the University of California–Davis Center for History, Society, and Culture; and the English Department Colloquium at Johns Hopkins University for inviting me to present my work in progress—and for helping me to make progress on it. In the course of talking about this book with people across the country, I've relearned the truth in the Bakhtinian truisms: the word I speak is half another's, and I don't quite know what I believe until I enter into dialogue with people who do not share my beliefs. For their kindness, hospitality, intelligence, and dialogism, I'm especially grateful to Tobin Siebers, Geoff Eley, Peggy Somers, Immanuel Wallerstein, Richard C. Lee, Philip Joseph, Gillian Silverman, Adam Lerner, Evan Carton, Fred Evans, Rafia Zafar, John McGowan, Heidi Kim, Ari Kelman, and Eric Rauchway.

To Leo Casey, I owe thanks for many online conversations and one long talk in a Park Slope coffeeshop in the dark days of 2002–03, and for sending me his work on Schmitt, Hobbes, Dewey, and Gramsci. To Michael Walzer, I owe a singular debt of gratitude: after I mistakenly identified him as a supporter of war in Iraq in a *Boston Globe* essay of September 2002 (indeed, just before he published an essay in which he concluded that "the administration's war is neither just nor necessary"), he responded not by telling me to get a clue but by graciously inviting me to write for *Dissent.*

Though I began planning to write this book in 2002–03, I did not have a chance to start working on it seriously until the National Humanities Center offered me an Assad Meymandi Fellowship for the month of March 2006. Some year-long Center fellows asked me what I could possibly do with a mere month of fellowship time; I can now tell them that I had four glorious weeks in which to read from morning until night, collect my thoughts, make my notes, and even—sometimes—sit in silence. I had not realized until I arrived in the Research Triangle (North Carolina) that I have never, at any point in my adult life, lived alone; but I can say with gratitude that the experience of sitting in silence and thinking after reading for eight or ten hours is really quite extraordinary. I thank Geoff Harpham for making that experience possible.

In the fall of 2007, Laura Shackelford was working as a postdoc at Penn State; she is now an assistant professor at the Rochester Institute of Technology. For months, Laura ran down every obscure reference in this manuscript, making sure that the material I'd cited really exists and can be found by other researchers. For her diligence and for the good cheer with which she tackled even the most elusive citations, I will be forever grateful.

Last but first, I thank Janet Lyon for discussing and debating these issues with me over the years and for being my partner in this as in all things, even where she disagrees with me about this, that, and the other; I thank Nick for being Nick, a reliable, sensible, and razor-sharp young man who will brook no nonsense about globalization and electoral politics; and I thank Jamie, as always, for being Jamie, and for reminding me that a world that embraces and empowers the Jamies among us is a world worth struggling for.

INTRODUCTION   ON TIME

THIS IS, I HOPE, an untimely book. Though I began thinking about it in the darkest days of the Bush-Cheney administration, 2002–03, I write these prefatory words in the opening moments of 2009, when those days now seem to many a hideous, aberrant period best forgotten. For after the historic events of 2008, all that is solid has seemed to melt into air: against all odds, the United States has elected its first black president, an exceptionally talented centrist-liberal with the unlikely name of Barack Hussein Obama, and much of the rest of the world has hailed his election as a hopeful sign that the Bush-Cheney regime will now be decisively repudiated, along with its corrosive lawlessness at home and abroad. And one of the reasons for Obama's election, perhaps, was the dramatic (if long-delayed) implosion of the housing and credit markets in the United States, which has sparked a truly global crisis in capitalism and bespeaks what Michael Lewis and David Einhorn call "the end of the financial world as we know it."

Why, then, bother with a book on the problems that continue to ail the U.S. left? However few leftists the Democratic Party may include, it seems undeniable that Democrats have finally broken the forty-year Republican stranglehold on the presidency (save for the electoral flukes known as Jimmy Carter and Bill Clinton, no darlings of the left they) and have at long last rendered the Deep South irrelevant to national politics; indeed, a map of U.S. counties that voted more heavily Republican in 2008 than in 2004 reveals a GOP that is strongest in the aging, overwhelmingly white districts of the lower Allegheny Mountains and the Ozarks—not a hopeful demographic sign for conservative strategists (Carter et al., "Shifts in the Map"). Still further south, the replacement of brutal fascist dictatorships in South America with democratically elected leftist leaders suggests that the tide has finally turned throughout the hemisphere, and the right is now on the defensive. Around the world, the collapse of the global financial system demonstrates the profound instability of unregulated capitalism. In such times, surely, a book on the left's troubles is out of step, out of place.

But I believe the argument of this book might be valuable precisely for its untimeliness; for it is a response not merely to an electoral cycle or to the world after 9/11 but to hard-left habits that have festered unaddressed for decades. Most of the books in the "what's wrong with the left" subgenre have, perhaps understandably, focused on world events since 2001, when al-Qaeda's attacks on the World Trade Center and the Pentagon—and the Bush-Cheney response to the attacks, culminating in the invasion of Iraq—shocked the world and induced crises for the left, both in the United States and throughout Western Europe. The phenomena I take up in *The Left at War*, however, predate and provide the conditions for the left's response to the Bush-Cheney Global War on Terror; they testify to the existence of a kind of cold war within the left itself, a cold war that turns hot—and becomes broadly legible—only when an actual U.S. war breaks out, whether in the Balkans in the 1990s or in Iraq after 2003. For example, it is now clear that there are severe divisions in the left over the concept of "humanitarian intervention," especially (but not exclusively) when the intervention in question is led by the United States and involves the U.S. military; but it is notable that most anti-interventionists, who opposed war in the Balkans (wrongly, I believe) and in Iraq (rightly, I believe), have had nothing compelling or cogent to say about massacres in Rwanda, Sudan, or the Congo, largely because no U.S. military force was involved one way or the other in those massacres.

My diagnosis of the left does not confine itself to its responses to U.S. foreign policy or to the world since 9/11; rather, I call attention to three important strands of recent leftist thought that underlie those responses.

The first, upon which I am hardly the first to remark, involves a kind of postcolonial bad conscience about criticizing such things as the Iranian persecution of gay men or the Taliban's treatment of women, on the grounds that such criticism (a) serves U.S. propaganda purposes and (b) replays the imperialist script of (in Gayatri Spivak's memorable phrase) white men saving brown women from brown men—or saving brown gay men, as the case may be. This strand of leftist thought goes back before 9/11 to intense debates about the relation of Western feminism to non-Western cultures, particularly with regard to controversial practices such as clitoridectomy or *sati*; it affected Western leftists' response to the 1979 Islamic revolution in Iran (dramatically, in the case of Michel Foucault; Afary and Anderson, *Foucault and the Iranian Revolution*) as well as to the fatwa pronounced against Salman Rushdie a decade later.[1] At least two factors are in play here, and at critical times they exacerbate each other: a pernicious and opportunistic form of cultural relativism, according to which even those nations that are signatories to the U.N. Declaration of Universal Human Rights are held to be so radically different from "us" that "we" cannot ethically assess their policies with regard to universal human rights; and a blinkered sense that the enemy of my enemy may turn out to be my friend, even if "my enemy" is the American right and their enemies include radical Islamists.

The second strand is almost never remarked on in this context; I hope this book will help remedy that. It involves a mode of belief, a way of believing, rather than a set of beliefs; it is the work of a *countercultural* left that sees popular politics as a game rigged by corporations and the process of winning popular consent as a form of "selling out." Of course, these are themselves beliefs, beliefs about the way public persuasion works in modern mass societies; but the countercultural left is marked more by its attitude toward public persuasion than by the specific content of any of its desires. It offers a dizzying range of ideas, mostly good ones, about everything from sustainable energy to fair labor and trade practices to alternative music and film; the only thing that constitutes it as a countercultural left is that it becomes uncomfortable whenever its ideas win the consent of more than a tiny fraction of the public. As long as its beliefs are shared by 2 or 3 percent of their fellow citizens, all is well; but the minute one of its ideas is adopted more widely, then the countercultural purists—call them the Two or Three Percenters—know that the field must necessarily be abandoned to the callow pragmatists and hangers-on who will compromise with anyone about anything in order to "cross over" to the masses.

The last strand entails a radical distrust of (amounting, in some circles, to an aversion to) modern ideas of liberal democracy and the Enlightenment tradition on which they rest. Only occasionally does this aspect of leftist thought emerge into public view, and then only when it is ignorantly condemned by the right as a form of Soviet apologetics. But there are no longer any serious U.S. leftists who hanker for the return of the Soviet Union; rather, the antiliberal left takes care to acknowledge the errors and atrocities of communism while insisting that the idea of liberal democracy's triumph, whether touted by Francis Fukuyama or Richard Rorty, represents a drastic foreshortening and constriction of the human political imagination. Mere liberal democracy, in other words, is thin gruel, served up by tepid wimps who can't imagine anything tastier or more satisfying. This is a supple and versatile complaint: on the one hand, it can be launched from anywhere, because the complainant never has to specify just what kind of society should replace the boring, procedural liberal democracy that constrains us; on the other, it can be mobilized to any end, even—at an extreme—to provide cover for profoundly antiliberal forms of government in the Islamic states or in the developing world.

Because this form of leftist thought is so widely misunderstood, I will provide one notable contemporary exponent of it rather than simply summarizing it, as I have for strands one and two. For many on the academic/theory left in the United States, Slavoj Žižek has become the contemporary political-theoretical intellectual par excellence; he is indisputably brilliant and insanely prolific, and no one else can combine his dazzling readings of Hitchcock films with romantic-revolutionary denunciations of "liberal-democratic hegemony." But more to the point, his dismissal of Hannah Arendt at the outset of *Did Somebody Say Totalitarianism?* offers some idea of his agenda for the left:

> Until two decades ago, Leftist radicals dismissed her as the perpetrator of the notion of "totalitarianism," the key weapon of the West in the Cold War ideological struggle: if, at a Cultural Studies colloquium in the 1970s, one was asked innocently, "Is your line of argumentation not similar to that of Arendt?", this was a sure sign that one was in deep trouble. Today, however, one is expected to treat her with respect. . . . This elevation of Arendt is perhaps the clearest sign of the theoretical defeat of the Left—of how the Left has accepted the basic co-ordinates of liberal democracy ("democracy" versus "totalitarianism," etc.), and is now trying to redefine its (op)position within this space. The first thing to do, therefore, is fearlessly to violate these liberal taboos: *So what* if one is accused of being "anti-democratic," "totalitarian" . . . (2–3; second ellipsis in original)

Underneath Žižek's formidable theoretical sophistication there is a quite simple knee-jerk reflex at work: if the opposition between democracy and totalitarianism favors the liberal-democratic West, then it is the job of leftist radicals to deny it. The proper democratic left response to this, whether undertaken from the West, East, North, or South, is to suggest that if the elevation of a figure like Hannah Arendt is the clearest sign of the theoretical defeat of the left, then it was a well-deserved defeat, too long in coming—however much one might sympathize with the twinge of radical nostalgia for the heady days when one could cow one's interlocutors in cultural studies symposia into an embarrassed silence by linking them to Arendt's work.

Toward the end of *Contingency, Hegemony, Universality,* a series of essays by and exchanges between Judith Butler, Ernesto Laclau, and Žižek, Laclau offers a simple challenge:

> In his previous essay, Žižek had told us that he wanted to overthrow capitalism; now we are served notice that he also wants to do away with liberal democratic regimes—to be replaced, it is true, by a thoroughly different regime which he does not have the courtesy of letting us know anything about. One can only guess. . . . Does he want to replace liberal democracy by a one-party political system, to undermine the division of powers, to impose the censorship of the press? (288)

Žižek's reply is remarkable for its inability to describe that "different regime": refusing "today's liberal blackmail that courting any prospect of radical change paves the way for totalitarianism," Žižek writes, "It is my firm conviction, my politico-existential premiss, that the old '68 motto *Soyons réalistes, demandons l'impossible!* still holds" (326). As a political platform, surely this leaves much to be desired—and surely that is precisely its point, to leave everything to desire.

FOR A DEMOCRATIC LEFT

The crimes of the Bush-Cheney regime beggar description. After 9/11, Cheney's authoritarianism and obsession with secrecy took a grotesque turn, with the development of the "one percent doctrine," (Suskind, *One Percent Doctrine*)[2] the conviction (buttressed by a reliance on conspiracy theorist Laurie Mylroie) that Saddam Hussein had some connection to the attacks, and, most grievously, with the development of a worldwide archipelago of torture sites from Guantánamo to Abu Ghraib and beyond. Bush-Cheney will—or, at least, *should*—be remembered as the worst president and vice president in U.S. history, with all of Richard Nixon's love of clandestine foreign operations and domestic spying programs but with none of Nixon's concessions to Keynesian economics or the social welfare state; they will also be remembered as the only administration to suspend habeas corpus *and* institute indefinite detention and torture as (unacknowledged) U.S. policy. Indeed, the atrocities committed by the Bush-Cheney administration around the globe, directly and through proxies (via "extraordinary rendition"), are so vile as to obscure many of the other travesties Bush and Cheney have visited on us—from their denials and evasions with regard to global climate change, to their totalitarian theory of the "unitary executive" that overrides the constitutional separation of powers, to their use of that theory to issue "signing statements" that undermine acts of Congress, to their payoffs to journalists and filming of faux "news" stories shipped to media outlets and run as free ads for administration policies, to their wholesale corruption of the Department of Justice.

Why, then, should such an analysis of the U.S. left be cogent now, after the post-Katrina public repudiation of Bush-Cheney, after the election of Obama and the repudiation of the revanchist right, after the onset of the global financial crisis? Because the left of which I write is indifferent to what it calls the "corporate duopoly" of electoral politics in the United States, believing the process to be at once hopelessly corrupted and peripheral to the larger, deeper movements of culture and society; it is not merely indifferent but actively hostile to Obama himself, casting him as a double-talking Republican and insisting—not without reason—that he will simply be a better manager of the American Empire. And because this left, welcoming the financial crisis as final confirmation of its long-held beliefs, has no effective answer to the global economic crisis, no investment—if you will pardon the phrase—in creating national and international regulatory systems that will prevent capitalism from eating itself and scorching the earth.

I have wondered for many years just what to call this left. "Far left" is clearly inadequate, for it suggests—to all too many leftists—that the user of the term is one of those pusillanimous "moderate" leftists (perhaps even a noxious "liberal") who shrinks from grappling with the hard truths of imperialism and exploitation; it leaves in place the idea that this left's evasiveness with regard to tyranny and genocide belong "on the left" in any sense whatsoever; and it cedes rhetorical ground to lefter-than-thou partisans who assume that "further left" simply means "more better." "Radical left" won't do, either, for some of the same reasons; it also plays into the left's long romance with radicalism, which runs from Ché Guevara t-shirts to solemn etymological assurances that radicalism gets "to the root" of the problem. More importantly, I have no desire to criticize radicalism *tout court*, since there are times—and the histories of the labor movement, the civil rights movement, and the "new" social movements of the 1960s furnish many examples of those times—when radicalism makes perfect political sense, even in pragmatic terms. Likewise, I do not designate this left as "anti-imperialist," because, as an anti-imperialist, I have no desire to undermine anti-imperialism; rather, I believe that much of this left uses the rhetoric of anti-imperialism as a cloak for something much less admirable, and I hope to bear out this charge in the course of this book. Is it then a *conservative* left, responding to every new global crisis by chanting forty-year-old mantras about being reasonable and demanding the impossible? A *reactionary* left, equivocating about the stoning of women rather than asserting universal human rights? An *academic* left, confined to a string of college campuses? None of these seems right; the last is especially problematic, since much of the radical left in the United States has nothing but contempt for the kind of poststructuralist theorizing common to the properly "academic" left.

Instead, I adopt the term "Manichean left." For the Manichean left, as for the Manicheans of the early Christian era, there are two forces in the world, those of good and evil, and everyone and everything that is not on one side is on the other. The opening chapter of this book furnishes a few examples of the phenomenon: if Israel is in the wrong, then Hezbollah must be in the right (and, as the Manichean-left slogan of the 2006 war in Lebanon had it, "we are all Hezbollah now"); to criticize the U.S. war in Afghanistan, one must defend the Soviet invasion of Afghanistan; and to oppose the U.S. war in Iraq, one has no choice but to support the Iraqi resistance. The term "Manichean," in such cases, is self-explanatory—though the reasons behind the Manicheanism are not, and will require some explanation as well as repudiation.

And yet I will not repudiate the entire left of the past forty years; far from it. Instead, I want this book to lead readers to go back and investigate some overlooked paths on the democratic left—primarily those of Ellen Willis, in the United States, and (more complexly) Stuart Hall, in the United Kingdom. I devote chapter 4 exclusively to Hall's work on Thatcherism, in the belief that it is not sufficiently recognized or understood by American leftists outside the small academic circles in which the history of British cultural studies is well known and oft-rehearsed; but I weave Willis's arguments on culture and society throughout the book as well, noting whenever possible the surprising and illuminating concordances between her thought and that of Hall. For Hall and Willis are not only writers in a democratic-socialist tradition that is itself deserving of greater public recognition; even within that tradition, they stand out for the original and brilliant way they discerned—and forged—the connections between cultural politics and global politics. And if I manage to convince my readers of nothing more than the proposition that the work of Stuart Hall and Ellen Willis deserves closer attention from liberals, leftists, and even some conservatives, I will consider this extended exercise in left self-criticism to have been worth the effort.

I would nevertheless like to convince my readers of a bit more than this, if I can. I would like to convince them that international or supranational forms of governance are going to be indispensable in the twenty-first century; and I would like to convince them that, when members of the Manichean left attacked the International Criminal Court as a "kangaroo court" for putting Slobodan Milošević in the dock, the defenders of Milošević worked to undermine an important, emergent form of internationalism. I would like to convince them that the United Nations was right, in 2005, to approve the idea that state sovereignty entails a "responsibility to protect" vulnerable people within state borders and that sovereigns who violate that responsibility by massacring their peoples forfeit their sovereignty; and I would like to convince them that members of the Manichean left who invoked Serbian sovereignty in the Balkans, and who opposed even U.N. weapons inspections and no-fly zones as violations of Iraqi sovereignty, worked to undermine another important, emergent form of internationalism. The nativist right wing tries to undermine such things all the time; it is horrified at the prospect that great powers might be constrained by international law, just as Margaret Thatcher was horrified at the 1998 arrest of Augusto Pinochet in the United Kingdom. But that's the nativist right's job—to use "sovereignty" as a rationale for anything and everything from preemptive war to indefinite detention and torture camps; the left's job should be to find ways of persuading people—even people who believe in the rightness of their nation—that there are better ways of governing the world. And that, most of all, is what I would like to convince you.

NOWHERE LEFT TO GO

THIS BOOK IS an attempt to bring the history of cultural studies to bear on questions of U.S. foreign policy and international relations. My topics range from Stuart Hall's work on the rise of Thatcherism to America's post-9/11 wars in Afghanistan and Iraq; from mid-1990s debates over multiculturalism and popular culture to late-1990s debates over war in Kosovo; from theories of ideology and hegemony to theories of humanitarian intervention and the "responsibility to protect." If this collocation of cultural studies and global conflict sounds strange, it is no doubt—as I argue in these pages—because much of the history of cultural studies, which began with the crisis of British imperialism in the Suez and the crisis of Soviet imperialism in Hungary, has been forgotten or trivialized in the past two decades.

The first half of my argument addresses debates that are familiar to observers of world politics after 9/11: the question of whether the United States should have responded to al-Qaeda with military action in Afghanistan, and the question of whether the United States should have then proceeded to invade Iraq. While it is truly remarkable—and speaks to a profound crisis in the left's self-definition—that people who opposed both wars and people who supported both wars can plausibly claim to be "on the left" (even as each camp denies the other's claim), I imagine that much of my readership will be well acquainted with the phenomenon and the polemics associated with it. The second half of my argument, however, may prove a bit more elusive to observers of world politics, even as it addresses debates that are familiar to scholars in cultural studies. For I argue that there are two dramatically different approaches to understanding the debates I discuss in the first half. One school of thought holds that American mass media, as the instruments of corporate oligarchy, "manufacture" popular consent for imperialist crusades abroad and reactionary social policies at home. The other school of thought holds that popular consent—even popular consent to imperialist crusades and repressive social policies, even popular consent granted by people who stand to gain

nothing from such crusades and social policies—is *won* rather than manufactured, and that it is won by means of struggles and strategies undertaken not only in the state apparatus but in the many and various institutions of civil society.

The consequences of these approaches are decisive, but their implications for international politics have not been well understood. Among
cultural studies theorists, for example, it is widely agreed that the first approach to the interpretation of politics and culture, which is associated
with an emphasis on political economy, is narrow and reductive: in its insistence that the meaning of a cultural artifact can be determined largely
by asking who owns the means of its production, it leads inexorably to
the conclusion that people misidentify their real interests because they are
led to do so by the corporate media. Critics of cultural studies, in turn,
claim that an inattention to political economy leads inexorably to the jejune conclusion that people always manage somehow to escape the logic
of the corporate media, even if only in the most oblique and private ways.

But I argue in these pages that the stakes are rather higher than this.
The advocates of analysis of "the political economy of the mass media" (to
cite the subtitle of Edward S. Herman's and Noam Chomsky's landmark
book, *Manufacturing Consent*), have an enormous interpretive advantage
over their opponents, and, indeed, over the rest of the field of cultural and
political critique, for they can always resort to the claim that their opponents (and everyone else in the field of cultural and political critique) are
ensnared in false consciousness. Thus Herman and Chomsky advance a
"propaganda model" of media, according to which "the media serve, and
propagandize on behalf of, the powerful societal interests that control and
finance them" (xi). By contrast, the neo-Gramscian school of thought associated with cultural studies can make no such claim about the power of
the corporate media to hornswoggle the masses: as Stuart Hall has noted,
"though there are people willing enough to deploy the false consciousness
explanation to account for the illusory behavior of others, there are very
few who are ever willing to own up that they are themselves living in false
consciousness! It seems to be (like corruption by pornography) a state always reserved for others" ("Toad in the Garden," 44).

A central feature of my argument, then, is the proposition that there
is a stark conflict between the work of Stuart Hall and the work of Noam
Chomsky. And at the center of that conflict, in turn, is the very concept of
"false consciousness"—and the crucial cultural and political work it per-
forms. For as Hall has long argued, the concept serves as a blanket excuse

for the left's failures to win over a significant fraction of the public: the left's problem lies not in the message or the messenger, on a Chomskian analysis, but in the system that prevents the message and the messenger from being heard. Indeed, the stronger the belief in the all-encompassing power of that system, the stronger the belief that the truth of a proposition can be gauged by its distance from the system.

This countercultural logic is one of my targets in this book, not only because it is inadequate to the way the world really works (in which one finds both cogent and insane propositions lurking at the same distance from the mainstream) but also because it has licensed the worst kind of moral contortions on the Manichean left—the kind in which leftists like Ed Herman and Diana Johnstone deny the crimes of Serbian ethnic cleansing and the regime of Slobodan Milošević on the grounds that the mainstream media are suppressing the truth about the Balkans; the kind in which conspiracy theorists ply their trade, safe in the knowledge that every challenge to their reasoning confirms their reasoning. The consequences for leftist thought in the United States have been devastating. At just the time when the United States needed a vigorous and widespread popular dissent from the depredations of the Bush-Cheney regime, the Manichean left stepped forward with a form of critique which holds that the United States is responsible for the emergence of al-Qaeda, that the war in Afghanistan is one of the most grotesque acts of modern history, and that anyone who demurs from these judgments is either an apologist for imperialism or a moral imbecile.

I believe that the Manichean left has lost sight of what should be the central emphases of the left: the advocacy of equality and freedom, the yin and yang of democratic theory and practice. I believe that the Manichean left has been willing to entertain (and sometimes even to sympathize with) any "anti-imperialist" who comes along to challenge the Western powers, from Milošević to Hassan Nasrallah of Hezbollah to Mahmoud Ahmadinejad. And I believe that some wings of the Manichean left have blurred the line between legitimate criticism of the murderous policies of the state of Israel (especially its ethnic cleansing of the Occupied Territories) and illegitimate and indiscriminate anti-Semitism. But the conflict I see between Hall and Chomsky bears only indirectly on these beliefs. The salient difference between Hall and Chomsky, as theorists of and on the left, involves how to think about political conflict.

For Chomsky, as for media theorists like Robert McChesney and social critics like Tom Frank, the reason that the left remains a tiny minority in the United States is that so many people are living in false consciousness about their true interests. According to this line of thought, only a few people have the time, the training, and the desire to pierce the veil of ideology and see the truth as in itself it really is. But this is *precisely* what Hall asks us not to believe about our fellow political animals. Yes, people are lied to by politicians and pundits, and, yes, the lies often take root: witness the millions of Americans who believe that Saddam Hussein was responsible for the attacks of 9/11 and that the United States uncovered weapons of mass destruction in Iraq. But by adopting the belief in "false consciousness" *as an axiom,* the left commits itself to a pernicious logic in which to win is to lose and vice versa: the more people disagree with you, the more right you must be—not only about those people and their illusions, but about the all-encompassing system in which they live, the System that prevents them from seeing the naked truth as we enlightened people do.

Pernicious though it may be, this logic is remarkably adaptable; it can be applied to almost any field of human endeavor, and when the left succumbs to the temptation, as it too often does, it usually does so in order to insist that the people have been blinded to the economic realities that should rightly determine their consciousness of the world. For example, in the left debates of the 1990s over "real politics" and "cultural politics," the proponents of the former held that the advocates of the latter were distracting people from realizing how conservative fiscal policies were working against them. In response, at the outset of her 1999 book, *Don't Think, Smile!,* Ellen Willis suggested that the appeal of "class-first" leftism lies partly in the fact that it can be hauled out again and again whenever the left suffers a political setback:

> When Ronald Reagan was elected in 1980, a wide assortment of liberals and leftists called for unity around a campaign for economic justice. Since then, as the country has moved steadily rightward, I have heard this call repeated countless times, along with many hopeful announcements of projects designed to put it into practice. Each time the right wins an egregious victory (as in the congressional elections of 1994), dozens of lefty commentators rush into print with some version of this proposal as if it were a daring new idea. . . . You would think that if economic majoritarianism were really a winning strategy, sometime in the past eighteen years it would have caught on, at least a little. Why has it had no effect whatsoever? Are people stupid, or what? (ix)

Stuart Hall could have supplied the answer: no, people are not stupid. As far as the class-first theorists and commentators are concerned, they have simply succumbed to false consciousness—like corruption by pornography (to draw on another subject of Willis's work, in which she refused the "false consciousness" theories of antiporn feminism), a state always reserved for others.

Of course, within the metaconflict over false consciousness are substantial conflicts about whether the Manichean left or the democratic left has a more adequate vision of the world. How does each wing of the left think about terrorism, about failed states, about human rights? The Manichean left has lately argued that the United States is a leading sponsor of terrorism, is itself a failed state, and uses the cover of human rights for a program of imperial conquest. The democratic left, for its part, is undeceived about U.S. crimes in the world and knows that, at its worst (though not always and everywhere), the United States does indeed clothe vile foreign policies in the language of "freedom" and "democracy"; but it insists that some forms of terrorism and some failed states have root causes other than those associated with U.S. imperialism, and that the promotion of human rights remains a legitimate task for theorists of international relations. *You Can't Be Neutral on a Moving Train,* we are told in a powerful documentary about the life and work of radical historian Howard Zinn; but as left internationalists learned in the 1990s, you can't be neutral in the middle of a genocide, either. For when the international community failed to act in Rwanda in 1994, it effectively weighed in on the side of the Interahamwe and the Impuzamugambi Hutu militia groups. At stake in the conflict between the Manichean left and the democratic left, in other words, is not just a theoretical dispute about how to conceive of hegemony, ideology, and the idea of false consciousness; there is also the question of how the international community should respond to crises in Rwanda, the Balkans, Sierra Leone, Zimbabwe, Sudan, and Afghanistan. Part of my argument in this book, accordingly, is that in response to post-Soviet crises of sovereignty and legitimacy around the world, the Manichean left has had nothing very pertinent or useful to say—except in the Balkans, where their part in the debate has actually been shameful: more concerned with opposing NATO than with addressing the phenomenon of "ethnic cleansing."

But why should such an argument about the Manichean left and the democratic left be hooked up to an argument about cultural studies? In the course of writing this book, I have heard many varieties of this question:

at a cultural studies conference not long after the invasion of Iraq, I heard one speaker after another declare that the time had come for cultural studies to turn away from culture and pay attention instead to neoliberalism. The economic base had returned at last, it seemed; it was determining in the last instance after all, and its name was neoliberalism. Finally, the monocausal explanation we had long mocked but secretly desired! And it's true, neoliberalism is a nasty thing, responsible for bad trade agreements and brutal austerity programs and the strengthening of plutocrats around the globe. But in a great deal of cultural criticism lately, it seems to be taking on the role of Explanatory Scheme of Last Resort—which is, once again, evidence of the kind of lazy leftist thinking Hall and Willis warned us against a generation ago. (There is also the uncomfortable fact that few academic-left critics of neoliberalism have bothered to make the case for neoliberalism's antidote, the expansion of the social welfare state, committed as they are to one or another variety of Foucauldian-anarchist critique.)

At other times, I've been asked whether cultural studies isn't *constitutively* out of the loop when it comes to thinking about global conflicts, insofar as its purview is the "cultural." To that objection, I have two answers. One is to suggest that cultural studies has always been devoted to the questions of how to understand the relation between cultural and economic phenomena and how cultural processes work toward political ends. (Lying deep inside those inquiries, in turn, is the very question of what constitutes the "cultural" and the "political.") The other is to cite an incisive essay Willis published not long before her untimely death, which argues that the global culture wars are nothing less than the seismic shocks of secular modernity in conflict with entrenched religious, sexual, and political traditions:

> The renewed cultural revolt known as "the 60s" had its epicenter in the United States, but its impact was felt worldwide. Feminism is a global movement, American mass culture with its invitations to sexual and other material pleasures is everywhere, and the vast increase in all manner of transnational interchange attendant on globalization ensures that almost nowhere on earth are people insulated from the challenges of secular cosmopolitanism to traditional religious and patriarchal authority as well as to nationalism and the preservation of local culture. The reaction, in turn, has not been confined to the United States and the Christian right. Militant fundamentalism in the Islamic

world and its European diaspora is the most conspicuous, violent form
of global backlash, but there is also right-wing Catholicism in Eastern
Europe, ultra-orthodox Judaism in Israel (and its Brooklyn diaspora),
evangelicism in Latin America and South Africa, Hindu and Sikh fundamentalism in India. ("Escape from Freedom," 9).

Cultural change and cultural conflict have profound implications for international politics, and the American democratic left should not let this
terrain of debate be dominated by the xenophobic right.

Following Willis's lead, then, I want to challenge both the democratic
and the Manichean left to think more seriously and more substantially
about the history of cultural studies, and I want theorists in cultural studies to think more seriously about the world of international relations. For
I want, above all, to try to imagine a new form of left internationalism. In
doing so, I want to make the case that in order to think globally, we need
to think culturally—and that in order to understand cultural conflict, we
need to think globally.

MANICHEAN HABITS OF MIND

In 2006, University of Chicago historian Moishe Postone published an
important essay in *Public Culture,* in which he argued that the Manichean
left's response to 9/11 consisted largely of "inadequate and anachronistic
'anti-imperialist' conceptual frameworks and political stances" left over
from "the dualisms of a Cold War framework that all too frequently le-
gitimated (as 'anti-imperialist') states whose structures and policies were
no more emancipatory than those of many authoritarian and repressive
regimes supported by the American government" (96). Postone further
argued that the Manichean left failed to take adequate measure—despite
their talk of "root causes" and "teaching moments"—of precisely who attacked New York and Washington on that day and why:

> The most general argument made was that the action, as horrible as it
> may have been, had to be understood as a reaction to American poli-
> cies, especially in the Middle East. While it is the case that terrorist
> violence should be understood as political (and not simply as an ir-
> rational act), the understanding of the politics of violence expressed
> by such arguments is, nevertheless, utterly inadequate. Such violence

is understood as a *reaction* of the insulted, injured, and downtrodden, not as an *action*. While the violence itself is not necessarily affirmed, the politics of the specific form of violence committed are rarely interrogated. Instead, the violence is explained (and at times implicitly justified) as a response. Within this schema, there is only one actor in the world: the United States. ("History and Helplessness," 97)

The same holds true, on a larger scale, for the 1979 Islamic Revolution itself (or, more precisely, the hijacking of the revolution by radical Islamists), which is sometimes understood on the Manichean left to be an understandable response to the CIA's overthrow of Mohammed Mossadeq in 1953; for while it is true that the Iranian revolution was deeply anti-American, thanks to U.S. support for the Shah and Savak, his brutal secret police, it is also true that Islamist radicalism has a longer trajectory and broader reach than that. Postone writes:

It is a serious error, for example, to interpret the felt grievances underlying a movement like al-Qaeda in narrow terms, as an immediate reaction to American policies and Israeli policies. This ignores too many other dimensions of the new jihadism. For example, when Osama bin Laden speaks of the blow inflicted on the Muslims eighty years ago, he is not referring to the founding of the state of Israel but to the abolition of the caliphate (and, hence, of the purported unity of the Muslim world) by Ataturk in 1924—long before the United States was involved in the Middle East and before Israel was established. It is noteworthy that the vision he expresses is more global than local, which is one of the salient features of the new jihadism, in terms of both the struggles it supports (transforming them into manifestations of a single struggle) and its driving ideology. And an important aspect of the global character of that ideology has been anti-Semitism. (98)

I think Postone is right on both counts: the Manichean left's response to the events of September 11 was in part a hangover from the Cold War, and it failed to come to terms with the history of Islamism or the specific motivations and desires of groups such as al-Qaeda. Moreover, Postone is right to take up the question of anti-Semitism and to distinguish it from legitimate criticism of the state of Israel:

Addressing anti-Semitism is crucially important when considering issues of globalization and antiglobalization, even if it can be subject to
misunderstandings because of the degree to which the charge of anti-
Semitism has been used as an ideology of legitimation by Israeli regimes in order to discredit all serious criticisms of Israeli policies. It is
certainly possible to formulate a fundamental critique of those policies
that is not anti-Semitic, and, indeed, many such critiques have been
formulated. On the other hand, criticism of Israel should not blind
one to the existence today of widespread and virulent anti-Semitism
in the Arab/Muslim world. . . .

This development should be taken seriously. It should neither be
treated as a somewhat exaggerated manifestation of an understandable
reaction to Israeli and American policies, nor should it be bracketed as
a result of the dualistically grounded fear that focusing on it can only
further Israeli occupation of the West Bank and Gaza. (98–99)

Postone argues that "the spread of anti-Semitism and, relatedly, anti-Semitic forms of Islamicism (such as the Egyptian Muslim Brotherhood and
its Palestinian offshoot, Hamas) should be understood as the spread of a
fetishized anticapitalist ideology which claims to make sense of a world
perceived as threatening" (101). Like Ellen Willis, Postone sees Islamism
and other forms of religious fundamentalism as reactionary backlashes in
the face of globalization, capitalism, and secular modernization.

And like Postone, Willis did not shy away from the question of anti-
Semitism in her discussion of the "root causes" of 9/11—even as she made
clear that her criticism of global anti-Semitism did not mute her criticism
of Israeli policy in the Occupied Territories. In her 2003 essay, "Is There
Still a Jewish Question? Why I'm an Anti-Anti-Zionist," Willis writes:

I believe that anti-Jewish genocide cannot be laid to rest as a discrete
historical episode, but remains a possibility implicit in the deep structure of Christian and Islamic cultures, East and West.

This last point is particularly difficult to argue on the left, where
the conventional wisdom is that raising the issue of anti-Semitism in
relation to Israel and Palestine is nothing but a way of stifling criticism of Israel and demonizing the critics. In the context of left politics, the dynamic is actually reversed: accusations of blind loyalty to
Israel, intolerance of debate, and exaggeration of Jewish vulnerability

at the expense of the real, Palestinian victims are routinely used to sti-
fle discussion of how anti-Semitism influences the Israeli-Palestinian
conflict or the world's reaction to it or the public conversation about
it. Yet that discussion is crucial, for there is no way to disentangle the
politics surrounding Israel from the politics of the Jewish condition.
Anti-Semitism remains the wild card of world politics and the light-
ning rod of political crisis, however constantly it is downplayed or denied. My anti-anti-Zionism does not imply support for Ariel Sharon's
efforts to destroy the Palestinians' physical, political, and social infra-
structure while expanding Jewish settlements in occupied territory; or
the disastrous policy of permitting such settlements in the first place;
or the right-wing nationalism cum religious irredentism that has come
to dominate Israeli politics; or, indeed, any and all acts of successive
Israeli governments that have in one way or another impeded negotiations for an end to the occupation and an equitable peace. Nor do I
condone the American government's neutrality on the side of Sharon.
But I reject the idea that Israel is a colonial state that should not exist. I reject the villainization of Israel as the sole or main source of the
mess in the Middle East. And I contend that Israel needs to maintain
its "right of return" for Jews around the world. (226)

It is in this context, I suggest, that we should regard a recent book,
published in the United States, that speaks of "Jews disproportionately
represented in the financial, political, professional, academic, real estate,
insurance and mass media sectors of the American economy" (Petras,
Power of Israel, 40). Surely, one would think, it is the work of a fringe
far-right figure like David Duke, or perhaps an unguarded moment from
a mainstream far-right figure like Patrick Buchanan. But then when one
finds that these ubiquitous Jews are to blame for the derailing of the antiwar movement with regard to Iraq, it becomes sickeningly clear that the
author of the book imagines that his critique of "Zioncons" is a critique
from the left:

> The leaders of the peace movement, both Jews and non-Jews alike,
> reject any effort to include Israel's genocidal war against Palestine for
> fear of alienating the "public" (read the major Jewish organizations)
> and the self-styled progressive Jews, who are ever protective of every-
> thing Jewish—even war crimes. Worse still, with few rare exceptions,
> the "progressive" Jewish critics of the war and Israel are forever and

adamantly determined to avoid criticizing the role of powerful Zionist policymakers in the government, their ties to Israel and the significant support they receive from the major Jewish organizations in all matters which pertain directly or remotely to Israeli interests. . . .

Jews in North America, South America and Europe are disproportionately in the highest paid positions, with the highest proportion in the exclusive, prestigious private universities, with disproportionate influence in finance and the media. It is clear that "anti-Semitism" is a very marginal global issue and, in point of fact, that Jews are the most influential ethnic group.

The tragic myopia or perverse refusal of Leftist Jews to face up to the prejudicial role of the major Jewish groups promoting the Israel First policy and imposing it on the electoral agendas substantially undermines their and our efforts to secure peace and justice in the Middle East and to forge a democratic U.S. foreign policy. (56–57)

The author, it turns out, is James Petras, a scholar of Latin American history and politics with a long and distinguished history on the anti-imperialist left in the Western hemisphere; but this argument is not a random aside in a book about U.S. crimes in Central America. Sadly, it is central to a book called *The Power of Israel in the United States,* published in 2006 by Clarity Press.

But should Petras seem too marginal a figure for analysis, let me turn to a passage from an academic leftist widely (and rightly) respected for his work on contemporary theory and postcolonialism, writing on the Balkans rather than on 9/11 or the Middle East. This passage comes from a book whose subtitle is *The Cultural Politics of Left and Right,* and in which the cultural politics of left and right are confounded almost from the outset:

It is not surprising that embedded in the term "East/West" is sedimentary evidence of a longstanding tendency in the West to associate the racial with the socialist other. . . . This previous common sense is what now allows many to take stock of the collapse of the Soviet (or "Eastern") bloc by noting that various nationalisms have taken over for socialism as the enemies of U.S. Realpolitik— one way of looking, certainly, at the bombing of Yugoslavia in the early 1990s, whose unruly Slavic actors (from the mainstream U.S. point of view) stand in quite readily for the Soviets in ways that go beyond their defiance of the U.S. government or their supposedly criminal actions. They are *like* the Soviets, they look like them to U.S. eyes, they speak a language "like" Russian, they have the same religion, they are not quite European in the same way as are our NATO allies, they are from the same peripheral region to the east of the Europe that counts. (Brennan, *Wars of Position*, 42, 44)

The author is University of Minnesota cultural critic Timothy Brennan, and the main title of the book is *Wars of Position*; here, in mapping the Balkan wars, Brennan asks us to believe that NATO intervened in the Balkans because the Serbs were racially unlike "us." (He also asks us to believe that the 1999 Kosovo war took place in the "early 1990s"—and as we will see in chapter 3, this fudging of historical detail allows the Manichean left to ignore the fact that Western Europe and the United States did nothing about Serbian aggression in the Balkans until it was far too late, thus effectively siding *with* Milošević for most of the 1990s and actually rewarding the Serbs at Dayton in 1995.) Presumably, for Brennan, U.S. eyes managed to recognize brothers and sisters in Bosnian Muslims and Kosovar Albanians, while somehow disavowing Serbs as the Soviet Other. One especially notes, with regard to Brennan's fanciful map of Americans' affective affiliations in the Balkans, the phrases "unruly Slavic actors (from the mainstream U.S. point of view)" and "their supposedly criminal actions." One is invited here to imagine that the Serbs had been indicted by the mainstream United States merely for their unruliness and their defiance, that the history of Serbian ethnic cleansing in the Balkans is of no account, and that the massacre in Srebrenica was merely *supposedly* criminal.

Brennan testifies eloquently to Postone's claim that "anti-imperialist" leftists are working with conceptual categories left over from the Cold War; but remarkably, Brennan's account of the Balkans doesn't even make sense in the terms on which Brennan predicates his book's argument. At the outset of *Wars of Position*, Brennan argues that in the West, anti-Muslim sentiment and anticommunism have much in common:

Prejudice toward left belief cultures tends to be overlaid upon more well-known imaginative geographies that were first developed in eighteenth- and nineteenth-century colonial discourses. They were perfected in the political showdown between left and right traditions during the interwar era (from which most of today's intellectual leads derive). An example might clarify what I mean: An article appeared in the *New York Times* in February 2005 titled "Europe's Muslims

May Be Headed Where the Marxists Went Before." Its purpose was to warn Europe's Muslims to end their "ideology of contestation" if they wanted to avoid Marxism's fate of irrelevance. This history of conso- nance between attacks on belief and attacks on culture is rarely ex- plored in any depth, however. The slippage from anti-red to anti-Mus- lim sentiments takes place to most observers, left and right, as though it were a wholly natural phenomenon. (xii)

If you start from the premise that anti-red and anti-Muslim sentiments are readily mapped onto each other by Western imperialists (shaky as that premise is, buttressed only by a *New York Times* essay whose content Bren- nan mischaracterizes),[1] it would seem impossible to argue that the United States and NATO came to the aid of Bosnian and Albanian Muslims be- cause they were like "us," whereas the Serbs too closely resembled the Soviets. Undeterred by the contradiction, Brennan glosses over the gory details of genocide and ethnic cleansing in the Balkans and assures us that his is "certainly" one way of looking at "the bombing of Yugoslavia."

By adducing the two disparate examples with which Petras and Bren- nan provide us, I hope to call attention to two intersecting phenomena: one, in the case of Petras, the adoption, on the Manichean left, of extremist positions on Israel more properly (though I wish I could say "exclusively") associated with the far right; two, in the case of Brennan, the adoption, on the academic left, of woefully underinformed and ideologically disfigured positions on the Balkans—positions that depend (for their cogency and their claim to the moral high ground) in part on their distinction from "liberal" internationalists (many of whom, like leftists Richard Falk and Ian Williams, are not accurately described as "liberals") whose opposition to ethnic cleansing is construed as craven capitulation to U.S. imperial- ism. One curious and noxious offshoot of the latter phenomenon is that writers who seek to position themselves on the putatively leftmost (most virtuous) side of a question often wind up substantially distorting the po- sitions of other writers on the left, construing them as complicit with any number of evils, up to and including the evil of mere liberalism.

It may seem strange at first that writers on the left, marginalized as they are in American political life, would seek to construe themselves as even more marginal than they already are, but this tactic of "removing the proximate first," as Brennan puts it (even as he engages in it), makes sense if you seek a very pure and very tiny left that consists only of lone voices in the wilderness. Indeed, in the course of his discussion of "the organizational imaginary" (and lack thereof) on the left, Brennan craftily positions himself to the left of fellow cultural critic Eric Lott:

> Making fun of [Richard] Rorty for droning on about the virtues of Ir-
> ving Howe even as Rorty busily ignores A. Philip Randolph (a good
> point there), Lott holds up for praise such "bona fide intellectuals" as
> Lani Guinier in order to demonstrate Rorty's narrow focus. But the in-
> vocation of Guinier in this context is odd. Whatever her considerable
> merits as a legal voting strategist, Guinier is a paradigm of Clinton lib-
> eralism, an uncritical fan of Janet Reno, her mentor, who is a politician
> that the Left and Right alike should have wanted in jail for her crimi-
> nal handling of the events in Waco. (*Wars of Position*, 167)

By the end of this overheated passage, Lani Guinier has been rendered almost as an accessory to the debacle at Waco; the metonymic skid of guilt-
by-association moves at near-light speed, so that by the time we're through
the paragraph, we may have forgotten that, in reality, Lani Guinier was
not a "paradigm of Clinton liberalism" at all. On the contrary, her serious
and devoted efforts to enforce the Voting Rights Act and enhance racial
justice in America's many rotten boroughs placed her so far outside the
Clinton paradigm that Clinton, to his eternal discredit, dropped Guinier's
nomination to the post of U.S. Assistant Attorney General for Civil Rights
even before the Senate had begun to review her. Clinton liberalism does
not find its paradigm in Lani Guinier; on the contrary, Clinton liberalism
finds its paradigm in the act of throwing Lani Guinier under the bus. But
because the object of the game here is to stake out a position to Lott's
"left" by citing the correct African American intellectual (Brennan sees
Lott's A. Philip Randolph and raises him a Lani Guinier: one can only
respond by seeing Brennan's raise and countering with Manning Marable,
Adolph Reed, or Robin D. G. Kelley), Guinier's work on voting rights
gets a dismissive, gestural subordinate clause so that we can get on to the
important work of associating her with Janet Reno and the horrific siege
of Waco.[2]

But Guinier is merely collateral damage in this attack; Brennan is after bigger game, upping the ante on Eric Lott's broad-brush indictment of
"Boomer Liberals" even as he acknowledges that Lott fails to address the
boomers' justified querulousness about the fragmentation and disorgani-
zation of the left. Thus, only one page before he associates Lani Guinier
with the siege at Waco, Brennan positions boomer avatar Todd Gitlin as

an imperialist stooge in a parade of liberal horribles that makes as much political sense as Lott's linking of Greil Marcus to Joe Klein:

> To talk about liberal racism and white ideology is never irrelevant, but in this context it misses a more important point. The subtlety of these particular charges obscures the real reasons one should have animus toward the boomer crew: Rorty's nativist patriotism, for example; Berman's right-wing fascination with left-wing causes and celebrities; Gitlin's Zionism and his apologies for U.S. imperial intervention in Iraq, Latin America, and elsewhere. What ought to be challenged is the claim of some of these fellows to *any* Left. (*Wars of Position*, 166)

I surmise that Gitlin is included in this lineup not for "his apologies for U.S. imperial intervention in Iraq, Latin America, and elsewhere" (for he was, of course, among the most vocal and visible opponents of war in Iraq, and he never supported any feature of U.S. imperial policy in Latin America), but because in 1995, he published *The Twilight of Common Dreams*, which placed him decisively on the wing of the left that (mistakenly, in my opinion) sought to blame "cultural" politics for the fragmentation of the left. Unfortunately, the positions of Lott's "boomer liberals" with regard to the cultural politics of 1995 do not map very well onto the terrain of George Bush's War on Terror: both Gitlin and Rorty opposed the Iraq war from the start, whereas Paul Berman wound up among the most prominent liberal advocates of war—insisting in venues such as *Slate* magazine and the *New York Times* that "this war has always been central to the broader war on terror" ("Will the Opposition Lead?"). I do not quite know what to to make of Brennan's reference to Gitlin's "Zionism," since, for all the thoughtcrimes he may have committed in *The Twilight of Common Dreams*, Gitlin has been consistently critical of the Likud wing of Israeli politics, fiercely opposed to its cheerleaders in the United States (ranging from Martin Peretz to Alan Dershowitz to Daniel Pipes) and a consistent opponent of Israel's settlements in the Occupied Territories.

Israel and Palestine are, of course, the third rail of left politics after 9/11, and, especially after the Lebanon war in the summer of 2006, the rhetoric of anti-Israel sentiment on the left became positively toxic. At the time, I maintained a blog that was devoted to culture and politics and all things relevant thereto, and in July I ventured to suggest that Israel's bombing of Lebanon was "disproportionate and profoundly counterproductive," following this in my comment section by saying that Israel's response to Hezbollah was "morally illegitimate" because of the degree of civilian casualties it entailed.[3] My general convictions are on the subject are as follows: I support a Palestinian state and full Israeli withdrawal from the Occupied Territories, and I think of the 1982 invasion of Lebanon and the 1995 murder of Yitzhak Rabin as unmitigated disasters for Israel, just as I think of the collapse of the Camp David talks in 2000, whatever the reason Yasser Arafat could not or would not respond to Ehud Barak's offer of land for peace (and however insufficient or incomplete that offer may have been, from some pro-Palestinian perspectives), as an unmitigated disaster for Palestinians. However, I also favor the disarmament of Hezbollah, and I believe that Israel has the right to respond to armed attacks—within reason. I quickly learned, therefore, that my condemnation of Israel's conduct in the 2006 war was not nearly good enough for some on the Manichean left. Within a mere six hours, my blog post had earned the following comment:

> Sort of like labelling the Nazi response to the Reichstag fire "German's [sic] disproportionate and profoundly counterproductive response to the latest Dutch anarchist outrages," isn't it?

When I objected to the implicit Israelis = Nazis trope animating this remark, my critic reappeared to explain that I had misunderstood him. It turned out that he was not likening the Israelis to Nazis; rather, he was likening me to Nazi apologists:

> But as you know very well, this trope is not a = b (Israelis = Nazis). The trope is x:a::y:b. Those who cluck their tongues about Israel's "overreaction" to Hizbullah terrorism are analogous to those who clucked their tongues about the NSDAP's "overreaction" to the communist torching of the Reichstag.
>
> 1933: "I agree, the Communist menace in Mitteleuropa must be stopped, but the Reichskanzler's reaction to the fire has been disproportionate and profoundly counterproductive."
>
> 2006: "I agree, Hizbullah's terrorism must be stopped, but the Prime Minister's reaction to the kidnapping has been disproportionate and profoundly counterproductive."
>
> Liberal moral cowardice, right across the board. Is there a difference? Sure. In 1933, the Center Party honorably refused to support the Reichstag Fire Decree. In 2006, HRC [Hillary Rodham Clinton]

has announced unequivocal support for this slaughter. No doubt you'll be sending her a check in two years' time. The plague take you all.

This is a stunning series of remarks, no doubt; but why should I resort, in a book such as this, to recounting exchanges in blog comment sections? We all know that the Internet is full of crazy people with too much time on their hands, and comment sections can be filled with the random effusions of angry anonymous trolls. The truly remarkable thing about this blog exchange, though, is that my interlocutor was one Professor Michael McIntyre. McIntyre was then the director of the International Studies Program at DePaul University, but he took the time to show up on my blog and tell me that I am akin to post-Reichstag Nazi apologists for not condemning Israel's bombing of Lebanon with the full-throated vehemence he considers appropriate. I thought at the time that this was a striking example of overheated lefter-than-thou Internet polemic, but I have since come to believe that what ought to be challenged, with a tip of the hat to Tim Brennan, is the claim of some of these fellows to *any* left at all.

But Israel-Palestine is not the only crisis to which the Manichean left has responded in this way. It has provoked some of the left's most regrettable spectacles in recent years, from the attempts by radical British academics to boycott Israeli universities and dismiss Israeli scholars from the boards of scholarly journals, all the way to the "we are all Hezbollah now" posters in the streets of London during the July 22, 2006, anti-Israel protest, to which George Galloway responded, "Hezbollah has never been a terrorist organization. I am here to glorify the Lebanese resistance, Hezbollah, and to glorify the resistance leader, Sheik Hassan Nasrallah" (quoted in "New Terror Law Comes into Force").[4] If Israel were the only issue, then perhaps rhetoric like this could be taken as the regrettable but understandable response to the forty years of occupation and persecution to which Palestinians have been subject, compounded by the breakdown of anything like a plausible peace process in this century as the policies of the United States and Israel in the Middle East have been controlled—as has too much of the public debate in the United States—by the hawkish right. (The extent to which nominally "pro-Israel" positions are now the preserve of radical Christian extremists in the United States should be of concern to anyone who has any interest in the legitimacy and the future survival of the state of Israel.) Unfortunately, however, the phenomenon in which the Manichean left takes up positions that should properly be associated with the far right is a good deal more widespread. Three remarkable examples will suffice for now.

BUSH AND BIN LADEN A COMPARATIVE STUDY

In February 2005, in the course of a rambling essay on Ward Churchill, Z magazine founder and publisher Michael Albert argued that although Osama bin Laden has a moral calculus that "sane people will reject," Bush and Cheney are still worse—on the grounds that they deliberately planned the invasion of Afghanistan ("Raise Your Voice but Keep Your Head Down"). Albert rued the fact that Ward Churchill, in suggesting that the World Trade Center dead deserved their fates, "provided right wingers fodder they could manipulatively use"; curiously, however, he then proceeded to provide right wingers with still more fodder:

> Since 9/11 at public talks I often compare George Bush and Osama bin Laden. I note that if you could have been a fly on the wall of the inner circle meeting rooms of the U.S. government leading up to the bombing of Afghanistan, I believe you would have heard no discussion, not even a minutes worth, taking into account the well being of the Afghan people in the face of possible massive starvation induced by our assault. Mass media at the time reported (on back pages only) that bombing Afghanistan could lead to five million deaths. No mainstream paper had a headline "United States contemplates killing millions to prove we are tough," though all knew it was true.
>
> I also indicate in the public talks that if I were to now have the opportunity to ask bin Laden how he could possibly have chosen to undertake the assault on the Twin Towers, despicable as this act was, I think he would probably understand the question and would reply, roughly, that he thought the gains (in trying to propel the United States into reactions that would provoke fundamentalism throughout the Mideast) were worth the price in human loss. Bin Laden, as evil as his designs surely were and are, would understand, that is, that there was something untoward that occurred on 9/11, piles of corpses, and that the negative deaths had to be weighed against what he saw as positive political gains. Sane people will reject his moral calculus, of course, but I am guessing that at least he had one.

On the other hand, I say in these talks that if I were to now have the opportunity to ask Bush and Cheney how they could possibly have chosen to undertake the bombing of Afghanistan, I think they would not even understand the question. They would not see any need to weigh off benefits against costs because they saw no costs. For them the general estimates made by all responsible parties that literally millions of Afghans might suffer starvation if bombing were to commence counted for naught. For them, Afghans are like bugs outside our front door are for the rest of us. To Bush and Cheney Afghans are expendable. Bush and Cheney have no moral calculus. They reduce humans to the status of fleas.

First, I note in fairness that Albert never explicitly expresses any "support" for or "solidarity" with bin Laden; he does not go nearly as far with al-Qaeda as Galloway will, one year later, with Hezbollah. Nevertheless, what precisely is the object of this bizarre thought experiment? The claim that the rationale for war in Afghanistan and attacks on al-Qaeda's training camps was really "United States contemplates killing millions to prove we are tough" is too childish for debate, but certainly (as I discuss more fully in the next chapter) there was a danger that the war could significantly aggravate the misery of millions of Afghans, and in fall 2001 it was not unreasonable to say so. But then why go so much further than this as to claim that bin Laden ranks a bit higher on the moral scale than Bush and Cheney *on the grounds that you have had an imaginary conversation with him?* Allow me to stress this aspect of Albert's essay for a moment, because there are two levels of foolishness at work here. The first involves the comparison itself, which was something of a standard trope among the Z-*Counterpunch* left at the time: Bush and bin Laden, twin fundamentalists—or, as Arundhati Roy had it, bin Laden as "the American president's dark doppelgänger" ("Algebra of Infinite Justice"). Albert merely ups the ante a bit, construing the American president's dark doppelgänger as just a tad morally superior to the American president himself.

But the second level of foolishness is mind-bending, insofar as this "guess" about bin Laden's moral calculus rests on nothing—no knowledge of his motives and designs, no understanding of Islamist radicalism, no empirical evidence whatsoever—outside of Michael Albert's imagination. What political effect is this kind of rhetoric supposed to produce? One can ask this question about Ward Churchill's "little Eichmanns" remark as well: as far as I know, very, very few Americans read Churchill's essay, "Some People Push Back," slapped their foreheads, and said, "by George, he's right! The World Trade Center dead *were* comparable to Eichmann—because, after all, some of them worked in global finance! Why didn't I see it before?"

I suspect that remarks like Albert's and Churchill's were not, finally, meant to turn ordinary Americans against the Bush-Cheney regime. Rather, they partake of both phenomena I described above—in which "left" intellectuals adopt extremist positions and proceed to compete with each other for the title of Most Oppositional.

ALL HAIL THE IRAQI *MAQUIS*

Characteristically, for leading figures on the Manichean left, it is not sufficient to oppose the Iraq war. Rather, one must support the Iraqi "resistance," whatever that is, and one must do so in the most emphatic terms possible:

> Washington's military-imperialist thrust into Central Eurasia, at first deplored by right-minded pillars of the status quo as an over-reaching adventure, has become the basis of a new world consensus: the hegemon must not be allowed to fail. The first, elementary step against such acquiescence is solidarity with the cause of national liberation in Iraq. The US-led forces have no business there. The Iraqi *maquis* deserves full support in fighting to drive them out. (Watkins, "Vichy on the Tigris," 17)

This is the conclusion of Susan Watkins's "Vichy on the Tigris," the lead essay of the July/August 2004 issue of the *New Left Review*. Here, the unproblematic penultimate sentence—that U.S.-led forces have no business in Iraq—sits uncomfortably between two thoroughly problematic ones. For why should opposition to the war entail support for the Iraqi "resistance"? That resistance, of course, was and is not one homogeneous thing; it consists of various strands and factions, some of which should not be endorsed by any secular leftist. But Watkins does not differentiate among Kurds and Ba'athists and Shi'ite clerics; nor does she lament (or even note) the fact that the U.S. invasion of Iraq strengthened the hand of some of the most reactionary and theocratic forces in the region. Rather, from her essay's title to its final sentence, she treats the resistance as if it were the French resistance of World War II. "Iraqi *maquis*" is a mellifluous phrase, I admit. But morally repellent all the same.

The corollary analogy, needless to say, is that the U.S.-led forces are like unto the Nazis, and frequent *Nation* contributor Daniel Lazare spelled it out in so many words in a debate with David Horowitz on the *Michael Medved Show* in December 2004.[5] The premise of the debate was drawn from Horowitz's 2004 book, *Unholy Alliance: Radical Islam and the American Left*, which, as you might imagine, accuses the American left of having forged an unholy alliance with radical Islam. Remarkably, Lazare, in toeing the "Vichy on the Tigris" line, manages to confirm Horowitz's argument— and then volunteers to "go further":

> MEDVED: Daniel Lazare, would you like to see the elections scheduled for January 30 in Iraq fail?
> LAZARE: I'm totally opposed to what the United States is doing in Iraq. Therefore, I would no more support U.S. elections than I would support German elections in France during World War II.
> MEDVED: So you're sticking with this comparison of the United States to Nazi Germany?
> HOROWITZ: He is, because he believes it in his soul.
> LAZARE: I believe it. I believe it entirely.

After Lazare utters this plaintive credo, Medved, who professes to find it "stunning," goes to commercial break, and when the debate resumes, Lazare proceeds to dig himself a bit deeper:

> MEDVED: Okay. This is what I find so clarifying about this. Very often, when I have people representing the Left on this radio show, they dissemble, they hide. You're straight out there. You've said unequivocally you think America today in Iraq and presumably around the world is like the Nazis under Hitler.
> LAZARE: Well, actually, I'll go further. No, I think David and you, too, Michael, have done a really great service. You really have clarified things really, very well. I don't say that Bush is Hitler. I'm not drawing an equation, obviously, but I am drawing a comparison. And not only am I drawing a comparison that his attack on Iraq was comparable to Hitler's on Poland, but I quite agree that the millions of people who took to the streets in protest against the invasion of

Iraq were motivated by this perspective. That was precisely why they took to the streets because they saw in Bush's actions a frightening parallel with the events that occurred, what, 65 years earlier in Europe. And so he's absolutely correct. I think Hitler had probably more reason to attack Poland than Bush had to attack Iraq.

MEDVED: David Horowitz?

HOROWITZ: Well, I hope people are listening because this is a validation of the case I have made in my book.

A bit later on, in response to Medved's question, "Are there any good guys currently engaged in trying to counteract the murderous Islamic extremists?" Lazare bravely nominates himself, saying, "You're actually talking to one of the few leftists, if I do say so myself, with the courage to defend the Soviet incursion in Afghanistan." It is a strange debate strategy, to be sure—confirming your antagonists' weakest and wildest charges, then going the extra mile to rank the invasions of Poland and Iraq so that the judgment comes out in Hitler's favor, then donning the drab and tattered garb of the Soviet apologist. But even more objectionable, perhaps, is Lazare's insistence that he speaks for all "the millions of people who took to the streets in protest against the invasion of Iraq." Even Horowitz, for all his mudslinging, never went as far as to suggest that antiwar protesters believed that the United States was the moral equivalent of Nazi Germany— except insofar as the Nazis possibly had some reason to attack Poland. So it is not quite fair to say that Lazare does Horowitz's and Medved's work for them in this debate; rather, Lazare also accomplishes a few rhetorical tasks that neither Horowitz nor Medved had attempted up to that point.

And yet Lazare is merely embellishing the argument often made by Watkins (and her husband, Tariq Ali); a slightly more nuanced version of that argument—one that acknowledged some of the complexities of the "resistance"—was made throughout 2004 by Arundhati Roy. Though Lazare (like Petras) is a relatively obscure figure in U.S. left politics (but unlike Petras, is a frequent contributor to the *Nation*), and though *New Left Review* remains marginal to most U.S. debates, Arundhati Roy is an icon, widely cited and revered by much of the antiwar movement around the globe. Interestingly enough, some of Roy's more widely cited remarks in support of the Iraqi resistance are couched as critiques of the idea of political purism: "I just feel that that resistance in Iraq is our battle too and we have to support it," she said in an August 2004 interview with Sonali

Kolhatkar for Z magazine. "And we can't be looking for pristine struggles in which to invest our purity" (quoted in Kolhatkar, "Superstars and Globalization"). I happen to agree with the latter half of this formulation; it is among the political lessons I draw from Stuart Hall's analyses of Thatcherism ("Toad in the Garden"). But the idea that we "have to" support the resistance in Iraq is quite another thing. In a lecture delivered not long before the Kolhatkar interview, Roy said:

> The Iraqi resistance is fighting on the frontlines of the battle against Empire. And therefore that battle is our battle.
> Like most resistance movements, it combines a motley range of assorted factions. Former Baathists, liberals, Islamists, fed-up collaborationists, communists, etc. Of course, it is riddled with opportunism, local rivalry, demagoguery, and criminality. But if we are only going to support pristine movements, then no resistance will be worthy of our purity. (Roy, "Tide? Or Ivory Snow?")

Roy is right in one respect: the "resistance" contains any number of people and factions no secular, feminist, gay-friendly democrat should support. But by this logic, perhaps it is worth supporting other compromised and unsatisfactory causes that are made of a motley range of assorted factions and riddled with opportunism, local rivalry, demagoguery, and criminality; perhaps it might even have been worth supporting the Democrats' efforts to unseat George Bush in 2004, since that movement included a few laudable secular, feminist, gay-friendly factions here and there. Unfortunately, Roy didn't agree that her logic applied to American politics in this way:

> It looks as though even if Americans vote for Kerry, they'll still get Bush. President John Kerbush or President George Berry.
> It's not a real choice. It's an apparent choice. Like choosing a brand of detergent. Whether you buy Ivory Snow or Tide, they're both owned by Proctor & Gamble.
> This doesn't mean that one takes a position that is without nuance, that the Congress and the BJP [Bharatiya Janata Party (India)], New Labor and the Tories, the Democrats and Republicans are the same. Of course, they're not. Neither are Tide and Ivory Snow. Tide has oxy-boosting and Ivory Snow is a gentle cleanser.

And, one might add, neither Tide nor Ivory Snow is really as "pure" as they claim, either.

Still, the contrast is striking: when the movement in question consists of a mainstream U.S. political party trying to defeat the consortium of autocrats, torturers, Christian fundamentalists, messianic neoconservatives, and Contra-funding 1980s retreads that made up the Bush-Cheney administration, we wash our hands of it and fall back on witticisms about laundry detergents; but when the political movement in question includes radical Islamist clerics and murderous Ba'athist thugs, we eschew ideological purity and practice a flexible coalition politics. Because, after all, their struggle is ours, and we have to support it.

FRINGE CONSIDERATIONS

Iraq, Israel-Palestine, and 9/11 have drawn most of the attention of the Manichean left, and with good reason. But there are plenty of other subjects on which that left has gone off the rails. One might, for instance, expect to find paeans to Mahmoud Ahmadinejad (including dewy-eyed invocations of him as "my Persian Prince") among writers on the radical Islamist right; but it should be alarming to learn that one of Ahmadinejad's biggest fans, Yoshie Furuhashi by name, is in fact the editor of the online magazine of the *Monthly Review,* one of the leading journals of the American socialist left since 1949 and currently the home of writers like Robert McChesney and John Bellamy Foster.

Likewise, it is no surprise to find Slobodan Milošević partisans among Serbian nationalists, arguing that Milošević was the victim of Western imperialism, bombed into submission and forced to appear before a kangaroo court; but it should be alarming to learn that the International Committee to Defend Slobodan Milošević was headed by Michael Parenti, still a respected figure on the *Z-Counterpunch* left, and included luminaries such as the late Harold Pinter and former U.S. Attorney General Ramsey Clark. Indeed, there is an offshoot of the "defend-Slobodan" enterprise on the *Z-Counterpunch* left, headed by Ed Herman and dedicated to the proposition that the massacre of roughly eight thousand unarmed Bosnian men and boys at Srebrenica in 1995 never really happened in quite the way reported by the mouthpieces of "Western propaganda" (which include, for Herman's purposes, the United Nations, Doctors Without Borders, and Human Rights Watch).

And in October 2007, the *Monthly Review* devoted an entire issue to what it called Edward Herman's and David Peterson's "definitive critique at this stage both of the U.S./NATO role in the exploitation and exacerbation of the Yugoslavian tragedy and of the 'Western Liberal-Left Intellectual and Moral Collapse' that made this possible." Furuhashi's work on the *Monthly Review* website is not confined to effusions about the anti-imperialist virtues of Ahmadinejad; she has also taken the lead in pointing out that antigenocide rallies for Darfur are driven by, among other things, the U.S. appetite for oil and "an odd alliance of evangelicals and establishment Jews" ("Notes from the Editors").[6]

These may sound like the fulminations of a fringe, the kind of thing one expects to see from people lining subway stations with wheat-paste posters that consist of stunning exposes of how the Trilateral Commission, with the help of the Rothschilds, killed famed martial artist Bruce Lee. But I have been careful, in selecting the preceding examples, to choose material only from publications—*Z, New Left Review, Monthly Review*—that are widely respected on the left. Indeed, many left fringes exist beyond these precincts, but I do not treat them here. I do not, for example, discuss the most infamous (and arguably the most vocal) of these fringes, the so-called Scholars for 9/11 Truth; nor do I address any aspect of the theory that the Bush-Cheney administration helped, passively or actively, to orchestrate the attacks of that day. Leaving aside the simplest point—namely, that if the Bush-Cheney administration *had* had a hand in those attacks, one would think that they would at least have gone to the trouble of making the link to Iraq and Saddam Hussein look plausible (thereby obviating the need for dark whispers about clandestine meetings in Prague between Mohammed Atta and an Iraqi agent and Iraqi attempts to purchase yellowcake from Niger)—I believe that 9/11 conspiracy theories should simply be allowed to take their rightful place alongside theories that John Hinckley's attempt to assassinate Ronald Reagan was staged, that the United States never really flew space missions to the moon, and that the CIA killed John Lennon. Many people will continue to believe these things regardless of what I write, and I do not see the point of engaging their beliefs.

For my purposes, it is quite bad enough that, when George Bush was greeted at his vacation ranch in Crawford, Texas, on the morning of August 6, 2001, by a CIA official bearing a briefing headlined, "Bin Laden Determined to Strike Inside U.S.," Bush responded by telling his briefer, "All right, you've covered your ass, now." It is quite bad enough that Bush then refused to testify before the 9/11 Commission under oath and had to be accompanied by Dick Cheney in giving secret testimony. Those facts, by themselves, are sufficiently damning, and they should have been sufficient to expel Bush and Cheney from office; they do not need to be embellished hysterically by people who are somehow convinced that the administration that gave you the epically botched response to Hurricane Katrina and the world-historical debacle in Iraq somehow pulled off one of the most elaborate and efficiently orchestrated terrorist attacks in history.[7]

Although the Scholars for 9/11 Truth have a few adherents here and there in academe's very-leftward precincts, they have nothing like the intellectual respectability of the publications I cite above. I therefore find them no more worthy of my attention here than are the followers of reclusive Revolutionary Communist Party Chairman Bob Avakian, whose writings are of some interest to members of his cult following, and whose cult following is of some interest to observers of the radical left, but who has no impact whatsoever on the direction of the left. Likewise, if I wanted to engage with the divagations of the radical left online, I would include figures like Louis Proyect, a Columbia University computer programmer whose name is well known to far-left listservs and blogs, and who is capable of writing things like, "To the credit of the late Slobodan Milošević and to Saddam Hussein, who now is on trial for his life in another kangaroo court, they never bowed down. In life and in death, these imperfect men will always remind us of the need to resist the injustice perpetrated by states acting out of perfect evil" ("Demonization and Death of Slobodan Milošević"). But for the purposes of this book, figures like Proyect, Avakian, and the "Truthers" are effectively off the radar. In these pages I discuss (briefly) only one such "fringe" group, Act Now to Stop War and End Racism (ANSWER), a curious offshoot of the neo-Stalinist Workers World Party, and only because this group managed to organize and set the agenda for the mass demonstrations against the Iraq war in 2002–03.

WHERE I'M CALLING FROM

Compiling such a list of leftist follies is no fun—and often leaves one's readers and interlocutors wondering whether the object of the compilation is to discredit the left altogether. I cannot imagine a reasonable reader who, upon completing this book, would attribute such a motive to me, since my purpose here is to defend and elaborate a democratic, international U.S. left that opposes U.S. world hegemony and seeks to create and enforce supranational means of securing human rights. Nevertheless, to dispel any unnecessary confusion, I conclude this chapter by explaining my angle of orientation.

I am on the social-democratic left with regard to domestic economic policy: "democratic" because I do not see how one can fully nationalize an economy without creating an enormous and repressive state apparatus, "social-democratic" because I believe that without a measure of practical *equality* with regard to fundamental human needs, *freedom* is just another word for nothing left to lose. On international matters I believe that we all bear the obligation to devise multilateral and global institutions to deter threats to peace (be they the Soviet invasion of Afghanistan, the Iraqi invasion of Kuwait, or the U.S. war in Vietnam) and to protect vulnerable populations everywhere on the planet—from tyranny, genocide, starvation, and scorched-earth neoliberalism. As I argue in *What's Liberal about the Liberal Arts?* I believe that all humans born should be considered to have equal claim on certain (ungrounded) human rights such as food, shelter, education, health care, and political representation; and because I believe that none of these rights should be contingent on an individual's capacity to use them or ability to pay for them, I support a strong public welfare state that makes public accommodation for people who would otherwise lack them. My regulative ideal is that of "participatory parity," and I believe that every form of discrimination based on race, gender, age, sexual orientation, and disability constitutes a violation of the principle of participatory parity. (I return to this in chapter 5, when I discuss "cultural" politics and "real" politics.) The ideal of participatory parity, as I understand it, entails not only a program of universal health care but also a defense of progressive taxation of income and investments, both to prevent the accumulation of great wealth in a few hands (and the consequent degeneration of democracy into plutocracy and oligarchy) and to create a social welfare state whose task it is to ensure that the life chances of individuals are not radically dependent on mere accidents of birth.

I am therefore more comfortable with normative political philosophy than I am with the kind of antinormative (or, as some critics have suggested, cryptonormative) critiques associated with poststructuralism (Anderson, "Cryptonormativism and Double Gestures"). For example, I like the formulation of "complex equality" that Michael Walzer sets out near the end of *Spheres of Justice:*

The appropriate arrangements in our own society are those, I think, of a decentralized democratic socialism; a strong welfare state run, in part at least, by local and amateur officials; a constrained market; an open and demystified civil service; independent public schools; the sharing of hard work and free time; the protection of religious and familial life; a system of public honoring and dishonoring free from all considerations of rank or class; workers' control of companies and factories; a politics of parties, movements, meetings, and public debate. But institutions of this sort are of little use unless they are inhabited by men and women who feel at home within them and are prepared to defend them. It may be an argument against complex equality that it requires a strenuous defense—and a defense that begins while equality is still in the making. But this is also an argument against liberty. Eternal vigilance is the price of both. (318)

Of course, it is always possible (and usually necessary) to argue that pluralistic liberal-democratic states are not pluralistic, liberal, or democratic *enough;* but in order to mount that argument, one has to accept the premise that there are pluralistic, liberal, and democratic norms that ostensibly pluralist liberal-democratic states are flouting. Nowhere is this clearer than in Judith Butler's essay, "Indefinite Detention," in which she brings the work of Michel Foucault and Giorgio Agamben to bear on Guantánamo. After the Bush-Cheney administration's establishment of Guantánamo as a detention center for "enemy combatants," the signing of the Presidential Military Order of November 13, 2001 ("Detention, Treatment, and Trial of Certain Non-Citizens in the War Against Terrorism"), and the U.S. government's suspension of habeas corpus (formally codified in the Military Commissions Act of 2006), one branch of the theory-left has drawn the obvious conclusion: *Carl Schmitt was right—sovereign is he who declares the state of exception.* Agamben thus appears as the prophet of our era, testifying to the proposition that nothing much has changed in the "liberal" West since the days when Roman law could declare anyone *homo sacer* and reduce him or her to "bare life." If the president of the United States can suspend the Constitution and override the separation of powers, surely the radical-left critics are right: behind the "liberal" facade of the industrialized democracies, there is a feral totalitarian power waiting to pounce. To the stateless detainees at Guantánamo, we say: 'twas ever thus.

However, Butler does not say this. Even as she (rightly) recognizes Guantánamo as a state of exception, she critiques the theory of the unitary executive on which it rests:

> It would seem that the state, in its executive function, now extends conditions of national emergency so that the state will now have recourse to extra-legal detention and the suspension of established law, both domestic and international, for the foreseeable future. Indefinite detention thus extends lawless power indefinitely. Indeed, the indefinite detention of the untried prisoner—or the prisoner tried by military tribunal and detained regardless of the outcome of the trial—is a practice that presupposes the indefinite extension of the war on terrorism. And if this war becomes a permanent part of the state apparatus, a condition which justifies and extends the use of military tribunals, then the executive branch has effectively set up its own judiciary function, one that overrides the separation of power, the writ of habeas corpus (guaranteed, it seems, by Guantanamo Bay's geographical location outside the borders of the United States, on Cuban land, but not under Cuban rule), and the entitlement to due process. It is not just that constitutional protections are indefinitely suspended, but that the state (in its augmented executive function) arrogates to itself the right to suspend the Constitution or to manipulate the geography of detentions and trials so that constitutional and international rights are effectively suspended. (*Precarious Life*, 63–64)

What is to be done when the state itself suspends the law? Butler's answer is surprisingly . . . liberal. It's worth explaining briefly why that's important. In *Contingency, Hegemony, Universality*, the series of exchanges among Butler, Laclau, and Žižek, which I briefly cited in the preface, Butler had argued, apropos of gay marriage, against "a view of political performativity which holds that it is necessary to occupy the dominant norm in order to produce an internal subversion of its terms. Sometimes it is important to refuse its terms, to let the term itself wither, to starve it of its strength" (177). In his closing remarks, Žižek cited that passage as license to refuse the terms of liberal democracy altogether and to insist that the left must rely on other terms (whatever these might turn out to be). In "Indefinite Detention," by contrast, Butler turns *precisely to the dominant norms of liberal democracy*—the U.S. Constitution, the separation of powers, the right to a fair and open trial—in order to argue that the regime of indefinite detention at Guantánamo is an *illegitimate* example of the use of sovereign power. Butler is right to do so, just as the Supreme Court was right to decide, in *Hamdan v. Rumsfeld* (2006), that the military commissions established to try the detainees at Guantánamo violated the Uniform Code of Military Justice and the Geneva Conventions. There is an important lesson here for the radicals of the theory-left. When a radical administration such as that of Bush and Cheney declares a state of exception and develops a theory of the unitary executive, liberal-democratic institutions turn out to be good things to think with; and appealing to the dominant norms of "constitutional and international rights" can be a very good thing to do.

My version of democratic socialism, then, like Walzer's, makes room for political pluralism and a constitutional or procedural form of liberalism that respects the separation of powers and the autonomy of civil society from the state; unlike Walzer's, my version is supplemented by what I have taken from the history of British cultural studies. As I note at the outset of this chapter, the claim might sound odd to democratic and Manichean leftists alike. But the history of cultural studies was always a geopolitical history: born at a time of postwar crisis and left realignment in 1956, cultural studies marked the British New Left's break with the calcified orthodoxies of the British Communist Party, aptly symbolized by the latter's defense of the Soviet Union's invasion of Hungary. And cultural studies attained its maturity, so to speak, in the late 1970s when members of the Birmingham Centre launched groundbreaking analyses of subcultural formations, mass media, and the incipient arrival of Thatcherite authoritarian populism. Subsequently, Stuart Hall's work in the 1980s carried on the tradition of cultural studies' independent leftism, rebuking hard-left Marxist orthodoxies while still holding out the hope of democratic socialism during the long Thatcherite winter. Any attempt to translate and revive Hall's work in the United States today that does not seek to rebuke our own calcified hard-left orthodoxies would be a disservice to the urgency and originality of that work.

Admittedly, far too little of this history has registered in American cultural studies—not to speak of American mass media. Stuart Hall is cited reverently in American cultural studies circles, yes, but not for his decisive rebukes of dogmatic British leftism; worse still, most left intellectuals in the United States, when they hear the phrase "cultural studies," think of solemn academic papers on popular culture in which the object is to show either that pleasure is good fun or that *Star Trek* fans are really quite clever in some ways. But the Birmingham mode of cultural analysis poses a compelling and underrecognized challenge to the Chomsky-Herman propaganda model of "manufacturing consent," which was and is dominant in American studies of mass media. Precisely because this challenge has gone unrecognized, communications theory on the American left went right along developing the two strands of argument to which cultural studies opposes itself—the first of which argues that mass media have a bad effect on people (particularly children, who are allegedly converted by television and video games into violent, amoral monsters), and the second of which argues that mass media are owned by corporations, and that this is, for all practical analytical purposes, all we really need to know about them.

For the past twenty or thirty years, theorists in cultural studies have made something of a cottage industry out of contesting the "media effects" and the "manufacturing consent" model of cultural analysis; and a libertarian (perhaps cryptolibertarian) wing of cultural studies, in which consumers are somehow empowered by their purchases (particularly if they wind up doing interesting things with the products they obtain), has widely and not inaccurately been portrayed as a form of naive critical populism. The history of cultural studies is far more complicated and contentious than this media-critique debate has suggested, however. I close this chapter, therefore, with the reminder that more than twenty years ago, in the pages of *Marxism Today,* Stuart Hall took his distance from the doctrinaire leftism of his day by decrying "that profound sectarianism which has always had a strong presence on the left and which I detect once again rising like the smog, as those who dare to put a question mark over our received wisdoms are instantly accused of treason, labelled as the enemy, or dismissed as 'pink professors misleading the left' (in Tariq Ali's recent, immortal phrase) and despatched into the outer darkness" (*Hard Road to Renewal,* 221). And I write not only to remind the left of the need, once again, to put a question mark over our received wisdoms but also to suggest, more constructively and more optimistically, that *another left is thinkable.*

ROOT CAUSES

IN SOME WAYS it may be pointless to criticize Noam Chomsky. Not because the criticism itself has no point, but because the response to criticism of Chomsky is so drearily predictable. His most devoted fans on the left treat all forms of criticism, no matter how careful, as "smears" and individual critics as "apostates";[1] his dedicated detractors on the right latch onto all forms of criticism as proof that Chomsky is anti-American, or anti-Semitic, or an apologist for Pol Pot. Some intellectuals on the democratic left wonder why anyone would take seriously someone as reductive as Chomsky, and some intellectuals on the left take those dismissals of Chomsky as proof that our intellectual class is deeply corrupt and that we therefore need Chomsky more than ever. (A variant of this dynamic can be found in arguments over the state of the discipline of international relations: when it is pointed out that few thinkers in international relations rely on Chomsky's work, that fact is taken as evidence not of Chomsky's shortcomings as a theorist but as evidence that Chomsky must be speaking some truths that the discipline of international relations does not want to hear. This line of argument has great "countercultural" appeal, as I argue toward the end of this chapter.)

The left critic of Chomsky, therefore, can expect to be met with two formulaic responses: on one side, knee-jerk defenses and counterattacks, some of which are strangely evasive (as when Chomsky's defenders claim that he is merely *quoting* a document rather than *endorsing* it, even though the citation in question is unambiguously meant to buttress Chomsky's argument); and, on the other side, "applause" from the wrong quarter, from the legions of Chomsky obsessives on the right (or in the center, or on the liberal left) who refuse to admit the myriad ways in which Chomsky's critiques of American foreign policy have been entirely correct.

I imagine that this chapter (and this book) will provoke a few such responses, as well as more salutary ones that, like some of the best exchanges I have had with Chomsky's supporters over the years, will lead me to reconsider the nature of Chomsky's appeal and the actual substance

of his remarks. But I open with this Chomsky Critic's Prolegomenon because Chomsky is, I believe, a uniquely iconic figure on the left. Not even
Edward Said and Michel Foucault have been so influential and so polar-
izing over the past forty years, though the pattern is the same for all three:
to some extent, the defenders of these figures engage in wagon-circling
and wholesale dismissals of critics and detractors precisely because so
many of the "critiques" of these figures have been ignorant, vicious, or
simply unhinged.[2] (The problem, of course, is that not all of the critiques
of these figures have been intellectually dishonest, and not all can be so
dismissed.)

Chomsky has drawn fire longer than either Said or Foucault, and on
more fronts; but he is not iconic for that reason alone. Rather, he has
amassed a record worthy, in some respects, of a Lifetime Achievement
Award—not only for his opposition to the Vietnam War and his support
for the people of East Timor but also for his championing of the Palestinian cause even when (as was often the case) no major U.S. media outlet
would touch the issue; for his searing condemnations of U.S. interventions in Central America in the 1980s, including his denunciation of the
mining of Nicaraguan harbors; and for his critiques of U.S. nuclear policy
and nuclear proliferation.[3] For all of these reasons, criticism of Chomsky
is criticism of an icon, and iconicity itself (his and others') is worthy of
further study.

As a political figure, Chomsky has occupied a space not unlike that of
Ralph Nader: whatever their recent shortcomings may be, their supporters
argue, they pale in comparison with the long and distinguished (and often
lonely) career of service to humanity for which they have been vilified by
the forces of evil. By contrast with the largely academic reception of Said
and Foucault, the intensity of feeling produced by Nader and Chomsky
on the American left is no doubt an aftereffect of the political conditions
in which left allegiances were formed more than a generation ago: in the
Bessemer furnaces of the 1960s, one might say, steel bonds were forged
that can never be broken. Little else, I propose, can explain the reluctance
of some on the left to reassess their heroes in the light of Chomsky's position on the Balkans (which I discuss in chapter 3) or Nader's avowed support for Bush in 2000 and his willingness to seek common ground with
Pat Buchanan in 2004.[4]

So, then, let me acknowledge the obvious at the outset: Chomsky is
an intellectual giant and an iconic figure on the left, and he has amassed a
long and distinguished career on both counts. Anyone who would criticize

Chomsky without first attempting to understand the sources of his appeal, I believe, is avoiding one of the most important intellectual lessons the British cultural studies tradition tried to teach: just as Stuart Hall adjured us to understand rather than to dismiss Thatcherism, I seek here to understand rather than dismiss Chomsky's work since 1999. And it must be admitted (by me, among others) as well that, in the immediate aftermath of 9/11, Chomsky said a number of entirely true and useful things: that, for example, the attacks demonstrated yet again the foolishness of "missile defense"; that they would very likely lead to a curtailment of civil liberties and a dramatic expansion of the apparatus of state surveillance within the United States; and that the most likely response from the Bush-Cheney administration would be—as he put it—"the one that probably answers bin Laden's prayers" by "escalat[ing] the cycle of violence, in the familiar way, but in this case on a far greater scale" (Radio B92 [Belgrade]).

Had Chomsky said no more than this, I would have no substantive quarrel with him. Quite the contrary: I would defend these remarks without qualification or hesitation. But he said much more, some of which, I contend, worked to vitiate his better arguments; indeed, even in the preceding passage, the "escalation" he speaks of is not the war in Iraq—which surely does constitute a horrific escalation of the violence of 9/11, quite apart from being an attack on a country and a regime that had nothing to do with 9/11—but, rather, the temporary interruption of aid convoys from Pakistan. Part of what made Chomsky's response to 9/11 so destructive to the U.S. left, then, was his extraordinary willingness—from the outset, from the very afternoon of the attacks, and for many months thereafter—to suggest that American actions from the al-Shifa bombing of 1998 to the interruption of Afghan aid convoys from September to November 2001 were far worse than anything that might happen as a result of the hijacking of civilian airliners and the conversion of them into flying missiles targeted at office buildings.

Chomsky has been criticized for these positions, and I hope to explain and expand such criticism here. But I do not do so simply to take issue with the positions themselves. Rather, I hope to show that they are part of an overall intellectual demeanor that is as important as the substance of the claims it forwards. One of the most salient and objectionable features of that demeanor is that Chomsky presents his claims as the only legitimate "left" positions in debate, not only by portraying the Western media and "intellectual elites" as a solid phalanx of propaganda-spewing and propaganda-swallowing apparatchiks but also by mischaracterizing or simply ignoring competing commentators on the democratic left, citing their work only when they are evidence of their apostasy or heresy. Thus, in the afterword of *Hegemony or Survival,* Chomsky makes the following claim about American post hoc justifications for the invasion of Iraq:

> The most exalted of these, conjured up after all pretexts for invasion of Iraq had to be abandoned, was the vision of bringing democracy to Iraq and the Middle East. By November 2003, this vision was taken to be the real motive for the war. Veteran correspondent and editor David Ignatius wrote that "this may be the most idealistic war fought in modern times—a war whose only coherent rationale, for all the misleading hype about weapons of mass destruction and al Qaeda terrorists, is that it toppled a tyrant and created the possibility of a democratic future." The president affirmed the vision in a widely lauded address a few days later.
>
> Reactions ranged from rapturous awe to criticism praising the nobility of the vision but warning that it may be beyond our means: the beneficiaries may be too backward, it might prove too costly. That this was the guiding vision, however, was presupposed as self-evident. News stories reported that "the American project to build a stable democracy in Iraq has encountered many obstacles." Commentators wondered whether "today's pseudo-Wilsonian campaign to make the Middle East safe for democracy" could really succeed. The harshest critics of the "neocons" conceded that their "decision to wage preemptive war in order to depose Saddam Hussein and trigger a democratic revolution across the Arab world has shaken the international system to its core." With considerable search, I have yet to find an exception. (246–47)

What does Chomsky mean in this last sentence? Surely it would be a mistake to try to read this claim literally. For if you ask whether it is actually true that, in response to Bush's claims of bringing democracy to Iraq, "reactions ranged from rapturous awe to criticism praising the nobility of the vision but warning that it may be beyond our means," you will almost certainly come to one of a small handful of plausible conclusions—either that Chomsky is deliberately overlooking the thousands of left, liberal, and progressive academics, bloggers, and journalists who never accepted this rationale for the war, or that he has not been apprised of the existence of the *New York Review of Books,* the *Nation, In These Times, Mother Jones,* the *Progressive,* or even the *American Prospect,* one sentence from which he cites, misleadingly, to suggest that even "the harshest critics of the 'neo-cons'" were little more than shills for the Bush-Cheney Administration.[5] It is also possible to conclude that Chomsky (however implicitly or ambiguously) is referring only to the mainstream media outlets that supported the war, but in that case his argument becomes tautological: most mainstream U.S. media did indeed support the war, and, in doing so, advanced one or another of the Bush-Cheney administration's justifications for it, from the alleged urgency of preventing Saddam from stockpiling and using weapons of mass destruction to the alleged boldness and benevolence of creating a model Arab democracy in the Middle East.

But it is far more useful, I submit, to read this claim—and many more like it—as if it were a kind of performative utterance, the purpose of which is to declare that *there is no need* to search for "exceptions" to the rule he lays down here. In other words, as a constantive utterance about the state of affairs in American political discourse, it is absurd; but as a performative utterance, it is not subject to the question of its truth of falsity. Rather, the question one should ask is what kind of response it invites from Chomsky's followers—what kind of political demeanor it licenses. On this score, the message is clear: *no one will tell you the truth about the war but me. Don't look for criticism of the rationale for war in Iraq or skepticism about the Bush and Cheney administration from the merely liberal left of magazines like the* American Prospect—*I have tried, and with considerable search, I have found none.* In Chomsky's interviews with the foreign press, this demeanor conveys a secondary but equally powerful message: *I alone have escaped from the United States to tell thee.*

The related claim that Chomsky's critics are apostates or careerists is more familiar than the phenomenon by which Chomsky suggests that he alone has escaped to tell thee; but it is worth remarking here insofar as it depends on a curious theory of false consciousness that is rarely called out by name. The claim is something of an article of faith among Chomsky's defenders: the reason progressive-left and democratic-left writers criticize Chomsky is that we are cravenly self-interested in some way—we want to advertise our mainstream credentials and thereby gain access to mass media, where we can be hailed as reasonable people who have seen the error of our youthful leftist ways. Sometimes we are accused of collaborating with the right by throwing a few radicals to the wolves or helping to suppress the masses who would surely rise up if only Chomsky were given the fair hearing denied him by elite U.S. media. In late 2002 an especially strong version of this latter argument appeared in *Social Text*, in which Fred Moten argued, chiefly in response to criticisms of Chomsky mounted by Geoffrey Galt Harpham in *Critical Inquiry* ("Symbolic Terror"), that the "renunciation" of Chomsky amounted to a renunciation of a broader public and another, better world:

> What is particularly interesting is that entrance into this sphere is now securable by enacting a new manifestation of the old ritual exclusion of a broader public. Again, this new ceremonial form has, as one of its prime features, the renunciation of Chomsky, which is now a kind of inoculation, a kind of visa required for entry into this republic of letters. But what is at stake is not Chomsky so much as the rest of the world that he has come to signify: the alternative public that he inhabits and helps to build, the ongoing enactment of (the drive for) another social life that finally constitutes the clearest evidence of his feelings. More properly, Chomsky has become something like a sign of the myriad other modes of political being that do not fall under the umbrella of elite American exceptionalism and whose flourishing in the midst of the present crisis—as the construction and sustenance of new and active networks of information and organization, as renewed forms of cultural and political resistance—has occasioned the disciplinary efforts of Harpham and his crew. For them, the Left critique of U.S. foreign policy that maintains its principles after and especially in the wake of September 11 must be denounced and held off or away like some kind of viral embarrassment. ("New International of Decent Feelings," 198)

As I demonstrate in this chapter, part of the critique of Chomsky mounted by "Harpham and his crew" involves precisely the question of whether he *has* maintained his principles. Moten's questions, earlier in the essay— "Why has Chomsky become such a problem? How do those who operate, as it were, under the protection of a kind of veil of the Left get so incensed by someone whose critique of capitalism, imperialism, and fascism has been so principled and uncompromising?" (192)—presume what Moten needs to demonstrate: namely, that Chomsky's critique of capitalism, imperialism, and fascism has been principled and uncompromising. (I return to the question of fascism when I discuss Chomsky's work on the Balkans in chapter 3.) But they enable Moten's critique of Harpham and his crew (whoever they may be), who (a) apparently claim a position on the left merely in order to operate under a veil of protection, perhaps as a Stealth Left, and (b) are nonetheless revealed, as Moten pierces the veil, as elite American exceptionalists trying vainly to snuff out the emergent folkways of the "alternative public" that is "flourishing in the midst of the present crisis." People like Harpham criticize Chomsky, in other words, not because they disagree with him for what might be entirely legitimate reasons but because they seek entry into an elite "republic of letters" whose imperial power they can deploy to discipline and punish the "flourishing" and "new" and "active" and "renewed" resistance. To criticize Chomsky is to participate in "the old ritual exclusion of a broader public," the public for which Chomsky stands; and liberals like Harpham are possessed by false consciousness, as they enact (and fail to realize that they enact) the logic of the oppressors.

A similar move is at stake whenever someone on the left accuses a liberal or progressive of indulging in the "left right equivalent thesis." The idea is that any liberal or progressive who announces his or her opposition to both Bush-Cheney and the far left does so for two primary reasons: first, to suggest that the two sides are equally cogent and powerful and, second, to position himself or herself in the vital center rather than on the left (and thereby to become eligible for all the goodies available to vital centrists). Thus, Robert Jensen, writing for *Counterpunch*, explains why liberals can't be trusted:

> Some of my best friends are liberals. Really. But I have found it is best not to rely on them politically.
>
> Bashing the left to burnish credibility in mainstream circles is a time-honored liberal move, a way of saying "I'm critical of the excesses of the powerful, but not like those crazy lefties." For example, during a discussion of post-9/11 politics, I once heard then-New York University professor (he has since moved to Columbia University) Todd Gitlin position himself between the "hard right" (such as people associated with the Bush administration) and the "hard left" (such as Noam Chomsky and other radical critics), implying an equivalence in the coherence or value of analysis of each side. The only conclusion I could reach was that Gitlin—who is both a prolific writer and a former president of Students for a Democratic Society—either believed such a claim about equivalence or said it for self-interested political purposes. Neither interpretation is terribly flattering for Gitlin. ("Why Leftists Mistrust Liberals")

Note that, for Jensen, there is no such thing as "criticism" of the left; there is only "bashing." And the reason liberals engage in such bashing is not that they simply disagree with this or that "left" position but because either they want to burnish their credibility in mainstream circles or they truly believe that the left is equivalent to the right. The possibility that liberals and progressives might disagree with a presidential administration that is at once criminal, plutocratic, and stupefyingly incompetent, on one side, and with a handful of leftist writers who make questionable or simply ridiculous claims on the other—and that criticism of the latter can indeed be as coherent and as valuable as criticism of the former—does not enter into Jensen's equation. Clearly, such liberals and progressives are possessed by false consciousness, as they enact (and fail to realize they enact) the logic of mainstream corporate sellouts.

Essentially, Jensen is accusing Gitlin of triangulation. The charge of triangulation, when leveled by the Manichean left at the democratic left, serves two critical functions. First, of course, it demands that there be no enemies to the left and insists on an asymmetrical relation in which it is just and necessary for Manichean leftists to distinguish themselves from all other leftists and liberals but somehow immoral for other leftists and liberals to distinguish themselves from the Manichean left. Second, it articulates this demand by associating the alleged "triangulator" on the democratic left with Clintonism and with the center-right Democratic Leadership Council strategy of adopting some Republican policies and talking points so as to "triangulate" between the far right and the moderate left. Accordingly, later in the essay Jensen writes, "when leftists and liberals form least-common-denominator coalitions, liberal positions dominate. There's no history of liberals moving to include left political ideas when right-wing forces are chased from power. Think Bill Clinton, here." And don't think of Franklin D. Roosevelt, who was pushed to the left by socialists and labor; don't think of a counterexample from the late 1960s when hard leftists dominated a liberal-left coalition and ran it right off the cliff, because you would probably need a Weatherman to know which way that wind blows.

CRIMES AGAINST HUMANITY THE CASE OF AL-SHIFA

On the afternoon of September 11, 2001, long before anyone knew how many people were killed in the attacks of that morning, Chomsky wrote:

> The terrorist attacks were major atrocities. In scale they may not reach
> the level of many others, for example, Clinton's bombing of the Su-
> dan with no credible pretext, destroying half its pharmaceutical sup-
> plies and killing unknown numbers of people (no one knows, because
> the U.S. blocked an inquiry at the UN and no one cares to pursue it).
> ("On the Bombings")

The actual pretext for the August 20, 1998, bombing of the Sudan, of
course, was that it was a retaliation for the August 7 al-Qaeda bombings of
U.S. embassies in Kenya and Tanzania that killed 224 people and wounded
hundreds more. Chomsky does not mention this, but he is right to say
that this pretext was not credible, for there does not seem to have been
any link between al-Qaeda and al-Shifa. (However, as Lawrence Wright
has written, "Bin Laden . . . initially said that the sites had been targeted
because of the 'invasion' of Somalia; then he described an American plan
to partition Sudan, which he said was hatched in the embassy in Nairobi.
He also told his followers that the genocide in Rwanda had been planned
inside the two American embassies" [*Looming Tower*, 308–09]. Perhaps,
therefore, Chomsky might have considered whether al-Qaeda's attack on
the embassies was undertaken with credible pretext.) And because there
is no plausible link between the embassy bombings and the bombing of
the al-Shifa plant, it is reasonable to say that the al-Shifa strike was a crime
against humanity, and that the United States' refusal to allow a chemical
weapons inspection of the bombing site by the United Nations was another crime.[6]

It is also true, as Chomsky notes later in this short piece, that "the
primary victims [of 9/11], as usual, were working people: janitors, secre-
taries, firemen, etc.," and that "the crime is a gift to the hard jingoist right"
("On the Bombings")—though, as I contend, it need not have been nearly
so generous a gift as the Manichean left helped it to become. But quite
apart from the question of whether the al-Shifa strike was justifiable, there
is the question of how, within hours of the attacks, Chomsky could have
declared that the consequent damage to human life arising from 9/11—in
its totality, from its effect on the American economy to its effect on the
workers breathing the air of lower Manhattan over the ensuing months—
"may not reach the level" of a criminal missile strike that killed one night
watchman in a factory that did not, despite Central Intelligence Agency
director George Tenet's insistence, manufacture chemical weapons.

Two things are worth remarking here. One is what I call the "timeless-ness" of the claim. By this I mean not that the claim will live forever more but that the claim inhabits *no time:* it does not need to wait for an actual tally of the bodies, because its primary effect is to shift the focus off 9/11 altogether and onto a debate about the cruise-missile bombing of the Su-dan. Two, the timelessness of the claim is the key to its unfalsifiability: even though years have now elapsed, and we can say with some certainty that the human toll of 9/11 did indeed exceed that of al-Shifa, Chomsky's claim has not become "wrong," because, after all, he did not definitively say that the attacks of 9/11 *would not* attain the scale of al-Shifa, only that they *may not.*[7]

Over the next few weeks, months, and years, Chomsky added to his initial claim an almost rococo series of elaborations. Starting from the fact that the al-Shifa plant manufactured antimalarial drugs and antibiot-ics, Chomsky asserted in a January 2002 interview with *Salon* magazine that the al-Shifa strike, "according to the estimates made by the German Embassy in Sudan and Human Rights Watch, probably led to tens of thousands of deaths" (quoted in Hansen, "Noam Chomsky"). Chomsky's claim was promptly repudiated by Carroll Bogert, communications direc-tor of Human Rights Watch, who wrote, "In fact, Human Rights Watch has conducted no research into civilian deaths as the result of U.S. bomb-ing in Sudan and would not make such an assessment without a careful and thorough research mission on the ground" (Bogert, "Letter to the Editor"). In response, Chomsky did not admit the error. Instead, he dog-gedly argued that Bogert bore him out: "There have been no serious stud-ies, by Human Rights Watch or anyone else, as I made explicit" (Chom-sky, "Letter to the Editor"). (Werner Daum, the German Ambassador to the Sudan from 1996 to 2000, had written in the summer 2001 *Harvard International Review* that "it is difficult to assess how many people in this poor African country died as a result of the destruction of the Al-Shifa factory, but several tens of thousands seems a reasonable guess" ["Univer-salism and the West," 19], but, alas, he had proffered that reasonable guess without providing any evidence for it. Meanwhile, neither Human Rights Watch nor Amnesty International nor Doctors Without Borders—none of whom were constrained by the U.S.'s reprehensible decision to block a U.N. investigation—undertook any on-the-ground assessment that would corroborate this estimate. Thus it was that Chomsky was able to adduce them as proof of his revised claim that "there have been no serious stud-ies.") But by that point, in January 2002, Chomsky himself had blamed the strike for far, far more than "several tens of thousands" of deaths. Indeed, much earlier, in his October 2001 reply to Christopher Hitchens in the *Nation,* Chomsky had insisted that

> To regard the comparison to September 11 as outrageous is to express extraordinary racist contempt for African victims of a shocking crime, which, to make it worse, is one for which we are responsible: as taxpayers, for failing to provide massive reparations, for granting refuge and immunity to the perpetrators, and for allowing the terrible facts to be sunk so deep in the memory hole that some, at least, seem unaware of them.
>
> This only scratches the surface. The United States bombing "appears to have shattered the slowly evolving move towards compromise between Sudan's warring sides" and terminated promising steps toward a peace agreement to end the civil war that had left 1.5 million dead since 1981, which might have also led to "peace in Uganda and the entire Nile Basin." The attack apparently "shattered . . . the expected benefits of a political shift at the heart of Sudan's Islamist government" toward a "pragmatic engagement with the outside world," along with efforts to address Sudan's domestic crises, to end support for terrorism, and to reduce the influence of radical Islamists (Mark Huband, *Financial Times,* September 8, 1998).
>
> Insofar as these consequences ensued, we may compare the crime in Sudan to the assassination of Lumumba, which helped plunge the Congo into decades of slaughter, still continuing; or the overthrow of the democratic government of Guatemala in 1954, which led to forty years of hideous atrocities; and all too many others like it. (Chomsky, "Reply to Hitchens")

Chomsky's more extravagant claims about al-Shifa were immediately challenged by United Federation of Teachers member and democratic leftist Leo Casey in an exchange on *ZNet.* On October 2, 2001, Casey argued that Chomsky's accounting of the Sudan was unsupported by any human-rights groups:

> It is also noteworthy that while international human rights organizations such as Amnesty International and the Human Rights Watch have taken note of the bombing of the factory, and called for independent inquiries into the U.S. claims that it was being used for the

production of chemical weapons, their reports on the situation in the Sudan, available on the Internet, contain no statements that even treat as credible and worthy of further investigation the claims that thousands of Sudanese might have died as a result of the bombing. What we have here is simply ungrounded assertion, without the slightest evidentiary proof. . . .

An ordinary academic pontificating on matters about which he was so poorly informed might have left the issue there. But not Chomsky. He goes on to blame the U.S. attack on this factory for every conceivable problem (and some inconceivable ones as well) in the Sudan and its surrounding region. Using a quote full of the most remarkable euphemisms, Chomsky informs us that the bombing of the factory brought to a halt "compromises" that might have ended the decades old "civil war" between Sudan's "warring sides." How the destruction of a single factory could have produced such remarkable results is never made clear in the particular passage Chomsky provides, but a fuller account is provided in the complete article from which it is excerpted. The full account, however, would strip the veneer right off the euphemisms, so Chomsky limits himself to the short selection. ("Unbearable Whiteness of Chomsky's Arguments")[8]

I return to Casey's treatment of that account (Hubard's *Financial Times* essay, "U.S. Cruise Missile Attack") in a moment; for now, I merely note that Chomsky not only challenged Casey's estimate of the al-Shifa fallout but argued that Casey's critique "offers some welcome opportunities to bring out more information about the terrible crimes he is laboring to conceal, and it helps us understand attitudes and techniques of apologists for crimes for which they share responsibility" ("Reply to Casey"). Chomsky proceeded to cite an October 2, 2001, *Guardian* essay by James Astill on the aftereffects of the Khartoum bombing:

First, let's clear away some of the initial debris that Casey scatters in his effort to obscure the central issues. To begin with, recall the "claim" of mine that initiated these interesting exchanges, for which Casey offers his curious paraphrase. The "claim" consists of a single sentence, in a composite response to inquiries from journalists, observing that the toll of the "horrendous crime" committed on Sept. 11 with "wickedness and awesome cruelty" may be comparable to the consequences of Clinton's bombing of the Sudan in August 1998. That plausible conclusion may be shocking to those who have been well-trained to consider their crimes against the weak to be as normal as the air they breathe. But as in innumerable other cases, the picture looks different at the other end of the guns. Dr. Idris Eltayeb, one of Sudan's handful of pharmacologists and chairman of the board of the pharmaceutical factory destroyed by U.S. missiles, says that the crime "was just as much an act of terrorism as at the twin towers—the only difference is we know who did it. I feel very sad about the loss of life [in New York and Washington], but in terms of numbers, and the relative cost to a poor country, [the bombing in Sudan] was worse" (James Astill, *Guardian*, Oct. 2, 2001).

Unfortunately, he may be right, even if we do not take into account "the political cost to a country struggling to emerge from totalitarian military dictatorship, ruinous Islamism and long-running civil war" before the missile attack, which "overnight [plunged Khartoum] into the nightmare of impotent extremism it had been trying to escape" (Astill). These political costs may have been even more harmful to Sudan than the destruction of its "fragile medical services," Astill concludes three years after the attack, confirming the reasoned judgment of *Financial Times* correspondent Mark Huband, which Casey tries hard to evade, and ludicrously attributes to me. ("Reply to Casey")

Chomsky is citing Astill accurately. But note the gestures at the beginning and the end of this passage: at the outset, deploying scare quotes like tongs, Chomsky disavows having made a "claim"; at the close, Chomsky insists that it is ludicrous to imagine that he endorsed Huband's account by citing it, even though he clearly cited it approvingly. The mechanics of citation and attribution here are exceedingly complex. As with his reliance on Werner Daum, Chomsky does not have to verify his source's statements, because he is not actually making them himself; rather, he is simply noting that they have been made.

The idea, of course, is to give cloistered and blinkered Americans some sense of what their country looks like on the other side of the guns. But the problem with this methodology is that one has to be extremely careful about who and what one cites at the other end of the guns. It is undoubtedly true that Dr. Idris Eltayeb felt and said that the al-Shifa bombing was worse than 9/11, and it is undoubtedly useful for Americans to hear this. But this does not go to the question of whether Eltayeb was *right* to feel and say so. Let me illustrate the problem by citing another voice from the other side of the guns, quoted a bit further on in Astill's article: "'America is reaping what it has sown. Hiroshima, Nagasaki, Korea, Vietnam, Iraq, Palestine: Muslims must fight this jihad together,'" Sheikh Mansoor Hussein told the faithful at last Friday's prayers. Up to and including the word "Palestine," the sheikh's words would not be out of place in *Z* or *Counterpunch*. But Chomsky did not cite them, because, as Astill notes, "after prayers, the sheikh claimed that 4,000 Jews did not show up for work at the World Trade Centre on September 11. 'We know who is responsible,' he said" (Astill, "Strike One"). As in innumerable other cases, the picture looks different at the other end of the guns. But sometimes, that picture is simply and demonstrably wrong.

This is not simply a question of which citation-within-a-citation (Chomsky-Astill-Eltayeb or Chomsky-Astill-Hussein) one prefers to cite; it is a much broader and more important question of what kind of evidence should be considered relevant to the assessment of crimes against humanity. And the astonishing thing here is that, for all his citations of people who offered support for his claim (or "claim") that the al-Shifa bombing was comparable with the assassination of Lumumba, Chomsky says nothing about how the political condition of the Sudan should be factored into the assessment. In his follow-up to Chomsky's reply, Casey writes:

> For all of the time and space he dedicates to invective about my "childish fabrications," my "consistent lying," and my "racist contempt" (I have apparently joined Hitchens in this category), not to mention my personal "responsibility" for the crime of killing tens of thousands of innocent Sudanese, Chomsky manages to avoid even one comment on the major issue I had raised in my original commentary—the nature of the Sudanese regime, its crimes against its African people and its connections to the bin Laden Al Qaeda organization (which participated, it appears, in some of those crimes in the southern Sudan). These are not insignificant realities, and they dwarf the bombing of the al-Shifa factory in their effect upon the Sudanese people.
>
> The Sudanese National Islamic Front (NIF) government came to power in a 1990 coup d'etat, and has pursued a genocidal war against its African peoples in the South which has been ongoing for nearly two decades, with a human toll in the millions—as high as 3 million in some estimates. It is an extreme fundamentalist regime, not unlike Afghanistan's Taliban, which has imposed fundamentalist

versions of religious shari'a law upon the country. Report after report of the United Nations and international human rights organizations have documented its abrogation of the rights of women, the denial of religious freedom and the suppression of freedom of expression and association; political repression is the norm. There is forced conscription of children as soldiers and the torture of children. (Human Rights Watch 1995 Report on "Children in Sudan: Slaves, Street Children and Child Soldiers" [www.hrw.org/reports/1995/Sudan.htm]) Not only is capital punishment regularly employed, but it has taken the forms of stoning and crucifixions. Government-sponsored Arabic "muraheleen" militia have engaged in a large and thriving slave trade, in which they take by force, enslave and sell Africans, primarily from the largest of the Sudan's ethnic group, the Dinka. (Human Rights Watch 1999 background Paper on "Slavery and Slave Redemption in the Sudan" [www.hrw.org/backgrounder/africa/sudan1.htm]) Add to all of this the use of food as a weapon of war described above, resulting in massive famine and starvation in the South. And to top that off, the Sudanese NIF government has been providing material aid and support to an insurgent group in northern Uganda, a Christian fundamentalist sect and cult known as the Lords' Resistance Army, which engages in similar practices there.

This is the government, Chomsky tells us, which was prepared to put aside its extreme fundamentalism, to end the genocidal war against its African people in the south and join in a war on terrorism—all but for the bombing of the al-Shifa factory. ("Let Us Not Inherit This Ill Wind")

Casey, I should add, agreed with Chomsky about the criminality of the al-Shifa strike:

A 50% loss [of lifesaving medicines] would be a significant loss, and that is why it is essential to continue to press the U.S. government, as Human Rights Watch and former U.S. President Jimmy Carter has done, among others, to provide compensation, should it be unable to provide supporting evidence for its claim that the factory was producing chemical weapons. But it is not a loss of such a magnitude that it was beyond the means of the Sudan to replace the lost medicine. A lot of the al-Shifa production involved medicine which is relatively easy to manufacture (chloroquine, aspirin), and thus could be shifted to one of the other five pharmaceutical factories in the capital city of the Sudan.

It is difficult to cast Casey as a defender of American imperialism or an apologist for crimes against humanity. Surely Casey did not challenge Chomsky in order to conceal terrible U.S. crimes; on the contrary, as he tried to make clear in his conclusion, he challenged Chomsky in order that we might come to as accurate an accounting of U.S. crimes as possible, and thereby direct our opposition to those crimes most compellingly. Chomsky's mode of analysis, writes Casey,

> needs to be criticized and opposed because insofar as it carries any influence, it undermines our capacity as citizens to compel the U.S. government to do the right thing in the world. . . .
>
> The problem here goes beyond the fact that the fundamentalist left opposes any U.S. government intervention, any use of armed force by the U.S. government, no matter how compelling and urgent the cause. Since the fundamentalist is opposed to any intervention, he is in no position to assume the vital role of ensuring that the form of the intervention taken by the U.S. government is consistent with the principles of the limited use of armed force: that it is directed at the state and its means of violence, and not at the people, that it makes every effort to protect innocent life and to free subjected people from their oppression. That is an essential task that democrats must assume in the upcoming days and months.

Chomsky's replies to such challenges, unfailingly and unfortunately, cast the critiques as evidence of the moral turpitude of the critic. In a September 2001 interview with David Barsamian, he said, "Though it is merely a footnote"—a footnote that, oddly enough, will take up fully eight pages of the early volume 9–11—

> the Sudan case is nonetheless highly instructive. One interesting aspect is the reaction when someone dares to mention it. I have in the past, and did so again in response to queries from journalists shortly after the 9–11 atrocities. I mentioned that the toll of the "horrendous crime" of 9–11, committed with "wickedness and awesome cruely" (quoting Robert Fisk), may be comparable to the consequences of Clinton's bombing of the Al-Shifa plant in August 1998. That plausible

conclusion elicited an extraordinary reaction, filling many web sites and journals with feverish and fanciful condemnations, which I'll ignore. The only important aspect is that that single sentence—*which, on a closer look, appears to be an understatement*—was regarded by some commentators as utterly scandalous. It is difficult to avoid the conclusion that at some deep level, however they may deny it to themselves, they regard our crimes against the weak to be as normal as the air we breathe. (Chomsky, *9–11*, 45–46; emphasis added)

And so, because it was difficult to avoid that conclusion, Chomsky did not do so; instead, he embraced it as the most likely reason for his critics' behavior. Thus people like Casey, who had argued that Chomsky's account of 9–11 and al-Shifa "undermines our capacity as citizens to compel the U.S. government to do the right thing in the world," are actually so amoral and corrupt as to accept unquestioningly—for who questions the air we breathe, unless he or she is breathing it in lower Manhattan in the fall of 2001?—our crimes against the weak. This is the line of thought, then, that led Chomsky to declare, in his reply to Hitchens, that "to regard the comparison to September 11 as outrageous is to express extraordinary racist contempt for African victims of a shocking crime."

Chomsky has never scaled back or moderated any of the claims; he has only added to them with time. In the afterword of *Hegemony or Survival*, Chomsky attributes to Jason Burke's study *Al-Qaeda* the argument that the al-Shifa bombing led to the rise of al-Qaeda as a force in Islamist politics:

> As Burke reviews, Clinton's 1998 bombings of Sudan and Afghanistan created bin Laden as a symbol, forged close relations between him and the Taliban, and led to a sharp increase in support, recruitment, and financing for Al Qaeda, which until then was virtually unknown. The next major contribution to the growth of Al Qaeda and the prominence of bin Laden was Bush's bombing of Afghanistan following September 11, undertaken without credible pretext as later quietly conceded. (Chomsky, *Hegemony or Survival*, 241)

In 2004, note, Chomsky was still claiming that the bombing of Afghanistan, like the bombing of al-Shifa, was undertaken without credible pretext and that this had been "conceded" by U.S. intelligence; but what's even more remarkable here is the claim—which, again, Chomsky cites in such a way as to allow his followers the claim that he is merely passing along uncontroversial information gleaned elsewhere—that all would have been well in the world (or at least much better), and bin Laden would have remained a marginal figure in it, if only the United States had not responded to the bombings of U.S. embassies in 1998.

As it happens, however, Jason Burke's history of al-Qaeda is far more nuanced than Chomsky makes it out to be; while Burke does indeed suggest that the Clinton administration's response to the embassy bombings offered bin Laden "confirmation that his controversial decision to start targeting America before the munafiq rulers in power in the Middle East was the right one," he also acknowledges, as Chomsky does not, that *the embassy bombings themselves* enhanced bin Laden's reputation among Islamists:

> To Islamic activists around the world, the bombings showed that bin Laden was not, as many had previously thought, merely a dilettante showboating rich kid who lived in safety in Afghanistan far from the tough struggle against the states' security apparatus in Saudi Arabia or Egypt or Jordan or Algeria. For aspirant activists all over the Islamic world, bin Laden, of whom many had not heard previously, became the focus of their ambitions. This conversion to cult status dramatically emphasized to local groups the symbolic and material advantages that alliance with him could bring. (Burke, *Al-Qaeda*, 181)

More generally, Chomsky takes from Burke the claim that "every use of force is another small victory for bin Laden" (Burke, *Al-Qaeda*, 290, quoted by Chomsky, *Hegemony or Survival*, 241) and draws from this the moral that "the proper reaction to terrorism" is "police work" combined with a resolve to "address the 'myriad grievances,' many legitimate, that are 'the root causes of modern Islamic militancy'" (Chomsky, *Hegemony or Survival*, 241).

Chomsky is finding in Burke only what he wants to see, however. Burke does argue that "every time force is used it provides more evidence of a 'clash of civilizations' and a 'cosmic struggle' and thus aids the militants in their effort to radicalize and mobilize" (*Al-Qaeda*, 290). But he is by no means committed to the view that police work and patient negotiation of "legitimate" grievances are the West's only options. "Of course the 'war on terror' should have a military component," Burke writes:

It is easy to underestimate the sheer efficacy of military power in achieving specific immediate goals. Hardened militants cannot be rehabilitated and need to be made to cease their activities, through legal processes or otherwise. But if we are to win the battle against terrorism our strategies must be made broader and more sophisticated. We must eliminate our enemies without creating new ones. Military power must be only one tool among many, and a tool that is only rarely, and reluctantly, used. Currently, military power is the default, the weapon of choice. (290–91)

I agree with this in every respect, just as I agree with Burke's reminder, two pages earlier, that "the cosmic nature of the aims of the militants make[s] them very difficult to counter. Dialogue with hardcore radicals is virtually impossible" (289).

But in an important sense, this painstaking parsing of Chomsky's claims about al-Shifa, and the degree to which he quotes his sources accurately or misleadingly, misses the larger point. To argue that Chomsky overestimated the death toll after al-Shifa and underestimated the role of Sudan's National Islamic Front, or to debate the value of citing either Carroll Bogert or Idris Eltayeb, is to quibble over the size of the trees while ignoring the forest. (And, according to Chomsky's reply to Casey, any such quibbling over al-Shifa is simply an attempt to obscure or conceal U.S. crimes.) So let me conclude this section as emphatically and unambiguously as possible: the U.S. cruise missile strike against al-Shifa managed to be both barbarous and deeply stupid at once, targeting a factory that not only had no connection to bin Laden or chemical weapons but was actually owned (as Werner Daum himself notes) by "a prominent opposition figure who had financed a newsletter in exile, and who even had on his payroll an old schoolmate who was a leader of the rebel Sudan People's Liberation Movement" ("Universalism and the West," 19).

But—and this is crucial—Chomsky presents al-Shifa *as if it is emblematic of the U.S. response to radical Islamism when, in fact, it was anomalous.* The image entailed in Chomsky's evocation of al-Shifa is a familiar one on the Manichean left: America the Terrible, lashing out blindly and murderously, napalming Vietnamese villages, mowing down Salvadoran peasants, carpet-bombing the wretched of the earth. But it doesn't match up very well with the United States that fled Somalia in 1993, refrained from responding to the bombings of the Khobar Towers in 1996 and the U.S.S.

Cole in 2000, and actually conducted extensive *police work* in response to the first attack on the World Trade Center in 1993.

Alongside al-Shifa, then, there is another story that could plausibly be told about the American response to violent provocations from radical Islamists, but the Manichean left does not speak of it—even when it insists that 9/11 called for police work rather than military action. In *The Looming Tower: Al-Qaeda and the Road to 9/11,* Lawrence Wright chronicles the attempts of U.S. intelligence agencies to track and combat Islamist terrorism, and he offers a compelling account of the interagency rivalries that crippled U.S. efforts to prevent terrorist attacks on American soil. Along the way, Wright has some laudatory words for certain U.S. attorneys:

> On May 29, 2001, in a federal courtroom in Manhattan, a jury convicted four men in the bombings of the American embassies in East Africa. It was the capstone of a perfect record of twenty-five terrorist convictions accomplished by the prosecutors of the Southern District of New York, which was headed by Mary Jo White, with her assistants Kenneth Karas and Patrick Fitzgerald. The struggle against Islamic terrorists had begun in 1993 with the first World Trade Center bombing. Eight years later, these convictions were practically the only victories that America could point to, and they were based upon the laborious investigations of the New York bureau of the FBI, particularly the I-49 squad. (382–83)

Wright calls the twenty-five convictions "genuine and legitimate achievements that demonstrated the credibility and integrity of the American system of justice" (383), and after the travesties of justice perpetrated by the Bush-Cheney administration, who could be so foolish as to disagree? Those convictions were won at a time when the United States still allowed suspects to petition for writs of habeas corpus; when U.S. policy prohibited torture and indefinite detention; and when the United States did not engage in "extraordinary rendition" of suspects to nations in which they would be tortured or indefinitely detained. They were won in open court, not in secret military tribunals convened for "enemy combatants."

This is a critical matter for democratic leftists, since we place great weight on the distinction between legitimate and illegitimate state policies and seek to criticize the latter by the standard of the former; for now, I simply note that Chomsky's response to 9/11 has not, to date, included a laudatory discussion of U.S. convictions of Islamist terrorists before 9/11.

Nor has anyone on the Manichean left argued that those convictions are genuine and legitimate achievements that demonstrate the credibility and integrity of the American system of justice. As a result, one is left to wonder what kind of American "police work" would have met with the Manichean left's approval after 9/11.

DOING THE RIGHT THING THE RADIO B92 INTERVIEW

But if I agree (as I do) with Leo Casey that Chomsky's analysis of al-Shifa actually undermines any attempt to provide a realistic assessment of U.S. crimes and thereby to try to compel the U.S. government to adhere to international standards of justice and law, then what mode of analysis and address might I prefer in its place? For an example, contrast Chomsky's rhetoric with that of Human Rights Watch Executive Director Kenneth Roth, who wrote to President Clinton in September 1998 to urge the United States to open an investigation into the missile strike and to compensate the Sudanese for the consequent damage. After quoting Section 8.5.2 of the Naval Handbook on advance warnings to protect noncombatants, Roth writes:

> It seems clear from statements you made, Mr. President, on August 28 and at other times, that consideration was given to the possibility that Sudanese civilians might be in the area bombed, and that you wanted to avoid injuring them. We believe the public is entitled to know whether consideration was given to the feasibility of warning civilians, and if that alternative was rejected, the reasons for its rejection.
>
> It would seem that a mere phone call fifteen minutes in advance might have given the Sudanese civilians enough time to evacuate the area. Given the type of weapons employed by the U.S. Navy, it would seem that this might have been done with no risk to U.S. personnel or to the success of the mission.
>
> In light of your stated concern with civilian injuries, it would be entirely appropriate as a humanitarian matter for the U.S. government to compensate those Sudanese injured and the survivors of the civilians killed in the bombing. There is already precedent for the U.S. to compensate civilians injured in a U.S. military attack without any concession of negligence or culpability. The U.S. provided compensation to the families of the persons on an Iranian civilian airliner mistakenly

shot down over the Persian Gulf, even though an internal U.S. investigation established that its forces did not act negligently. In Sudan, also, the U.S. should compensate civilians who for no fault of their own were injured in the U.S. military strike. ("Letter to Clinton")

Roth can hardly be faulted for "racist contempt" of the victims of the missile strike; on the contrary, he expresses concern for the unintended effects of bombing and cites a precedent in which the United States has compensated civilians even though an internal investigation did not find U.S. forces at fault. But note that Roth does not—here, elsewhere in his letter, or elsewhere in Human Rights Watch documents—attempt to claim that the strike is the rough equivalent of the assassination of Lumumba or that it prevented wide-scale peace from breaking out in Sudan, Uganda, and the entire Nile Basin. For Roth is writing to persuade an American president to do the right thing, and Chomsky is not. What, then, is Chomsky trying to do instead?

This is not an idle question; it is central to the analysis of Chomsky's appeal. Look, for example, at how Chomsky answered the relatively straightforward query, "Why do you think these attacks happened?" as put to him on September 18 by Radio B92 in Belgrade. (This interview has enjoyed considerable popularity on the Internet, and it was one of the first of Chomsky's utterances to be taken as the definitive leftist word on 9/11.) It is a long answer, and I interrupt it at a couple of points for commentary and clarification:

> To answer the question we must first identify the perpetrators of the crimes. It is generally assumed, plausibly, that their origin is the Middle East region, and that the attacks probably trace back to the Osama Bin Laden network, a widespread and complex organization, doubtless inspired by Bin Laden but not necessarily acting under his control. Let us assume that this is true. Then to answer your question a sensible person would try to ascertain Bin Laden's views, and the sentiments of the large reservoir of supporters he has throughout the region. About all of this, we have a great deal of information. Bin Laden has been interviewed extensively over the years by highly reliable Middle East specialists, notably the most eminent correspondent in the region, Robert Fisk (London *Independent*), who has intimate knowledge of the entire region and direct experience over decades. A Saudi Arabian millionaire, Bin Laden became a militant Islamic leader in the war to

drive the Russians out of Afghanistan. He was one of the many religious fundamentalist extremists recruited, armed, and financed by the CIA and their allies in Pakistani intelligence to cause maximal harm to the Russians—quite possibly delaying their withdrawal, many analysts suspect. . . .

Here again, we have a gratuitous, speculative claim for which Chomsky himself does not take direct responsibility, attributing it instead to "many analysts." As with his partial citation of Mark Hubard with regard to al-Shifa, Chomsky goes well beyond the ordinary claim that the United States was playing with fire in funding the "Afghanis." It is well known, in liberal and leftist circles, that in 1998 former National Security Adviser Zbigniew Brzezinksi took credit for luring the Soviets into Afghanistan, asking, "What is most important to the history of the world? The Taliban or the collapse of the Soviet empire? Some stirred-up Muslims or the liberation of Central Europe and the end of the cold war?" (Brzezinski, Interview, 274).[9]

Though this sounds like a damning (and monstrously callous) admission of American complicity with the rise of the Taliban, it is hard to know whether to take Brzezinski at his word. In *Ghost Wars: The Secret History of the CIA, Afghanistan, and Bin Laden, from the Soviet Invasion to September 10, 2001,* Steven Coll disputes the claim:

> Years later Brzezinski would tell an interviewer . . . that he had "knowingly increased the probability" that the Soviets would intervene in Afghanistan by authorizing the secret aid. Brzezinski implied that he had slyly lured the Soviets into a trap in Afghanistan. But his contemporary memos—particularly those written in the first days after the Soviet invasion—make clear that while Brzezinski was determined to confront the Soviets in Afghanistan through covert action, he was also very worried that the Soviets would prevail. Those early memos show no hint of satisfaction that the Soviets had taken some kind of Afghan bait. Given this evidence and the enormous political and security costs that the invasion imposed on the Carter administration, any claim that Brzezinski lured the Soviets into Afghanistan warrants deep skepticism. (581)

Still, whether or not Brzezinski deliberately goaded the Soviets into an invasion, the fact remains that the United States did support the Islamist mujahedeen in the years that followed.

That kind of global gamesmanship, in which the United States combats totalitarian forces in one area of the world by supporting totalitarian forces (remarkably, even more regressive and brutal ones) elsewhere in the world, is objectionable on its face: the United States might well be criticized for attempting, as many analysts have phrased it, to ensnare Soviet forces in a quagmire at the expense of the people of Afghanistan.[10] But Chomsky is not making that criticism; he is making the far more extraordinary criticism that Soviet forces *would have withdrawn prior to 1989* if not for that meddlesome U.S. intervention, which, like the al-Shifa strike, apparently had a far more devastating effect on the region than anyone has yet surmised—not only inflaming an already volatile part of the world but actually preventing the emergence of an incipient peace in the region. Like the claim that the attacks of 9/11 may not approach the al-Shifa bombing in scale, it is not merely counterintuitive but unfalsifiable.

Turning back to the Belgrade interview:

> . . . though whether he personally happened to have direct contact with the CIA is unclear, and not particularly important. Not surprisingly, the CIA preferred the most fanatic and cruel fighters they could mobilize. The end result was to "destroy a moderate regime and create a fanatical one, from groups recklessly financed by the Americans" (*London Times* correspondent Simon Jenkins, also a specialist on the region).[11]

Though Chomsky cites Jenkins on the rise of the Taliban in Afghanistan, he does not discuss the initial Soviet invasion of Afghanistan (or Pakistani and Saudi sources of funding for the mujahedeen). All we know from this account is that the United States may have delayed the Soviets' withdrawal—and that the CIA deliberately (and not surprisingly) chose the most fanatic and cruel fighters they could mobilize. With regard to those fighters, however, Chomsky's well-earned suspicions of the evil designs of the CIA may have led him to be rather too credulous with regard to the Islamist hype about the mujahedeen, who, as warriors, were more of an annoyance than a Delta Force, fixated more on martyrdom than on military victory. As Lawrence Wright notes:

> For the journalists covering the war, the Arab Afghans were a curious sideshow to the real fighting, set apart by their obsession with dying. When a fighter fell, his comrades would congratulate him and weep

because they were not also slain in battle. These scenes struck other Muslims as bizarre. The Afghans were fighting for their country, not for Paradise or an idealized Islamic community. For them, martyrdom was not such a high priority.

Rahimullah Yusufzai, the Peshawar bureau chief of the *News,* a Pakistani daily, observed a camp of Arab Afghans that was under attack in Jalalabad. The Arabs had pitched white tents on the front lines, where they were easy marks for Soviet bombers. "Why?" the reporter asked incredulously. "We want them to bomb us!" the men told him. "We want to die!" (*Looming Tower,* 124)

If, indeed, the CIA chose these deadly fighters in order to cause maximal harm to the Russians, surely at some point the agency must have wondered whether it had gotten its money's worth. For Wright challenges the very idea that the mujahedeen were responsible for the Soviets' defeat: "In fact the war was fought almost entirely by the Afghans themselves. Despite [Abdullah] Azzam's famous fatwa and bin Laden's subsidies, there were never more than three thousand of these outsiders—who came to be known as the Arab Afghans—in the war against the Soviets, and most of them never got out of Peshawar" (121; Jason Burke confirms this account in *Al-Qaeda,* 60–61).

Chomsky then elaborates on the wider travels of the mujahedeen in the 1980s and 1990s:

These "Afghanis" as they are called (many, like Bin Laden, not from Afghanistan) carried out terror operations across the border in Russia, but they terminated these after Russia withdrew. Their war was not against Russia, which they despise, but against the Russian occupation and Russia's crimes against Muslims. The "Afghanis" did not terminate their activities, however. They joined Bosnian Muslim forces in the Balkan Wars; the U.S. did not object, just as it tolerated Iranian support for them, for complex reasons that we need not pursue here, apart from noting that concern for the grim fate of the Bosnians was not prominent among them. (Radio B92)

Here, Chomsky's gesture toward "complex reasons"—which he understands fully but need not pursue here—obscures the fact that the United States did indeed object to the presence of "Afghanis" in Bosnian Muslim forces and called for their withdrawal from the region in the Dayton Peace

Accords; the mujahedeen were required by Article III of Annex 1A of that document (the "Withdrawal of Foreign Forces" section of the "Agree-ment on the Military Aspects of the Peace Settlement") to leave Bosnia by January 14, 1996. But in Chomsky's account of the Balkans, U.S. support for Islamists was part of the master plan from the start. More important, Chomsky implies that U.S. policy in the Balkans was not, in fact, a mess of contradictions, foot-draggings, and shows of support for Milošević right through the Dayton Accords, but, rather, a straightforward and simple policy of a piece with U.S. support for Islamists in Afghanistan: *it was all part of the plan, you see.*

As discussed here in chapter 3, Chomsky claims that "in the early 90s, primarily for cynical power reasons, the United States selected Bosnian Muslims as their Balkan clients, hardly to their benefit" (9–11, 79), but he neglects to explain precisely which great power reasons were disposi-tive in inducing the United States first to select such unlikely clients and then to allow those clients—because concern for their grim fate was not prominent among the reasons for American support—to be butchered by the thousands for most of the rest of the decade. Chomsky then attributes to bin Laden a series of grievances against the United States:

> Bin Laden is also bitterly opposed to the corrupt and repressive re-gimes of the region, which he regards as "un-Islamic," including the Saudi Arabian regime, the most extreme Islamic fundamentalist re-gime in the world, apart from the Taliban, and a close U.S. ally since its origins. Bin Laden despises the U.S. for its support of these regimes. Like others in the region, he is also outraged by longstanding U.S. support for Israel's brutal military occupation, now in its 35th year: Washington's decisive diplomatic, military, and economic intervention in support of the killings, the harsh and destructive siege over many years, the daily humiliation to which Palestinians are subjected, the expanding settlements designed to break the occupied territories into Bantustan-like cantons and take control of the resources, the gross violation of the Geneva Conventions, and other actions that are rec-ognized as crimes throughout most of the world, apart from the U.S., which has prime responsibility for them. And like others, he contrasts Washington's dedicated support for these crimes with the decade-long U.S.-British assault against the civilian population of Iraq, which has devastated the society and caused hundreds of thousands of deaths while strengthening Saddam Hussein—who was a favored friend and

ally of the U.S. and Britain right through his worst atrocities, including
the gassing of the Kurds, as people of the region also remember well,
even if Westerners prefer to forget the facts. (Radio B92)

This forgetfulness certainly does not speak very well of those Westerners. But Chomsky's emphases seem somewhat awry here; the first two
sentences clearly invite the interpretation that bin Laden's disdain for U.S.
support of Saudi Arabia stems from the fact that the United States has allied itself with "the most extreme Islamic fundamentalist regime in the
world, apart from the Taliban" and that bin Laden therefore has a critique
of U.S. foreign policy that corresponds to that of American leftists.[12] The
second pair of sentences go even further and make bin Laden sound almost like Chomsky himself—deeply and righteously opposed to the brutal Israeli occupation in sentence three, and outraged in sentence four over
the contrast between U.S. support for Israel and U.S. sanctions against
Iraq.[13] Yet Chomsky does not acknowledge that the Islamic regimes that
bin Laden would like to install would be even more repressive than those
he seeks to supplant; though bin Laden is "bitterly opposed to the corrupt and repressive regimes of the region," he is opposed to them from the
right—not because he has weighed them in the scales of secular, pluralist,
democratic ideals and has found them wanting.

Chomsky then proceeds to cite a *Wall Street Journal* article surveying
the views of "wealthy and privileged Muslims in the Gulf region (bank-
ers, professionals, businessmen with close links to the U.S.)" and reports
that "they expressed much the same views: resentment of the U.S. policies of supporting Israeli crimes and blocking the international consensus
on a diplomatic settlement for many years while devastating Iraqi civilian
society, supporting harsh and repressive anti-democratic regimes throughout the region, and imposing barriers against economic development by
'propping up oppressive regimes.'" To this array of beliefs, Chomsky contrasts the simplistic West:

The U.S., and much of the West, prefers a more comforting story. To
quote the lead analysis in the *New York Times* (Sept. 16), the perpetrators acted out of "hatred for the values cherished in the West as freedom, tolerance, prosperity, religious pluralism and universal suffrage."
U.S. actions are irrelevant, and therefore need not even be mentioned
(Serge Schmemann ["What Would 'Victory' Mean?"]). This is a con-
venient picture, and the general stance is not unfamiliar in intellectual

history; in fact, it is close to the norm. It happens to be completely at variance with everything we know, but has all the merits of self-adulation and uncritical support for power.

This paraphrase makes it sound as if the *Times* "analysis" consisted exclusively of shallow jingoism and tabloid-quality cheerleading: indeed, U.S. actions are irrelevant and need not even be mentioned! But Chomsky isn't being remotely fair to Schmemann's article—perhaps, one wonders, in order to assure his listeners and his readers that he and he alone has the courage to mention "U.S. actions," just as he and he alone doubted the Bush-Cheney administration's rationale for war in Iraq. As a matter of fact, however, Schmemann quite clearly noted that anguished debate had begun about the appropriate scale of the U.S. response:

> Now and again, the fear that the pressure for action would lead to an erosion of America's own values could be heard through the acrid smoke.
> "Not to respond would be unthinkable: it would diminish and demean American leadership and would surely invite further attacks," wrote Charles G. Boyd, a retired Air Force general, in Wednesday's *Washington Post.* "But to react excessively or inaccurately would put us on the same moral footing as the cowards who perpetrated yesterday's attack." ("What Would 'Victory' Mean?")

And Schmemann proceeded to put the attacks, and the possible U.S. responses, in global perspective:

> Yet the wake-up call was so violent that raw vengeance threatened to take the place of serious discussion. Though debate is bound to resume on the wisdom of building a costly defense against missiles now, the challenge went beyond deciding where to put the money. An effective war on international terrorism would require a fundamental revision of American national security strategy, as well as an admission that America cannot go it alone.
> And dealing with terrorism rather than just terrorists surely requires not only stamping out cells, but understanding the poverty and hopelessness in which recruits are found, as well as the conflicts that, left unresolved too long, foster deep and lasting hatreds. It requires understanding that these are often forces Americans themselves have helped

set loose, as when the United States armed and financed Afghan rebels against the Soviet Union.

Just to keep things straight: those words are Schmemann's, not Chomsky's. Schmemann continues:

"We need to understand that this kind of operative thrives in a place like Afghanistan or Pakistan, that their humanitarian crises pose a tremendous security threat to the entire world, and that this requires a completely new response, that it requires intelligence, diplomacy—and yes, if the perpetrator is identified, a military response," argued Jessica Stern, a lecturer at Harvard's Kennedy School of Government who has conducted extensive studies among the soldiers of various holy wars.

The war also requires an appreciation of the complexity of Islamic militancies and the governments that sponsor them. Israel's most respected columnist, Nahum Barnea of Yedioth Ahronot, said he was troubled by the Israeli politicians who now hope that the United States will step in and deliver the definitive blow to Islamic terrorism. The same complex of politics, grievances and hatreds that have confounded the Israelis will confront the Americans, he said: "There's no black and white in the war against terrorism. In order to fight the Taliban you need help from Iran. Or you can fight Iran, but then you have to confront the Russians, who are helping them get nuclear weapons. Or you can fight Iraq, but then you need support from Syria, which supports Hezbollah and George Habash." . . .

And it will require a recognition that America cannot go it alone. The people who attacked the United States on Tuesday attacked it as the leader of the first world, not as an island of prosperity. Moreover, the long-term, global campaign that the ensuing struggle demands, whether in crushing terror cells or alleviating the conditions that created them, will require extensive cooperation not only from NATO, but from agencies like the United Nations.

I do not believe that it is possible to characterize Chomsky's summary of Schmemann's article—let alone his claim that it has "all the merits of self-adulation and uncritical support for power"- as intellectually honest or responsible. But it makes sense as part of a rhetorical strategy in which the *New York Times* is cast as a weapon of mass deception and intellectuals

like Chomsky appear as lone voices in a wilderness of consent-manufac-
turing mass media.

Chomsky's response to his interviewers' second question is more restrained—and yet more problematic:

> Q: What consequences will they have on U.S. inner policy and to the
> American self reception?
>
> A: U.S. policy has already been officially announced. The world is be-
> ing offered a "stark choice": join us, or "face the certain prospect of
> death and destruction." Congress has authorized the use of force
> against any individuals or countries the President determines to
> be involved in the attacks, a doctrine that every supporter regards
> as ultra-criminal. That is easily demonstrated. Simply ask how the
> same people would have reacted if Nicaragua had adopted this doc-
> trine after the U.S. had rejected the orders of the World Court to
> terminate its "unlawful use of force" against Nicaragua and had ve-
> toed a Security Council resolution calling on all states to observe
> international law. And that terrorist attack was far more severe and
> destructive even than this atrocity. (Radio B92)

The salient items here are the strange claim that every *supporter* of the use
of force regards such a response as "ultra-criminal" and the equally strange
claim that the U.S. mining of Nicaraguan harbors, which was rightly condemned by the World Court and rightly protested (with regard both to
substance and procedure) by Nicaragua, was "far more severe and destructive" than the events of 9/11. One begins, at this point, to wonder
whether there is any U.S. violation of international law that does not dwarf
al-Qaeda's strikes against the Pentagon and the World Trade Center.

The next question elicited a claim that resonates on the radical left to
this day. Drawing on a report from the *New York Times* of September 16,
Chomsky said:

> The U.S. has already demanded that Pakistan terminate the food and
> other supplies that are keeping at least some of the starving and suf-
> fering people of Afghanistan alive. If that demand is implemented,
> unknown numbers of people who have not the remotest connec-
> tion to terrorism will die, possibly millions. Let me repeat: the U.S.
> has demanded that Pakistan kill possibly millions of people who are
> themselves victims of the Taliban. This has nothing to do even with

revenge. It is at a far lower moral level even than that. The significance is heightened by the fact that this is mentioned in passing, with no comment, and probably will hardly be noticed. We can learn a great deal about the moral level of the reigning intellectual culture of the West by observing the reaction to this demand.

This passage is the basis of the later claim that the United States is responsible for five to seven million deaths because of the interruption of those Pakistani food convoys between September and November of 2001, and I return to this claim in the following pages. For now, however, I simply note it and move to Chomsky's final answer from the Radio B92 interview:

Q: "The world will never be the same after 11.09.01." Do you think so?

A: The horrendous terrorist attacks on Tuesday are something quite new in world affairs, not in their scale and character, but in the target. For the U.S., this is the first time since the War of 1812 that its national territory has been under attack, even threat. Its colonies have been attacked, but not the national territory itself. During these years the U.S. virtually exterminated the indigenous population, conquered half of Mexico, intervened violently in the surrounding region, conquered Hawaii and the Philippines (killing hundreds of thousands of Filipinos), and in the past half century particularly, extended its resort to force throughout much of the world. The number of victims is colossal. For the first time, the guns have been directed the other way. The same is true, even more dramatically, of Europe. Europe has suffered murderous destruction, but from internal wars, meanwhile conquering much of the world with extreme brutality. It has not been under attack by its victims outside, with rare exceptions (the IRA in England, for example). It is therefore natural that NATO should rally to the support of the U.S.; hundreds of years of imperial violence have an enormous impact on the intellectual and moral culture.

Many people around the world look back to the day on which Le Monde declared "nous sommes tout américains" and see in that gesture an admirable statement of solidarity with the victims of a terrible crime, a moment of solidarity that the Bush-Cheney administration squandered in its drive to invade Iraq and trample the United Nations. Others, like Chomsky, saw that moment of Euro-American unity, expressed both by ordinary citizens and by NATO's invocation of Article V ("an attack on one is an attack on all"), as the culmination of hundreds of years of imperial violence that had an enormous—and, we may presume, deleterious—effect on the intellectual and moral culture of democratic societies. The history of Western oppression is all too real, of course; there is no need for a critic of Chomsky to become an apologist for Western imperialism. But it is not at all clear that the events of 9/11 represented a reversal of the guns that were used to slaughter Native American peoples and conquer Mexico.

THE MOOD AT HOME

Much of what I have written above is old news. The interviews and debates date from the fall of 2001, and are surely familiar—if not overfamiliar—to some readers. Why, then, is it worth the trouble to revisit them now, to parse Chomsky's claims about al-Shifa and his post-9/11 interviews so carefully, long after the United States has embarked on truly horrific crimes around the globe, from Guantánamo to Abu Ghraib? Simply because they set the rhetorical terms and the political agenda for the Manichean left's response to the world after 9/11—and, in so doing, created the parameters for what would count in those precincts *as* a "left" response. Anyone who wants to imagine another American left, therefore, is obliged to go back over these field-defining principles and dicta in order to see how we got here—and why we should go someplace else.

And yet, on its own terms, Chomsky's response to 9/11 makes a certain kind of sense: it is a radical denunciation of the United States, undertaken without consideration of its occasion and without even the slightest of nods toward the consequences of actions by other forces in the world—from the Soviet invasion of Afghanistan to the depradations of Milošević in the Balkans to the history of NIF rule in the Sudan. There are no concessions here to petty American sensibilities—to the sense of shock, of loss, of bereavement—or to the fear of follow-up attacks, particularly among New Yorkers who had known since 1993 that radical Islamists had also devised plans to take out the city's bridges and tunnels. There are no words about the grainy details of the attack and the topography of lower Manhattan with its capillary networks of subways and commuter trains (one branch of the PATH, of course, went directly to the World Trade Center, and the officials—PATH Deputy Director Victoria Cross Kelly and trainmaster Richie Moran, who directed one incoming train to skip the stop at the World Trade Center (WTC) and another train to discharge passengers in New Jersey and arrive empty at the WTC to facilitate evacuation—may have saved thousands of lives) (Cohen et al., "Catastrophe and the Public Service"), the consideration of which, if treated with the logic Chomsky applied to Afghanistan, Sudan, and Nicaragua, might have troubled the moral calculus by which he had determined that the number of victims of 9/11 was surpassed by far more heinous hypothetical deaths that might have occurred elsewhere. But what's especially perplexing about this rhetorical performance is that, here and elsewhere, Chomsky closes with the insistence that *he is actually trying to appeal to people whose opinions might help determine the course of future action:*

> How the West chooses to react is a matter of supreme importance. If the rich and powerful choose to keep to their traditions of hundreds of years and resort to extreme violence, they will contribute to the escalation of a cycle of violence, in a familiar dynamic, with long-term consequences that could be awesome. Of course, that is by no means inevitable. An aroused public within the more free and democratic societies can direct policies towards a much more humane and honorable course. (Radio B92)

Chomsky strikes this note repeatedly in these early interviews, as when he tells Z editor Michael Albert on September 22, "What the administration does will depend, in part at least, on the mood at home, which we can hope to influence" (*9–11*, 64). But it is not easy to explain why any left strategist would go about trying to influence "the mood at home" in this way.

For the record, criticism of Chomsky's rhetorical strategies is not confined to tepid liberals and mainstream pundit-aspirants who fear the unvarnished truth of America's role in world affairs and believe that "the mood at home" can be influenced only by stepping lightly over American crimes. Writing in the Marxist online journal *Politics and Culture* in 2002, Scott Wible filed a largely sympathetic review of Chomsky's *9–11* (sufficiently sympathetic, for example, to label liberal Louis Menand a "conservative" for Menand's criticism of Chomsky) that nonetheless registered some discomfort with Chomsky's style of address:

> Throughout much of the text, Chomsky leaves little room for political debate within his analysis—you're either moral, rational, and with

him, or you're "feverish and fanciful" in condemning him (46). No-where does the reader find a glimpse of the varied moral and ethical perspectives that the U.S. citizens have struggled to create as the Bush administration seems prepared to mobilize the military for an attack on Iraq. Take, for instance, Chomsky's assertion that there are two kinds of citizens of the Western world, those who intend "to reduce the probability of further atrocities" and those who want to "react with extreme violence, and expect to escalate the cycle of violence, leading to still further atrocities such as the one that is inciting the call for re-venge" (26). There are certainly more than two ways of thinking and talking about the White House's use of military force and diplomacy in its "War on Terrorism," but Chomsky's sharp delineation effectively shuts down necessary engagement with the majority of Westerners that he believes have failed to retain "their sanity and moral integrity."

The relevant question, of course, is whether Chomsky is serious about try-ing to influence public opinion on a larger scale or whether he has simply given up on engaging the majority of Westerners on the grounds that they are a lost cause—but, perhaps, for a saving remnant.

In all fairness, it should be mentioned that some of Chomsky's state-ments in 9–11 follow from the inanity of the questions put to him, and Chomsky deserves some credit for batting away some of the silliest. For example, the Italian Communist journal Il Manifesto asks, "Could you say something about connivance and the role of American secret service?" ap-parently suggesting that the attacks were planned from within the United States but unaware of what the American "secret service" consists of. Chomsky diplomatically replies, "I don't quite understand the question" (17–18). But nevertheless, some rather odd passages make it into the book all the same. To Albert, Chomsky says, "many who know the con-ditions well are also dubious about bin Laden's capacity to plan that in-credibly sophisticated operation from a cave somewhere in Afghanistan" (59–60). This bizarre claim—attributed, one notes, to "many who know the conditions well"—wound up being repeated almost word for word by Michael Moore in Dude, Where's My Country? (16), thereby cementing the impression that some figures on the American left will repeat practically anything Chomsky utters, no matter how speculative or preposterous.

Later in the same interview, Chomsky makes a remark that he repeats often in the following years: that the U.S. response to 9/11 is historically unique, for the British response to Irish Republican Army bombings was "to consider realistically the background concerns and grievances, and try to remedy them" (*9–11, 62*) and that, in the U.S. response to the Oklahoma City bombing, "there were efforts to understand the grievances that lie behind such crimes and to address the problems" (63). In reality, by contrast, the British response to the IRA included Bloody Sunday; Operation Demetrius, establishing internment without trial for suspected Irish nationalists; the wrongful imprisonment of the Guildford Four, the Birmingham Six, and the Maguire Seven; and the ten deaths by starvation in the Irish Hunger Strike of 1981—to reference only those aspects of British repression that date from 1971, leaving aside the history of British oppression in Ireland since the Battle of the Boyne. The U.S. response to Oklahoma City included the execution of Timothy McVeigh and the passage of severe new antiterrorism laws, laws that have since been regularly castigated by the left for their erosion of civil liberties. It is not as if the U.S. Department of Justice, in the course of its investigation into the Oklahoma City bombing, decided to convene a book club on William Pierce's racist screed *The Turner Diaries* in order to "understand the grievances" of white supremacists like McVeigh. Perhaps, by contrasting the American response to al-Qaeda with his fanciful characterization of the British response to the IRA, Chomsky is attempting, by way of a curious *détournement* of American exceptionalism, to suggest that other nations' responses to terrorist violence have been comparatively rational. But whatever his aim, he leaves himself looking woefully ignorant about the actual history of the British response to the IRA.[14]

One of the longest-lived and best-known of Chomsky's early arguments has to do with the interruption of the aid convoys from Pakistan. The quotation has made its way around the Internet, resonating on blogs and websites around the world:

> The U.S. has demanded that Pakistan kill possibly millions of people who are themselves victims of the Taliban. This has nothing to do even with revenge. It is at a far lower moral level even than that. The significance is heightened by the fact that this is mentioned in passing, with no comment, and probably will hardly be noticed. We can learn a great deal about the moral level of the reigning intellectual culture of the West by observing the reaction to this demand. (Radio B92)

As with the Serge Schmemann essay that appeared on the same day, the *New York Times* article from which this claim is drawn (Burns, "Pakistan

Antiterror Support") is considerably more complex than Chomsky suggests.[15] But more important, for my present purposes, is the way this claim metastasized from September 2001 onward. Almost immediately, it became the basis for Chomsky's even more famous claim, in an October 18 speech at the Massachusetts Institute of Technology, that the United States was engaged in a "silent genocide" in Afghanistan:

> According to the *New York Times* there are 7 to 8 million people in Afghanistan on the verge of starvation. That was true actually before September 11th. They were surviving on international aid. On September 16th, the *Times* reported, I'm quoting it, that the United States demanded from Pakistan the elimination of truck convoys that provide much of the food and other supplies to Afghanistan's civilian population. As far as I could determine there was no reaction in the United States or for that matter in Europe. I was on national radio all over Europe the next day. There was no reaction in the United States or in Europe to my knowledge to the demand to impose massive starvation on millions of people. The threat of military strikes right after September—around that time forced the removal of international aid workers that crippled the assistance programs. Actually, I am quoting again from the *New York Times*. . . .
>
> Well we could easily go on—but all of that—first of all indicates to us what's happening. Looks like what's happening is some sort of silent genocide. It also gives a good deal of insight into the elite culture, the culture that we are part of. It indicates that whatever, what will happen we don't know, but plans are being made, and programs implemented, on the assumption that they may lead to the death of several million people in the next couple of weeks. Very casually with no comment, no particular thought about it, that's just kind of normal, here and in a good part of Europe. ("The New War against Terror")

Again, we find the gesture of the lone truth-telling intellectual in a crowd of casual mass murderers: *no one brings these facts to light except for me.* But, actually, there was a great deal of comment about this at the time and throughout the fall of 2001. Aid organizations continually criticized the United States for its ineffectual (and PR-driven) food drops from the air, and many liberal and progressive commentators debated the likely humanitarian costs of the war.[16] What happened, however, in some of that debate, was that Chomsky's claims were debated on the merits. In

November 2001, progressive journalist Laura Rozen wrote, in *Salon*, about the debates within those humanitarian aid organizations about whether their initial predictions were warranted:

> But aid experts say that the agencies' repeated alarms about the impact of the U.S. military campaign against the Taliban on relief efforts have ignored the fact that more food has been reaching Afghanistan since the U.S. bombing began than was before—a lot more.
>
> "More aid has gone into Afghanistan in the past month than in the past year," says John Fawcett, a longtime humanitarian relief worker who studies the politics of aid. "The aid agencies cried wolf. They said the bombing will stop us from delivering humanitarian aid. It will create 1.5 million refugees. Well, in fact, the result of the bombing is there are 150,000 new refugees—one-tenth of what they expected, and there's been a tenfold increase of humanitarian aid getting in, because everybody's focused on the problem now."
>
> The lead U.N. food agency, the World Food Program (WFP), has been getting 2,000 tons of food a day into Afghanistan—up from 200 tons a day before Sept. 11, Fawcett notes. The WFP confirms that. ("Crying Wolf, or Doing Their Job?")

Lest Fawcett sound as if he is belittling or trivializing the aid agencies, I note that Rozen's article immediately added, "Fawcett says aid groups shouldn't be criticized for sounding the alarm about Afghanistan's horrific humanitarian plight. 'It's aid groups' job to cry wolf. We know that. And the WFP is doing a good job. They have been very flexible' in a situation of constant flux on the ground in Afghanistan.'"

From a Chomskian perspective, it is always possible to dismiss Rozen's account as a particularly deceptive piece of mass-media propaganda. But through November and December, other aid workers testified that the fall of the Taliban had benefited their work considerably. Mark Bartolini, vice president of the International Rescue Committee, told the *Times*, "had this war not occurred, we wouldn't have had the access we have now—the best access in the past decade" (quoted in Weiner, "Now, the Battle to Feed"). In December, the World Food Program's Jordan Dey told the BBC, "We are serving six million people in Afghanistan and that is using between 2,000 and 2,500 trucks, barges, rail cars, and even airplanes. We are moving record amounts of food into Afghanistan this month" (quoted in "Kandahar 'No Go'"). In the *Washington Post*, U.N. World Food Program

Executive Director Catherine Bertini told reporter Marc Kaufman, "There will be no famine in Afghanistan this winter. There will be deaths, because the country was in a pre-famine condition before the war started. But it will be isolated, and not large-scale"; Andrew S. Natsios, administrator of the U.S. Agency for International Development, added, "I thought and feared earlier I would be facing a famine next spring, but now I believe we will not. It was caught at an early stage, despite the war" (quoted in Kaufman, "Massive Food Delivery").

According to a mid-2002 report by the media watchdog group Fairness and Accuracy in Reporting, less hopeful claims about humanitarian relief in Afghanistan were indeed underreported in the U.S. press, as was the fact that the United States ignored U.N. Human Rights Commissioner Mary Robinson's request for a cease-fire in October 2001, as well as the three-day cease-fire in November, observed by the Taliban and the Northern Alliance in order to allow UNICEF to conduct its polio immunization program in Afghanistan (Ackerman, "Afghan Famine"). But Chomsky's skepticism about these claims ran far ahead of FAIR's. About the fall of the Taliban, he wrote in February 2002, "When Taliban forces did finally succumb, after astonishing endurance, opinions shifted to triumphalist proclamations and exultation over the justice of our cause, now demonstrated by the success of overwhelming force against defenseless opponents. Without researching the topic, I suppose that Japanese and German commentary was similar after early victories during World War II" ("War in Afghanistan"). Leaving aside the question of why Chomsky would hail the "astonishing endurance" of the Taliban, I confine myself to noting Chomsky's equation of American commentary on the overthrow of the Taliban with Japanese and German commentary on the early victories of the Axis powers in World War II. (Recall here Dan Lazare telling Michael Medved and David Horowitz, "I think Hitler had probably more reason to attack Poland than Bush had to attack Iraq.")

It is critical, at this point, to understand how Chomsky himself understands his own claim with regard to "silent genocide": for as far as he is concerned, he did not properly make any claim at all. Thus in late 2003, Chomsky replied as follows to a reader of the *Independent* (U.K.) who asked, "Where is the 'silent genocide' you predicted would happen in Afghanistan if the U.S. intervened there in 2001?"

That is an interesting fabrication, which gives a good deal of insight into the prevailing moral and intellectual culture. First the facts: I predicted nothing. Rather, I reported the grim warnings from virtually every knowledgeable source that the attack might lead to an awesome humanitarian catastrophe, and the bland announcements in the press that Washington had ordered Pakistan to eliminate "truck convoys that provide much of the food and other supplies to Afghanistan's civilian population." (Interview)

This is an important exchange. As we have seen above, in his speech at MIT, Chomsky had actually said, "*Looks like what's happening is* some sort of silent genocide." This does not appear to be a prediction; rather, it looks very much like a straightforward "description" or an "account" of an ongoing silent genocide. In response to this 2003 question (from one Mike Dudley of Ipswich), however, Chomsky insists that he was "report[ing] the grim warnings from virtually every knowledgeable source that the attack might lead to an awesome humanitarian catastrophe."

There are three things going on in this reply to Mr. Dudley: one, Chomsky insists he was merely repeating warnings made by others; two, Chomsky offers a change of mood, so to speak, from the indicative to the subjunctive, as well as a retrospective change of tense from the present to the future (that is, from "looks like what's happening," which is what he said, to something more like "looks like what other people say might happen," which is what he now claims to have meant); and three, Chomsky takes the question (as he did with Leo Casey's critique of his claims about the al-Shifa bombing) as evidence of the moral depravity of the questioner. Apparently, only someone immersed in the prevailing moral and intellectual culture (with all that implies) would ask Chomsky about his *prediction* of a silent genocide.

After 2003, Chomsky modified his not-claim still further, arguing that the risk of starvation *should have been* called a silent genocide: in *Hegemony or Survival,* he writes,

> "Studied lack of interest" in the likely consequences of war for the population of the country to be invaded is conventional. The same was true, when, five days after 9-11, Washington demanded that Pakistan eliminate "truck convoys that provide much of the food and other supplies to Afghanistan's civilian population," and caused the withdrawal of aid workers along with severe reductions in food supplies, thereby leaving "millions of Afghans . . . at grave risk of starvation"—risk of what should properly have been termed "silent genocide." (128–29)

The second citation here is to an essay by Samina Ahmed ("The United States and Terrorism"), then a senior analyst in the Pakistan/Afghanistan Project at the International Crisis Group; it appeared in the journal *International Security* in late 2001. Ahmed's essay notes that "in Afghanistan, continued reliance on force is far less likely to promote U.S. antiterrorism objectives in the long run than is humanitarian assistance for the economic reconstruction of that war-ravaged country. Massive international assistance is urgently needed to avert a looming humanitarian crisis—the result of civil war, famine, and drought—that U.S. military operations have exacerbated" (92). But it is worth noting that while Chomsky cites Ahmed's concern for Afghanistan's civilian population, he studiously refrains from citing her verdict on the war, further down on the same page: "The removal of the Taliban regime was in the interests of the United States and the Afghan people. International terrorism was funded by their drug economy. Anti-U.S. terrorists received the Taliban's sanctuary and support, while their distorted brand of Islamic orthodoxy deprived the Afghan people of their civil rights" (92).

So far, we have the following: Chomsky did not predict a silent genocide, he did not describe an ongoing silent genocide, and yet the risk of starvation in Afghanistan should have been termed a silent genocide. Now that we understand this much, we need to understand why it is crucial to assess U.S. actions in Afghanistan with regard to the *risk* of humanitarian catastrophe rather than with regard to the *actual occurrence* (or nonoccurrence) of humanitarian catastrophe. And to understand that, we need to look to the Cuban Missile Crisis. Elsewhere in *Hegemony or Survival,* Chomsky writes:

> It is the merest truism that choices are assessed in terms of the range of likely consequences. We understand the truism very well when considering the actions of official enemies but find it hard to apply to ourselves. There are many illustrations, including recent U.S. military exercises. Aid agencies, scholars, and others who properly warned of the risks in Afghanistan and Iraq were ridiculed when the worst, fortunately, did not come to pass. At the same level of moral imbecility, one would rush into the streets every October to sing praises to the Kremlin, while ridiculing those who warned of the dangers of placing missiles in Cuba and persist in condemning the criminal lunacy of the act. (78)

Here as throughout his career, Chomsky insists that Americans fail to understand such truisms because they exempt themselves from the moral accounting those truisms require and apply them asymmetrically (and hypocritically) to their enemies.

Allow me, then, to take Chomsky's analogy to the Cuban Missile Crisis on its merits and to add the mere truism that choices are also assessed in terms of *actual* consequences. It is not clear, on that score, what a sober post hoc assessment of the temporary interruption of Afghan aid convoys has to do with rushing into the streets every October to sing praises to the Kremlin, but this much *is* clear: Chomsky's position on Afghanistan is not "I relied on the reports of aid workers as relayed by the *New York Times*, and though (thankfully) the worst predictions did not come to pass, I still oppose the war on Afghanistan on moral grounds." This is a position I would disagree with but would certainly respect. Rather, Chomsky's position is that people who reassessed the moral calculus of the war in Afghanistan after the fall of the Taliban—that is, after the most dire warnings did not come to pass—are *moral imbeciles,* the equivalent of people who would praise the Kremlin (on an annual basis, no less) for precipitating the Cuban Missile Crisis.

As with Chomsky's inscrutable invocation of the British response to the IRA, it is impossible to tell whether he means the Soviet analogy seriously. Aside from the elementary point that certain actions may have terrible consequences, I can discover no sense in which the war that deposed the Taliban is like the Soviet gamble that very nearly led to an intercontinental nuclear exchange—in other words, to the possible destruction of all human life on the planet. For even if the U.S. invasion of Afghanistan heightened the possibility of (but did not ultimately bring about) massive civilian starvation, there is no plausible moral sense in which this possible consequence is comparable with the possible consequence of global thermonuclear war.

Chomsky may be forgiven, in some quarters, for trying to cast American actions in the most extreme terms, even when those actions do not have the consequence of the "silent genocide" Chomsky neither predicted nor described. But his analogy to the Cuban Missile Crisis is especially ill considered. For insofar as the United States and its allies helped to disrupt the alliance between al-Qaeda and Pakistan's Inter-Services Intelligence (ISI), the 2001–02 war in Afghanistan may well have prevented al-Qaeda from obtaining access to Pakistan's nuclear arsenal and thereby decreased the likelihood of tactical nuclear warfare, whereas the Soviet placement of nuclear weapons in Cuba clearly increased the likelihood of global nuclear warfare. One only wishes, on this score, that the United States had *more effectively and permanently* disrupted the alliance between al-Qaeda and Pakistan's ISI.

THE Z MATRIX

By the mid-2000s, then, Chomsky's initial claims about 9/11 and the war in Afghanistan had hardened into dogma—and had been further festooned with ancillary accusations that not only underscored the initial claims but raised the rhetorical stakes by casting all those who doubted or challenged those claims as cowards, imbeciles, and moral reprobates. As a result, the proper "left" party line on Afghanistan had become not that the war had failed to establish a stable non-Islamist regime in the country and had failed to keep the Taliban at bay, but that, as Chomsky phrased it in a 2006 interview, "Afghanistan, if we look at it, is one of the most grotesque acts of modern history" (Stephen, Interview with Chomsky).

It is on those grounds, then, that Z magazine founder Michael Albert, taking Chomsky's cue, performed the delicate series of calculations that ended in the conclusion that bin Laden ranked somewhat higher on the moral scale than George Bush and Dick Cheney—not because of the war in Iraq, the string of secret torture camps, or the assault on civil liberties and the separation of powers at home, but solely because of the possibility of Afghan starvation in late 2001 ("Raise Your Voice but Keep Your Head Down"). But to fault Chomsky or Albert for failing to tailor their remarks to a U.S. audience is to miss the point. For although they gesture repeatedly at the project of shifting public opinion, repeating to each other that "what the administration does will depend, in part at least, on the mood at home, which we can hope to influence," it should be clear that these rhetorical strategies—inflating the al-Shifa bombing and the interruption of aid convoys to the point at which they rival the Holocaust, attributing the actions of bin Laden and al-Qaeda almost wholly to "root causes" traceable to U.S. policy—are not likely to win the hearts and minds of Americans. To read Chomsky and to blame him for not leading "the mood at home" to the left is, I suggest, to misread Chomsky entirely.

Instead, I suggest we should read Chomsky's claims precisely as *countercultural* claims on our collective political attention. And to understand

Chomsky as countercultural icon, we need to understand the contours and premises of countercultural thought. In their bracing and witty (and leftist) critique of the countercultural left, *Nation of Rebels: Why Counterculture Became Consumer Culture* (published in Canada under the title *The Rebel Sell*), Canadian philosophers Joseph Heath and Andrew Potter offer *The Matrix* as a Debordian countercultural fantasy:

> The inhabitants of Zion, in *The Matrix*, are a concrete embodiment of how countercultural rebels since the '60s have conceived of themselves. They are the ones who have been awakened, the ones who are free from the tyranny of the machines. And the enemy, in this view, is those who refuse to be awakened, those who insist on conforming to the culture. The enemy, in other words, is *mainstream society*.
>
> Morpheus sums up the countercultural analysis perfectly when describing the Matrix: "The Matrix is a system, Neo. That system is our enemy. But when you're inside, you look around, what do you see? Businessmen, teachers, lawyers, carpenters. The very minds of the people we are trying to save. But until we do, these people are still a part of that system and that makes them our enemy. You have to understand, most of these people are not ready to be unplugged. And many of them are so inured, so hopelessly dependent on the system, that they will fight to protect it." (7–8)

Let me be clear about my citation of Heath and Potter: I am not claiming that Noam Chomsky somehow patterned his political commentary and his rhetorical style after a science-fiction movie that came out in 1999. Rather, I am saying that the best way to make sense of Chomsky's rhetorical style, in combination with his insistence that he is trying to influence "the mood at home," is to suggest that his manner of trying to influence the mood at home is of a piece with his propaganda thesis of mass media. When you're inside the mass media's propaganda machine, you look around, what do you see? Media elites and their corporate masters, reporters, newscasters, mainstream intellectuals, new mandarins. The very minds of the people we are trying to save. But until we save them, these people are still a part of that system and that makes them our enemy. Besides, most of those people are not ready to be unplugged, and many are so inured, so hopelessly dependent on the system, so immersed in the *prevailing moral and intellectual culture,* that they will fight to protect it. That is why we must continue to insist that the bombing of al-Shifa and the invasion of Afghanistan were crimes against humanity far greater than anything that has been perpetrated by al-Qaeda.

In other words, Chomsky's mode of address to American readers after September 11 makes sense if, and only if, one starts from the assumption that one's fellow Americans are Matrix dwellers who have had the al-Shifa bombing and the possibility of mass starvation in Afghanistan erased from their memories by elite media mandarins and policymakers who have no concern whatsoever for the lives of the Sudanese or the Afghans—or, indeed, anyone who is not an American. What is needed, if that is the case, is not a nuanced series of arguments weighing the costs and benefits of various avenues of response to al-Qaeda's attack and parsing the rise of Islamic radicalism in the Arab world; what is needed is a kind of shock therapy, a blue pill, that will cause the scales to fall from the eyes as one's readers and listeners come to grips with the horrible truth that their government contemplated killing millions to prove it was tough, and that its leading newspaper rallied the sheeplike commentariat with news "analyses" that had all the merits of self-adulation and uncritical support for power.

It so happens that many of my fellow Americans know little about the al-Shifa bombing and are unaware of or indifferent to U.S. policies that increase the misery of the innocent and powerless in countries they can't even find on a map. For some of those people, reading Chomsky can be a tonic for the uninitiated—as long as they don't dismiss Chomsky altogether. But as shown in this chapter, when one goes beyond Chomsky to his sources and to competing sources—be they Jason Burke, Samina Ahmed, Leo Casey, Lawrence Wright, Serge Schmemann, or the text of the Dayton Accords—a much more complex picture results. Certainly, there is something to be said for shock therapy; doubtless this accounts for much of Chomsky's following. But there is also something to be said for running down sources and appreciating political arguments in their full complexity. Readers who don't do this, those who insistently take Chomsky's every word on faith, wind up as acolytes.

It is in this sense that one can speak of Chomsky's approach as a leftism of *style*—a style in which initially plausible or merely speculative claims (about al-Shifa or the interruption of aid convoys) are elaborated and inflated to the point at which they command the assent of only a tiny handful of true believers. In countercultural politics, this is a good thing; the greater the number of people who disagree with you, the more clearly and bravely you must be speaking truth to power. As Chomsky fan

Robert Barsky puts it in *The Chomsky Effect: A Radical Works beyond the Ivory Tower,* "the effect he is looking for . . . is an anarchist-inspired one: to stimulate the 'rabble' to creative action that accords with their own views and experiences. He has at times regrets that his effect is rejected or ignored in popular media, but on other occasions rightly points out that if he were held up as an icon in these corporate-controlled outlets he'd have to question the degree to which his message was appropriately dissenting" (104).

Chomsky's work on 9/11, in other words, does not seek to persuade; it seeks to galvanize. Its ideal (or assumed) reader would seem to be someone who had had no idea of the history of U.S. imperialism: no idea that, before 9/11, the United States virtually exterminated the indigenous population, conquered half of Mexico, intervened violently in the surrounding region, and conquered Hawaii and the Philippines, killing hundreds of thousands of Filipinos. That reader needs to be informed about U.S. history in the starkest possible terms, apparently, before one can embark on a proper analysis of al-Qaeda and September 11. Readers and listeners who reject the analysis, consequently, can safely be dismissed as American exceptionalists, apologists for imperialism, fantasists, system-dependents, and moral imbeciles who, for a variety of reasons, prefer to dwell in the Matrix and will defend their delusional existence to the death; whereas readers and listeners who heed the call, who undertake the journey necessary to understand that the war in Afghanistan was one of the most grotesque acts of modern history, will constitute the few, the free, the proud members of Zion, laboring under duress and against tremendous odds to save humanity from its greatest scourge.

It should be no wonder that Chomsky is popular not only among radical leftists but among young anarchists and post-punks, for the logic at work here is very much the logic of the alternative music scene: Chomsky's value is partly a function of his marginality to mainstream political commentary. That is, the extent to which Chomsky is ignored or vilified by the mass media becomes the index of his intellectual integrity: he is considered a fringe figure by the architects of the Matrix precisely because he tells the unpleasant and unvarnished truth. By the same token, principled critics of the Iraq war like Mark Danner and Todd Gitlin (by "principled" I mean that they opposed the war on principle rather than with regard to its conduct, and never accepted the argument that the war could have succeeded if only it had been fought differently), can be set aside precisely because their work appears in "establishment" venues like the

New York Review of Books and *American Prospect.* Those publications, like the despised Democratic Party itself, are for crossovers and sellouts. This is why, on the countercultural left, the argument that Chomsky's analyses are not taken seriously by established scholars of international relations makes no headway whatsoever: for as it is with the mainstream respectability of mass media, so, too, is it with the mainstream respectability of international relations scholars who have studied Sudan or Afghanistan or Islamism or the Balkans in great detail. If Chomsky is overlooked or maligned in such quarters, by such people, surely he must be doing something right.

Indeed, the fact that Chomsky is overlooked or maligned by international relations scholars, as well as the vast majority of Matrix-dwelling Americans, is, on some accounts, proof not only of his rightness but of his *popularity.* It is a strange argument, as we saw in Fred Moten's critique of Geoffrey Harpham, but Z magazine stalwart and sometime Chomsky co-author Ed Herman made it in capsule form in his November 2002 critique of "Cruise Missile Leftists" ("CMLs"):

> One problem with the CMLs is that, not really being on the left, they have lost sight of what the left is all about. The left's criterion of success is not the extent to which it is listened to or heard, irrespective of message content; it is its success in getting a left message across (and on some issues, like "free trade," and the merits of overseas military ventures [except in the heat of battle and under a furious elite propaganda barrage], the "radical left" is far closer to mainstream opinion than is the "decent left," and it is listened to on those issues by ordinary citizens when they can be reached).

The parenthesis-within-the-parenthesis is the key to the passage's pair of complex and delicate contortions. The first of these is the idea that the radical left is actually closer to mainstream opinion than are the 90 percent of Americans who supported a military response in Afghanistan— or that they *would* be closer to mainstream opinion if not for the Matrix Mass Media, which manufactures popular consent with its furious elite propaganda barrage and keeps the people from realizing that they are lying in a pod of pink goo. The second is the dogged insistence that the left's criterion of success is the degree to which it is listened to by ordinary citizens and gets its left message across—except when those people can't be reached. And when the left isn't listened to on those issues, the problem lies neither in the left nor in the message: the problem lies with the Matrix, which, in the heat of battle, deploys its furious elite propaganda barrage, duping people who would otherwise realize in a heartbeat that the al-Shifa bombing was far worse than 9/11, that the fall of the Taliban constituted a terrible crime against humanity, and that Europe rallied to the support of the United States after 9/11 chiefly because hundreds of years of imperial violence have had an enormous impact on the West's intellectual and moral culture.

Then again, it may be a terrible misreading of Chomsky's arguments to consider them as being addressed to Americans in the first place. Though Chomsky continually appeals to his fellow Americans, insisting that the choice between terror and justice is "one that is very largely in the hands of the American people" ("What a Fair Trial for Saddam Would Entail"), it is notable that he is hailed far more widely and warmly outside the United States than within. His reputation, from South America to Europe to the Middle East and South Asia (I am not sure about Africa and East Asia), is that of America's leading dissident intellectual, if not America's *only* dissident intellectual. Certainly, his interviews with international media immediately after 9/11, and many of his interviews in the foreign press in the following years, have bolstered that reputation. It is possible, then, that his appeals work by way of a series of relays: the preceding invocation of the power of the American people, for example, was actually published not in the United States but in the *Toronto Star*, at the end of an article which argues, sensibly enough, that a fair trial of Saddam's war crimes would have to acknowledge U.S. military aid to Iraq right up to the Iraqi invasion of Kuwait. Here are the final two paragraphs:

> The Bush administration has openly declared its intention to dismantle what remained of the system of world order and to rule the world by force, with Iraq as a demonstration project.
>
> That intention has elicited fear and often hatred throughout the world, and despair among those who are concerned about the likely consequences of choosing to remain complicit with the current policies of U.S. aggression at will. That is, of course, a choice very largely in the hands of the American people.

The essay is dated January 25, 2004. Perhaps, then, this is not a call *to* the American people to rise up and cast off the government that is eliciting such fear and hatred around the world; perhaps it is a declaration *about* the American people, who may well—and did, later that year—choose to remain complicit with the current policies of U.S. aggression at will. If that is the case, then Chomsky would be writing not to persuade his fellow citizens but to castigate them.

In some ways there is nothing wrong with castigating them: it is true, after all, that a populace that votes for Bush *after* the revelations of Abu Ghraib thereby becomes complicit with the atrocities of Abu Ghraib. Some prominent Americans, as we learned in the presidential race of 2004, were positively enthusiastic about that complicity; during Senate hearings on the matter in May 2004, Sen. James Inhofe of Oklahoma declared that he was "probably not the only one up at this table that is more outraged by the outrage than we are by the treatment" (quoted in "GOP Senator Labels Abused Prisoners 'Terrorists'"). About that much, it is safe to say that Senator Inhofe was correct, and that many Americans on the right enthusiastically support the torture of terror suspects. Furthermore, it is altogether understandable that Chomsky—or any other left intellectual in the United States—would seek a global audience for global matters and would find a welcome home writing for publications in saner Western countries where Bush's approval rating never went above 20 percent. My point here is simply that much of one's assessment of Chomsky's rhetorical strategy must turn on the question of whether he is speaking *to* or *about* Americans.

I have saved the most obvious objection to Chomsky's post-9/11 work, however, for last. It would have been entirely possible for any committed leftist intellectual, in the hours and days after 9/11, to express his or her fears about the likely reprisals against Muslims in the United States, the curtailment or abridgment of civil liberties, and the possibility of terrible escalation on the part of the Bush-Cheney administration—*without suggesting that past U.S. actions with regard to Chile, Vietnam, Central America, the Cherokee or the Sioux had anything to do with the attacks.* Linking the attacks of 9/11 to past U.S. actions against groups other than al-Qaeda, even to place the attacks "in context" rather than to justify them, quite clearly suggested that a cosmic debt was being repaid, that the number of U.S. victims is colossal, and that, for the first time, the guns have been directed the other way. (That is, I think that if we read Chomsky's "the guns have been directed the other way" line literally, it suggests precisely what it seems to suggest: *well, it's about time.*)

Rather, left intellectuals could have pointed out that the forces arrayed against us were not oppressed Palestinians or East Timorese but, rather, a gang of violent patriarchal theocrats—and, remembering that discretion is sometimes the better part of valor, they could have blunted the degree to which the attacks became, in Chomsky's words, "a gift to the hard jingoist right" by pointing out that al-Qaeda has more in common with the hard jingoist right in the United States than with any conceivable leftist project. Anti-imperialist left intellectuals would have been aided in this enterprise by the hard jingoist right itself, one wing of which was calling for mass murder on an unprecedented scale, and the other wing of which was arguing *in so many words* that America had it coming. In the pages of the *National Review,* Rich Lowry wrote:

> We know the states that harbor our enemies. If only Osama bin Laden and his 50 closest advisers and followers die in the next couple of weeks, President Bush will have failed in a great military and moral challenge of his presidency.
>
> The American response should be closer to something along these lines: identifying the one or two nations most closely associated with our enemies, giving them 24-hours notice to evacuate their capitals (in keeping with our desire to wage war as morally as possible), then systematically destroying every significant piece of military, financial, and political infrastructure in those cities. ("Against Cruise Missles")

The left would not have had to wait long to let the hard jingoist right reveal itself in all its profound ugliness; Lowry wrote those words on September 12, 2001. The next day, two of the leading "religious" figures from America's far right sat down to agree with each other as to where the blame should be laid:

> JERRY FALWELL: And I agree totally with you that the Lord has protected us so wonderfully these 225 years. And since 1812, this is the first time that we've been attacked on our soil and by far the worst results. And I fear, as Donald Rumsfeld, the Secretary of Defense, said yesterday, that this is only the beginning. And with biological warfare available to these monsters—the Husseins, the Bin Ladens, the Arafats—what we saw on Tuesday, as terrible as it is, could be miniscule if, in fact—if, in fact—God continues to lift the curtain and allow the enemies of America to give us probably what we deserve.

PAT ROBERTSON: Jerry, that's my feeling. I think we've just seen the an-
techamber to terror. We haven't even begun to see what they can
do to the major population.

JERRY FALWELL: The ACLU's got to take a lot of blame for this.

PAT ROBERTSON: Well yes.

JERRY FALWELL: And, I know that I'll hear from them for this. But,
throwing God out successfully with the help of the federal court
system, throwing God out of the public square, out of the schools.
The abortionists have got to bear some burden for this because
God will not be mocked. And when we destroy 40 million little innocent babies, we make God mad. I really believe that the pagans,
and the abortionists, and the feminists, and the gays and the lesbians who are actively trying to make that an alternative lifestyle, the
ACLU, People For the American Way—all of them who have tried
to secularize America—I point the finger in their face and say "you
helped this happen."

PAT ROBERTSON: Well, I totally concur, and the problem is we have
adopted that agenda at the highest levels of our government. And
so we're responsible as a free society for what the top people do.
(Robertson, Interview with Falwell)

How hard would it have been, I wonder, for Chomsky and his followers to refrain from suggesting that bin Laden's grievances about U.S.
foreign policy overlapped in some respects with their own and point
out, instead—as did Ellen Willis in the *Nation* ("Bringing the Holy War
Home")—that the patriarchal, homophobic theocrats who attacked us
had far more in common, ideologically, with Falwell and Robertson than
with anyone on the left?

The hatred of America's liberal ideals has since become a common
theme on the American right, from Ann Coulter's equation of liberalism
with treason (*Treason*) to Sean Hannity's insistence that we are fighting
against liberalism (*Deliver Us from Evil*) to Bill O'Reilly's recent literary
jihad against America's "secular-progressive" forces (*Culture Warrior*) to
Dinesh D'Souza's full-blown argument that al-Qaeda attacked us out of
legitimate outrage at the freedom of American women, atheists, gays, and
lesbians (*Enemy at Home*). The attacks themselves may have been a gift
to the hard jingoist right, in the sense that their domestic consequences
surely included a renewed (yet *another* renewed) insistence on military
strength and an outpouring of patriotic gore. But the hard jingoist right,

left to its own foul devices, would have done a great deal to repel ordinary Americans and would have allowed the left to make the simple point that we consider the struggle against violent patriarchal homophobic theocrats abroad part and parcel of the struggle against violent patriarchal homophobic theocrats at home—as evidenced by the Falwells and Robertsons who were pointing the finger at us and saying, "you helped this happen." One wing of the left tried to make this point—but it was not the wing dominated by Chomsky and *Z*.

In October 2001, for example, nationally syndicated leftist cartoonist Dan Perkins ("Tom Tomorrow") captured the right mode of rhetorical address with perfect pitch. There's much to love in these six panels, starting from its premise—that American leftists, in the face of an attack from Islamist radicals, should actually *defend* America's secular liberal traditions. But what makes the strip brilliant is its ironic acknowledgment—ironic because blanketed by the giant American flag and by Uncle Sam—that those traditions are under assault from the Christian right and the

Republican base and must be wrested from the people fraudulently lay-
ing claim to them. It was easy enough for the Manichean left to mock the
Bushes (George and Laura) for their shallow and opportunistic invocation
of the liberation of Afghan women from the Taliban; no doubt that invocation will long be remembered as one of the lowest-hanging fruits ever
recorded in the history of rhetoric. But it was another thing entirely—apparently, an impossible thing, like praising the attorneys of the Southern
District of New York for their successful prosecutions of Islamist terrorists—for the Manichean left to imagine itself calling a series of women,
gays and lesbians, racial minorities, and atheists to testify to "our basic
American values."

Because the flag was such a charged symbol after 9/11, especially for
veteran culture warriors who remembered it as a symbol of support for
the Vietnam War, it is especially important to distinguish Tom Tomorrow's deployment of the flag from Todd Gitlin's ("Ordinariness of American Feelings") and Marc Cooper's ("Liberals Stuck in Scold Mode") contemporaneous insistence in the fall of 2001 that antiwar protestors should
have made their patriotic allegiances clear before embarking on criticism
of the administration's conduct after 9/11.[17] Following a line of thought
laid down by Richard Rorty in the 1990s (*Achieving Our Country*) (a line
of argument to which I return in chapter 5), Gitlin and Cooper chastised
the Manichean left for (among other things) its lack of patriotism; but, by
the logic of the argument I am developing here, that was the wrong line
of thought to pursue, for it hardened that wing of the left in its conviction
that "mainstream opinion" attributed the attacks simply to al-Qaeda's "hatred for the values cherished in the West as freedom, tolerance, prosperity,
religious pluralism and universal suffrage," and that such an explanation
was, as Chomsky said, "completely at variance with everything we know"
though it has "all the merits of self-adulation and uncritical support for
power" (Radio B92). For the Manichean left, Gitlin's and Cooper's appeals to American patriotism were prima facie evidence that such appeals
were craven accommodations to power; but because Tom Tomorrow's appeal to American values clearly—and ironically, because tacitly—suggests
that (a) secular humanist ideals should properly be international ideals
and (b) American leaders are traducing them even as they invoke them,
there is a qualitative difference between this cartoon and Gitlin's and Cooper's analyses of patriotism and the left.

Again, let me take a moment to state the obvious: I am not suggesting that the left should have responded to 9/11 with a series of brilliant

cartoons. I *am* suggesting that Tom Tomorrow's cartoon availed itself of two rhetorical strategies to which the Manichean left did not have— or did not allow itself—recourse: the defense of American traditions of secular liberalism, and the argument that the Bush-Cheney government was betraying those traditions. There are doubtless many reasons why the Manichean left could not make these moves, but I can name two. First, they were unable to deploy the images of Uncle Sam and the flag, even ironically, because at one level they did not believe that American secular liberal ideals were a legitimate standard of measure. That feature of Manichean leftism has been noted before, misrecognized as "anti-Americanism." It stems instead, I suggest, from a belief that any appeal to specifically *American* ideals of secular liberalism smacks of American exceptionalism (and everything entailed therein, up to and including imperialism and genocide). The second is more obscure, and more alarming: at a deeper level yet, Manichean leftists were unable to appeal to America's best secular liberal traditions because *they did not believe any such appeal would matter.* For all their ritual invocations of how the course of history lay in the hands of an "aroused public within the more free and democratic societies," they did not believe that the United States could behave as anything *other than* a vicious imperialist power.

I would not make such an argument about the Manichean left had I not encountered it in the course of an online debate with Ed Herman (the full exchange is available in the *ZNet* archive). In late 2002, Herman responded to a *Boston Globe* essay in which I tried to criticize both the liberal hawks' enthusiasm for war in Iraq and the *Z-Counterpunch* left's opposition to war in Afghanistan. In a passage aimed at the liberal hawks, who were already championing the war as a liberatory crusade, I argued that the claim that American forces would be welcomed as liberators would be undermined by the invasion itself:

> Most likely the hard left's myopia and intransigence will not matter to most Americans—that is, those who never trusted the judgment of Chomsky or *Z Magazine* in the first place and don't see why it matters now that anti-imperialists have lost a "credibility" they never had in some quarters. But the reason it should matter, even in parts of America where there are no campuses, no anti-Sharon rallies, and no subscribers to *Counterpunch*, is that the United States cannot be a beacon of freedom and justice to the world if it conducts itself as an empire. (Bérubé, "Peace Puzzle: Why the Left Can't Get Iraq Right")

I was trying, to use a shopworn phrase, to hoist the liberal hawks on their own petard, to show that their own exceptionalist rhetoric would be undermined by the neoconservative Project for the New American Century on which they had embarked. And I believed I was arguing, in so many words, that the war in Iraq would be "utterly devastating to those few souls who still dream that the course of human events should be judged—and guided—by principles common to many nations rather than by policies concocted by one." When Herman replied to that argument in a *ZNet* exchange precipitated by my response to his "Cruise Missile Leftists" essay, however, he emphatically rebuffed my suggestion that the United States could act as anything *but* an evil empire:

> In the November article on the cruise missile leftists I quoted Bérubé's statement that "the United States cannot be a beacon of freedom and justice to the world if it conducts itself like an empire." That is, he believes acting like an empire is a matter of choice; that the U.S. leadership can "say no," and is not obliged to carry out a foreign policy that serves the interests of its dominant corporate elite. If it did establish a system of National Security States in Latin America, supported Marcos, Suharto, Mobutu (etc.), and has pressed Structural Adjustment Policies on dozens of poor countries, it didn't have to do that. It could dedicate itself to doing good. This is not only silly, it is plain imperial state ideology, and wonderfully suited for apologetics for imperial interventionism. (Herman, "Much More Severe Problems on the Cruise Missile Left")[18]

For Herman, the idea that the United States has a "choice" not to act like an empire is not merely "silly" but "plain imperial state ideology." Clearly, in debating someone like me, he is dealing with some addled imperialism-apologist still trapped in the Matrix. And yet it is an astonishing admission: according to the logic Herman provides here, even a President Ralph Nader would have invaded Iraq.

Arguments like Herman's demonstrate why it is a mistake to consider his wing of the left anything other than an intellectually conservative bloc for whom world events are somehow fated by the inexorable laws of empire. Admittedly, Herman's mode of analysis keeps things nice and simple: when the United States takes military action in the Balkans or in Afghanistan, it is behaving as an imperialist power; when it restores Aristide to power in Haiti, it is behaving as an imperialist power; and when it does nothing in Rwanda or Darfur, it is behaving as an imperialist power. But I submit that this kind of simplicity is not a virtue.

By contrast, the democratic left to which I belong believes that acting like an empire *is* a matter of choice, and that—to steal a page from the Book of Bush—it does matter who the "decider" is. We believe that U.S. foreign policy can be more destructive or less destructive, more unilateral or more multilateral, more cooperative with emerging international laws and norms or more contemptuous of them. We believe, in short, that the United States can be more just or more vicious—and that democratic processes and public debate are vitally important in determining which direction U.S. foreign policy will go. We also believe that popular opinion can resist—and, in the past decade, has managed to resist—a furious elite propaganda barrage, and that it is worth trying to devise rhetorical and political strategies that will continue to win Americans away from the agendas of the right. As discussed in chapter 4, these were among the arguments that Stuart Hall tried to mount against the doctrinaire left of the Thatcher era. But first, we must retrace the steps that led the Anglo-American left into Iraq—where both the Manichean left and the liberal-hawk interventionist left revealed their conceptual and political weaknesses.

IRAQ THE HARD ROAD TO DEBACLE

IN 2001 I supported the war in Afghanistan—initially with trepidation. At the time, I was worried that the U.S. response would be wanton and indiscriminate, killing tens or hundreds of thousands of civilians. I despised the fact that the Bush-Cheney administration would be responsible for the U.S. response; I was worried as well that the Soviet invasion might turn out to be a precedent, and U.S. and allied forces would be bogged down in a quagmire for years to come. I was worried that retaliatory strikes against al-Qaeda might further radicalize the Taliban's allies in Pakistan's Inter-Services Intelligence (ISI). But I did not think that retaliatory strikes were wrong in principle or that the attack would violate international law; I was worried on consequentialist grounds alone. When, therefore, the Taliban fell, the aid convoys resumed, and Pakistan's radicals seemed largely to be held in check, I believed that the left's most dire predictions had not come to pass and that, although too many Afghan civilians were dead or wounded, many more had been delivered from the clutches of one of the foulest, most brutal regimes in the world. By early 2002, therefore, I was stunned to find that the Manichean left would not retract any of its initial claims about the war; on the contrary, they intensified them, regardless of whether they had been consequentialist or principled claims.[1]

Still, I have no desire to portray myself as the leftward boundary of the thinkable with regard to Afghanistan. There were and are many opponents of that war whose positions I respect; some of those opponents were right, not only with regard to the likely long-term consequences of the war (chiefly, their belief that the war would be but a prelude to a much wider war in the Middle East and would not serve to capture Osama bin Laden or stabilize Afghanistan) but also with regard to the Bush-Cheney administration's utter disdain for the framework of international law, which was signaled almost immediately by the U.S. refusal to seek U.N. approval (which it could have obtained with ease) for retaliatory military action. Some critics on the left, for instance, argued that the events of 9/11 should have been treated as a massive crime rather than an act of war and that al-Qaeda, as a stateless agent, should have been pursued by international legal, diplomatic, and police procedures rather than by the military model of war between opposing states.

That argument has great merit; indeed, if al-Qaeda had not established a parasite-host relationship with the Taliban, effectively operating in Afghanistan as the military arm of a rogue government in a failed state, I would agree with it. However, al-Qaeda's base of operations in Afghanistan, together with its close relationship with the Taliban, rendered it something of an anomaly for an internationalist framework: a terrorist group controlling a state and harboring the potential to destabilize neighboring Pakistan as well, thus potentially giving Islamist radicals access to nuclear weapons. Those circumstances, I believe, warranted an immediate military response—but only to unseat the Taliban and destroy the base at Tora Bora and the associated terror training camps. Once that objective had been accomplished, I agree that post-9/11 al-Qaeda operations—in Bali, Madrid, London, and elsewhere—should have been treated as international crimes committed by a stateless syndicate. I agree also that the attack on Tora Bora was badly botched, as was Operation Anaconda three months later, though I doubt that Bush or Cheney made a conscious decision to let bin Laden slip away on the grounds that he was worth more in propaganda value alive than dead.[2] And under no circumstances would I agree that any of al-Qaeda's attacks provided warrant for an invasion of Iraq.

The actual calls for war, at the time, should have given any reasonable person pause. From the bloodthirsty ravings of right-wing pundits to the highest echelons of the military, who chose as their mission name "Operation Infinite Justice" (a phrase that might have come from the domain of 1970s'-era Saturday-morning children's cartoons, and which expanded on Clinton's equally juvenile "Operation Infinite Reach," the cruise missile response to al-Qaeda's 1998 embassy bombings), the early pro-war position was so vile and repugnant that the right's yearning for wanton slaughter nearly convinced me of the virtues of indiscriminate pacifism. But like many others on the left who eventually supported the war, I did not think for a moment that my support implied any support of right-wing pundits, military planners, or the Bush-Cheney administration itself—any more than a conviction that Nazism should have been opposed by military force commits one to lifetime membership in the fan clubs of Winston Churchill or Josef Stalin. For that matter, support for the war in Afghanistan does not imply support for the massacre of civilians and the establishment of secret detention and torture camps, any more than support for the Allied struggle against Nazi Germany implies support for the firebombing of Dresden. Yet opponents of the Afghanistan war did not refrain from deriding pro-war leftists as imperialist-apologist stooges "aligning with power," just as pro-war leftists did not refrain from deriding anti-war leftists as simply "anti-American."

But despite the fact that the 9/11 attacks were targeted, after all, against the United States, the question of one's pro- or anti-Americanism was and is a red herring. Thus, when Todd Gitlin wrote in exasperation of the excesses of the Chomskian left in the pages of *Mother Jones,* his well-earned critique of their doctrinaire opposition to U.S. foreign policy was vitiated by his suggestion that the American left needs to take patriotism more seriously: "After disaster comes a desire to reassemble the shards of a broken community, withstand the loss, strike back at the enemy. The attack stirs, in other words, patriotism—love of one's people, pride in their endurance, and a desire to keep them from being hurt anymore" ("Blaming America First").[3] That claim, in turn, allowed the Chomskian left to dismiss Gitlin (and everyone who agreed with his analysis of the far left) as flag-waving, jingoistic proponents of American exceptionalism. That unfortunate road had been paved in the 1990s with Richard Rorty's attacks on the "unpatriotic" left; both before and after 9/11, Rorty's liberal nationalism, oscillating between pragmatic and patriotic modes, worked to undermine his commitment to what he often called, invoking Tennyson's "Locksley Hall," the "Parliament of Man, Federation of the World."[4]

But the American debate over how best to oppose al-Qaeda need not have turned on the question of patriotism at all. A more careful and accurate reading of the history of Islamist radicalism since the founding of the Muslim Brotherhood in 1928 would have shown that the United States was not Islamism's only opponent, and, in fact appeared on the Islamist radar relatively late in the game. Recognition of this global aspect of Islamism should have sufficed to prevent any leftist who supported a military response to al-Qaeda from making the mistake of thinking that they had to join their neighbors in flying the flag and affixing "power of pride" stickers to the rear bumpers of their cars in order to demonstrate their true-blue 100 percent Americanness. On the contrary, the recognition of Islamism's global reach should have reinforced the American left's commitment to internationalism, just as the recognition of Islamism's ideological commitments should have reinforced the American left's commitment to the ideals of secular democracy. On this score, Chomsky, as a secular democrat, could easily have made common cause with any number of liberals and progressives to his right. And if any specific defense of American secular democracy were needed, liberals and leftists could have mounted one, as I suggest in chapter 2, in the mode of Tom Tomorrow—by appealing precisely to those political, religious, and sexual freedoms that Islamists *do* hate about the United States and which are anathema to the American religious right (and to fellow travelers like Dinesh D'Souza) as well.

In other words, when I say I do not want to portray myself as the leftward boundary of the thinkable, I mean that I have substantial grounds for rapprochement with a number of antiwar positions with regard to Afghanistan. Those who expressed concern for the lives of civilians were right to do so, for the events of 9/11 did not give the United States the right to kill any innocent civilian anywhere in the world. Those who expressed concern for the framework of international law were right to do so, for Bush-Cheney's foolish rebuff of the United Nations was a sign of much worse antidiplomatic arrogance to come, at a time when the United States needed as many allies as possible. Those who argued that the United States came to the table with such dirty hands that it could not be trusted to conduct a retaliatory operation against al-Qaeda raised a legitimate (but debatable) point—one that could conceivably be conceded if there were other readily available means for expeditiously routing the Taliban and destroying al-Qaeda's base of operations (for although I believe that these things needed to be done, I would have been happy to see them done by other nations in our stead). And those who argued that 9/11 was a crime rather than an act of war raised a legitimate (but debatable) point, one that could well be conceded once the Taliban was overthrown and al-Qaeda's base of operations destroyed.

But it is one thing to make arguments such as these and quite another to insist that the war in Afghanistan amounted to a silent genocide that was one of the most grotesque acts of modern history. It is critical, therefore, even now, to distinguish between plausible and implausible—or, if you prefer, credible and incredible—rationales for opposing war in Afghanistan. I also want to make it clear that those of us who supported that war did so partly out of *concern for* international institutions; our interpretation of the legitimate needs of international institutions merely differed (however substantially) from that of the antiwar camp.[5] (For instance, we tend to think that the antiwar camp, reading Afghanistan backward from Iraq, significantly underestimates the degree of international support for military retaliation against al-Qaeda immediately after 9/11 and, accordingly, the degree of international legitimacy that retaliation enjoyed.) We supported the removal of the Taliban on the grounds that they were working hand in glove with al-Qaeda, and we think of the Taliban not as a counterforce to (or creation of) U.S. imperialism but as a gang of violent, tyrannical theocrats; we were and are defenders of secular democracy, not "cruise missile leftists" or apologists for imperial intervention. We believe, for instance, that it is intellectually dishonest to brush off the question of the fate of Afghan women under the Taliban by mocking Laura Bush's sudden late-2001 conversion to international feminism; we believe that the leftists and liberals who decried the treatment of Afghan women under the Taliban before 9/11 had it right the first time and that there is no need to sneer at the possibility of enhanced life chances of Afghan women after the fall of the Taliban simply because the American right opportunistically appeals to them. As for the resurgence of the Taliban in recent years, we believe that this is further evidence of the unspeakable foolishness of the war in Iraq and that it demonstrates quite clearly that the crime committed in Afghanistan by the United States after 9/11 is not one of imperialism but one of malign neglect.

Indeed, one of the most useful potential arguments against war in Iraq was a corollary of the liberal-progressive argument that war in Iraq represented a disastrous diversion from al-Qaeda and Afghanistan: namely, that the Bush-Cheney administration's abandonment of the search for bin Laden and the enterprise of nation-building in Afghanistan (which should have been undertaken precisely to prevent a return to the conditions that led Afghanistan to state failure in the first place—and to demonstrate decisively to the Muslim world that the United States did not desire a wider war against Islam or Arab states in general) was proof positive that the neoconservative plan for nation-dismantling-and-rebuilding in Iraq would be a debacle. Those who opposed war in Iraq pointed out, with good reason, that if war were approved only by the United States, United Kingdom, and a handful of smaller allies (such as Spain, Poland, and Australia), it would clearly violate international law; in addition, Kenneth Roth of Human Rights Watch argued forcefully that an invasion of Iraq could not plausibly be considered a "humanitarian intervention." (I discuss Roth's position in more detail at the end of this chapter.)

Those were good, sound, principled reasons to oppose the war in Iraq, and I endorse them fully. But in the court of U.S. public opinion they might have been paired with pragmatic consequentialist reasons as well, apart from the obvious and parochial appeal to American self-interest in the form of the war's likely human and financial toll for the United States. In saying this I do not mean to minimize the damage that has been done to the United States by the Iraq war, or the far greater damage done to Iraqis; nor do I mean to overlook the fact that Bush and Cheney were unwilling to countenance any but the most Pollyannaish predictions about the war's outcome, and they moved quickly to fire anyone, civilian or military, who made the mistake of offering a reasonable assessment of the war's likely costs (although in retrospect, even those early predictions, like economic advisor Lawrence Lindsay's suggestion that the war might cost $200 billion, seem almost unimaginably dewy-eyed). I mean only that the diversion of troops and funding from Afghanistan to Iraq should have been seen, *even at the time,* as prima facie evidence that the Bush administration would conduct its military campaigns as if it were playing a board game in which one "occupies" a country simply by moving one's pieces into it and pushing one's opponent's pieces off the board—without regard to rebuilding the country's physical infrastructure, political superstructure, and institutions in civil society. In recent years, it has become routine to hear supporters of war in Iraq argue that the war would have been justifiable if only it had been fought in the "right" way (whatever that might be); I do not credit that argument, and I am not making a similar argument about Afghanistan, because I regard the casus belli in Afghanistan as legitimate. Rather, I am arguing that the war in Iraq is *precisely* what went wrong with the war in Afghanistan.

Needless to say, however, those Manichean leftists who opposed war in Afghanistan could not avail themselves of any pragmatic arguments about what the diversion of troops and funding from Afghanistan would mean. Because they regarded Afghanistan as an illegitimate war, they could not very well complain that Iraq represented a "distraction" from it; it would have been absurd, for instance, for Chomsky to oppose war in Iraq on the grounds that it would distract the United States from the important business of conducting a silent genocide in Afghanistan. Instead, the Manichean left wound up unwittingly reinforcing the premise of the Iraq war set out by the Bush-Cheney administration: that Iraq and Afghanistan were part of the same struggle, two battles in one war. And by the same token, liberal hawks, in going along with the Bush-Cheney administration, managed to reproduce the logic of the Manichean left as well; except that where the Manicheans saw Afghanistan and Iraq as wars

of imperialist aggression, the neoconservatives and the liberal hawks regarded them as wars of national liberation.

I say more about how the Manichean left and the liberal hawks worked
to produce and sustain each other at the close of this chapter; first, however, I need to explain how—and why—the Manichean left and the democratic left wound up adopting such drastically different rationales against
war in Iraq in 2002–03. And the answer, I suggest, lies in the relatively obscure left debates over the war in Kosovo and the conflict in the Balkans
during the preceding decade.

THE BALKANIZED LEFT

All traditional alignments of left and right became useless in the Balkans.
"Anti-imperialist" leftists and Serbian nationalists and (closer to home)
paleoconservatives like Pat Buchanan and foreign policy "realists" like
James Baker opposed any intervention in the Balkans; democratic leftists
and Margaret Thatcher and Susan Sontag and John McCain and most of
the editorial board of the *New Republic* favored it. For that reason, I propose that we think of Kosovo as the place where the tactic of "guilt by
association" died. And though Kosovo was, in retrospect, the place where
I decided the antiwar left had taken a decisive wrong turn, once again, I
do want to acknowledge that many arguments against the U.S.-NATO war
in Kosovo were cogent and reasonable—and that, as with Afghanistan, I
not merely acknowledge but agree with some of them. For example, the
actual conduct of the war, involving high-altitude bombing, was appalling; the willingness of NATO to proceed without U.N. Security Council
authorization was troubling; and the many failures of diplomacy before
the war—from the foot-dragging that preceded the Dayton accords to the
bumbling that followed, right through to negotiations at Rambouillet—
were galling.

Indeed, some writers who supported intervention, such as Ian Williams, admitted as much. As Williams wrote in his review of Tariq Ali's
edited collection, *Masters of the Universe? NATO's Balkan Crusade:*

> Even many vociferous supporters of intervention were worried about
> the international legal implications of taking action without U.N.
> approval, and also about the form of the intervention. High-level

bombing increased risks of civilian casualties in order to save politically inconvenient military casualties for the U.S., and the refusal until the final stages to consider ground troops, almost certainly prolonged the war and allowed Belgrade to go ahead with its atrocities.(Williams, "More Agitprop Than Reasoned Argument")

"There is no doubt," Williams adds, "that American diplomacy has become almost an oxymoron under Clinton." Although it was tempting for some liberals in the Bush years to look back on oxymoronic Clintonian diplomacy as the good old days, Williams reminds us that the Clinton administration's series of responses and nonresponses to the depradations of the Milošević regime are eminently blameworthy:

> It is clear that the U.S. was dragged unwillingly and half-heartedly into the Balkans, and that on this occasion it was European leaders who dragged it in. It is also true that if the U.S. had made a credible threat of action at any time almost from the shelling of Vukovar onwards, let alone in Kosova, it would have stopped Milošević in his tracks. Indeed the U.S. position has consistently been the very reverse of Teddy Roosevelt's: it has been to shout loudly and to carry a light-weight olive branch rather than a big stick. The strident Madeleine Albright cries "wolf" again and again abroad, while Clinton and the Congress at home worry about the political costs of a single casualty.

As for the question of U.N. approval, Williams notes:

> Every Russian attempt to condemn NATO was overwhelmingly defeated in every U.N. forum—including the Security Council. It is of course true that the U.S. has abused and continues to abuse its veto power in the U.N. But does that make it any more moral for Moscow to thwart the wishes of the majority of member states?
>
> Milošević's regime is under U.N. sanctions and has been the subject of over 50 U.N. Security Council Resolutions and innumerable statements. The Council unanimously set up an International Tribunal to try the perpetrators of what they agreed had been egregious war crimes. Only months before the bombing, the Security Council endorsed Milošević's agreement to reduce troop numbers in Kosova— and to stop killing and expelling Kosovars. He broke the agreement and the U.N. resolution.

As with Afghanistan, I try to distinguish plausible from implausible anitwar arguments: I agree that the Kosovo war set a dangerous precedent, insofar as it led some liberal advocates of "humanitarian intervention" to conclude that the Security Council's refusal to approve of war in Iraq was no moral or procedural barrier to the war. But the worst arguments that concern me here, as they were mounted by the Manichean left, had nothing to do with the United Nations. They included the argument that intervention in Kosovo could not possibly have been motivated by humanitarian concerns, because humanitarian concerns would also have required intervention in East Timor; the argument that Milošević was targeted by neoliberal free-marketeers and their servants in government because he was Europe's last socialist; the argument that the United States chose the Albanians as their allies in the Balkans for "cynical power reasons"; and—a bit further over the edge—the argument that the 1995 massacre at Srebrenica, which the International Criminal Tribunal for the Former Yugoslavia has officially designated as "genocide," did not happen as reported.[6]

The first three of these arguments have been made, at various times, by Chomsky himself; the whitewashing of Srebrenica, by contrast, is associated more with Diana Johnstone and Ed Herman, the latter of whom has founded a "Srebrenica Research Group" dedicated to overturning the findings of the "Western media" (as well as the United Nations, the International Criminal Tribunal for the former Yugoslavia [ICTY], and aid agencies).[7] From the perspective of the democratic left, this initiative is especially grotesque; Ellen Willis, writing in the late 1990s, suggested that "the idea of American imperialism . . . fuels a strain of reflexive anti-interventionist sentiment whose practical result is paradoxical dithering in the face of genocide" (Don't Think, Smile! 15). She might have added that, for some especially addled leftists, the idea of American imperialism leads not to "dithering" but to a frantic determination to join the Srebrenica Research Group and the International Committee to Defend Slobodan Milošević—that is, not to dithering about genocide but to outright genocide denial.

To date, Chomsky has recommended Johnstone's work without agreeing with it; but he has not questioned Johnstone's specific arguments, nor has he criticized the work of the Srebrenica Research Group.[8] The tenor of his thinking on the subject, however, can be gathered from a June 2006 interview with the New Statesman in which Chomsky spoke disparagingly of the trial of Slobodan Milošević before the International Criminal Court:

The worst crime was Srebrenica but, unfortunately for the International Tribunal, there was an intensive investigation by the Dutch government, which was primarily responsible—their troops were there—and what they concluded was that not only did Milošević not order it, but he had no knowledge of it. And he was horrified when he heard about it. So it was going to be pretty hard to make that charge stick. (Stephen, Interview with Chomsky)

Chomsky did not go as far as to join the International Committee to Defend Slobodan Milošević, chaired by Michael Parenti, but his extraordinary willingness to take at face value the claim that Milošević was ignorant of *and horrified by* the massacre at Srebrenica is noteworthy in itself, especially because the April 2002 report of the Netherlands Institute for War Documentation (NIOD), to which Chomsky refers here, does not quite say what Chomsky claims it does:

> It is also not known whether Milošević had any knowledge of the continuing Bosnian-Serb offensive that resulted in the occupation of the enclave. After the fall of the enclave, Milošević made no mention to that effect to the U.N. envoy Thorvald Stoltenberg—he was too much of a poker player to reveal anything. On the other hand, Milošević did express himself clearly later, in 1996, when he dropped the question to a group of Bosnian-Serb entrepreneurs as to "what idiot" had made the decision to attack Srebrenica while it hosted international troops when it was obvious that, in any event, the enclave would eventually have been bled dry or become depopulated. It is not clear to what extent that statement had been intended to clear his responsibility for those events. (Netherlands Institute for War Documentation, *Srebrenica,* part 3, chapter 6, section 9)[9]

I suppose that one can insist (though I would not) that there is no significant difference between NIOD's "it is not known whether Milošević had any knowledge" and Chomsky's "Milošević had no knowledge." One thing is clear, however: there is nothing in the NIOD report to suggest that Milošević was "horrified" by Srebrenica.

When in the past Chomsky's account of the Balkans has met with skepticism from people who are largely sympathetic to his critiques of U.S. foreign policy, Chomsky's response has not been pretty. For example, Adrian Hastings, a renowned theologian and author of *SOS Bosnia* who was actually trapped in the siege of Sarajevo, reviewed Chomsky's *The New Military Humanism* in 2001 and found it inadequate on a number of fronts. What makes Hastings's review notable, for my purposes, is that it begins by announcing that "the present reviewer finds himself in substantial agreement with the author in regard to the general character of modern American foreign policy, which he agrees is largely abhorrent" ("Not a Book about Kosovo"). Having established that he is no shill for American imperialism, Hastings proceeds to call attention to some of the more remarkable lacunae in Chomsky's book:

> What is most striking to a Balkanist about this book is what is left out. There is no discussion of the character, aims and methods of Milošević, no attempt whatever to place the war in Kosovo in the context of a decade of wars—in Slovenia, Croatia and Bosnia—and very little attempt even to portray what had actually happened in Kosovo in the twenty years before 1999. If anyone suffers from the disease of seeing the world as so centred in Washington that nothing else really matters, that person is Chomsky. It is a little surprising to find that the names of Sarajevo, Vukovar and the like never appear. Where he does refer to previous events in ex-Yugoslavia he often gets them wrong, uncritically accepting Serbian propaganda or using any conceivable quote to hammer the West. . . .
>
> The book offers no plausible response to the question what alternative there was to a NATO intervention, an intervention for which it all the same remained very difficult to obtain approval. Doubtless without intervention there would not have been hundreds of thousands of Kosovars fleeing the country within weeks, but there were already—as Chomsky admits—several hundred thousand internal refugees and an extensive policy of torching Albanian homes. There is no reason to think that this would not have continued and grown worse. . . . Chomsky repeatedly claims that the bombing "failed" in that it greatly escalated the refugee flow; but its failure in that regard was only temporary. It in fact ensured the rapid return of the refugees, undoubtedly to miserable conditions but not to worse conditions than they had experienced in the months before the bombing, and essentially to a situation which would improve rather than indefinitely deteriorate.

The recent history of the Balkans is murky and tangled, to be sure, and conflicting reports about refugees and atrocities abound. Hastings

employs the logic of most left supporters of intervention in Kosovo—
namely, that Milošević's actions in the region constituted the third act of a
long-running tragedy and needed to be stopped before they produced yet
another humanitarian catastrophe. It is possible for reasonable people to
contest the logic of waging war to prevent catastrophe, I acknowledge, and
possible to suggest that the bombing was not the best method by which
to try to avert that catastrophe, insofar as high-altitude bombing produces
its own humanitarian catastrophes. But what is most bizarre about Chomsky's account, possibly, is the claim that "in the early 1990s, primarily for
cynical power reasons, the U.S. selected Bosnian Muslims as their Balkan
clients." One is left to wonder why, if indeed the United States had selected such unlikely clients as pawns in a global power game, the United
States acquiesced in their slaughter, their "grim fate," for so long. Hastings
writes:

> Even in regard to the question, why did NATO decide to act, Chom-
> sky is not convincing. For years Milošević had remained NATO's cho-
> sen instrument for maintaining peace of a sort in ex-Yugoslavia. To the
> disgust of many of us, that remained the case at Dayton in 1995. On
> a Chomsky-style account of Machiavellian American policy, coupled
> with supine European acquiescence in whatever Washington wanted,
> there is no reason why the attitude of the West should have changed.
> It was easy enough to go on portraying the KLA as "terrorists" who
> had rightly to be crushed—and some in Washington long remained
> attracted to that position. Chomsky's attempted explanation in terms
> of Serbia being "an annoyance, an unwelcome impediment to Wash-
> ington's efforts to complete its substantial take-over of Europe . . . as
> long as Serbia is not incorporated within US-dominated domains, it
> makes sense to punish it for failure to conform" (p. 137) strikes one as
> bizarre. Why was this "impediment" only discovered in 1999 and not
> in 1992 or 1995?

"It is absurd," Hastings adds, "to pontificate about why there was intervention in Kosovo in 1999 while saying nothing about Vukovar in 1991,
Sarajevo, Tuzla, Bihac and Srebrenica in the following years." Then, Hastings takes up the question of whether, in fact, Kosovo represented not
merely a change in U.S.-U.K. policy in the Balkans but a new form of
internationalism:

Finally, is there no truth at all in the claim for a new "moral internationalism," even a "military humanism" about which Chomsky is so scornful? That there has been no transformative moral revolution in places where deeply entrenched policies remain in place is clear enough, especially in regard to parts of the world where Washington feels little interested in the sentiments of its European allies. Nevertheless Kosovo is not the only indicator of a change of mood, of the sort of moral interventionist internationalism which has come to be associated particularly with Tony Blair. Thus East Timor is one of the case studies thrown in by Chomsky to illustrate the charge of mass slaughters "thanks to the support of the U.S. and the U.K."; but in fact, after a quarter of a century of doing nothing, the "international community" in precisely the same year as Kosovo did engineer the independence of East Timor. There was certainly some sort of "new" interventionist policy at work here. It involved the U.S. relatively little and was mainly led by Australia, though British support was considerable. Again, "military humanism," essentially British, has brought a degree of effective intervention in Sierra Leone, which may well have saved the country from total ruin and is certainly backed by most of its citizens.

Hastings's invocation of a "sort of moral interventionist internationalism which has come to be associated primarily with Tony Blair" makes the point that Blair's Labour Party broke with the Conservative quietism "controlled by Hurd and Rifkind" and supported by Major; this is an important argument, and I will underscore its American counterpart in a moment. But in the wake of Iraq, surely the idea of Blair as a moral interventionist serves Chomsky's argument far better than Hastings's: for the path to Iraq, according to the Manichean left, began in Kosovo and confirms their belief that Kosovo, too, was an illegal and imperialist war.

Nonetheless, after Sierra Leone and before Iraq, it was indeed possible to imagine a new moral internationalism; Chomsky refused to do so and actually replied to Hastings's argument about the history of the Balkans by assailing the argument's "depravity." The question was put to Chomsky by a sympathetic reader:

How would you respond to this criticism? Why *didn't* NATO act against Serbia in 1992 or 1995, esp. after "Vukovar in 1991, Sarajevo, Tuzla, Biha, and Srebrenica in the following years" as Hastings asks?

Hastings says "the decisive underlying factor [for NATO intervention] was the war in Bosnia and belated contrition in the West for its own appalling record in that regard. . . . It was the sense of guilt over the long agonies of the siege of Sarajevo, together with the speedy ending of the war once the West did intervene, which so powerfully fuelled the resolve to stop its repetition."

This was Chomsky's reply:

At this point, the argument descends to what can only be called "depravity." I do not use the term lightly. How would we respond to some apologist for Saddam Hussein who praises him for offering a large monetary gift to victims of Israeli atrocities during the Intifada, explaining his benevolence on grounds of "belated contrition" for his "appalling" failure to protect Palestinians in earlier years, e.g., during the U.S.-backed Israeli invasion of Lebanon, which left perhaps 20,000 dead? We know exactly how to evaluate the claim of the Saddam apologist. We ask what else Saddam was doing at the same time, or before, to demonstrate his profound humanitarianism in some case from which he does not directly benefit. The logic is the same in this case, and a more than sufficient answer is given in the book under review, in a chapter entitled "assessing humanitarian intent." A look at a book of mine shortly after, "A New Generation Draws the Line," carries the record of U.S.-British crimes well past the end of the war in Kosovo. It is understandable that Western intellectuals should prefer not to look at the crimes for which they share responsibility, and to prate about the high moral values of their leaders. But not very pretty.[10]

Not very pretty, indeed. The Saddam-U.S. analogy would not stand up in a high school debating tournament, primarily because there is no meaningful parallel between offering money to victims of Israeli atrocities and trying to stop a wave of ethnic cleansing; but it does provide Chomsky a handy way of putting the U.S.-backed Israeli invasion of Lebanon (and the crucial phrase "Israeli atrocities") onto the table of a discussion of the Balkans—and then to turn the table on Hastings, who, no longer an opponent of genocide, is revealed here as a purveyor of "depravity." It is good to know that Chomsky does not use the term lightly.

In a later interview, Chomsky uses a number of other terms unlightly when speaking of Hastings:

It is also worth adding that the hypocrisy of the pretense of concern for the fate of the Kosovar Albanians is so colossal that it takes a really well indoctrinated educated class to suppress it. To mention only the obvious (discussed in *New Military Humanism*, but scrupulously ignored by outraged reviewers), at the very same time, the U.S. and U.K. were not only tolerating comparable or worse atrocities, but were actively participating in escalating them—including a major case that was not "at the borders of NATO," as the [*sic*] Hastings and others like him lamented, but right within NATO. To "overlook" all this and shed tears for the victims of the crimes of others takes a really impressive level of vulgarity and disciplined subordination to power.[11]

In citing "comparable or worse atrocities . . . right within NATO," Chomsky refers here to Turkish oppression of the Kurds—which, in fact, Hastings had scrupulously addressed; he had even held out hope that a moral internationalism would address the Kurdish question as well. Hastings had written: "Nevertheless it [moral internationalism], and the ever-growing body of international public opinion demanding global justice, are contagious. Once it is seen to work in some places, the impact spreads and it becomes more difficult for any power to act in a wholly contrary manner. In the longer run even the Kurds may benefit." But the question here should not be whether Chomsky has done justice to this or that one of Hastings' arguments. The question should be whether Chomsky has done justice to intellectual argument itself, in casting Hastings's arguments as examples of "a really impressive level of vulgarity and disciplined subordination to power." I have already noted Chomsky's habit of calling his interlocutors cowards, imbeciles, and moral reprobates; here, I want simply to note that he has dismissed, in roughly similar terms, a critic who agrees with him that modern American foreign policy is "largely abhorrent."

After a few years of asking Chomsky fans how they square Chomsky's demeanor in such exchanges with the conviction that Chomsky is a lonely beacon of reason and morality in the West, I have met with two kinds of response: one from people who know Chomsky primarily through his work on Vietnam and Central America, and who profess general admiration for him while acknowledging that they have not followed the debates over the Balkans (murky and tangled as they are), and another from people who have followed debates over the Balkans very well and are convinced that Chomsky has been, as ever, completely in the right. The latter group will hardly be convinced by anything I write here. But for those who are capable of being persuaded that there is something quite wrong with Chomsky's position on the Balkans, I try here to offer an explanation for how the Manichean party line went so badly awry. It is commonly argued (as in Hastings's review and Moishe Postone's more recent essay, "History and Helplessness") that the Manicheans' mistake lies in seeing the United States as the primary actor in world affairs; if the United States is indeed the evil empire, then all its opponents are worthy (to one degree or another) of our support. But with Kosovo, I think something considerably stranger is going on as well.

The Manichean version of the "anti-imperialist" position not only insists that U.S. intervention in the Balkans was not humanitarian; it also insists, as part of its overall critique of U.S. foreign policy, that U.S. intervention in the Balkans was not anomalous. It is worth considering this latter claim in its own right. The Balkans were an area in which the United States had no compelling strategic interests (not even that famous, if amorphous, pipeline), and in which, as Hastings correctly notes, the United States was initially content to back Milošević as it has any number of thugs and tyrants. But the election of the Blair government in the United Kingdom, the appointment of German Foreign Minister Joschka Fischer, and the world's growing awareness of the shameful history of U.N. inaction, not only in the Balkans but in Rwanda, led the United States and the European powers to reverse course in the former Yugoslavia. A congeries of unlikely forces and unlikely alliances produced Kosovo—including, for example, the long-running Monica Lewinsky sideshow that eroded Clinton's political capital at home and made it all but impossible for the United States to commit ground troops (even as Clinton's actions in the Balkans were derided by left and right alike as "wag the dog" diversions from Monicarama). This is precisely the supposition that the Manichean left will not entertain: for them, there are no anomalies in world affairs, no reversals of policy. As Ed Herman explained, the empire has no choice but to behave as an empire. There are no anomalies, and there are no changes of course—just great powers with their cynical power reasons.

Thus, when Washington is finally prodded into action in the Balkans, Chomsky has but two strategies at his disposal. One, to argue that the Bosnian Muslims were U.S. clients all along and that there were no disagreements in official Washington about the choice of "clients" or the manner in which we would treat them (that is, with appalling indifference for most of the decade). Two, to ignore the actual history of the Balkans before Kosovo, except to suggest that Milošević and the Serbs had been the real victims all along—their crimes magnified by the Western media and the provocations of the Bosnians and Kosovar Albanians downplayed by Washington's formidable propaganda machine. It is not merely that the Manichean left cannot bring itself to support a military action undertaken by the United States. That much is true, but alongside this political phenomenon lies a theoretical one (to which I return in chapter 4): the Manichean left is unwilling to credit—or, possibly, is incapable of understanding—conflict *within* the governing classes of the United States and the United Kingdom, and it construes substantial policy disagreements between opposing parties as mere ruling-class shadow-boxing. The Gramscian understanding of "hegemony" as developed by Raymond Williams, Stuart Hall, Ernesto Laclau, and Chantal Mouffe in the 1970s and 1980s, in which historic blocs are made up of a complex patchwork of conflicted and contradictory elements, is simply not part of the Manichean left's theoretical apparatus. Likewise, there is no place in the Manichean analysis of the Balkans for a theory in which the political realm has some degree of autonomy from the economic. When, for example, Chomsky claims that the Kosovo war was waged "because Serbia was not carrying out the required social and economic reforms, meaning it was the last corner of Europe which had not subordinated itself to the U.S.-run neoliberal programs, so therefore it had to be eliminated," he is not merely engaging in some slyly selective quotation of Strobe Talbott's foreword to John Norris's book *Collision Course: NATO, Russia, and Kosovo* (although he certainly is doing that); he is also insisting that the "cynical power reasons" behind U.S. policy are all about the money in the end (Chomsky, "On the NATO Bombing of Yugoslavia").[12]

The fact that Kosovo cannot be explained in such simplistic terms, then—the fact that it quite clearly demonstrates the complexity of geopolitical life, the conflicts within various factions of the West's ruling classes, and the extent to which political debate cannot be brutally reduced to the economic plane—is, on my reading, one of the things that drives Chomsky and company into such frenzies of denunciation and denial. Hence Chomsky's bizarre retort, when asked to reply to Hastings's argument about the policy shift in the West between 1991 and 1999, that Hastings's position is analogous to that of a Saddam apologist praising the great man for offering money to victims of Israeli atrocities during the Intifada. Chomsky does not have to account for the shift in U.S. and European policy because, as far as he is concerned, there has been no policy shift at all, nor could there have been, except in the minds of people who have attained a really impressive level of vulgarity and disciplined subordination to power.

Additionally, there are two small side benefits for Manichean leftists who seek to avoid historical and political specificity in their analysis of the Balkans. The first is that they are thereby enabled to argue, in Naderite fashion, that there is not a dime's worth of difference between the major parties in the United States—and, in Chomskian fashion, that U.S. foreign policy since 1945 has been one long unbroken reign of terror regardless of who holds the reins of state power.[13] It is true, of course, that Democratic administrations and Harvard liberals propelled us into Vietnam. But with regard to the Balkans, the standard leftist line about the "corporate duopoly" of "Demoblicans and Republicrats" runs up against the inconvenient truth that most American conservatives and Republicans opposed the Kosovo war. With regard to the Balkans, in other words, there wasn't a dime's worth of difference between the two major parties—except that one party largely supported U.S. intervention and the other one didn't. As Phyllis Schlafly proudly noted at the time:

> The media spinmeisters have been trying to put Republican Members of Congress on the griddle because they were critical of Clinton's war and refused to support it. History will show that they were absolutely right to vote against Clinton's military actions in Yugoslavia.
>
> By large majorities, Republican Members of Congress went on record against Clinton's war: 93% voted to require Congressional approval before ground troops were sent in, 86% voted against the bombing, 80% voted against sending peacekeeping troops, 58% voted to withdraw U.S. forces after the bombing started, and 64% voted to forbid the use of defense appropriations for Yugoslavia without specific Congressional approval. ("Cox Report Is a Real Whodunit")

Schlafly's remarks bring us to the second side benefit of the Manichean left's analysis of the Balkans: in refusing to acknowledge the policy differences between the two major parties and the new political formations supporting the war, they are thereby enabled to remain silent on the new political formations *opposing* the war. Take note, here, of Schlafly's insistence that the negotiations at Rambouillet were designed to drive Milošević from the table:

Jack Kemp said it exactly right in an editorial entitled "A Web of Deceit" (*Washington Times,* June 27, 1999). He called Clinton's war "a debacle, an international Waco, which no amount of spinning by NATO and the media can erase." Kemp called the war "unnecessary, illegal and unconstitutional from the beginning. It failed on every score to achieve the goals articulated to justify it, exacerbated the very problems it sought to remedy and created new problems that will plague America and the Balkans for years to come." Kemp pointed out that "the bombing and the killing and destruction it wreaked in Yugoslavia were absolutely unnecessary to achieving the final terms of the current agreement." Clinton could have gotten the same or even a better deal at Rambouillet if he had wanted to, but he flung an ultimatum on Milošević that no sovereign country could accept, namely, that he accept NATO troops occupying Belgrade and independence for Kosovo in three years. After 80 days of bombing, Milošević withdrew from Kosovo, but only after NATO abandoned those demands.

This is precisely the argument made by the contributors to Tariq Ali's *Masters of the Universe?* and, as Williams indicated in his review, the argument is nonsense no matter who makes it: "[Peter] Gowan trots out one of the most consistent canards, that the clauses in the Rambouillet agreement giving privileges to NATO troops in Yugoslavia were a cunning ploy to force the Serbs to reject the agreement. In fact the Serbian delegation never raised, or tried to modify, what was pretty much of a boiler-plate 'status of forces' agreement" ("More Agitprop Than Reasoned Argument").

The connection between Gowan and Schlafly has nothing to do with the politics of guilt by association; as I argued above, the Balkans deranged all the usual political alliances, so this confluence is not especially remarkable in and of itself. It is worth noting only in light of the Manichean belief that there aren't any important differences between the major parties in the United States. For with regard to the war in Kosovo, the bipartisan alliance in U.S. foreign policy matters was not found between Democrats and Republicans; it was found, instead, between the far left and the far right. However, if you choose to believe that the U.S. ruling classes were united behind the vicious imperialist bombing of Yugoslavia, then you don't have to account for the existence of far-right antiwar allies like Phyllis Schlafly—or Tom DeLay, or Patrick Buchanan—any more than you have to take stock of realist Republican allies like James Baker or libertarian Republican allies like Jack Kemp. You thereby avoid the difficult theoretical matter of trying to account for those segments of the U.S. ruling class that agree with your analysis of Kosovo word for word.

SOVEREIGNTY AND ITS DISCONTENTS

A full accounting of the prelude to Kosovo is well outside the bounds of this book; indeed, it would require (at least) a book of its own.[14] After the fall of the Berlin Wall in 1989 and the breakup of the Soviet Union in 1991, the early stages of the crisis in the Balkans were compounded by state failures in Somalia and Rwanda—neither of which (unlike the Balkans) could be attributed to the end of the Cold War. Like later postcolonial African crises in Sierra Leone, Congo, Liberia, Zimbabwe, and Sudan, the catastrophes in Somalia and Rwanda (despite their different histories and trajectories) lit up one of the critical features of the post-Soviet global landscape: the fact that the threat of superpower confict, and superpower conflict mediated by third-party proxy states, had been superseded by the emergence of state failure as a threat to world peace and stability.

Accordingly, left intellectuals and progressive journalists began to seek frameworks and structures for understanding the phenomenon of state failure and how the international community could best respond to it.[15] The "response" of which I speak, I should note immediately, did not have to be a military one; even in the horrific genocide in Rwanda, where over 800,000 (mostly Tutsi) were killed by extremist Interahamwe and Impuzamugambi Hutu, U.N. forces could have done the world a positive service simply by jamming or destroying Rwandan government radio.

The international outrage and dismay at the failure of the United Nations to act in Rwanda—a failure whose domestic American version involved the refusal of any government official to utter the word "genocide"—has been well documented and helped set in motion a new form of left internationalism. There were two curious features of this new left internationalism, however: one was that, as we have seen, not every faction on the left was on board with it, because some saw it simply as a stalking horse for American imperialism; and the other was that, unlike the left internationalisms over the preceding 150 years, this one did not depend on the existence (real or hypothetical) of an international proletariat. It was not a Marxist internationalism—or, for that matter, a socioeconomic internationalism of any kind. Rather, it was a moral and legal internationalism, seeking change not in the base but in various superstructures: the United Nations, international criminal tribunals (in Rwanda and the Balkans), truth and reconciliation commissions (in South Africa), and an International Criminal Court. The intervention in Sierra Leone was one of the high-water marks of this internationalism; another was a Spanish court's indictment of Augusto Pinochet in 1996, followed by Pinochet's arrest in Britain in 1998 and his Chilean indictment in late 2004; still another, of course, was the liberation of East Timor. Though the new internationalism has occasioned much debate on the left, the vast majority of its most vocal and dedicated opponents are on the right. The U.S. opposition to the International Criminal Court is one of the many shameful blots on our recent record, but it makes sense if you realize that a good part of the Republican electorate in the United States loathes even the United Nations with unbridled passion and hates and fears anything that threatens U.S. domination of world affairs. (Hard as it may be to imagine, their complaint is that the United Nations has not been *beholden enough* to U.S. interests.) A political party whose major figures routinely sneer at the United Nations can hardly be expected to countenance something as radical as an International Criminal Court in which Dick Cheney, among other U.S. policymakers, would take his rightful place in the dock alongside Pinochet and Milošević. And it should have been no surprise that the far-right fanatic known as Osama bin Laden targeted Bali in part out of his sense of outrage at the Australian-led U.N. intervention in East Timor: "Australia was warned about its participation in Afghanistan," bin Laden said in his late 2002 audiotape taking responsibility for the Bali bombing, "and its ignoble contribution to the separation of East Timor" (quoted in Watson, "Reclaiming the Muslim Empire").[16]

"Moral internationalism" is the cause, one might say, of a "human-rights left"; and I imagine that it is not well understood, in popular discussions of left internationalism in the United States, partly because it has so few points of contact with more salient lefts such as the environmentalist left or the antiglobalization left. For most young American activists, certainly, being "on the left" in a global sense more commonly means being familiar with Naomi Klein's *No Logo* and *The Shock Doctrine* or Medea Benjamin's Global Exchange and Code Pink than with Human Rights Watch, more drawn to G8 protests than to the plight of Iranian dissidents. I do not mean to disparage other forms of left internationalism; climate change and the workings of multinational capital are both, in their separate ways, truly global issues, and anyone who calls attention to carbon emissions and sweatshops is working on the side of the angels. But I am not sure that human-rights issues always get the attention they deserve from left internationalists in the United States; I am not sure that the defense of the U.N. Universal Declaration of Human Rights inspires quite as many activists as do street demonstrations against the World Trade Organization. And I am quite sure that American "leftists" who defame Samantha Power as a mouthpiece for war and imperialism and who denounce Salman Rushdie for his response to the fatwa issued by the Ayatollah Khomeini are effectively working to undermine the human-rights internationalism that should be the foundation of any global left with regard to genocide and freedom of expression.

In an obvious sense, of course, the human-rights left is working at a severe disadvantage. The idea of enforcing the Universal Declaration of Human Rights or supporting the causes of political dissidents living under tyrannical regimes seems all too thin and abstract, a matter of checkbook altruism, a paltry thing when compared with the immediately and dramatically pressing crises of global poverty, brutal inequality, ecological devastation, and climate change. What is the life of a single dissident, let alone the status of a piece of paper, when one contemplates the possibility of permanent, irreversible damage to the planet and the reality of billions of human beings living in utter abjection? What is the value of an opposition newspaper in a distant country when one realizes that one's sneakers have been manufactured by child laborers earning pennies a day? It is no wonder that the global left tends to emphasize equality over freedom—for freedom seems like an ephemeral, epiphenomenal thing contrasted to the bare facts of bare life, to the wretchedness of the wretched of the earth, to the essential requirements for life's sustenance and sustainability; and to some young left activists, liberal advocates of political freedom sound like earnest, misguided wonks working to craft ever-finer versions of laws that forbid rich and poor alike from sleeping under the world's bridges. Pledging allegiance to international norms and standards in the political realm must seem, to some people on the environmentalist and antiglobalization left, like pledging allegiance to an international system of weights and measures.

Then, too, there is the profound insult to moral internationalism in having "human rights" championed by a United States that practices torture and indefinite detention—and that, in violation of the Universal Declaration, fails to consider food and health care as basic human entitlements. And yet, and yet: the case must be made that political freedom and international institutions are more important to economic sustenance and ecological sustainability than most people (and most nations) have realized to date. It is quite true, for example, that some international conflicts are conflicts over resources—not excepting oil—and it follows that stronger international institutions stand a better chance of resolving such conflicts peacefully than weak international institutions trying vainly to referee a war of all against all. Likewise, tyrannies have proven to be exceptionally poor stewards of the earth and only moderately successful, at their very best, at combating misery; indeed, at their worst, as in Saddam's Iraq, Karimov's Uzbekistan, and Pinochet's Chile, they have opened new frontiers in human immiseration. Though the human-rights left is working at a disadvantage when competing for the hearts and minds of young activists, and though its commitments may seem to some too thin a gruel for human consumption, it nevertheless works on the crucial assumption that the best chances for human flourishing, in every sense of the term, are to be found in democracies with a high degree of political transparency and accountability. The fact that the United States can be weighed in those scales and found wanting is obvious, and merely underscores the point that the United States should be more democratic and more transparent than it is; moreover, as I argue in chapter 4, there is a virtue to the "thinness" of international norms and standards, insofar as they may be able to dilute "thicker" commitments to blood and soil and nation.

Under ordinary circumstances, the conflict between the human-rights left and the Manichean left would be matter for a seminar discussion or perhaps an energetic conference or two; certainly, that's how the conflict played out between 1999 and 2001, when it could have been construed as a series of arguments carried on between the writers for *Dissent* magazine and *Z*. In 2002–03, however, the conflict became fundamental to an important, if ill-understood, division in the rationales with which people on the left opposed war in Iraq. That division played out behind the scenes of the rallies, so to speak, in a series of essays and books that had little to do with the reasons that motivated the vast majority of Americans who attended antiwar rallies up through and including the enormous New York demonstration of February 15, 2003 (an event which I attended as well); the only things that united most rallygoers, as far as I could tell, were the conviction that war in Iraq was a very bad idea and the (related) belief that the Bush-Cheney administration was either mistaken, delusional, or deliberately deceptive (or some combination thereof) with regard to the necessity of the war and its likely outcome. But the relative obscurity of the conflict among left intellectuals does not diminish its intellectual importance; on the contrary, the conflict remains with us today and constitutes one of the critical issues over which the left remains at war.

The moral-internationalist, human-rights left has sought, in fine, to find ways to contest—and, in extreme cases, override—the Westphalian system of state sovereignty and the principle of self-determination. To that end, in recent years it has developed the concept of a "responsibility to protect," an international norm devised principally by former Australian foreign minister Gareth Evans. The responsibility to protect, or "R2P," grew out of the International Commission on Intervention and State Sovereignty inaugurated by Canada in 2000, was endorsed by 191 U.N. member states in 2005, and was subsequently affirmed in April 2006 by U.N. Security Council Resolution 1674 on the Protection of Civilians in Armed Conflict. The R2P website sets out the guidelines for "humanitarian intervention":

> The Responsibility to Protect describes an evolving concept about the duties of governments to prevent and end unconscionable acts of violence against the people of the world, wherever they occur.
>
> The international community has a responsibility to protect the world's populations from genocide, massive human rights abuses and other humanitarian crises. This responsibility to prevent, react to and rebuild following such crises rests first and foremost with each individual state. When states manifestly fail to protect their populations, the international community shares a collective responsibility to respond. This response should be the exercise of first peaceful, and then, if necessary, coercive, including forceful, steps to protect civilians.
>
> The Responsibility to Protect means that no state can hide behind the concept of sovereignty while it conducts—or permits—widespread harm to its population. Nor can states turn a blind eye when these events extend beyond their borders, nor because action does not suit their narrowly-defined national interests. (Responsibility to Protect, "Introduction to R2P")

The advocates of R2P see it as a step beyond nationalism on the way to forming something like a Federation of the World in defense of the planet's most vulnerable populations; R2P's detractors see it as imperialism with a humanitarian-interventionist face.[17] In a fascinating discussion of sovereignty and its discontents, John Brenkman argues that R2P actually has Hobbesian roots, insofar as Hobbes's theory of sovereignty presumes the sovereign's obligation to protect the people who have contracted to form a state—and that it offers a decisive rebuke to theories of sovereignty advanced from the right by Carl Schmitt and from the left by Giorgio Agamben:

> Sovereignty is traditionally defined primarily or solely as a nation's right not to have other nations interfere in its internal affairs. The revisionists argue that the definition of sovereignty should include a government's *responsibility to protect* the people over whom it is sovereign. A murderous despotic regime or a regime engaged in ethnic cleansing or genocide has, according to this definition, violated or defaulted on its own sovereignty. Other nations are justified, in some sense even obligated, to take upon themselves this responsibility to protect until it can be restored within the country's own political system. The horizon is to *restore* sovereignty.
>
> No one seems to have noticed that this admirable innovation in cosmopolitan thinking resurrects the essence of sovereignty presupposed by Hobbes! Hobbes' axiom is not Schmitt's *Sovereign is he who declares the state of exception*. Rather, Hobbes' axiom implicitly is *Sovereign is he who protects the multitude*. (*Cultural Contradictions of Democracy*, 153–54)

Brenkman does not add, however, that the Hobbesian axiom can be twisted in such a way as to produce the Schmittian, as when George Bush declares a state of exception at Guantánamo on the grounds that he is protecting American civilians by subjecting terror suspects to torture and indefinite detention. But then, this point underscores how important it is to distinguish legitimate from illegitimate forms of "protection," legitimate from illegitimate forms of sovereignty. And it underscores the broader point that because the Schmitt/Agamben framework does not readily recognize illegitimate forms of sovereignty, it is useless when it comes to contesting Guantánamo—or the human-rights abuses of despotic and totalitarian regimes. That is why Judith Butler (*Precarious Life*) had to turn to the norms of liberal democracy in order to critique the state of exception Bush had declared in Guantánamo.

Occasionally, the complex international-relations dispute over the status of sovereignty found its way onto the public stage of antiwar events, as when the Not in Our Name! antiwar statement of 2002, in the course of condemning the war in Afghanistan, insisted that "peoples and nations have the right to determine their own destiny, free from military coercion by great powers" ("Statement of Conscience against War and Repression"). The human-rights left may have had little overlap with the environmentalist left and the antiglobalization left; but in 2002–03 it ran smack into the Manichean left's dogged defense of state sovereignty. That defense of sovereignty must have sounded attractive to many on the left as long as it involved opposition to military coercion by the great power known as the United States; but it was, nonetheless, a strange position for "leftists" to find themselves in. One strains to imagine a late-1930s "Not in Our Name" petition dedicated to the principle that Spain and Germany must be left to determine their own destinies, free from military coercion by great powers, or, even worse, an early-1980s left devoted to the principle that El Salvador should be allowed to determine its own fate by means of civil war because the world did not have any business interfering in that sovereign state's internal affairs.

The antiwar movement, accordingly, was split with regard to Iraq: one side argued that weapons inspections, revised sanctions, and no-fly zones were acceptable and prudent alternatives to war, and the other side argued that *any* of the above—even inspections and no-fly zones—were unacceptable violations of Iraqi sovereignty. Thus, for example, in his 2003 book, *Full Spectrum Dominance: U.S. Power in Iraq and Beyond,* University of Texas professor and United for Peace and Justice antiwar organizer Rahul Mahajan articulated the Manichean left's critique of those leftists who, by his account, opposed war in Iraq for reasons that were not properly leftist:

> At exactly the time of maximal ferment, both domestically and internationally, the antiwar movement in the United States was afflicted with a variety of self-appointed spokespeople who were very careful to tell us the right and wrong ways to oppose the war. For Todd Gitlin, Marc Cooper, Michael Walzer, Michael Bérubé, and others, it was right for us to oppose the war on Iraq because it was poorly thought out, because it was a "distraction" from the war on terrorism, and similar reasons; it was and is not all right to question the fundamental goodness of America's role in the world, it wasn't all right to oppose the war on Afghanistan, and it wasn't all right to oppose the sanctions on Iraq or to argue that Iraq posed no significant threat beyond its borders.

As Walzer wrote in the *New York Review of Books,* "Defending the embargo, the American overflights, and the U.N. inspections: This is the right way to oppose, and to avoid, a war." That's the embargo that destroyed a society, the American overflights combined with bombing that were the prelude to a war, and the U.N. inspections that prepared the way for that war by disarming the targeted enemy.

Without delving too much into their tendentious reasoning, or into their total lack of contribution to any antiwar movement, their continuing role now is very clear. They were and are trying to keep the antiwar movement both from becoming a more sustained movement and from being an anti-imperialist movement, two considerations that are linked. (191–92)

Some aspects of Mahajan's argument are crude caricature: it is absurd to charge people like Gitlin, Walzer, Cooper, and myself with believing that it "is not all right to question the fundamental goodness of America's role in the world." (Although such formulations do important work for the Manichean left, insofar as they enable the pretense that they and they alone are critics of American foreign policy.) Mahajan's claim that "it wasn't all right to oppose the war on Afghanistan" is a bit disingenuous, since, as his own argument makes clear, as far as the antiwar movement's leadership was concerned, it wasn't all right to *support* the war on Afghanistan; people who did support that war, but not war in Iraq, were an "affliction" to the movement. And, of course, Mahajan refuses the argument that war in Iraq is "a 'distraction' from the war on terrorism" for the reasons I mentioned at the outset of this chapter: for the antiwar leadership, retaliatory strikes against al-Qaeda's base of operations were illegitimate, imperialist ventures as well.

But Mahajan's less polemical and more "serious" points are actually far more disturbing than his swipes at Walzer et al. The argument that "Iraq posed no significant threat beyond its borders," for example, *was* made by people like Gitlin, Walzer, and me, proposing the "containment" of Saddam rather than war. However, we recognized and tried to address two objections to containment: the "weapons of mass destruction" (WMD) argument and the human-rights argument. With regard to weapons of mass destruction, people in our wing of the antiwar camp believed that the best answer to WMD scaremongering (whether such scaremongering came from Bush's now-notorious 2003 State of the Union address[18] or Kenneth

Pollack's *The Threatening Storm: The Case for Invading Iraq* [2002]) was to let UNSCOM do its job. Mahajan, by contrast, criticizes U.N. weapons inspections on the grounds that they "prepared the way for . . . war by disarming the targeted enemy." Most antiwar liberals and progressives supported weapons inspections as an alternative to war, and we saw nothing wrong with disarming Saddam; Mahajan denies the legitimacy of inspections and disarmament altogether. He was strongly seconded in this denial by Ed Herman, who, in the second installment of his series on the "Cruise Missile Left," argued that the so-called CMLs "believe that the inspections regime is reasonable and should be allowed to continue to seek out and remove those weapons. . . . These views are not 'left' at all, they are 'moderate' apologetics for imperial violence" ("Cruise Missile Left, Part 2").

And with regard to the human-rights case against Saddam, people in our wing of the antiwar camp believed that Kanan Makiya's desire for forcible regime change should be answered rather than dismissed; whereas Mahajan's argument, in its refusal to take seriously any human-rights claim against Saddam's inconceivably brutal regime, not only defaults on a moral obligation but also, in doing so, leaves the door wide open for liberal hawks to advance their version of a "humanitarian intervention" rationale for the invasion of Iraq. Precisely by putting Saddam's state sovereignty over every other consideration, by opposing weapons inspections and the no-fly zones that protected the Kurds, and by dismissing even a completely overhauled sanctions regime that would take chlorine and other essential items off the "dual use" list so that Iraqis could purify the water supply the United States and its allies had deliberately degraded in 1991—by doing all this, the Manichean left led many otherwise intelligent liberals to believe that the antiwar camp was useless or worse when it came to taking seriously an internationalist claim against Saddam's crimes against humanity.

The sanctions against Iraq require a discussion unto themselves. Opposition to inspections and no-fly zones was the work of ideological extremists; but opposition to sanctions was widespread on the left—and with good reason. Compared with the widely hailed sanctions against South Africa, for instance, which helped render South Africa a pariah state and contributed significantly to the end of the era of apartheid, the sanctions against Iraq were a dismal failure on every count: they paradoxically strengthened Saddam's grip on power while exacerbating the misery of Iraqi citizens. They were such a dismal failure, indeed, as to throw into crisis the idea of sanctions tout court, leaving internationalists with the dilemma of how to put pressure on rogue states by peaceful means when sanctions prove counterproductive. In a scathing critique published in *Harper's* just five months before the war, Joy Gordon ("Cool War") pointedly called the sanctions a "weapon of mass destruction"; earlier in 2002, Arne Tostensen and Beate Bull published a more general and academic discussion of sanctions and sanction theory, "Are Smart Sanctions Feasible?" in which they acknowledged that "in the Iraqi case, the presumption that the sanctions would enable opposition forces to exert sufficient pressure on the incumbent regime to bring it into compliance clearly has been proven wrong. Whereas this has been an effective approach in some cases—most notably, in South Africa—in others it quite simply is not" (376). They concluded that "sanctions can represent a prelude to war" (399), rather than an alternative to war, and that even "smart" sanctions may not suffice to do the job of enforcing international norms: "smart sanctions may simply not be 'smart enough' to achieve their stated objectives and will therefore remain an instrument that only causes further violations of economic and social rights on a large scale (as well as integrity rights in extreme cases)" (403).

To these critiques of the Iraqi sanctions, Chomsky adds a still more grievous charge: that far from failing to enable an Iraqi opposition to exert pressure on Saddam, the sanctions actually prevented Iraqis from overthrowing Saddam after the 1991 rebellion was put down:

> That Iraqis might have taken care of their own problems had it not been for the murderous sanctions regime was suggested by the Westerners who knew Iraq best, the respected international diplomats Denis Halliday and Hans von Sponeck, who administered the U.N. oil-for-food program in Iraq and had hundreds of investigators reporting from around the country. Halliday resigned in protest in 1998, condemning the sanctions as "genocidal." Von Sponeck resigned two years later, for similar reasons. The speculation that Saddam Hussein's tyranny was sustained by the sanctions was strengthened by postwar U.S. government investigations, which revealed that the government was being held together virtually by Scotch tape. Subjective judgments about the matter, however, are of little interest. Unless people are at least given the opportunity to overthrow a tyrannical regime, no outside power has the right to carry out the task. (*Failed States*, 57–58)

Chomsky is right that Saddam's tyranny was strengthened after the Gulf War, and he is right that Halliday and von Sponeck resigned and condemned the sanctions as murderous and counterproductive. (As did Jutta Burghardt, the head of the U.N. World Food Program in Baghdad.) Halliday, indeed, told *Al-Ahram Weekly* in 2002, "I believe if the Iraqis had their economy, had their lives back and had their way of life restored, they would take care of the form of governance that they want, that they believe is suitable for their country" (quoted in Abdou, "Scylla and Charybdis"). As Michael Jansen of the Lebanese newspaper the *Daily Star* reported, Halliday also proposed

> a 13-point plan which includes the resumption of U.N. monitoring of Iraq's weapons program; imposition of "smart" sanctions on arms-producing states to prevent Iraq from obtaining prohibited weaponry; an end to the "demonization" of Iraq and its president; dialogue with Baghdad; lifting of economic sanctions; release of oil equipment to repair the country's severely damaged oil industry; investment in the devastated economy; postponement of reparations payments which consume 30 percent of gross oil revenues; and an end to the daily Anglo-U.S. bombing sorties which Iraq says have killed 300 of its civilians and wounded more.
>
> Halliday, who had made a career in the U.N. and held the rank of assistant secretary-general before he resigned, admitted to this correspondent in an interview that he was not "very happy" with his plan. But he said it had been designed to "help Washington and London to get out of this dreadful mess they have gotten themselves into" by insisting on sanctions until Saddam disappears from the scene. (Jansen, "Denis Halliday")

Halliday's plan—particularly when compared with Bush's "liberation" of Iraq—looks like sanity itself; but it is unclear, from their remarks on the sovereignty of Iraq, whether Chomsky or Mahajan would accept the legitimacy of U.N. weapons inspections and "smart" sanctions on arms sales to Iraq. More to the point, the argument that the sanctions prevented the overthrow of Saddam, whether advanced by Chomsky or by Halliday, overlooks (a) the degree of factionalism and religious sectarianism hampering the formation of an effective Iraqi opposition, and (b) the fact that when the U.S. government *did* call on Iraqis to overthrow their tyrannical regime, they were butchered by Saddam well before the sanctions regime had killed a single Iraqi child. The blood of that failed rebellion is arguably on the hands of the United States and its allies in the first Gulf War. For sometimes, it appears, a nation's people can be so brutally and systemically oppressed that they *do* need external assistance in order to overthrow a tyrannical regime; certainly, one hopes that Chomsky's argument that "no outside power has the right to carry out the task" does not apply to U.N. action in East Timor.

Reasonable people can disagree about the endgame of the Gulf War, in which the United States and its allies opted for containment and sanctions rather than regime change in Baghdad. But it is crucial to note that the confusions of the Manichean left with regard to Iraq go back much further than the sovereignty debates of 2002. For the Manichean left opposed U.N. sanctions not merely because they had killed so many innocent Iraqi children (particularly before Saddam's belated adoption of the oil-for-food program in 1997); they opposed sanctions because they regarded the first Gulf War as illegitimate and any U.N. sanctions, as the consequence of that war, as illegitimate as well. Does it follow that the Manichean left approved of Saddam's invasion and annexation of Kuwait? By no means; on the contrary, the Manichean left diligently and rightly derided U.S. officials such as April Glaspie, who had informed Saddam in 1990 that the United States would not interfere if Saddam invaded Kuwait. It noted that Glaspie's meeting with Saddam was yet another piece of evidence of U.S. hypocrisy in the region, dating back to the "tilt" in Iraq's favor after the Iranian Revolution, when in 1982 President Ronald Reagan's administration suddenly removed Iraq from its list of terror-sponsoring states.[19] That move, as every schoolchild now knows, yielded copious shipments of American-manufactured conventional and chemical weapons to Baghdad and a cheery picture of then-Middle East Special Envoy Donald Rumsfeld shaking hands with his new friend Saddam Hussein.[20]

And why did the United States tilt toward Iraq and turn against Iran in the first place? According to Chomsky, "to punish Iran for overthrowing the murderous tyrant, the shah, imposed in 1953 by the U.S. and U.K. coup that destroyed the Iranian parliamentary system" (*Failed States*, 169). About the criminality of the coup against Mossadegh, Chomsky is quite right. But in suggesting that the United States opposed post-revolutionary Iran simply because it wanted to punish the country for overthrowing the Shah, Chomsky is altogether glib, overlooking not only the West's legitimate interest in opposing the spread of Islamism but also (astonishingly, since it seems tailor-made for a Chomskian analysis) Washington's naked realpolitik interest in making sure that the popular Islamist regime in Tehran did not threaten the stability of its allies in the corrupt plutocratic regime in Riyadh.

All that time, it was never clear just what the Manichean left wanted to *do* with its opposition to U.S. policy. It opposed U.S. support for Iraq in the 1980s, as well it should have, even if it was unsure what to make of Iran; it opposed the first Gulf War as well, despite that war's approval by the United Nations; and about the disastrous abandonment of the Kurds and the Shi'ites in the wake of the first Gulf War, as the United States watched Saddam slaughter the very people President George H. W. Bush had urged to rise up and overthrow the tyrant, the Manichean left has had nothing coherent to say. In *Hegemony or Survival,* Chomsky surmises that the United States allowed the rebellion to fail because "the uprising would have left the country in the hands of Iraqis who might have been independent of Washington" (140). This suggests an extraordinary mixture of confusion and omniscience, not only on Chomsky's part but also on Washington's: apparently, the United States called for the overthrow of Saddam and then was content to see the uprising fail because of the likely "independence" of a post-Saddam government. It is not clear why, if the United States feared leaving Iraq in hostile hands that would be independent of Washington, it decided to leave Saddam in power. Nor is it clear, in Chomsky's analysis, what form that hypothetical post-Saddam independence would take; that is, Chomsky does not specify whether this Washington-independent Iraq would be an Islamist state or a democratic-socialist utopia—or something else altogether. As a result, I am not sure what the United States is being faulted for with regard to its response to the 1991 uprising, but I suspect the answer is something like *everything it can conceivably be faulted for:* for supporting and for opposing Saddam, just as it is to be faulted for supporting and for opposing bin Laden.

Curiously, Chomsky does not acknowledge that, despite Washington's complicity in the survival of Saddam's despotism, the postwar no-fly zones secured a remarkable and laudable degree of independence for the Kurds of the north. Still, in a sense, the Manichean left's incoherence on Iraq is preferable to the neoconservatives' very definite plans for Iraq, as first articulated in the 1998 Project for the New American Century letter to then-president Clinton.[21] For the Manichean left has never been anywhere near state power in the United States and has never had to ask itself how President Noam Chomsky, Secretary of State Rahul Mahajan, and National Security Advisor Edward S. Herman would have responded to an abortive Iraqi uprising in 1991, or to Iraq's annexation of Kuwait in 1990, or to the revolution in Iran in 1979.

And yet the sovereignty problems remain. In response to the first Gulf War, Chomsky opposed the war *and* criticized the United States and its allies for failing to assist the 1991 uprising, even though the United States and its allies would not have had the opportunity to assist the uprising (nor would the uprising have happened) if not for the war. Chomsky's position on the overthrow of Saddam in the second Gulf War takes a similar shape: having opposed the war, he would seem to be in no position to celebrate the overthrow and capture of Saddam. At most, one imagines, those who opposed the war (like me) can say only that while we acknowledge the importance of Saddam's capture, we believe that the invasion that made it possible did terrible and unnecessary damage both to international law and to Iraq itself, and that the war has not, on balance, made the Middle East or the world a better and safer place. Chomsky, however, takes a somewhat different line. In *Hegemony or Survival,* he argues that "unless the population is given the opportunity to overthrow a brutal tyrant, as they did with other members of the rogue's gallery supported by the U.S. and U.K., there is no justification for resort to outside force to do so" (249; he repeats the argument in similar language in *Failed States,* 57–58); but earlier in the book, Chomsky had insisted that the fall of Saddam is cause for "rejoicing":

> Those concerned with the tragedy of Iraq had three basic goals: (1) overthrowing the tyranny, (2) ending the sanctions that were targeting the people, not the rulers, and (3) preserving some semblance of world order. There can be no disagreement among decent people on the first two goals: achieving them is an occasion for rejoicing, particularly for those who protested U.S. support for Saddam before his invasion of Kuwait and again immediately afterward, and opposed the sanctions regime that followed; they can therefore applaud the outcome without hypocrisy. (*Hegemony or Survival,* 143)

Most opponents of the war in the Walzer-Gitlin camp had the intellectual honesty to admit that our position—favoring containment over invasion—would leave Saddam in place, and we agonized over whether we were right to consider this the lesser evil. (I return to this point when I discuss one of the more notable lacunae in George Packer's *The Assassins' Gate.*) But for Chomsky there is no need to agonize: the invasion was illegal and immoral, and no outside force has the right to overthrow a tyrant, and yet the overthrow of the tyrant can be applauded "without hypocrisy."

In *Hegemony or Survival,* however, the strain is so evident that Chomsky feels the need to repeat the claim in an afterword, declaring that "the invasion did depose Saddam Hussein, an outcome that can be welcomed without hypocrisy by those who strenuously opposed U.S.-U.K. support for him through his worst crimes, including the crushing of the Shi'ite rebellion that might have overthrown him in 1991, for reasons that were frankly explained but are now kept from the public eye" (248). Once more, just to be clear: no hypocrisy is involved in this position. Just a supple form of doublethink, in which not only the invasion but even UN-SCOM inspections and no-fly zones are denounced as imperialist violations of Iraqi sovereignty, and in which it is nonetheless possible to rejoice at the overthrow and capture of the sovereign when it occurs.

DIRTY FUCKING HIPPIES

Two important things happened on the American political landscape in 2001–03: the antiwar movement was hijacked (and, worse, *led*) by a tiny group of authoritarian ultraleftist thugs, and the pro-war forces (conservative, centrist, and liberal) managed to marginalize antiwar sentiment even when it had nothing to do with tiny left-sectarian grouplets.

The first development proceeded as follows. While no one was looking, a bizarre, beyond-the-fringe neo-Stalinist sectarian group, the Workers World Party (WWP)—originally formed in 1959 to defend the Soviet invasion of Hungary and to denounce Nikita Khrushchev's revelations of Stalin's crimes at the Twentieth Party Congress in 1956, and now announcing its support of Kim Jong Il and North Korea—began organizing "peace" demonstrations. There were plenty of speeches about Cuba and Mumia Abu-Jamal, along with the occasional chant of "Palestine must be free from the river to the sea" and denunciations of U.S. imperial aggression in Afghanistan, but little in the way of offering ordinary Americans clear reasons to oppose the incipient war in Iraq. The WWP front group in charge of the early demonstrations, ANSWER (Act Now to Stop War and End Racism) did manage to organize some impressively large rallies, inspiring flattering parallels to the early antiwar demonstrations of the Vietnam era: for a time, the antiwar left could legitimately credit itself with having drawn hundreds of thousands of protestors to Washington, D.C., before a war had even begun.

The vast majority of attendees at those demonstrations, of course, had no idea what ANSWER was or what the history and agenda of the WWP might be; they simply wanted to prevent what they (rightly) believed would be a disastrous and illegal war, and in doing so, those attendees did a service to democracy and to the American nation. ANSWER itself, however, was another matter. For those of us who knew the group's history and agenda, the prewar period looked like a perfect political storm: the hard right in charge of the world's most powerful nation, its millennial schemes supported by a complaisant and often jingoistic press; liberal and progressive intellectuals willing to traduce their own internationalist ideals in support of a nearly unilateral war in Iraq on "humanitarian" grounds; and an "antiwar" movement led by a group that could not have been more counterproductive for a democratic left if it had been personally crafted by Karl Rove and FOX News. Though the antiwar demonstrations were impressive in size, ideologically, the political contrast with the early Vietnam era is vivid—and would be risible if it were not so sad. The first major antiwar demonstration of the Vietnam era took place in Washington, D.C., in 1965, organized chiefly by Students for a Democratic Society— which, notably, insisted that there be no expressions of sympathy for the Viet Cong and no overheated references to American "imperialism" at the event. In retrospect, it almost seems as if the fringe left of the WWP designed the post-9/11 rallies precisely as a long-festering protest against their marginalization a generation earlier: this time around, the "radicals" would be front and center, chanting about imperialism and Zionism and the plight of the Cuban Five.

On the right, however, things were even worse—not only because the American right is many times more powerful than the WWP left in terms of access to money, media, and the apparatus of state, but also because the American right proceeded to unleash some of its most xenophobic and murderous fantasies. Echoing Rich Lowry's call for the destruction of entire capitals (in the service of "morality"; "Against Cruise Missiles") and Ann Coulter's infamous call to jihad ("We should invade their countries, kill their leaders and convert them to Christianity"; "This is War") were hundreds of right-wing commentators who sometimes seemed to vie to outdo each other for sheer cruelty and stupidity. As Jonah Goldberg of the *National Review* cavalierly wrote in April 2002:

I've long been an admirer of, if not a full-fledged subscriber to, what I call the "Ledeen Doctrine." I'm not sure my friend Michael Ledeen will thank me for ascribing authorship to him and he may have only been semi-serious when he crafted it, but here is the bedrock tenet of the Ledeen Doctrine in more or less his own words: "Every ten years or so, the United States needs to pick up some small crappy little country and throw it against the wall, just to show the world we mean business." That's at least how I remember Michael phrasing it at a speech at the American Enterprise Institute about a decade ago (Ledeen is one of the most entertaining public speakers I've ever heard, by the way). ("Baghdad Delenda Est, Part Two")

The collapse of the American news media must be seen in this context. It is not, as Chomsky suggested, that *no one* questioned Bush's rationale for war in Iraq by late 2003; on the contrary, by then, many reporters and commentators had questioned the WMD rationale and disputed the premise of "Operation Iraqi Freedom." Even *Time* magazine was speculating that Bush's elaborate photo op on U.S.S. *Lincoln*—featuring the "Mission Accomplished" banner and a flight suit that made MSNBC pundit Chris Matthews swoon and Nixon henchman G. Gordon Liddy wax poetic about the size of Bush's genitalia—would come to be seen as a political liability (Dickerson, "Bush's 'Bannergate' Shuffle").[22]

But about the complicity of American mass media in the runup to war, Chomsky is not wrong: by 2003, the American press, television networks, and cable news channels had done a most impressive job of mainstreaming even some of the most vicious right-wing pundits and positions and marginalizing even the most tepid forms of liberal dissent. (Likewise, in 2005, in response to criticism of U.S. practices in Guantánamo, the Pentagon created a disinformation organization comprised of military experts who offered administration-friendly "analysis" for television, and the networks and cable outlets played along.)[23] Nor was it only a matter of TV cable outlets giving platforms to Ann Coulter and Jonah Goldberg and entire programs to fringe ranters like Glenn Beck and (briefly) Michael Savage; the nation's two leading newspapers were critical components of war hysteria as well. Judith Miller's reports on Iraq for the *New York Times,* which served largely as press releases for Ahmad Chalabi's version of the world, damaged that paper's credibility far more extensively than a newsroomful of Jayson Blairs; columnist Tom Friedman, whose bellicose support of war in Kosovo was an embarrassment to the cause of humanitarian intervention ("Every week you ravage Kosovo is another decade we will set your country back by pulverizing you. You want 1950? We can do 1950. You want 1389? We can do 1389 too"), unleashed his inner bully once again, telling Charlie Rose that one crucial rationale for war was that the United States needed to burst the "bubble" of Islamist radicalism by taking out an Arab state and telling Arab extremists, "Suck. On. This."[24]

Meanwhile, the *Washington Post*'s editorial page editor, Fred Hiatt, turned his paper's op-ed section into something like a highbrow neocon version of the *Washington Times*.[25] Indeed, the *Post* op-ed pages started the drumbeat for war in Iraq the moment the Taliban fell: in November 2001, the *Post*'s resident liberal, Richard Cohen, was writing essays like " . . . And Now to Iraq," which included the following immortal paragraph:

> Richard Perle, the former Reagan administration official and the Ze-lig-like character who appears over the shoulder of countless op-ed writers, makes a good point (over my shoulder) when he says that the danger is not merely that Iraq will go nuclear but also that it will hand off the device to some terrorist with a suitcase. Then, as with anthrax, we will not be able to find the source.

That column has the virtue, such as it is, of reminding us that the anthrax scare of fall 2001 was widely understood in official Washington to be the work of Saddam Hussein—though why Saddam would want to target postal workers and tabloid editors and Democratic elected officials like Tom Daschle was not made clear at the time. Instead, in response to the anthrax-that-must-be-from-Saddam, Richard Cohen, with Richard Perle at his shoulder, spun out his fears of Iraqi-nukes-in-a-suitcase, and the *New Republic* issued a cry for war:

> "I will show you fear," the poet wrote, "in a handful of dust." The hand-fuls of dust have been appearing in Boca Raton and New York and Washington, and the fear is loose in the land. . . .
>
> In the shattering weeks since September 11, it has been definitively proven that Americans have courage. The time has come to weaponize it. ("After Fear")[26]

The announcement that "demolishing Hussein's military power and liberating Iraq would be a cakewalk" appeared in the *Post*, of course, courtesy of Reagan-era retread Kenneth Adelman, no doubt writing with his colleague Richard Perle at his shoulder ("Cakewalk in Iraq"). But the *Post* did not confine itself to championing the cause for war. Like so much of the Beltway circuit, it worked overtime to smear and discredit even the most sober and restrained critics of its war fever. As Glenn Greenwald pointed out on his acclaimed blog, *Unclaimed Territory* ("Only a Fool") in November 2006, after Colin Powell's speech to the United Nations on February 5, 2003—the speech from which Powell's reputation as a statesman will never recover—Richard Cohen had this to say: "The evidence he presented to the United Nations—some of it circumstantial, some of it absolutely bone-chilling in its detail—had to prove to anyone that Iraq not only hasn't accounted for its weapons of mass destruction but without a doubt still retains them. Only a fool—or possibly a Frenchman— could conclude otherwise" ("Winning Hand for Powell"). Howard Dean, Greenwald notes, responded differently:

> Secretary Powell's recent presentation at the U.N. showed the extent to which we have Iraq under an audio and visual microscope. Given that, I was impressed not by the vastness of evidence presented by the Secretary, but rather by its sketchiness. He said there would be no smoking gun, and there was none.
>
> At the same time, it seems to me we are in possession of information that would be very helpful to U.N. inspectors. For example, if we know Iraqi scientists are being detained at an Iraqi guesthouse, why not surround the building and knock on the door? If we think a facility is being used for biological weapons, why not send the inspectors to check it out? ("Defending American Values—Protecting America's Interests")

Dean's suggestion about inspectors would surely be dismissed by Rahul Mahajan and Ed Herman as Imperialism Lite, but it represented the position of those of us who believed in letting the inspectors determine whether, in fact, Iraq had stockpiles of WMD. For all that, Greenwald recalls, Dean was dismissed as both a lightweight and a madman:

> Cohen—the "liberal" *Post* columnist—spent the rest of the year viciously mocking Dean as a McGovernite pansy who has no experience in Washington and thus knows absolutely nothing about complicated foreign affairs.

On September 18, 2003, Cohen said that "if the Bush team could digitally create the perfect patsy candidate it would be Dean." On November 11, 2003, Cohen said: "The conventional wisdom is that Dean is George McGovern all over again. I do not quibble," and that Dean "encapsulates the deep hatred among some Democrats for our president." ("Only a Fool")

The master of this genre, in those heady days, was the late Michael Kelly—who responded to Al Gore's measured (and altogether prescient) critique of the Bush administration in September 2002 with a column that declared Gore to be "someone who cannot be considered a responsible aspirant to power" ("Look Who's Playing Politics"). Gore, in a September 23 speech, had argued that "we should focus our efforts first and foremost against those who attacked us on September 11th and who have thus far gotten away with it" rather than turn our attention to Iraq, even as he insisted that "all Americans should acknowledge that Iraq does indeed pose a serious threat to the stability of the Persian Gulf region, and we should be about the business of organizing an international coalition to eliminate his access to weapons of mass destruction" ("Iraq and the War on Terrorism"). Kelly responded like so:

> Politics are allowed in politics, but there are limits, and there is a pale, and Gore has now shown himself to be ignorant of those limits, and he has now placed himself beyond that pale.
>
> Gore's speech was one no decent politician could have delivered. It was dishonest, cheap, low. It was hollow. It was bereft of policy, of solutions, of constructive ideas, very nearly of facts—bereft of anything other than taunts and jibes and embarrassingly obvious lies. It was breathtakingly hypocritical, a naked political assault delivered in tones of moral condescension from a man pretending to be superior to mere politics. It was wretched. It was vile. It was contemptible. But I understate. ("Look Who's Playing Politics")

This unhinged rant was not the work of an unemployed twentysomething blogger working in his parents' basement, his keyboard covered in powdered Doritos cheese. It was not the work of one of the spittle-flecked hatemongers of right-wing talk radio. It was the work of a man who, at various points in his career, was tapped to edit the *National Journal,* the *New*

Republic, and the *Atlantic Monthly* and who thereby served as a gatekeeper to two of the nation's outlets of "serious" opinion. And in 2002–03, this is what much "serious" opinion in the United States sounded like.

Thus far, I have given far less space to the tirades of the right than to the stumbles of the left (even though the former set the tone for the country's march to war), because neither the democratic left nor the Manichean left took their cue from those tirades; that role fell to the liberal hawks. The liberal hawks did not merely sign on for war in Iraq; intellectually, they did remarkably destructive work to political debate in the United States. First, and most disastrously, they accepted Bush's basic premise for war: that the attacks of 9/11 "changed everything," so that we needed to respond—preemptively where possible—not merely to the loose network of Sunni extremists who attacked us but to the full complement of our many antagonists in the Middle East. Though they rarely gave in to the kind of WMD hysteria exemplified by Richard Cohen, they argued strenuously—more strenuously, in many cases, than the Bush administration itself—that Iraq should be considered a "humanitarian intervention" and a war of national liberation. They then used that argument to ridicule the antiwar left—by which they meant not only those who considered strikes against al-Qaeda to be an imperialist abomination but also those who were raising simple, prudent Deanian-and-Gorean questions about the rationale for war in Iraq. In so doing, they managed to constitute themselves as the leftward boundary of the thinkable (marginalizing both the Manichean left and the democratic left) and to reinforce the argument that war in Iraq was of a piece with war in Afghanistan. And thereby, the liberal hawks depended both on the logic of the Bush administration (for support) *and* on the logic of the Manichean left (as a foil). Indeed, the liberal hawks and the Manichean left wound up producing and reinforcing each other; as I note at the outset of this chapter, just as it is in both camps' interest to pretend that Kosovo, Afghanistan, and Iraq were all part of the same enterprise, both groups share the goal of aligning supporters of war in Kosovo and Afghanistan with supporters of war in Iraq.

The case for a wider war—against Islamist extremism in general, but also against all the antidemocratic forces in the Arab world—was made most energetically by Paul Berman. Having offered a diligent and insightful reading of Islamism in the first half of his 2003 book, *Terror and Liberalism,* in which he showed that some of the "root causes" of 9/11 lay in the writings of Sayyid Qutb and Islamism's debt to European fascism, Berman made that reading the basis for a call to arms against Iraq. Later, when the Iraq war was just over a year old, Berman followed up with an editorial in the *New York Times* titled "Will the Opposition Lead?" There, he argued as follows:

> The war in Iraq may end up going well or catastrophically, but either way, this war has always been central to the broader war on terror. That is because terror has never been a matter of a few hundred crazies who could be rounded up by the police and special forces. Terror grows out of something larger—an enormous wave of political extremism. . . .
>
> The Sept. 11 attacks came from a relatively small organization. But Al Qaeda was a kind of foam thrown up by the larger extremist wave. The police and special forces were never going to be able to stamp out the Qaeda cells so long as millions of people around the world accepted the paranoid and apocalyptic views and revered suicide terror. The only long-term hope for tamping down the terrorist impulse was to turn America's traditional policies upside down, and come out for once in favor of the liberal democrats of the Muslim world. This would mean promoting a counter-wave of liberal and rational ideas to combat the allure of paranoia and apocalypse.
>
> The whole point in overthrowing Saddam Hussein, from my perspective, was to achieve those large possibilities right in the center of the Muslim world, where the ripples might lead in every direction. Iraq was a logical place to begin because, for a dozen years, the Baathists had been shooting at American and British planes, and inciting paranoia and hatred against the United States, and encouraging the idea that attacks can successfully be launched against American targets, and giving that idea some extra oomph with the bluff about fearsome weapons. The Baathists, in short, contributed their bit to the atmosphere that led to Sept. 11.[27]

There are four important features of this argument. One, the assertion that Iraq has always been central to the broader war on terror. This claim not only endorses the Bush administration's view that Iraq has been the real enemy all along; it fully embraces the Bush-Cheney concept of a war on "terror."[28] Two, the use of the term "larger extremist wave" to conflate the secular totalitarianism of the Ba'ath Party with the Islamist radicalism of al-Qaeda: Berman's formulation would leave the United States—like the mad Cuchulain of Irish myth—fighting a wave, an image that neatly manages to evoke an endless, futile war. Three, the strange belief that the Bush administration had somehow decided to support "the liberal democrats of the Muslim world": perhaps people like Berman had made this decision, but Bush and Cheney quite clearly had not. And four, the claim—attenuated, to be sure—that the Ba'athists had something to do not with 9/11 itself but to the "atmosphere" that led to it.

Together, these four features demonstrate that liberal hawks such as Berman did not merely support the war in Iraq; they supported an entire wave of positions held by the Bush administration, on top of which the war itself was but a kind of foam. Unfortunately for Berman, a significant challenge to all these assumptions had been issued a few weeks earlier— not by Chomsky, either, but by former counterintelligence expert Richard Clarke, who had said, on CBS's *60 Minutes,* "Osama bin Laden had been saying for years, 'America wants to invade an Arab country and occupy it, an oil-rich Arab country.' We stepped right into Bin Laden's propaganda" (quoted in Cocco, "Bush's 9/11 Myths Endanger U.S.") With all due respect to Berman, I submit that Richard Clarke is more knowledgeable than he with regard to bin Laden and the larger extremist waves in the Middle East.

Berman does not always fare well in George Packer's 2005 book, *The Assassins' Gate,* particularly when Packer recalls him saying that postwar Iraq would look like something out of Berman's *A Tale of Two Utopias:* "He kept comparing the situation in post-totalitarian Baghdad to Prague in 1989. I kept insisting that Iraq was vastly different: under military occupation, far more violent, its people more traumatized, living in a much worse neighborhood" (*Assassins' Gate,* 160).[29] But Packer, who describes himself as one of "the tiny, insignificant camp of ambivalently prowar liberals, who supported a war by about the same margin that the voting public had supported Al Gore" (87), nonetheless extends to Berman a form of intellectual respect that he denies to most of the antiwar movement—the discussion of which occupies a mere six pages in a richly detailed 450-page book. For all its brevity, Packer's discussion of the antiwar movement is highly revealing and should serve to remind us that, although the camp of "ambivalently prowar liberals" was indeed tiny, it was hardly insignificant.

Recounting his interview with Eli Pariser of MoveOn, Packer takes a reasonable remark of Pariser's and follows it with a paragraph devoted to undermining Pariser's credibility. Noting that Pariser is "unfailingly polite and thoughtful," and that in this and other ways "he seemed to exist so that the rest of the country couldn't dismiss the antiwar movement as a fringe phenomenon of graying pacifists and young nihilists" (84), Packer writes:

> Pariser told me, "I just don't know that it makes sense for us to risk everything that we're risking both in terms of international stature and in terms of the lives of our military people for a vague idea that people think it could be better without this guy."
>
> There was a case to be made for this nuanced view, and it moved millions of Americans. But the first thing to notice was its essential conservatism. Containment preserved the status quo along with a notion of American virtue. Pariser descended on his father's side from Zionist Jews who helped found Tel Aviv, and on his mother's from Polish socialists. But the aggressive antifascism that once characterized young people on the left had given way, in the wake of Vietnam and the green movement, to a softer, more cautious worldview that often amounted in practice to isolationism. The antifascist wars of our own time—in Bosnia and Kosovo—never strongly registered with Pariser's generation of activists. When I asked whether the desires of Iraqis themselves should be taken into account, he said, "I don't think that first and foremost this is about them as much as it's about us and how we act in the world." (84–85)

By the time Packer has demonstrated Pariser's "conservative" commitment to "isolationism" with this regrettably America-first remark, a lot of serious damage has been done.

First, Pariser has been trotted out as the exception to the rule, or what Packer calls "the most appealing face of the movement" (84): unlike those graying pacifists and young nihilists, he is *thoughtful*. This is such a common trope in contemporary American political discourse that the liberal blogosphere now ironically refers to leading antiwar spokespersons like Pariser and Howard Dean as "dirty fucking hippies" (since this is how they are often treated in mainstream political discourse) and notes bitterly that their words on Iraq remain worthless compared with those of the Very Serious People who promised us a rose garden and a cakewalk.[30]

Second, the term "conservative" is trotted out as a scare word: What thoughtful antiwar activist or intellectual wants to be known as *conservative*? But, of course, the term as used here does not mean "aligned with political conservatives," who supported George Bush and the Iraq war in overwhelming numbers. It means something more like "cautious," and under that heading, surely it behooved Packer to note that, by the time he was writing his book, Eli Pariser's brand of caution had shown itself to be something smarter and more worthy of respect than simple "isolationism." Even a parenthetical admission on Packer's part that Pariser had had the cost/benefit analysis basically correct would have been nice.

Third, Pariser's inattentiveness to "the desires of Iraqis"—though one wishes that he'd replied to Packer's question by surmising that most Iraqis would not, in fact, welcome Americans as liberators, and that Kanan Makiya, for all his eloquence, was not a representative sample of Iraqi opinion—is ascribed to his lack of interest in the antifascist wars in the Balkans. This is good red meat for the Manicheans and reinforces their claims that the liberal hawks' enthusiasm for war in Iraq was inspired by Kosovo.[31] Packer had mounted this argument before, in his December 2002 *New York Times Magazine* cover story that profiled the liberal hawks and attributed their faith in American military action to the lessons of the Balkans ("Liberal Quandary over Iraq"). That article was one of the more influential pieces of political journalism to come from the left in 2002; perhaps it is only professional modesty that leads Packer, a few years later, to construe his camp of pro-war liberals as "insignificant." In reality, his camp set the terms for discussion of the antiwar position in much of the liberal wing of the media, and he repeats those terms in this description of the February 15, 2003, New York rally in *The Assassins' Gate:* "The movement's assumptions were based on moral innocence—on an inability to imagine the horror in which Iraqis lived, and a desire for all good things to go together, for total vindication. War is evil; therefore, the prevention of war must be good" (86). The movement had some terrible leadership in ANSWER, yes. And perhaps Packer is right that some of the demonstrators failed to contemplate the horror of life under Saddam; we will never know, since Packer did not interview any. But when Packer writes, "the protestors saw themselves as defending Iraqis from the terrible fate that the United States was preparing to inflict on them," he unwittingly reminds us that the protestors did not, in general, deserve to be dismissed as softheaded peaceniks who wanted all good things to go together. For the protestors, whatever else their faults, saw themselves *correctly* as trying to defend Iraqis from the terrible fate that the United States inflicted on them.

I focus on Packer not because he was the worst of the liberal hawks but because he was one of the best: few people on the pro-war left took the idea of Iraqi liberation as seriously as he did, and though he relied too heavily on the passion of Kanan Makiya, he has been among the most self-critical supporters of the war in recent years.[32] Unfortunately, he did not always take the arguments of the war's opponents quite so seriously, and that failure accounts for two very curious moments in *The Assassins' Gate*.[33] The first is Packer's account of a November 2002 panel at New York University, in which he summarizes the remarks of Michael Walzer before moving to Makiya's stirring reply:

> "The Iraqi opposition is something new in Arab politics. It can be encouraged or it can be crushed just like that. But think about what you're doing if you do crush it. I rest my moral case on the following: If there is a sliver of a chance to what I just said happening, a five to ten percent chance, you have a moral obligation, I say, to do it."
>
> The room exploded in applause. The other panelists looked startled. Against the reasonable arguments of these reasonable people, Makiya was offering something more attractive—the face of hope, however slender.
>
> "It's very hard to respond," Walzer said.
>
> It was hard because a man like Walzer didn't want to stand in the way of a dream like Makiya's. He didn't want to be on the other side of a great moral question. "I would not join an antiwar movement that strengthened the hand of Saddam," Walzer told me later, and when I asked whether there could be an antiwar movement that didn't, he admitted, "it's very hard to think of what form it could take." (*Assassins' Gate*, 83)

Here, Packer suggests that neither Walzer nor any of the other panelists had an answer for what we might call, following Cheney's One Percent Doctrine, Makiya's Five to Ten Percent Challenge. But as Todd Gitlin pointed out on the blog TPM (Talking Points Memo) Café in October 2005, in a "book event" devoted to *The Assassins' Gate*, Packer purchased this suggestion at a steep discount, by ignoring remarks that had addressed Makiya's argument directly—just before Makiya made it. The remarks happened to have been made by one Todd Gitlin, and on TPM Café, Gitlin referenced them first by saying, in a "Dear George" letter:

> I want to speak up for the part of the antiwar movement to which I belonged, and belong—the part that did not take the easy way out, the

part that was not morally innocent, the part that was also not on principle pacifist, the part, in other words, that weighed the great benefits that would accrue to Iraq if Saddam Hussein fell against the damage that war on Iraq would do to the necessary fight against jihadists, and not least to Iraq, too, and found the war wanting in the scales. ("War Movement and the Antiwar Movement")

He then reproduces some of the text of his speech that evening:

If wishes were arguments, the strongest argument for an American war would be the most ambitious, which is Kanan Makiya's—the wish that by deposing Saddam Hussein and occupying Iraq, the U. S. would install the first democratic regime in the Arab world, a regime that, in turn, would undermine the autocratic consensus that governs the region, reverse the Islamist movement and foster the growth of anti-Islamist tendencies elsewhere. Such an outcome is devoutly to be desired. I take it especially seriously coming from Kanan Makiya, from whom I've learned more about the monstrous tyranny of Saddam Hussein and the Ba'ath party than from anyone else. And I have to say: If only the wish sufficed.

But the world in which the wish would suffice is not the world we live in. An American war in Iraq is very unlikely to bring it about. What it is far more likely to bring about is carnage and a boost to terror. The risks are far too great to justify war. Wars get out of control and are, after all, hellish. That is why they must be matters of last resort. In Iraq's neighborhood, there are simply too many ways in which this particular war could get out of control. The scenario most likely to bring about the use of weapons of mass destruction is precisely the one George W. Bush has been angling for: an attack on Saddam Hussein's regime. The scenario most likely to bring about terror attacks— even on Americans—is precisely the same. The scenario most likely to win recruits for al-Qaeda is precisely the same. Against Saddam Hussein's future threats, there are substantial, not merely rhetorical, alternatives. The case for containment is strong. Smart sanctions (not the current blunderbuss kind), maintenance of the no-fly zones, and inspections with teeth are the alternatives to war.

So the antiwar movement should accept that the U.N.-imposed inspections are legal, proportionate to the threat, and therefore just. The unanimous Security Council resolution mandating inspections is a testament not only to Bush's power but to the strength of the case. The proportionate threat of force to ensure that inspectors have access to whatever they wish to inspect is justified. The use of force for "regime change" is not proportionate, nor is it justified by the Security Council.[34]

Ironically, Gitlin had opened his remarks that evening by saying, "political decency consists not just in taking the right position but in being willing to face contrary positions, face them at their strong points, not win arguments cheaply." Almost three years later, at the TPM Café, some version of that sense of political decency was doubtless what prevented Gitlin from saying explicitly that this is the standard traduced by Packer's account of the New York University panel.

Likewise, when it comes time to discuss the likely postwar scenarios in Iraq—which were weighed by so many people in the antiwar camp, in so many various ways—*The Assassins' Gate* produces another curious moment. Throughout the book, Packer is scathing in his criticism of the Bush administration's arrogance and incompetence, and offers devastating accounts of how the Cheney-Rumsfeld Axis of Arrogance and Incompetence ensured that postwar Iraq would be one tactical disaster after another. But Packer closes his chapter on "Special Plans" on a note so false as to disrupt the entire composition:

> As for the postwar plan, there was no need to worry. The president had already been told what he wanted to hear—by his vice president and national security advisor, by his secretary of defense and his secretary's deputies, by Kanan Makiya and other exiles, by his ardent supporters in the think tanks and the press, by his own faith in the universal human desire for freedom. And so the American people never had a chance to consider the real difficulties and costs of regime change in Iraq. (*Assassins' Gate*, 147)

The American people never had a chance to consider the real difficulties and costs of regime change in Iraq. One would have thought that much of the antiwar movement consisted of people considering the real difficulties and costs of regime change in Iraq, regardless of what George Bush's echo chamber was telling him; indeed, debates about the real difficulties and costs of regime change in Iraq were part of the warp and woof of prewar debate in the United States.[35]

One of the most substantial contributions to that debate was James Fallows's November 2002 cover story for the *Atlantic Monthly,* "The Fifty-First State?" And while Fallows's essay would not win much applause from the readers of Z, since Fallows himself supported the war, it belies Packer's claim that Americans just didn't have the chance to discuss the difficulties and costs of regime change. In his interviews with dozens of military and political analysts, Fallows scrupulously airs the arguments of the war's opponents, including those of retired Air Force general Merrill McPeak, who opposed preemptive war, and John Dower, historian of the U.S. occupation of Japan, who opposed the war "vehemently," in Fallows's words, because of its lack of international support. Throughout the essay, Fallows entertains the possibility that the war might issue in a U.S. occupation that would last for decades. As far as I know, that issue of the *Atlantic Monthly* was not classified as secret by Cheney's office; I believe it was readily available on newsstands throughout the country. Meanwhile, in other venues, one military figure after another weighed in on the difficulties and costs, from retired General Anthony Zinni to Army Chief of Staff General Eric Shinseki—as Packer himself notes earlier in that very chapter.

As Michael Walzer might say, it's very hard to respond to a passage such as this. But I can suggest that it is, in its odd way, the liberal-hawk counterpart to Noam Chomsky's claim that no one in the mainstream American press questioned Bush's rationale for war in late 2003. In each case, the rhetorical field is miraculously evacuated of interlocutors and competitors: in Chomsky's version, the American media never managed to muster any skepticism at the idea that "Operation Iraqi Freedom" was all about Iraqi freedom, and everyone marched in lockstep with Bush's rationale for war; in Packer's version, the antiwar movement failed to ask the hard questions about the war, and the American people never had the chance to debate the real difficulties and costs of regime change.

These lacunae are important not only because they reveal the limitations of the liberal prowar position but also because they highlight the eerie symbiosis between the liberal hawks and the Manichean left. The Manicheans need the hawks in order to justify their own opposition to military action in Kosovo and Afghanistan, and the hawks need the Manicheans in order to justify their belief that opponents of war in Iraq weren't sufficiently nuanced or sophisticated to grapple with the problems posed by a brutal authoritarian like Saddam. And lying between the two camps, antiwar critics like Walzer and Gitlin, Dean and Gore, were dismissed as insufficiently serious (by the hawks) or apologists for imperialism (by the

Manicheans). The "liberal" wing of the mass media largely sided with the hawks. That dynamic persisted well into the war's fourth year, when the Beltway punditocracy threw up its collective arms in horror after Connecticut Senator Joe Lieberman was defeated in a Democratic Party primary by little-known antiwar candidate Ned Lamont; the conventional wisdom offered by writers such as Jacob Weisberg and Jon Chait was that the Lamont vote signaled the return of the McGovernite wing of the Democratic party, which, in Beltway punditspeak, means something like love-ins and Weatherman bombings, Yippies and Grateful Dead concerts—and, of course, acid, amnesty, and abortion.[36] The point should be obvious: a political climate in which a figure like Ned Lamont is considered to be just beyond the leftward boundary of the thinkable simply for defeating the Democrats' most vocal pro-war senator in a primary (a senator who, moreover, has made a career out of attacking and undermining other Democrats, and who then proceeded to campaign for John McCain in 2008) is a climate in which no "serious" commentator has to pay the slightest attention to any critique from the democratic left.

The liberal hawks, therefore, were useful to constituencies on both sides: to the right, they gave "bipartisan" cover to a preemptive and unnecessary war, and to the further reaches of the left, they proved once again, as in Vietnam, that "liberals" are merely U.S. imperialists in sheep's clothing. The Manicheans derided the liberal hawks as facile cheerleaders for Bush; the liberal hawks repaid the compliment by deriding the Manicheans as facile isolationists and peaceniks strengthening Saddam's hand. The Manichean opposition to war in Afghanistan was used by the liberal hawks to delegitimate a far more popular opposition to war in Iraq; and the liberal hawks' enthusiasm for war in Iraq was used by the Manicheans to delegitimate far more justifiable wars in Afghanistan and Kosovo.

TO THE EUSTON STATION

The symbiosis between the Manicheans and the hawks is one reason why the liberal hawks' importance, in this political formation, is out of all proportion to their actual size. In a review essay on Nick Cohen's *What's Left? How Liberals Lost Their Way,* Johann Hari writes:

> The pro-invasion left was always a small battalion, made up almost
> entirely of journalists and intellectuals who believed toppling the

Taliban and Saddam Hussein was a good idea—even if the only leader available to lead the charge was George W. Bush. Yet almost since the first statue of Saddam fell to the ground, it has been losing troops— to the antiwar side, to a sullen AWOL silence, or to despair. So far, there have been retractions from Peter Beinart, Norman Geras, David Aaronovitch, and more; only a few lone fighters remain, like Japanese troops hiding in the forest, unaware their war has been lost. ("Choosing Sides," 79)[37]

Hari is right about the relative size of the "pro-invasion left" in the United States and the United Kingdom; it is genuinely astonishing, in view of the attention paid to liberal hawks such as Beinart, Berman, Packer, and Michael Ignatieff (and to politically unclassifiable hawks, such as Hitchens), that so many liberal and left internationalists opposed the Iraq war—including some liberal and left internationalists who criticized the leadership of the antiwar camp. A partial list would include, aside from Walzer, Cooper, and Gitlin, Timothy Garton Ash, Martha Nussbaum, Jürgen Habermas, Michael Tomasky, Samantha Power, David Corn, Seyla Benhabib, Charles Taylor, Fred Dallmayr, Saskia Sassen, Ronald Dworkin, Mark Danner, Richard Falk, Mary Kaldor, Ian Buruma, Ellen Willis, Danny Postel, Josh Cohen, David Held, Doug Cassel, Ian Williams, Amartya Sen, Michael Lind, Cass Sunstein, Ken Roth, Marcus Raskin, Richard Rorty, Stephen Holmes, Tzvetan Todorov, Thomas McCarthy, Kwame Anthony Appiah, the editors of *Nation,* the editors of *Boston Review,* the editors of *openDemocracy,* the editors of *American Prospect,* and the editors of the *New York Review of Books.* Surely such a lineup of journalists and intellectuals is worth acknowledging, even when they are counterbalanced by Christopher Hitchens at his most voluble.

But then, Hitchens's very volubility was part of the Manichean-versus-hawk dynamic. Over the course of a mere twenty months, Hitchens went from writing a series of searing critiques of the Manichean left to his own sectarian form of Manicheanism, embracing George Bush and mocking the Dixie Chicks as "fucking fat slags" for telling a British audience that they were embarrassed to be from Texas.[38] In the United Kingdom, Nick Cohen followed in the Hitchensian slipstream; and as Cohen's book *What's Left?* demonstrates, the symbiotic link between the follies of the pro-invasion left and the follies of the Manichean left are somewhat clearer on the other side of the Atlantic, where blogs like Lenin's Tomb (written by Socialist Workers Party member Richard Seymour) and figures like George Galloway openly trumpet their sympathy for some of the most reactionary forces in the Arab world, from Saddam to Hezbollah. The British far left has thereby precipitated a crisis of leftist identification and purpose to which writers like Cohen and Geras responded by writing and promoting the "Euston Manifesto" of 2006—a document which, for all its laudable invocations of internationalism and universal human rights, takes no position on Iraq except to announce that it is not the job of the left to analyze the debate over the war:

> The founding supporters of this statement took different views on the military intervention in Iraq, both for and against. We recognize that it was possible reasonably to disagree about the justification for the intervention, the manner in which it was carried through, the planning (or lack of it) for the aftermath, and the prospects for the successful implementation of democratic change. We are, however, united in our view about the reactionary, semi-fascist and murderous character of the Baathist regime in Iraq, and we recognize its overthrow as a liberation of the Iraqi people. We are also united in the view that, since the day on which this occurred, the proper concern of genuine liberals and members of the Left should have been the battle to put in place in Iraq a democratic political order and to rebuild the country's infrastructure, to create after decades of the most brutal oppression a life for Iraqis which those living in democratic countries take for granted—rather than picking through the rubble of the arguments over intervention.[39]

The mention of "rubble" is especially unfortunate, since it evokes the actual state of some Iraqi cities more readily than it characterizes the record of the arguments over intervention, and it suggests that the Eustonians are extending to themselves a kind of blanket amnesty program in which even those who supported the invasion wholeheartedly will continue to be those who arrogate to themselves the right to set the terms for "left internationalism" in the future.

But perhaps the tone and approach of the "Euston Manifesto" become more comprehensible once one realizes the extent and severity of the local Manichean phenomenon to which it is responding. There is no prominent American parallel, for instance, to Susan Watkins's cheerleading for the "Iraqi *maquis*" ("Vichy on the Tigris"), and no American counterpart to Perry Anderson's characteristically magisterial declaration, in the September–October 2002 issue of the *New Left Review,* that the supporters of war in Kosovo are even more contemptible than Bush-Cheney-Rumsfeld themselves:

> The doctrine of pre-emption is a menace to every state that might in future cross the will of the hegemon or its allies. But it is no better when proclaimed in the name of human rights than of non-proliferation. What is sauce for the Balkan goose is sauce for the Mesopotamian gander. The remonstrants who pretend otherwise deserve less respect than those they implore not to act on their common presumptions. ("Force and Consent," 30)

Part of what drives Anderson's thundering dismissal of actions taken "in the name of human rights" is the strange belief that Kosovo should be understood as an example of "the doctrine of pre-emption"—a belief that requires one to ignore the history of the Balkans prior to 1999, as Adrian Hastings pointed out in his review ("Not a Book about Kosovo") of Chomsky's *New Military Humanism.* But such are the terms of the current historical conjuncture: the authors of the "Euston Manifesto" are right to reject Galloway, Lenin's Tomb, and the *New Left Review* as exemplars of a deeply reactionary strain of "radical" left thought; but the terms in which the manifesto offers itself as opposition actually confirm Anderson's charge—as does, more dramatically, the woeful career of Tony Blair himself—that the road to Baghdad begins in the Balkans. Likewise, the fact that Michael Ignatieff championed intervention in the Balkans, and then insisted that Iraq, too, was a "humanitarian" mission, put the still-emerging ideals of liberal internationalism on the defensive, and left the very idea of "humanitarian intervention" in tatters.

Ignatieff plays a role here not unlike that of George Packer: he was one of the most idealistic and substantial liberal intellectuals who supported war in Iraq, as opposed to the volatile Hitchens and the blustering Friedman. The damage done to liberal internationalism by Ignatieff, accordingly, is all the greater, because Ignatieff sincerely believes in (indeed, helped to develop) the idea of an international "responsibility to protect."[40] In insisting that the Iraq war should be understood as a fight against tyranny, Packer and Ignatieff consistently managed to avoid sounding the discordant note of bloodlust that crept into (and thereby vitiated) the appeals to Iraqi liberation mounted by hawks like Friedman and Hitchens. For that reason, paradoxically, Ignatieff and Packer testify to a terrible development for advocates of international human rights: with regard to war in Iraq, the best arguments had the worst effects.

The best argument—the one that demanded the most serious attention from the left—was that the war would liberate millions of innocent people from the rule of a psychotic tyrant and his equally psychotic progeny. (This is why it was a mistake for Edward Said to dismiss Kanan Makiya as "a man of vanity who has no compassion, no demonstrable awareness of human suffering . . . a man of pretension and superficiality" [Said, "Misinformation about Iraq"]. Makiya could have been all this and worse still, a wanton kicker of dogs, and his call to liberate Iraq would still have merited a substantial response.) As a corollary, the idealists believed, a free Iraq would reduce by one the number of pariah states in a volatile region that were willing to use or distribute weapons of mass destruction. But the argument about WMD was an argument about security rather than an argument about freedom—and, of course, the question of whether Iraq had WMD to use or distribute was a matter that could have been addressed by letting UNSCOM inspectors do their work.[41] Lowest on the moral scale lay the argument that war in Iraq constituted revenge for the attacks of 9/11 and the argument that the West needed to humiliate a major Arab nation in order to prevent further attacks. But precisely because those arguments are so despicable, their proponents did no damage to the idea of humanitarian intervention and the ideal of international human rights; that task was left to people such as Packer and Ignatieff, who proved to be entirely too blithe about the importance of multilateral consensus and the possibility that the idea of "humanitarian war" just might, someday, be misapplied.

It is worth pointing out to the Manichean left, whenever the opportunity presents itself, how many liberal and left internationalists refused the terms set by Packer and Ignatieff on one side and Chomsky and Anderson on the other. And it is worth reminding all parties that in January 2004, Ken Roth of Human Rights Watch issued a detailed and convincing report, titled "War in Iraq: Not a Humanitarian Intervention," which acknowledged that "Human Rights Watch has on rare occasion advocated humanitarian intervention—for example, to stop ongoing genocide in Rwanda and Bosnia" but which decisively slammed the door on any attempt to use the 1988 Anfal (in which 100,000 Kurds were killed) or the suppression of the 1991 Intifada as retroactive grounds for international action. I quote at length in order to give some idea not only of the substance of Roth's argument but also of its intellectual rigor:

If Saddam Hussein committed mass atrocities in the past, wasn't his overthrow justified to prevent his resumption of such atrocities in the future? No. Human Rights Watch accepts that military intervention may be necessary not only to stop ongoing slaughter but also to prevent future slaughter, but the future slaughter must be imminent. To justify the extraordinary remedy of military force for preventive humanitarian purposes, there must be evidence that large-scale slaughter is in preparation and about to begin unless militarily stopped. But no one seriously claimed before the war that the Saddam Hussein government was planning imminent mass killing, and no evidence has emerged that it was. There were claims that Saddam Hussein, with a history of gassing Iranian soldiers and Iraqi Kurds, was planning to deliver weapons of mass destruction through terrorist networks, but these allegations were entirely speculative; no substantial evidence has yet emerged. There were also fears that the Iraqi government might respond to an invasion with the use of chemical or biological weapons, perhaps even against its own people, but no one seriously suggested such use as an imminent possibility in the absence of an invasion.

That does not mean that past atrocities should be ignored. Rather, their perpetrators should be prosecuted. Human Rights Watch has devoted enormous efforts to investigating and documenting the Iraqi government's atrocities, particularly the Anfal genocide against Iraqi Kurds. We have interviewed witnesses and survivors, exhumed mass graves, taken soil samples to demonstrate the use of chemical weapons, and combed through literally tons of Iraqi secret police documents. We have circled the globe trying to convince some government—any government—to institute legal proceedings against Iraq for genocide. No one would. In the mid-1990s, when our efforts were most intense, governments feared that charging Iraq with genocide would be too provocative—that it would undermine future commercial deals with Iraq, squander influence in the Middle East, invite terrorist retaliation, or simply cost too much money.

But to urge justice or even criminal prosecution is not to justify humanitarian intervention. Indictments should be issued, and suspects should be arrested if they dare to venture abroad, but the extraordinary remedy of humanitarian intervention should not be used simply to secure justice for past crimes. This extreme step, as noted, should be taken only to stop current or imminent slaughter, not to punish past abuse.

In stating that the killing in Iraq did not rise to a level that justified humanitarian intervention, we are not insensitive to the awful plight of the Iraqi people. We are aware that summary executions occurred with disturbing frequency in Iraq up to the end of Saddam Hussein's rule, as did torture and other brutality. Such atrocities should be met with public, diplomatic, and economic pressure, as well as prosecution. But before taking the substantial risk to life that is inherent in any war, mass slaughter should be taking place or imminent. That was not the case in Saddam Hussein's Iraq in March 2003.

It would be something of a challenge, no doubt, for George Packer, Christopher Hitchens, or Nick Cohen to dismiss this form of opposition to the Iraq war as unserious. And it would be no less a challenge for Noam Chomsky, Perry Anderson, or Rahul Mahajan to dismiss it as an apologia for imperialism. But until the liberal hawks and the Manicheans are displaced, and the polemical link from Kosovo to Afghanistan to Iraq broken, this kind of argument will not get the hearing it needs and deserves—and the conceptual parameters of left internationalism will not change for the better. Indeed, in some precincts on the American and British left, the human-rights positions of people like Kenneth Roth will not even be understood as left positions—or as forms of internationalism alongside those of the environmental and antiglobalization movements. The task for the democratic left, then, is to forge a human-rights internationalism that offers resolute opposition to mass murder and genocide, which is where the Manichean left has failed, while being diligently respectful of international coalitions and institutions, which is where the liberal hawks have failed.

The left suffered for decades because one branch of its family tree was willing to tolerate a certain degree of tyranny if it advanced the material well-being of the peasants or proletariat; for that left, all talk of balancing *égalité* with *liberté* was so much bourgeois blather. The left does not now need another branch whose position on tyranny is that tyranny is bad, but tyrants can only be legitimately overthrown by their victims; in practice, this position amounts to saying *we oppose tyranny around the globe, but not to the extent of actually doing anything about it.* Such is the effect of the Manichean left's defenses of state sovereignty: in deriding the "responsibility to protect" as an apologia for imperialism, the Manichean left simply abandons every political dissident and victim of oppression whose comrades and supporters are not strong enough to overthrow their tyrannical regime on their own. And yet, liberals and democratic leftists in the United States need to remember that much of the world has had quite enough of blundering, well-intentioned Americans. Their task—*our task*—is therefore to forge genuinely international and multilateral means of articulating and enforcing a fundamental international norm, a norm from which even the United States will not be exempt: *sovereign is he who protects the multitude.*

CULTURAL STUDIES AND POLITICAL CRISIS

IN THIS CHAPTER I turn from debates over war in Iraq, Afghanistan, and Kosovo and offer a reexamination of Stuart Hall's work on Thatcherism almost a generation ago. This is an oblique turn for two reasons. First, Hall has not played a major role in the debates over Afghanistan and Iraq on the British left, and he does not offer a precise or detailed position on state sovereignty and R2P that sets out the principles under which international human-rights interventionism is justified. Second, Hall's position on war in Afghanistan is not my own, though it is one of the positions which, as I describe them in chapter 3, I consider entirely reasonable. (Moreover, Hall has no affiliation with the wing of the British left that saw intervention in the Balkans as an imperialist persecution of Milošević, the Last Socialist.) In remarks published in *Soundings* within a few months of the attacks, Hall took a nuanced and multifaceted approach to what he called the "new world disorder" (Hall et al., "New World Disorder," 12).

I remark on three features of that approach here. First, Hall spoke as a left secularist and appealed to one of Edward Said's most cogent arguments about Islamism: "There is much to be said for Edward Said's position, which is that it is time for secular people on the left to say that there is something particularly dangerous about the combination of technology and fundamentalism. That is to say, the means of the delivery of violence without cost, combined with the messianic capacity to mobilise around a kind of absolute, is a very dangerous combination" (10). Second, he argued for treating 9/11 as an international crime:

> If you ask me what ought to have happened after 11 September: I am opposed to what has happened, in particular the indiscriminate bombing of the population of Afghanistan and the rush to unsanctioned violence. I would say it would have been important to define the terrorism of that moment as a crime against humanity—that is to say, to attempt to pursue it and its perpetrators with a genuine form of

justice. That would have required some form of international justice by which it could be judged, and some process which could have suspended the definition of who was responsible until proper evidence had been gathered. I am not suggesting this would have been easy— it was inevitable that the Americans would want to see some sort of immediate response. But the dangerous point which we have arrived at now is that, whenever difficult situations like this arise, the fragile means by which some international order could be put together of a more democratic type—that is to say, recourse to the United Nations, the International Court of Human Rights, or the International Court of Justice, citing arguments against violence against the person, etc.— are quickly circumvented, left behind, bypassed. (10–11)

As I suggest in chapter 3, I agree strongly with the appeal to international frameworks and institutions here, but maintain nevertheless that the symbiosis between al-Qaeda and the Taliban and the existence of Tora Bora and terror training camps warranted an immediate (and strictly limited) military response. Hall also overlooks (as do most proponents of a police response to 9/11) one decisive aspect of the relation between the Taliban and al-Qaeda: though he rightly suggests that charging al-Qaeda with a crime against humanity would require "some form of international justice by which it could be judged," he does not ask whether it would also have required some institution of *Afghan* justice by which it could be adjudicated. As John Brenkman points out, the problem in Afghanistan was not merely that the Taliban "were being propped up by al-Qaeda as much as they were giving it sanctuary" (*Cultural Contradictions of Democracy*, 91) (and that leftists who believed that the Taliban would cooperate with a criminal investigation were almost impossibly naive), but that it is impossible to appeal to reliable policing mechanisms in a failed state:

> A police action also presupposes that a policing power holds a relatively effective monopoly on legitimate violence in the territory where the criminals operate and hide. Afghanistan was not such a place. Had the Taliban rulers of Afghanistan arrested Osama bin Laden and his network, then indeed the international juridical apparatus, even Afghan courts, could have played a role. Without that, the pursuit of al Qaeda inside Afghanistan required a level of organized force more akin to war than policing. (81)

I agree that such a level of organized force was required in Afghanistan, but, of course, neither Brenkman nor I argue that it licenses the bombing of civilian populations. Moreover, I agree with Brenkman that

> beyond that first phase, however, the struggle against al Qaeda and international terrorism required a complex multilateral effort of police work, a long-term engagement in Afghanistan to stabilize the country and break up al Qaeda and the Taliban, and a still largely neglected program to foster economic and political reform in several Arab and other Muslim countries. Neither the Bush doctrine nor the Powell doctrine was suited to such tasks. (40)

Third and last, Hall turned to the Muslim response to 9/11, and, walking a fine line, sought to appeal to moderates on the grounds that "effective alliances" with Muslims require that Muslims refuse to put up a united front against the West:

> It is not a war against Islam: but that doesn't require us to say that every way in which Muslim people respond to the crisis is by definition always okay. I want to identify three aspects—and I say this in friendship to my Muslim friends—in which I find that response inadequate [actually, he proceeds to enumerate only two]. It is inadequate to quote the Qur'an. All the world religions say we ought to get on with our neighbours. It is a predominant theme in the Bible. But this has never prevented Christians from hacking other Christians and other peoples to death, while quoting the Bible. The whole point about fundamentalism is that you can always find something in the Bible to quote as you destroy your enemy. So it doesn't help to tell me that the Qur'an, like the Bible, says don't hit them.
>
> Secondly, it is not enough to say that all Muslims are brothers. The Muslim world, like every other, is deeply divided by oppositions, between secular versus religious trends, between different interpretations of the holy word. Muslims have themselves to face the fact that the appeal across the board to a universal umma does not correspond to the real world. It is a kind of evasion of the real world. This is not a legitimation of the attacks against Afghanistan. It's simply to say that Muslims who take the position I take—namely, that I'm opposed to the Taliban *and* to the attacks launched by al Qaida, and I don't think Afghanistan should be bombed to smithereens—would be strengthened

in their case if they explicitly recognised internal conflicts within Islam itself. Without that, it seems to me, we can't strike effective alliances with them. (11–12)

These are careful and judicious remarks, and the argument about divisions within Islam has no counterpart in the record of the Manichean left's early responses to 9/11. There are other important points missing from Hall's analysis, however, and these were supplied a few months later by Ellen Willis, in the provocatively titled essay "Why I'm Not for Peace," published in April 2002 in *Radical Society,* an outgrowth of the *Socialist Review.* Though Willis expressed her strong support for a military response, she was undeceived about the difference between the response she desired and the response of the Bush administration:

The objections I have had from the beginning—and still have—are not to the fact of our war in Afghanistan but to the way we've conducted it. I object in general to our modus operandi of avoiding American casualties by depending on air power and using local troops as our proxies. If we have a legitimate stake in a war we should take responsibility for it by putting our own troops on the ground. Bombs, however "smart," inevitably hit civilians and should be kept to the absolute minimum necessary to destroy an opponent's military capacity—yet even after the Taliban's collapse, and under conditions of maximum confusion between soldiers and civilians, we kept on bombing. As for the decision to let the Northern Alliance fight our war, the predictable result is that the warlords are back in control, the provisional government has no means of enforcing its authority, and rampant banditry is once again the rule. In interview after interview with ordinary Afghans, they plead for an international presence to establish law and order. Yet for all its lip service to reconstruction, the United States refuses to send troops or allow other countries to send them in anything like the numbers needed.

My frustration, in other words, is not that we took action in Afghanistan but that we have not done enough. We should have fought the ground war and occupied Kabul; organized an international force to disarm the warlords, protect ordinary citizens, and oversee the distribution of aid; demanded that secularists be included in the negotiations for a new government and that basic women's rights be built into a new structure of law. If this is "imperialism"—in the promiscuous contemporary usage of that term—I am for it: I believe it is the prerequisite of a stable peace. (14–15)

But if Willis was clear about the failures of the Bush administration ("the shock of the attack itself was compounded by the aftershock of realization that all the decisions about how to respond to it would be made by the most reactionary presidential administration in my lifetime" [13]), she was just as clear about the assumptions of the Manichean left:

> At the heart of the matter is an unspoken meta-argument: that America is a sinful country, and must achieve redemption through nonviolence. Violence committed against us is the wages of sin. To strike back in kind is to continue to collect the geopolitical equivalent of bad karma, inevitably provoking more "blowback." Sow the wind, reap the whirlwind.
>
> The crudest expression of this attitude—the claim that terrorism is retaliation for specific U.S. policies—does not pass cursory inspection. It trivializes the Islamic fundamentalist movement, which has quite bluntly declared its dedication to destroying unbelievers and their morally corrupt societies, to imagine it would be mollified by the withdrawal of American troops from the Persian Gulf or the lifting of sanctions against Iraq. (16)

Like Moishe Postone, Willis knew better than to ascribe 9/11 simply to American actions and anti-American reactions. And like Postone, she did not discount American actions; instead, she asked whether 9/11 followed inevitably from them—and, if so, what the United States should do in response:

> The broader claim that we are responsible for our vulnerability has resonance because it's at least partly true. After all, it's incontestable that America's tunnel-vision cold war policy of building up radical Islamists to fight the Soviet Union has blown back on us. Overall, our government's commitment to the notion that the business of America is global business, its championing of neoliberal policies that exacerbate economic inequality, its alliances with "stable" autocratic regimes and allergy to any democratizing movement with a leftist tinge have done their part to foment the economic and political resentments that fundamentalist demagogues exploit.

Suppose, then, that this were the whole story: America's malfeasances unleashed a monster. Why would it follow that we should not fight back? On the contrary, wouldn't we have even more responsibility to confront the golem we created? (16)

Willis did not stop at countering the "blowback" argument; crucially, she made a broader case against the kind of global cultural backlash represented by Islamism and insisted on the importance of global feminism to the struggle against that backlash:

> The religious totalitarianism Al Qaeda represents . . . is the latest flashpoint in the ongoing, worldwide culture war that began in the eighteenth century: intertwined with the spread of capitalism, though by no means synonymous with it, the ideas of freedom, equality, separation of church and state—and their more recent application to our sexual and domestic lives—have penetrated everywhere, eroding traditional patriarchal institutions and rigid social controls. (17)

(As discussed later in this chapter, Willis and Hall had a common sense of the cultural contradictions of capitalism.)

Most importantly, Willis faulted the United States not only for its tunnel-vision Cold War chess-games but also for its inattention to women's human rights around the globe; in so doing, she eerily echoed Chomsky's citation of bin Laden's bitter opposition to the "corrupt and repressive regimes of the region"—without suggesting that bin Laden's opposition to repressive regimes had any point of contact with her own:

> I would argue that the U.S. government has contributed to its present predicament not only by exercising but also by abdicating its power. Our bracketing of theocratic despotism and the persecution of women as non-issues in our international relations—a cultural-political blind spot as well as a matter of corporate realpolitik—has substantially strengthened the hand of radical fundamentalists no longer willing to confine their atrocities to their own population. (Consider our complaisance toward Saudi Arabia, or our tepid response to the death sentence pronounced on Salman Rushdie.) Which is to say that the old imperialism model does not hold, either economically or culturally— and that the left badly needs a new and more nuanced analysis of the role of the nation-state in world affairs. (17)

This welcome indictment of the U.S. government's inattention to theocracy and women's oppression around the world overlooks one of the few foreign-policy victories of the domestic American left—the successful campaign by American women's groups to prevent the Clinton administration from recognizing the Taliban. But otherwise, it is a bracing reminder of the standards of freedom and equality that should be brought to bear on any society, from the flawed one of the United States to the truly horrific one of the Taliban; and Willis's insistence on the theocratic persecution of women cannot conceivably be dismissed as shallow and opportunistic, as was Laura Bush's invocation of the rights of Afghan schoolgirls. Perhaps, indeed, it was Willis's lifelong and distinctive commitment to the cultural and political freedom of women that enabled her to see Islamism not merely in realpolitik terms but as part of a cultural struggle spanning centuries and continents, and to put the question of "sexual and domestic lives" on the table in a way no male leftist managed to do after 9/11.

Still, despite the fact that I agree more with Willis than with Hall on Afghanistan, and the fact that Hall's work on Thatcherism included no explicitly feminist analysis of how the New Right reshaped public policy and the domestic sphere, I make the oblique turn to Hall for substantial reasons. I draw on Hall's body of work on Thatcherism because it responded to a historical moment in which Americans can recognize a distant mirror of the early years of the twenty-first century: an energetic right wing at the helm of the state; a befuddled and demoralized "opposition" party not offering much in the way of opposition; and a doctrinaire, out-of-touch "left" repeating shopworn slogans and blaming their failures on the power of ruling-class ideology and the corporate media to dupe the masses into docile subservience.

Hall's analysis of Thatcherism offered a blistering critique of New Right racism, authoritarianism, and scorched-earth economic libertarianism. But it also identified certain entrenched and counterproductive habits of mind on what he called, alternatively, the "hard left" or the "fundamentalist left," habits of mind that are with us still—and that need, as Willis well understood, to be critiqued anew. Not for the sake of "theory" (though Hall composed a compelling and capacious theory of "hegemony" by way of accounting for Thatcherism), and certainly not for the sake of "triangulating" between left and right; rather, Hall embarked on his project in part to urge the left to rethink, from the ground up, what it means to be "on the left."

NEW LEFT REVIEW

As Dennis Dworkin has argued in detail in *Cultural Marxism in Postwar Britain: History, the New Left, and the Origins of Cultural Studies,* British cultural studies was born in a time of political crisis for the left: the Suez crisis, on the one hand, and the Soviet invasion of Hungary, on the other, led left theorists such as E. P. Thompson, Stuart Hall, Richard Hoggart, and Raymond Williams to form a "New Left," breaking with the ossified and autocratic British Communist Party over Hungary while opposing Britain's last-gasp imperial adventure in the Middle East. The contemporary parallel suggests itself immediately: a formation of left intellectuals who oppose the U.S.'s desperate gamble in Iraq but who also refuse the reactionary, knee-jerk position in which all opponents of the United States and United Kingdom are entitled to some measure of support, however "critical" that support may be. But though this parallel is obvious, I want to look elsewhere in the history of cultural studies.

The period of the late 1950s and early 1960s, critical though it was for British leftists seeking new and more adequate ways of conceptualizing culture and society, did not produce the kind of sustained analysis of its own moment that would offer contemporary American readers a useful theoretical past. Rather, the early work of British cultural studies was somewhat diffuse—the New Left itself did not last more than a few years—and its major scholarly breakthroughs, from Williams's *Culture and Society* to Thompson's *Making of the English Working Classes* (itself an extended response to Williams's *Long Revolution*), had more to do with the history of England (and the discipline of history itself) than with the immediate crisis of the left. That crisis, as Dworkin shows, was the condition of possibility for the rethinking of British history and the "Condition of England": the Conservative Party seemed to have swept the political field of the 1950s, and in postwar Britain, the revolutionary proletariat showed no signs of seizing control of the means of production anytime soon. Quite the contrary: the working classes seemed largely to agree with the Conservative slogan, "you've never had it so good," and the mixed-economy social-democratic elaboration of the postwar welfare state seemed to have blunted the left's most searing critiques of capitalism. At the time, however, British cultural studies' most substantial theoretical responses to this state of affairs offered more in the way of debates over the conceptualization of class struggle in the eighteenth and nineteenth centuries than in debates over the contemporary direction of British politics—even though the conceptualization of class struggle in the eighteenth and nineteenth centuries had important resonances for the contemporary direction of British politics.[1]

Over the next two decades, cultural studies blossomed into a distinct intellectual tradition, even if it avoided characterizing itself as a "discipline." It underwent a heady period of theoretical ferment, consequent on the translation into English of some of the major writings of European structuralism and Marxism, and developed pathbreaking analyses of race and youth culture in postwar Britain. The moment on which I want to focus here grew out of that tradition: in the late 1970s through the 1980s, Stuart Hall managed to combine the theoretical ferment of 1970s British Marxism with cultural studies' analyses of race and youth culture, and he devised an analysis of Thatcherism so rich and subtle that it is still routinely misunderstood and underappreciated by many American left intellectuals—when it is not ignored altogether. I revisit that analysis here not only to make its terms available for debates on the American left after 9/11 but also to point out the many things Hall did *not* do, the many left-reflex gestures in which Hall did *not* engage. And along the way, I show that Hall's analysis of Thatcherism and the rise of the British New Right also offered a series of stunning rebukes to left orthodoxy that renewed the initial New Left break of 1956, and which need to be remembered now. They need to be remembered partly for their complex and subtle understanding of the New Right, to be sure, but even more urgently for their conviction that the ascendancy of Thatcherism represented not just the New Right's long march through the institutions and consequent reconfiguration of popular common sense but, in many senses, a failure for the left.[2]

That failure was partly an economic failure, a failure to respond to the worldwide recession of the mid-1970s; the Labour government of James Callaghan is roughly similiar to the Democratic presidency of Jimmy Carter in this respect, save for the fact that the British trade unions were considerably stronger than their American counterparts. But it was also a failure of political imagination, Hall charged, on the part of both Labour and the left; a failure of strategy and organization, as Thatcherism captured popular discontent and remade it into the fuel for an ambitious attack on the welfare state; and even a failure of theoretical sophistication, as orthodox leftists continued to speak of the crisis of capitalism and the phenomenon of mass unemployment as if these phenomena would inevitably benefit the left. This last failure will sound odd to some American leftists, convinced as they are that the problem with the left is an excess rather than a dearth of theoretical sophistication, especially in academic precincts; but as Hall argued time and again, at the moment of Thatcher's ascendancy the left too often responded with some of the rustiest devices in its intellectual toolshed—repeating the mantra that the ruling class owns the ruling ideas, insisting that the fate of the economy would determine the political struggles of the day, and, disastrously, writing off the phenomenon of working-class conservatism as false consciousness.

Hall devoted much of his work on Thatcherism to urging his fellow leftists to update or throw out those rusty devices. Above all, he argued that the Marxist reliance on a simplistic idea of "ideology" left it theoretically complacent and politically useless. In response, the Marxist left typically accused him of dissolving material realities in a bubbling postmodern-deconstructionist vat of "discourse" (even though Hall took pains to distinguish his positions from those of both postmodernists and deconstructionists). When, for example, Hall was asked in 1983, "In what sense would you still describe yourself as a marxist? What, if anything, do you retain from Marx?" he replied:

> I choose to keep the notion of classes; I choose to keep the notion of the capital/labor contradiction; I choose to keep the notion of social relations of production, etc.—I just don't want to think them reductively. . . . My critique of marxism attempts to dethrone marxism from its guarantees, because I think that, as an ideological system, it has tried to construct its own guarantees. And I use the word "ideological" very deliberately. I think of marxism not as a framework for scientific analysis only but also as a way of helping you sleep well at night; it offers the guarantee that, although things don't look simple at the moment, they really are simple in the end. You can't see how the economy determines, but just have faith, it does determine in the last instance! The first clause wakes you up and the second puts you to sleep. It's okay. I can nod off tonight, because in the last instance, though not just yesterday or today or tomorrow or as far as I can see forward in history, but in the last instance, just before the last trumpet, as St. Peter comes to the door, he'll say, "the economy works." I think those are very ideological guarantees. And as soon as you abandon that teleological structure under marxism, the whole classical edifice begins to rock. ("Toad in the Garden," 72–73)

Hall developed this line of thought into the landmark essay, "The Problem of Ideology: Marxism without Guarantees," for as he saw it, the problem

of ideology had everything to do with the "ideological" belief that somebody or something was hornswoggling the working classes into misiden-
tifying with ruling-class interests instead of taking their cues from the in-
the-last-instance determining economic base.

In "The Problem of Ideology," Hall builds on his earlier reading of
Marx's 1857 "Introduction" to the *Grundrisse,* in which he had argued that
"ideology" arises from one's necessarily partial view of a system too vast
for any one vantage point to comprehend:

> If you use only "market categories and concepts" to understand the
> capitalist circuit as a whole, there are literally many aspects of it which
> you cannot see. In that sense, the categories of market exchange ob-
> scure and mystify our understanding of the capitalist process. . . .
>
> Is the worker who lives his or her relations to the circuits of capital-
> ist production exclusively through the categories of a "fair price" and
> a "fair wage" in "false consciousness"? Yes, if by that we mean there is
> something about her situation which she cannot grasp with the cat-
> egories she is using; something about the process as a whole which is
> systematically hidden because the available concepts only give her a
> grasp of one of its many-sided moments. No, if by that we mean that
> she is utterly deluded about what goes on under capitalism.
>
> The falseness therefore arises, not from the fact that the market is
> an illusion, a trick, a sleight-of-hand, but only in the sense that it is an
> *inadequate* explanation of a process. (Hall, "Problem of Ideology," 37)

I return to Hall's conceptualization of "the market" below; for now, I offer an explanation of why this understanding of "ideology" matters to the
argument.

For at first, this analysis seems to suggest that ideology is Delusion
Lite rather than full-blown Delusion: a structural misunderstanding of
that which remains invisible in capitalist categories rather than a complete
misunderstanding of capitalism altogether. Yet when this analysis is combined, as Hall combines it, with a Gramscian understanding of hegemony
in which there is no necessary correspondence between the ruling class
and the ruling ideas and in which the ruling classes themselves have no
single "interest," and then with Ernesto Laclau's and Chantal Mouffe's understanding (borrowed in turn from Russian theorists V. N. Volosinov and
Mikhail Bakhtin and articulated most fully in *Hegemony and Socialist Strategy*)[3] of the "multiaccentuality of the sign," the result is something that, for

intellectuals on the left, should have broken the (ideological) link between ideology and false consciousness once and for all.

Hall puts it rather more polemically in the essay "The Toad in the Garden: Thatcherism among the Theorists." Over the next few pages, I quote from this essay at some length, because the argument is absolutely fundamental for any rethinking of left orthodoxy:

> The traditional escape clause for classical marxism . . . is the recourse to "false consciousness." The popular classes, we must suppose, have been ideologically duped by the dominant classes, using what *The German Ideology* calls their "monopoly over the means of mental production." The masses, therefore, have been temporarily ensnared, against their real material interests and position in the structure of social relations, to live their relation to their real conditions of material existence through an imposed but "false" structure of illusions. The traditional expectation on the Left, founded on this premise, would therefore be that, as real material factors begin once more to exert their effect, the cobwebs of illusion would be dispelled, "reality" would be transferred directly into working-class heads, the scales would fall from workers' eyes, and Minerva's Owl—the great denouement promised by the *Communist Manifesto,* as the socialization of labor progressively created the conditions for mass solidarity and enlightenment—would take wing at last (even if timed to arrive approximately 150 years too late). (43)

But by the early 1980s, Hall notes, even mass unemployment—which had surpassed the previously unthinkable number of three million in the United Kingdom, after analysts had predicted mass defections from the Conservative Party once the number hit two million—has not yet launched Minerva's Owl. And that, he argues, is partly because "mass unemployment" is, to all of the masses except our employed or unemployed selves, not only a material state to be experienced but also a *sign to be read,* which is why obscure Russian Marxist-formalist theories about the "multiaccentuality of the sign" should matter to left intellectuals everywhere:

> This explanation has to deal with the surprising fact that mass unemployment has taken a much longer time than predicted to percolate mass consciousness; the unemployed, who might have been expected to pierce the veil of illusion first, are still by no means automatic mass

converts to laborism, let alone socialism; and the lessons that can be drawn from the fact of unemployment turn out to be less monolithic and predictable, less determined by strict material factors, more variable than supposed. The same fact can be read or made sense of in different ways, depending on the ideological perspective employed. Mass unemployment can be interpreted as a scandalous indictment of the system; or as a sign of Britain's underlying economic weakness about which mere governments—Left or Right—can do very little; or as acceptable because "there is no alternative" that is not more disastrous for the economy; or indeed—within the sociomasochistic perspective that sometimes appears to be a peculiarly strong feature of British ideology—as the required measure of suffering that guarantees the remedy will work eventually because it hurts so much (the Britain-is-best-when-backed-to-the-wall syndrome)! The logics of ideological inference turn out to be more multivariate, the automatic connection between material and ideal factors less determinate, than the classical theory would have us believe. (43)

Hall makes a similar point about the multivalence of political signs in his 1981 essay, "Notes on Deconstructing 'the Popular,'" where he argues that "the people," as a term, can be appropriated for the right just as effectively as for the left; while the left chants "power to the people," for instance, the right can be busy—as was Thatcherism—constructing "the people" as something that needed to be "disciplined more, ruled better, more effectively policed, whose way of life needs to be protected from 'alien cultures.'"[4]

Having thus thrown cold water on one of the left's most "popular" tropes, Hall proceeds (as I note at the outset of chapter 1) to suggest that standard Marxist invocations of the people are not merely ideological but—to use a loaded word—somehow *false:*

> It is a highly unstable theory about the world which has to assume that vast numbers of ordinary people, mentally equipped in much the same way as you or I, can simply be thoroughly and systematically duped into misrecognizing entirely where their real interests lie. Even less acceptable is the position that, whereas "they"—the masses—are the dupes of history, "we"—the privileged—are somehow without a trace of illusion and can see, transitively, right through into the truth, the essence, of a situation. Yet it is a fact that, though there are people

willing enough to deploy the false consciousness explanation to account for the illusory behavior of others, there are very few who are
ever willing to own up that they are themselves living in false consciousness! It seems to be (like corruption by pornography) a state
always reserved for others. ("Toad in the Garden," 44)

The repudiation of ideology as "false consciousness" did not occur in a
theoretical vacuum. It was an immediate—if gradually elaborated—response to what Hall (rightly) considered the British left's misreading of
Thatcherism's rise and its popular appeal. The failure of Labour, like the
failure of the Carter presidency in the United States, was obvious; economic stagnation, energy crises, rising inflation combined with rising unemployment (heretofore considered a near-impossibility in the classical
macroeconomic model) signaled what we now know as the beginnings of
the long slow decline of real wages since 1973 and the political fragmentation of the working classes since the 1960s. Add to this volatile mix of
instability and discontent a racist backlash (developing a few years later
in the United Kingdom than the United States, but crystallized at similar moments by Enoch Powell and George Wallace, respectively) and the
emergence of a "law and order" right (its Nixonian version matched a
decade later by Thatcher), and you've got all the ingredients necessary for
the collapse of Labour/Democrats and the emergence of a new kind of
Conservative/Republican.

Hall is undeceived about the origins of this new formation: it was, in
part, the result of years of hard work by the British New Right (led by Sir
Keith Joseph as its chief architect), and Hall places special emphasis on
the dexterity with which the New Right revived libertarian economics and
placed it front and center. "Keynesianism," Hall writes in his 1979 essay
"The Great Moving Right Show," "was the lynch-pin of the theoretical ideologies of corporatist state intervention throughout the postwar period,
assuming almost the status of a sacred orthodoxy or *doxa*" (*Hard Road to
Renewal*, 46). One can almost hear Richard Nixon proclaiming that we are
all Keynesians now. But, as it turned out, we weren't all Keynesians just
yet:

To have replaced it in some of the most powerful and influential apparatuses of government, in research and the universities, and restored
in its place the possessive individualist and free-market nostrums of
Hayek and Friedman is, in itself, a remarkable reversal. Ideological

transformations, however, do not take place by magic. For years bodies like the Institute for Economic Affairs have been plugging away in
the margins of the Conservative Party and the informed public debate
on economic policy, refurbishing the gospel of Adam Smith and the
free market, undermining the assumptions of neo-Keynesianism, planning and projecting how the "competitive stimulus" could be applied
again to one area after another of those sectors which, as they see it,
have fallen into the corporatist abyss.

Gradually, in the more hospitable climes of the 1970s, these seeds
began to bear fruit. First in the learned journals, then in the senior
common rooms, and finally in informal exchanges between the "new
academics" and the more "sensitive" senior civil servants, a monetarist
version of neo-classical economics came to provide the accepted frame
of reference for economic debate. ("Toad in the Garden," 46–47)

In one respect, the argument of this passage may be familiar to us now: it
is the British version of the story of the movement of the libertarian-plu-
tocratic wing of the right from the think tanks to the mainstream press to
the halls of power, and it has its American counterpart in the story of how,
after Barry Goldwater's epochal defeat in 1964, institutions like the Heri-
tage Foundation, the American Enterprise Institute, and the Cato Institute
helped provide so-called movement conservatives with a new arsenal of
ideas with which to attack the New Deal of Franklin D. Roosevelt and the
Great Society of Lyndon Johnson.[5]

But although this narrative trajectory is familiar to us *now*, most
American leftists lagged a decade or more behind Hall in understanding
the intellectual base of the New Right's long march through the institutions it had itself created. And this aspect of Hall's work should serve as a
partial rebuttal to doctrinaire British Marxists who complained that Hall's
account of Thatcherism was too "discursive," and to American leftists who
consider Hall's work too theoretical and abstract: Thatcherism, for Hall,
was not simply a matter of new languages "hailing" new "subject positions" and creating a new form of politics out of the ether. Nor was the
promotion of neoliberal economics simply dreamed up one day by swink-
ing demons in think tanks and foisted on an unsuspecting public. It involved serious intellectual and organizational work, combined with canny
cooptations of the racist anti-immigrant backlash, vague longings for traditional "English" ways of life, and discontent with the machinery of state
bureaucracy. And even though its success depended in part on Labour's

weakness, Thatcherism was not, Hall insisted, a mere swing of the pendulum or an ordinary electoral correction; it involved a rewriting of the social contract and an undoing of the postwar compromise between capital and labor.

In *Policing the Crisis: Mugging, the State, and Law and Order,* Hall—together with Chas Critcher, Tony Jefferson, John Clarke, and Brian Robert—had not only predicted Mrs. Thatcher's victory the following year but "anticipated the conservatives' domination of British politics since the late 1970s" and offered "an all but prophetic reading of future trends," as Dworkin puts it (*Cultural Marxism,* 174). Though this prophetic reading is now (with good reason) part of the Legend of Cultural Studies, two things about Hall's early work on Thatcherism need to be stressed here. One is that Hall correctly saw Thatcherism as an ideological hodgepodge, to which he gave the names "regressive modernization" and "authoritarian populism"; the other is that Hall offered not only descriptions of Thatcherism that were superior to those of colleagues on the left but also a series of theoretical and political challenges *to* colleagues on the left. "The Great Moving Right Show," for instance, is usually remembered as an essay about—well, about the British right's great moving right show. And so it was. But it also argued that the contradictory nature of Thatcherism opened a window onto the contradictory and unstable nature of hegemony itself, and it insisted that this feature of Thatcherism was being badly misread by the British left. "Thatcherite populism," Hall noted, "is a particularly rich mix. It combines the resonant themes of organic Toryism—nation, family, duty, authority, standards, traditionalism—with the aggressive themes of a revived neo-liberalism—self-interest, competitive individualism, anti-statism" (*Hard Road to Renewal,* 48).

That rich mix was potent enough, on both sides of the Atlantic, to persist for well over a decade, to the point at which Samuel Luttwak could write, in 1994, "It is only mildly amusing that nowadays the standard Republican/Tory dinner speech is a two-part affair, in which part one celebrates the virtues of unimpeded competition and dynamic structural change, while part two mourns the decline of the family and community 'values' that were eroded precisely by the forces commended in part one" ("Why Fascism Is the Wave of the Future," 6). Let it be noted that Hall had the contours of that dinner speech down pat, even before it was first delivered at any Republican or Tory fundraiser. But let it also be noted that Hall opened "The Great Moving Right Show" in an air of great impatience with the intransigence of the traditional left. The essay was (like many of the essays collected in *Hard Road to Renewal*) published in *Marxism Today*, to a readership of fellow leftists, and it wastes no time throwing down the gauntlet:[6]

> The full dimensions of this precipitation to the right still lack a proper analysis on the left. The crisis continues to be read by the left from within certain well-entrenched, largely unquestioned assumptions. Our illusions remain intact, even when they clearly no longer provide an adequate analytical framework. Certainly, there is no simple, one-to-one correspondence between a "correct" analysis and an "effective" politics. Nevertheless, the failure of analysis cannot be totally unrelated to the obvious lack of political perspective which now confronts the left.
>
> In spite of this there are still some who welcome the crisis, arguing that "worse means better." The "sharpening of contradictions," comrades, together with the rising tempo of the class struggle, will eventually guarantee the victory of progressive forces everywhere. Those who hold such a position may enjoy untroubled nights; but they have short political memories. They forget how frequently in recent history the "sharpening of contradictions" has led to settlements and solutions which favoured capital and the extreme right rather than the reverse. (*Hard Road to Renewal*, 40)

The second paragraph is worth reprinting as a broadside and taping to the backs of every American leftist who welcomed the 1968 election of Nixon, the 1980 election of Reagan, or the 2000 Supreme Court appointment of Bush. But Hall is not done. After critiquing "those who dismiss the advance of the right as 'mere ideology,'" he traces the left's political shortcomings back to its theoretical shortcomings:

> Yet another common response is an extension of this last position. It argues that the current "swing to the right" is only the simple and general expression of every economic recession. On this view, there are no significant differences between the present and any other variant of Tory philosophy. "Thatcherism," "Baldwinism," etc.—each is only a name for the same phenomenon: the permanent, unchanging shape of reactionary ideas. What is the point of drawing fine distinctions?
>
> Such arguments are especially characteristic of a certain hard-headed response from the "hard" left. All this analysis, it is implied, is

unnecessary. The committed will not waste time on such speculations, but get on with the job of "engaging in the real struggle." In fact, this last is a position which neglects everything that is specific and particular to this historical conjuncture. It is predicated on the view that a social formation is a simple structure, in which economic conditions will be immediately, transparently and indifferently translated onto the political and ideological stage. If you operate on the "determining level," then all the other pieces of the puzzle will fall into place. The idea that we should define a conjuncture as the coming together of often distinct though related contradictions, moving according to different tempos, but condensed in the same historical moment, is foreign to this approach. (41)

I can imagine—indeed, I have heard—the objection that in passages like these, Hall is either (a) flailing at straw-man *reductio* Marxists or (b) irrelevant to the American political scene, in which there aren't any "hard" leftists who take such a simple view of politics as to ignore "often distinct though related contradictions, moving according to different tempos." Perhaps, then, it would be helpful to contrast Hall's mode of analysis with that of a prominent American leftist, who recently offered the following account of our own crisis:

The third crucial sign of America's failure, he says, is that "there's a *huge* gap between public opinion and public policy. Both political parties are well to the right of the population on a host of major issues, and the elections that are run are carefully designed so that issues do not arise."

But Americans still voted overwhelmingly for either Bush or Kerry in 2004, didn't they? "I don't know if you watched the presidential debates. I didn't but my wife [they have been married since 1949] did. She has a college Ph.D. and taught for 25 years at Harvard and is presumably capable of following arguments. She literally couldn't tell where the candidates stood on issues, and people didn't because the elections are designed that way." By whom? "The public relations industry, because they sell candidates the same way they sell toothpaste or lifestyle drugs." Who are their masters? "Their masters are concentrations of private capital which invest in control of the state. That funds the elections, that designs the framework." (Stephen, Interview with Chomsky)

The voice, of course, is that of Chomsky, and the interviewer is Andrew Stephen; the interview is the very same June 2006 *New Statesman* in which Chomsky offered the opinion that Slobodan Milošević had no knowledge of Srebenica and was horrified when he learned about it. The claim that an intelligent observer could not distinguish between Bush and Kerry during the debates is mere boilerplate and does not require a serious rebuttal (hint: Kerry was the one not wearing a wire). What does concern me here, rather, is the theory that the frameworks of electoral campaigns can be explained ultimately by reference to concentrations of private capital; about that theory all one can say, after reading Hall, is that it is admirable for its simplicity, and for its capacity to help us sleep well at night, offering the guarantee that, although things don't look simple at the moment, they really are simple in the end.

The contrast between Hall and Chomsky is just as stark, and just as obvious, with regard to the role of the media in establishing and maintaining a historic bloc: where Chomsky argues (with Ed Herman) that the corporate media manufacture the consent of the dominated masses, Hall regards the "propaganda" thesis as just one more leftist bromide—an excuse, like that of "false consciousness," for failing to grapple with the complexity of a specific historical conjuncture. In "Gramsci's Relevance for the Study of Race and Ethnicity," for example, Hall insists not merely that hegemony is unstable and fragmentary but also that it cannot be accounted for by relying on the concept of the ruling class (and its control of the means of mental production):

> We must take note of the multi-dimensional, multi-arena character of hegemony. It cannot be constructed or sustained on *one* front of struggle alone (for example, the economic). It represents a degree of mastery over a whole series of different "positions" at once. Mastery is not simply imposed or dominative in character. Effectively, it results from winning a substantial degree of popular consent. . . . What "leads" in a period of hegemony is no longer described as a "ruling class" in the traditional language, but a historic bloc. This has its critical reference to "class" as a determining level of analysis; but it does *not* translate whole classes directly on to the political-ideological stage as unified historical actors. The "leading elements" in a historic bloc may be only one fraction of the dominant economic class—for example, finance rather than industrial capital; national rather than international capital. Associated with it, within the "bloc," will be strata of the subaltern and

dominated classes, who have been won over by specific concessions and compromises and who form part of the social constellation but in a subordinate role. The "winning over" of these sections is the result of the forging of "expansive, universalizing alliances" which cement the historic bloc under a particular leadership. Each hegemonic formation will thus have its own, specific social composition and configuration. That is a very different way of conceptualizing what is often referred to, loosely and inaccurately, as the "ruling class." (424)[7]

The passage is abstract, but the import is clear: mastery is not simply imposed or dominative in character; consent is not simply manufactured by a ruling class and its monopoly over the means of mental production. Rather, the rich mix of Thatcherite populism succeeded in redefining the terms of British politics because it *actively made sense* to those defined by that bloc, and the discourses cobbled together by its hegemonic project were persuasive rather than coercive.

In "Toad in the Garden," in the course of a long and sinuous theoretical excursus about the necessity of understanding how new "subject positions" are created by historical conjunctures, Hall tosses in this wry and illuminating aside: "Of course, there might be an essential Thatcherite subject hiding or concealed in each of us, struggling to get out. But it seems more probable that Thatcherism has been able to constitute new subject positions from which its discourses about the world make sense, or to appropriate to itself existing, already formed interpellations" (49). It is a brilliant passage, chiding the British left for thinking of working-class recruits to Thatcherism as if they were characters in *The Invasion of the Body Snatchers,* taken over suddenly by Thatcherite pods; its American translation would consist of a warning to the U.S. left not to think of the emergent Reagan Democrats as always-already reactionaries who were simply waiting out the 1970s until they could spring to life in 1981. And yet Hall's negotiation of Gramsci's complex understanding of the workings of hegemony in civil society and Louis Althusser's markedly less complex structuralist-Marxist determinism (Hall even calls the latter a form of "functionalism" at one point [48]) is perhaps a bit slippery here; while he cannily mocks the idea that the New Right simply called us to cast off the liberal shells of ourselves, he seems to suggest that new subject positions were and are, in fact, created by discourses.[8]

But should anyone find this talk of "subject positions from which [Thatcherism's] discourses about the world make sense" too poststructuralist or abstract for their tastes, I call attention to this key formulation a few pages earlier in Hall's essay:

> The first thing to ask about an "organic" ideology that, however unexpectedly, succeeds in organizing substantial sections of the masses and mobilizing them for political action, is not what is *false* about it but what is *true*. By true I do not mean universally correct as a law of the universe but "makes good sense," which—leaving science to one side—is usually quite enough for ideology. (46)

Leaving the well-deserved swipe at Althusser to one side (in the sotto voce line about "science"),[9] I propose that, for people who want to think seriously about political formations and coalitions, despite the many differences between the historical conjuncture of Thatcherite Britain and the Bush-Cheney era in the United States, these remain words to live by.

But there is one crucial thing that Hall's analysis of Thatcherism does *not* do: even as it eschews "worse-is-better"ism and disdains the usual left alibis for the success of the right, it never—not once—indulges in the rhetorical game of pretending that there isn't a dime's worth of difference between the Labour and Conservative parties of 1979. Though Hall was far from satisfied with Labourism, and (later on) positively contemptuous of Tony Blair's "Third Way," and though he was often ambivalent about the relation between the intellectual left and party politics as such, he also wrote witheringly of the "crisis of political organization which has afflicted the left since Leninism lost its magic in 1956, and since 1968 when to be 'radical' meant, by definition, to be 'radically against *all* parties, party lines and party bureaucracies'" (*Hard Road to Renewal*, 181).[10] The tongue-in-cheek reference to Leninism's "magic" alludes, of course, to the original emergence of the British New Left—and the somewhat more somber reference to 1968 alludes to the pervasive antiestablishmentarianism that rendered so much of the late-1960s editions of the New Left fractious, violent, and incoherent. The result, Hall suggests, is that "this problem of 'party' represents an unsurpassed limit in the politics of the left today: we seem able neither to return to nor pass across" (181).

Despite that ambivalent yearning for and aversion to party politics, however, Hall never makes any effort to elide (or split) the differences between Thatcherism and its predecessors on the left—or on the right. Quite the contrary: his project was to urge the left to grapple with the lessons of Thatcherism, and it was absolutely central to that project that we come to understand Thatcherism as a radical break with business as usual, a radical departure from the postwar consensus on the welfare state. We need to come to that understanding, for Hall, not only in order to comprehend Thatcherism in all its aspects and guises but also in order to learn how best to roll it back and marginalize it. We could, alternatively, chant to ourselves that *the people, united, will never be defeated.* But that strategy will serve only to lull us back to sleep. As Hall puts it in the 1985 essay, "Realignment—For What?" the ossified routines of the "hard left" are part of what a new New Left needs to overcome:

> What is wrong with the habits and positions—or model—which have shaped the "hard left," as I have been defining it? Basically, that model has committed us over the years to an analysis which no longer has at its centre an accurate description of contemporary social, economic or cultural realities. Second, it has attached us to a definition of how change occurs in society which in no way adequately reflects the actual social composition of the class forces and social movements necessary to produce it or the democratic realities of our society. Third, it is no longer able to politicize and develop the majority experiences and dispositions of the popular forces which the left must enlist. Fourth, it is wedded to an automatic conception of class, whereby the economic conditions can be transposed directly on to the political and ideological stage. (*Hard Road to Renewal,* 242)

This list of particulars, especially the last, should be familiar to us now. But Hall follows them with a stringent critique of something we might call "hard left culture" itself:

> It is deeply linked to a politics of gesture, whereby it is better to lose heroically than to win. It blackmails everyone into the leapfrog game of "lefter-than-thou" which is so often the main if not the only business actually conducted at meetings of the left. Its conception of socialism remains profoundly statist—Fabian or Soviet style. It has never really squared up to the profound damage done to the left by the experience of actual existing socialism. It has lost the capacity to advance a convincing political vision of a more egalitarian, more open, more diverse, more libertarian, more democratic, more self-organizing form of socialism conceived in relation to the actual historic trends at work in the world today. That is what is really meant by the "hard left." (242–43)

The point could not be clearer: for Hall, an integral part of the hard road to renewal was ruthless criticism of the hard left. One can only imagine the howls of outrage from what remains of the hard left in the United States were a paid-up Gramscian theorist to publish such an essay in *Mother Jones* or the *Nation* today. But then, one strains to imagine a self-identified Gramscian theorist in the United States publishing such an essay in *Mother Jones* or the *Nation* in the first place.

IS IT HEGEMONIC YET?

It is widely agreed that Stuart Hall developed a complex neo-Gramscian theory of hegemony and of Thatcherism. However, at the time, there was no universal agreement as to just what Hall was saying about Thatcherism as a hegemonic formation in British politics. Some leftists—usually the targets of Hall's critiques—were apoplectic (and remained apoplectic for years) that Hall urged the left to learn from Thatcherism; as Hall put it in the conclusion to *Hard Road to Renewal*, "it is a sign both of the defensiveness and the residual sectarianism afflicting many parts of the left that it misreads an injunction to analyse 'Thatcherism' for a recommendation to swallow it whole" (272). Others defended the Althusserian Marxist project against Hall's attempts to leaven it with his reading of Gramsci and his interests in race and ethnicity; and still others complained that Thatcherism wasn't nearly as popular as the phrase "authoritarian populism"—or Hall's project in general—seemed to suggest. This last objection, the most plausible-sounding of the three, involved a serious misunderstanding of Hall's project, and because that misunderstanding is important not only to its moment but to the period of the second term of the Bush-Cheney administration, when the American left remained flummoxed at the phenomenon of a far-right president whose approval ratings languished in the 20s and low 30s for more than two years but who nonetheless managed to set much of the political and ideological agenda for American politics, I dwell on it briefly before moving to a consideration of Hall's work on the left's relation to the state, to the nation, and to international crises.

If Hall is to be read as a left theorist who claimed that Thatcherism dominated every aspect of British life, implemented its programs seamlessly, and brought the post-1973 economy to heel while reversing Britain's century-long decline, then Hall can be—and should be—dismissed fairly easily. But this dismissal depends on a debilitating misreading of what

Hall meant when he said that Thatcherism was a "hegemonic" project, and it depends on a severe misreading of what a "hegemony" might consist of. To paraphrase Hall, hegemony is not a stable, unitary, or permanent state; it is composed of multiple and contradictory elements, not all of which are moving at the same speed, so to speak, or working equally effectively. And it does not forestall dissatisfaction and dissent; far from it.

In adapting Nicos Poulantzas's term "authoritarian statism" and dubbing Thatcherism "authoritarian populism," Hall was not saying that Thatcherism *was actually popular;* he was saying that, like its American cousin, Reaganism, it combined a commitment to free-market/monetarist economics with a dramatic enhancement of the police powers of the state—*and did so in the name of the people.* As Hall put it in his 1979 Cobden Trust Human Rights Day Lecture, "make no mistake about it: under this regime, the market is to be Free; the people are to be disciplined" ("Drifting into a Law and Order Society," 5). The conundrum is familiar to Americans, no doubt, as the right wing's largely successful crusade to get government out of the boardroom and into the bedroom. But what mystifies both the British and the American left, to this day, is the fact that some—not all, not always a majority, but often more than enough—people are actually moved and persuaded by this appeal to "the people." Whether because they believe that the people to be policed are people other than themselves (darker and poorer, usually), or because they believe that abortion is immoral, or because they believe that gay civil unions are a threat to the traditional family, or because they believe that popular culture is encouraging These Kids Today to become violent thugs and sex addicts, they adopt socially conservative positions and support socially conservative politicians who appeal to them *as* "the people" and counterpose them to "the elites" or "the bureaucrats."

Hall argued that there are two points the left needs to grasp if it is to contest this phenomenon effectively. The first point is that, mirabile dictu, pointing out the contradiction between the New Right's passion for economic deregulation and its fetish for policing the private realms of love and sexuality doesn't actually render the combination ineffective. As Hall put it, "the left sometimes finds the role of the state in the current period of Thatcherism hard to understand since it continues to represent itself, ideologically, as unremittingly 'anti-statist.' In part, this is because the left continues to believe that ideology is unified, uncontradictory and coherent—its coherence guaranteed by the unified class interests it is supposed to reflect" (*Hard Road to Rewewal,* 85). This explanation is "partial," however, because some of the left *does* understand the incoherence of the New Right; the problem for those leftists is that the political terrain is not set up like a high school debating contest, and liberal-left wonks who think they can inflict fatal harm on their opponents by pointing out inconsistencies and contradictions are doomed to frustration and failure. "It is highly contradictory terrain," Hall wrote in a 1986 assessment of Thatcherism's social agenda:

> There is no clear evidence that ordinary Conservative folk—let alone the Conservative Party chairman—are actually giving up the so-called permissive society. It seems, from the scanty evidence we have, that this is even less the case with the younger generation. How, then, can we explain the discrepancy between what Thatcherite children are actually doing with and to one another, and what Thatcherite parents are represented as wanting or not wanting their children to be taught in schools? (90)

Not by resorting to the idea of "false consciousness," that much is sure; rather, by understanding that effective political movements can be chock full of all kinds of nasty contortions and contradictions. For instance, the United States has managed to develop and sustain an entire cottage industry of antifeminist women writers who argue that women should return to traditional domestic roles as wives and homemakers, and who have developed this argument over the course of very successful and lucrative careers as media spokespeople and public intellectuals.

Alternatively, one could make a case that some aspects of the "permissive society" are worth defending explicitly, particularly if they "permit" things like women's reproductive rights, interracial marriage, and openly gay and lesbian relationships; this was precisely Ellen Willis's line of argument throughout the 1980s and 1990s. With regard to the contradiction between official conservative mores and actual conservative practices, Willis writes:

> Conservatives have stigmatized and dangerously restricted access to abortion but have not been able to arouse popular support for outlawing it. Nor has rampant hysteria about teenage sex restored the old taboos. Despite periodic censorship campaigns, open sexuality, feminist assumptions, and the iconography of multiculturalism permeate the popular media, including TV programs watched by millions;

Dan Quayle's attack on *Murphy Brown* made him look sillier than his spelling. What were once radical ideas and sensibilities have been selectively assimilated not only by liberals but by a wide and politically varied swath of the population: gay Republicans demand the right to marry in the name of family values; white suburban teenagers embrace rap music and hip-hop style; evangelical Christian women roll their eyes at the Southern Baptist convention's call for wifely submission to male leadership—and in some cases their churches even leave the convention. In short, American cultural values are in flux, and Americans, pulled in conflicting directions, are ambivalent—which is why the culture wars have gone on so long and been so inconclusive. (*Don't Think, Smile!* 26)

The salutary aspects of the "permissive society" are worth underscoring, as is the seeming contradiction between conservative social policy and social practice. All too often, American progressives and leftists understand the New Right free-market/social conservative agenda as a shell game, whereby the real action takes place with regard to deregulation, tax cuts, and privatization, and the foolish masses are roped along with an agenda that opposes abortion, gay marriage, and flag-burning. The idea, in other words, is that the "contradiction" is no contradiction at all; there is a clear hierarchy between the economic wing of the New Right and the social-conservative wing, with the former holding the strings that make the latter dance.

But this position, too, assumes a much more straightforward and uncomplicated relation between ideology and practice on the New Right than is in fact the case. The contradictions between economic and social conservatism are quite real, and there is no Conservative Central Command that dispatches opponents of abortion and gay marriage to select voting districts in order to soften up the people for the real assault, the repeal of the capital gains tax. And as I show in chapter 5 when I discuss Tom Frank's *What's the Matter with Kansas?* the American left's failure to grasp the relations between cultural and economic conservatism not only results in a retreat to the idea of "false consciousness"; it also leads to some muddled thinking about the pros and cons of the "so-called permissive society," such that Frank himself winds up blaming social permissiveness for the right's political successes.

In the United Kingdom, the left's failure to understand what Hall meant by "authoritarian populism" has led commentators like Chris Rojek, author of a book-length study of Hall's career, to object that "in none of the three elections won under Thatcher's leadership did the Conservatives secure more than 44.9 percent of the vote" (152). That 44.9 percent was good enough for eleven years of rule, followed by seven more with John Major as prime minister; but it does not matter whether Thatcherism won the hearts and minds of majorities or supermajorities. What matters is whether Thatcherism remade the political landscape so that its opponents had to address the New Right agenda of deregulation and "value for money" in its own terms. What matters is that in 1979, one-third of all trade union members voted Conservative—presaging the appearance of the Reagan Democrats of the 1980s. It is worth remembering, too, that of the four elections won by Ronald Reagan and George W. Bush, only one was a landslide; Reagan and Bush, like Thatcher, mounted hegemonic projects that often failed to win the support of a majority of the electorate. (The corollary objection that Thatcher's success owes something to Labour's weakness, far from vitiating Hall's argument, underlines it.) Responding to the complaint that Thatcherism didn't change every aspect of British life, Hall wrote in 1986:

> Thatcherism has never been "hegemonic" if by that we mean that it succeeded in unifying a major social bloc and "winning the consent" of the great majority of the subordinate classes of society and other key social forces to a major task of social reconstruction. Especially if we conceive "hegemony" as a permanent, steady state of affairs.
>
> What we have always argued is that it had a "hegemonic project." It was designed to renovate society as a whole. And, in doing so, it understood that it must organize on a variety of social and cultural sites at once, both in society and in the state, on moral and cultural, as well as economic and political terrain, using them all to initiate the deep reformation of society. It has not achieved the goal of securing a period of social and moral ascendancy over British society, whose problems remain as yet too deep and intractable for such an enterprise. But it remains, by dint of a more "directive" form of authoritarian populist politics, the leading force in British political life. (*Hard Road to Renewal,* 91)

In the same essay ("No Light at the End of the Tunnel"), Hall also acknowledged that Thatcherism's failure to win wider popular assent to its social programs required the party to respond with some good old-fashioned chicanery:

The growing unpopularity of the authoritarian style of Thatcherite politics finds its reverse side in the open manipulation of public opinion.
Where a populist consensus cannot be won, it must be seduced into
place. The massaging of the unemployment figures by Lord Young's
department is remorseless. . . . Not to put too fine a point on it, lying and double-dealing have become part and parcel of the politics of
Thatcherism, just as they have long been the hallmark of Reaganism.
(*Hard Road to Renewal*, 86–87)

Most of the major criticisms of Hall's account of Thatcherism, then,
tend to miss the mark. Hall did not believe that Thatcherism was entirely
successful; on the contrary, he was keenly attentive to its economic shortcomings and to popular resistance to the "regressive" half of its regressive
modernization. Hall did not treat Thatcherism's hegemony as always-already achieved, nor did he imagine that its attempts to win popular consent were completely clean and above-board. As Hall wrote in one of his
most pugnacious essays, "Authoritarian Populism: A Reply to Jessop et al."
(1985, responding to a *New Left Review* essay by Bob Jessop, Kevin Bonnett, Simon Bromley, and Tom Ling):

I have never advanced the proposition that Thacherism has achieved
"hegemony." The idea, to my mind, is preposterous. What I have said
is that, in sharp contrast to the political strategy of both the Labour-
ist and the fundamentalist left, Thatcherite politics are "hegemonic" in
their conception and project: the aim is to struggle on several fronts
at once, not on the economic-corporate one alone; and this is based
on the knowledge that, in order really to dominate and restructure a
social formation, political, moral and intellectual leadership must be
coupled to economic dominance. . . . I have several times pointed out
the yawning discrepancy between Thatcherism's ideological advances
and its economic failures. . . .

But I also warned that Thatcherism had won power on "a long leash"
and would not be blown off course "by an immediate crisis of electoral
support." I added that it would be perfectly possible for Thatcherism
to "fail" in delivering a solution to Britain's economic crisis, and yet to
"succeed" "in its long-term mission to shift the balance of class forces to
the right." Big capital, I suggested, has supported Thatcherism because
it sees in it "the only political force capable of altering the relations of

forces in a manner favourable to the imposition of capitalist solutions." In that sense, I argued, "the long-term political mission of the radical right could 'succeed' even if this particular government had to give way to one of another electoral complexion." To that extent, I concluded, "Thatcherism has irrevocably undermined the old solutions and positions." That analysis was offered in 1980, but I believe it to have been fundamentally correct and to have been confirmed by subsequent developments. (*Hard Road to Renewal*, 154–55)

Likewise, the American right of the 1980s failed to deliver solutions to the nation's post-1973 economic crises, and, in insisting on tax cuts for the wealthy while overtaxing low-income and middle-income taxpayers and raising sales and excise taxes, precipitated a series of fiscal crises of its own making; yet it succeeded in shifting the balance of class forces to the right. There are lessons here both for American liberals and leftists—liberals who fail to understand that success, for a project that is "hegemonic" in scope, is not to be measured in displacing a particular government with one of another electoral complexion; and Chomskian leftists who, despite their occasional gestural remarks about trying to win the hearts and minds of the American people, have no interest in mounting a project that is "hegemonic" in conception and project, because hegemony is bad.

The phrase "fundamentalist left" seems chosen deliberately here—for it appears at the outset of the essay, where Hall writes of Poulantzas's final work in terms that leap to the fore today:

> The actual term "authoritarian populism," however, only emerged in 1978 after I read the concluding section to Nicos Poulantzas' courageous and original book, *State, Power, Socialism*, which was also—tragically—his last political statement. There, Poulantzas attempted to characterize a new "moment" in the conjuncture of the class democracies, formed by "intensive state control over every sphere of socioeconomic life, combined with radical decline of the institutions of political democracy and with draconian and multiform curtailment of so-called "formal" liberties, whose reality is being discovered now that they are going overboard" [203]. (I especially relished the final phrase, since it put me in mind of how often the fundamentalist left is scornful of civil liberties until they find themselves badly in need of some.) (*Hard Road to Renewal*, 151)

The phrase—and Hall's "relish" for it—makes it clear that Hall's "fundamentalist left" is that antiliberal branch of the left that characteristically dismisses civil rights and human rights as mere liberal-bourgeois concerns. This is perhaps its only point of contact with what might plausibly (if controversially) be called a "fundamentalist" left today—that is, the addled wing of the left that is willing to cut some slack to anyone who nationalizes an industry or stands up to the Evil Empire, up to and including Fidel Castro, Slobodan Milošević, Hugo Chávez, Mahmoud Ahmadinejad, and Sheik Hassan Nasrallah of Hezbollah. And it should be no mystery why that fringe of the left finds itself so incapable of theorizing a fluid form of hegemony that operates both in the state and in civil society, disdainful as it is of the very institutions of civil society and the very liberal-bourgeois idea of preserving institutions' and individuals' relative autonomy from state power.

THE STATE OF THE NATION

Up to this point I have traced Hall's thought largely to mark out my areas of agreement with its critiques of false consciousness and leftist purism, and to draw the appropriate intellectual contrasts with the work of the Chomskian left in the United States. As I move to discuss Hall's account of the state and the nation, however, I begin to reach the limits of his work in the period of Thatcherism—the political limits against which his critiques of orthodox Marxism run up, and the theoretical limits of trying to think Gramscian cultural studies in terms of the "national-popular."

Hall's relation to the state was rich and ambivalent: on one hand, he attacked the orthodox left's reliance on statism with characteristic brio, as we have seen in his remarks about how "its conception of socialism remains profoundly statist—Fabian or Soviet style" and his charge that "it has never really squared up to the profound damage done to the left by the experience of actual existing socialism." These are bold claims, and not entirely accurate about the history of the broad anticommunist left; moreover, one does not want to enforce a "mother, may I" clause throughout every precinct of the left, according to which one is not allowed to advocate for universal health care or paid family leave without first apologizing for Stalin and Mao. That said, Hall should be applauded for facing foursquare the question of how the legacy of Stalinism had alienated working people from socialism—and for doing so well before the Berlin Wall came down. For example, in his 1981 essay, "The Battle for Socialist Ideas in the 1980s," Hall took his stand for Solidarnosc:

> One of the reasons why the terrain for socialist ideas is so stony is the fact, the legacy, the experience of Stalinism. By this I mean something quite different from the usual simple-minded anti-communism. Nevertheless, I do think that when they speak to people drawn and attracted to socialism, socialists today have something to explain, to account for: why the attempt to transform some societies in the image of socialism has produced this grim caricature. . . . People are willing to contemplate pulling up what they know by the roots *only* if they can have some rational hope, some concrete image of the alternative. At the beginning of the century, the language of socialism was full of hope, indeed of a perhaps too naive scientific guarantee about the future. But the actuality of Stalinism and its aftermath has added the tragic dimension to the language of socialism: the stark possibility of failure. The socialist experiment *can* go wildly and disastrously wrong. It *can* produce a result which is both recognizable as "socialism" and yet alien to everything intrinsic to our image of what socialism should be like. It can deliver consequences against which socialists may have to stand up and be counted. This is a deep and wounding paradox— and a damaging weakness which every socialist first has to dismantle before he or she can persuade people in good faith to come to our side and assume positions alongside us in the struggle. In our struggle to realise a proper kind of socialism, we have first to explain—not explain away—the *other* kind: the kind where, in the name of the workers' state, the working class is actually shot down in the streets, as is happening at this very moment to Polish Solidarity in Gdansk. (*Hard Road to Renewal*, 184)

The echo of the British New Left's initial, post-Hungary repudiation of Soviet apologetics should be obvious.

On the other hand, Hall always understood the object of his critiques to be organized political parties seeking or wielding state power; unlike many of his counterparts on the countercultural left (and despite his own distance from campaigning and organizing), he never gave up on electoral politics and never minimized the importance of public policy. In fact, one of the reasons Hall maintained such an ambivalent relation to the state was that he had become convinced that state bureaucracies themselves were

not conducive to a popular-front leftism: "The actual experience which
working people have had of the corporatist state," he wrote in "The Great
Moving Right Show," "has not been a powerful incentive to further support for increases in its scope" (*Hard Road to Renewal*, 51). A few years
later, in the essay "The State—Socialism's Old Caretaker," he expands on
the rational core of popular anti-statism:

> The state which gives out benefits also snoops on its recipients. Then
> there is the size and scale of the administrative side of the state, cou-
> pled with its bureaucratic mode of operation. People, when they are
> being "done good to" by the state, increasingly *experience* it, in real-
> ity, as being "put in their place" by the state: by "experts" who always
> know better, or state servants who seem oblivious to the variety of ac-
> tual needs on the other side of the counter. The feeling is very deep
> that the way the welfare state works makes people into passive, greedy,
> dependent clients much of the time, rather than people claiming rights
> from a state which is supposed to be their own, representing them
> against the logic of the market. (*Hard Road to Renewal*, 226)

To American ears, the last sentence may sound as if Hall is channeling
centrist Democrats and "Republican-Lite" pundits rather than the British working classes; but in fact, he is drawing on a centuries-old tradition of political resistance within the British working classes, the tradition
of "lost rights" elaborated by Marxist historians such as Dona Torr and
Christopher Hill.[11] That tradition, as Hall argues in "No Light at the End
of the Tunnel" in 1986, provided the ground for much of the rejection of
Thatcherism even during its reign, "remind[ing] us how deeply rooted democracy, in a broad sense, still is in British political culture and the limit
this sets to any political force which attempts to push the long, historic,
democratic gains of the British people back too far" (*Hard Road to Renewal*, 84). But it also places real limits on any effort on the part of democratic socialists to use the instruments of the state to redress inequality,
as Hall acknowledged in "Socialism's Old Caretaker": "The problem for
the left is that the dissatisfactions with the state are real and authentic
enough—even if Thatcherism misdescribes them and misexplains them.
Thatcherism did not invent them—even if its remedies for the problem
are fictitious. Further, it exposed a weakness, a critique, of the existing system which the left had made too little of: the deeply *undemocratic* character of state-administered socialism" (*Hard Road to Renewal*, 227).

This goes well beyond the usual simple-minded anticommunism. It gets to the heart of any left politics worthy of the name: for if the left does not stand for freedom and equality, it stands for nothing—and quickly collapses. Freedom: not only from tyranny but also from the entrenched hierarchies of rank and class, as well as freedom from fear, freedom from religious persecution, freedom of speech, freedom from want, freedom for every individual to realize his or her capabilities to the best of his or her abilities or desires. Equality: so that individuals whose life chances are diminished by any form of stigma or oppression, from poverty to race to gender to age to sexual orientation to disability, can look to the public sphere and the public sector for succor when necessary. The problem lies, and always has lain, in the question of how to advance the agenda of equality without impinging unnecessarily on the prospects of freedom; and whenever the left forgets or ignores this problem, it leaves the door wide open for opportunists, free-market libertarians, and authoritarian populists promising to get "government" out of the way of the pursuit of happiness.[12]

While insisting on the importance of political campaigns and social policies, therefore, Hall emphatically contested the idea that the hopes of the left should be invested exclusively in the state. He suggested, instead, that a popular left should seek to reinvigorate a public conception of the public realm itself: "I feel sure," he wrote in "Socialism's Old Caretaker,"

> that socialism cannot exist without a conception of *the public*. We are right to regard the "public sector," however little it represents a transfer of power to the powerless, as an arena constructed against the logic of capital. The concept of "public health" *is* different from the idea of private medicine because it deals with the whole environment of health, which is more than the sum of individual bodies—a *social* conception of health as a need, a right. "Public transport" is not simply a practical alternative to private transport because it embodies conceptions of equal access to the means of mobility—to movement around one's environment as a publicly validated right. The idea of "public space" signifies a construction of space not bounded by the rights of private property, a space for activities in common, the holding of space in trust as a social good. In each case the adjective *public* represents an advance in conception on the limits of possessive individualism, of liberal thought itself. In this conception of the public and the social, socialism is still ahead. And the public can only be carved out of

market space, capital's space, by the engine of state action. (*Hard Road to Renewal,* 230)

"On the other hand," he adds, crucially, "'the public' cannot be identical with the state."

Instead, Hall argues, the left should diversify its holdings, so to speak, and look to civil society and the expansion of the meanings and practices of "democracy" to include popular access to every kind of social good. The fairer distribution of social goods, in turn, will enhance the participatory parity of citizens, and the idea of participatory parity—though Hall does not use the phrase—is central to the debate over "cultural" politics and its relation to public policymaking. In Hall's formulation, the expansion of democracy (in this sense) will actually work to undo the calcification of state-administered programs. In its final paragraph, "Socialism's Old Caretaker" concludes:

> The democratization of civil society is as important as dismantling the bureaucracies of the state. Indeed, perhaps the most important lesson of all is the absolute centrality to all socialist thinking today of the deepening of democracy. Democracy is not, of course, a formal matter of electoral politics or constitutionalism. It is the real passage of power to the powerless, the empowerment of the excluded. The state cannot do this for the powerless, though it can enable it to happen. They have to do it for themselves by finding the forms in which they can take on the control over an increasingly complex society. Certainly, it does not happen all at once, through one centre—by simply "smashing the state," as the sort of socialist thinking which is fixated in the state would have it. It has to happen across a multiplicity of sites in social life, on many different fronts, including, of course, the state itself, whose tendency to concentrate power is precisely what constitutes it as a barrier to socialism. (231)

Hall's conception of democracy places him, to his credit, far from thinkers like Paul Berman, who, even in the course of attempting to rally the like-minded to defend democracy from Islamist radicalism in *Terror and Liberalism,* defines democracy as a matter of institutional forms—and does so sketchily, at that: "free elections, political parties, opposition newspapers, a system to defend individual freedom, and that sort of thing" (162).[13]

More generally, and more importantly, Hall is wrestling with what now appears, in retrospect, to have been a profound crisis in the history of Western Marxism—the problem of how to think about freedom and equality in terms of democracy and socialism. In his 2007 interview with Colin McCabe, Hall remarks that "the most unexpected thing" about the period of Thatcherism "is the collapse of the social democratic, the socialist left, as a result of the collapse of the Soviet Union in which they'd never believed. It was incredible. *Marxism Today,* which has never been a Stalinist or pro-Soviet journal, winds up when the wall comes down!" (McCabe, "Interview with Hall," 36). It was mystifying, to be sure: finally freed of the albatross of Soviet communism, which the right had hung for decades around the necks of anyone who suggested that people's access to basic social goods should not be dependent on their ability to pay for them, the socialist left in the West suddenly buckled. In *The Cultural Contradictions of Democracy,* John Brenkman offers what I take to be the best one-page summary of why this happened:

> Why did Marxism have the ground cut from beneath it with the collapse of Soviet communism even though it had lent little or no support to the Soviet Union? All during the Cold War, Western Marxism forged a two-pronged discourse in search of a socialist vision that repudiated both American-led capitalism and Soviet-dominated totalitarianism. One prong criticized capitalism and the excesses of Western anticommunism lying behind repressive domestic policies (from McCarthyism in the 1950s to West Germany's antiterrorist campaign in the late '70s) and neo-imperialist foreign policies (Vietnam, Chile, Nicaragua). Democracy per se was simply taken for granted, all the more so because of its reassuring stability and security in most Western countries, while the anticommunist excesses were blamed for inhibiting the creation of a more egalitarian society. The other prong denounced state socialism and imagined that every revolt in the Soviet bloc (Hungary, Czechoslovakia, Poland) was, despite its inevitable brutal repression by the Soviets, the harbinger of the eventual transformation of state socialism into something democratic. The two prongs complemented one another, as mutual alibis, so to speak: anti-anticommunism presupposed democracy while rejecting capitalism; antitotalitarianism presupposed socialism while rejecting bureaucracy and one-party rule. The rejection of capitalism, bureaucracy, and one-party rule seemed then to confirm the presupposition that socialism and democracy belong

together. Meanwhile, the standoff of the Cold War itself deferred the crucial unanswered question: by what path could liberal democracy become socialist or state socialism democratic? When the Soviet system collapsed and the Cold War ended, Western Marxism had to face two uncomfortable truths: state socialism had never been reformable, and democracy has no intrinsic affinity with socialism or even social justice conceived in egalitarian terms. (65–66)[14]

One of the reasons Hall's work in the 1980s remains so resonant today, I suspect, is precisely that Hall confronted this dilemma squarely at exactly the moment when neoliberalism's attack on the welfare state and the endstages of Soviet decline were about to converge and produce the world we now know—while most of his orthodox Marxist colleagues were doggedly insisting that the inexorable laws of history would bear them out if only the left had the courage to stay the course. Those colleagues, no doubt, now account for the development of what Moishe Postone called the "inadequate and anachronistic 'anti-imperialist' conceptual frameworks and political stances" that have defined the Manichean left since 9/11 ("History and Helplessness," 96). Hall, to his credit, understood that the crisis for Western Marxism in the 1970s and 1980s was not going to disappear once mass unemployment caused the workers to rise up and throw off their chains; and if he did not resolve that crisis, it is merely because the crisis was, as Brenkman argues, unresolvable.

But having said this much, I should add that the more immediate problem with Hall's formulation of socialism and democracy, nuanced as it is, is that while it usefully deflects attention from the state to civil society (without neglecting the state altogether), it displaces the problem of freedom and equality onto "the public"—while keeping it bounded by the *nation*. I do not wish to be misunderstood here: Hall's appeals to "nation" are different in kind not only from reactionary, nativist flag-waving but also from most of the liberal American nationalists who called for a more patriotic left both before and after 9/11. Throughout his long career, Hall has combatted exclusionary and racist constructions of national identity, and he may fairly be credited with helping to bring about a profound rethinking of British national identity.[15] But the lesson he drew from Thatcher's inability to dismantle the National Health Service (NHS)— "Mrs Thatcher's 'Maginot line,'" as he put it in 1986 (*Hard Road to Renewal*, 81)—was that popular sentiment could be articulated to socialism by means of a conception of the common good, and that "common good," and the invocation of the "public health" *as* a common good, relies on the boundaries of the welfare state.[16]

In the concluding essay of *The Hard Road to Renewal* (on the final page, to be exact), Hall returns to the NHS as the ground for a left politics of human solidarity: "If [the left] knew how to articulate these new forces within the great levelling experience of illness, which hits everyone sooner or later irrespective of wealth or class or sexual preference, it would soon discover that society, looked at in a more diversified way, is not at all 'passive' about new needs in the field of health and medical care" (282). This is, once again, very close to a "capabilities" approach to democracy, one that foregrounds the centrality of illness and disability to the life chances of individuals and insists that we all have common cause in recognizing our common frailty. And it has much to recommend it: Americans should recall, at minimum, that William Kristol's famous 1993 memo calling on Republicans to kill even the inadequate Clinton health-insurance plan was predicated not on the argument that universal health coverage would fail but on the argument that it would *work*—and that voters would therefore be grateful to Democrats for years to come.[17]

Kristol's argument, in fine, was that any health care plan passed during a Clinton presidency would move the Maginot line leftward: where conservatives now fulminate that Social Security has such broad support as to be untouchable, future generations of conservatives, the American sons and daughters of Thatcherism, would fulminate that national health had become untouchable. Such a state of affairs, in which Americans think of national health care as a social good held in common, is clearly anathema to the privatizing and atomizing impulses of conservative and neoliberal ideologues. Yet this argument for national health, in the end, is only an argument for *national* health. It would be an extraordinary achievement if American progressives could win that much of the argument, true enough; but it would not address the larger question of how to rally popular support for the left when international politics are at stake. And nowhere are the tensions in Hall's neo-Gramscian "national-popular" leftism clearer than in the aftermath of the Falklands War, to which I now turn.

BEYOND A BOUNDARY

"The left, opposed to the war in a principled stand, is nevertheless isolated, silenced by the usual media blackout" (*Hard Road to Renewal,* 69).

So wrote Hall in the 1982 essay, "The Empire Strikes Back," his account of the Falklands crisis. The words will resonate for American critics of the Iraq war, no doubt, as will Hall's concluding paragraph on the collapse of the Labour opposition:

> More scandalous than the sight of Mrs Thatcher's best hopes going out with the navy has been the demeaning spectacle of the Labour front-bench leadership rowing its dinghy as rapidly as it can in hot pursuit. Only, of course—here, the voice of moderation—"not so far! Slow down! Not so fast!" (74)

And yet if there is one thing Hall can be legitimately faulted for in his critique of Thatcherism, it is his account of the Falklands War of 1982. Not because he opposed it—I consider that an eminently reasonable position, myself—but because he undertheorized it. I mean this in two senses: first, he remained focused chiefly on domestic matters regarding the fate of the social welfare state and did not write very much about Thatcherism's foreign policy or its role in the Reagan Epoch of the Cold War. He admitted as much in the introduction to *Hard Road:* "I do not give sufficient attention to the issues of defence and foreign policy, war and peace" (3). It cannot be said, then, that Hall was unaware of this weakness, but it can be said that it places limits on how one can adapt his work on Thatcherism for the United States after 9/11. And second, Hall "undertheorized" the Falklands by failing to explain precisely *what* principle the left stood for; in the course of neglecting this critical question, Hall wound up falling back on precisely the kind of "false consciousness" thinking he eviscerated with regard to domestic policy. It is as if, in Hall's composite analysis of Thatcher's first term, the British people were not duped by Thatcherite anti-statism in the economic sphere but *were* duped by the sight of the Union Jack flying from atop the ships of the New Armada.

Some of Hall's most intriguing and useful remarks about the Falklands are found not in "The Empire Strikes Back" (although I devote most of this section to this essay, for reasons that will become clear) but in the question-and-answer section of "The Toad in the Garden." This may require some explanation. "The Toad in the Garden," which I have been taking as one of Hall's most important theoretical essays on Thatcherism, was not published until 1988 (coincidentally, the same year *The Hard Road to Renewal* appeared) as part of the volume *Marxism and the Interpretation of Culture,* edited by Cary Nelson and Lawrence Grossberg. But the essay was originally a talk delivered five years earlier at the "Marxism and the Interpretation of Culture" conference at the University of Illinois at Urbana–Champaign—the conference that was the foundation for the book and also the template for the 1990 "Cultural Studies Now and in the Future" conference. The question-and-answer following Hall's talk, therefore, reads something like a time capsule from the summer of 1983; it was reportedly composed not merely of questions asked of Hall after his presentation at the conference but also of questions put to Hall over the course of the summer seminar that accompanied the conference. Some of Hall's remarks on "nation" and national belonging in that long series of exchanges, therefore, are addressed by way of the Falklands crisis.

The principal question, of course, is whether the left can wrest the discourse and the imagery of the "nation" away from the right. As one questioner puts it:

> You have, on other occasions, stressed the key role of discourses of the nation in Thatcherism—for example, in the way the nation was mobilized for the Falklands war. But how does one decide whether the struggle over terms like "the nation" is possible to win? What is the strategic question one raises here? Can the Left engage in significant ideological struggles against Thatcherism around the nation, or is it so likely that the Left is going to lose that we had better find other issues? ("Toad in the Garden," 64)

Hall's response is worth following at considerable length, not only for the admirable clarity of its opening paragraph but also for the increasing murkiness of the succeeding paragraphs:

> You could make the same argument about law and order. You could argue that you cannot possibly engage with the issues that are concealed in the slogans of law and order because they always deliver results that are of a deeply conservative and reactionary kind. Then, one after another the domains of public argument are snatched away from you; you can't touch any of them because they all seem to be articulated, organized and structured in such a way as to deliver a victory to the other side.
>
> . . . The problem is that, as against the way the ideological terrain is historically articulated around the nation, it seems an abstract argument to ask ordinary people in the street, who are being appealed

to powerfully in terms of the concrete experience of their sons sailing away on the Falklands task force, to reidentify, against the flag, with the Argentine people. It's totally outside their horizon. They've never heard of it; they have no living connections with it. The only way they know the Argentine is as the team that always beats us at football. There is not a lot of mileage in "We are one with the Argentines!" as a popular slogan.

I'm talking, then, about the kind of long groundwork or prepara- tion that is necessary. Does any nation build solidarity with another nation when it doesn't know what it is? I suspect not. I suspect inter- nationalism comes out of people having a sense of their own national, popular, or community identity, which allows them to build bridges to other people. After all, differences of national history, culture, and identity have to be recognized. The Argentines *do* have different in- terests from us. They do have quite a good claim to the Falklands, for example. So these are not easy contradictions to reconcile. But the building of solidarity has to come out of an actual, grounded sense of where *we* belong and fit into the world, a sense that is different from the old national-imperial one.

It is a very risky strategy, and I'm not recommending it. I recom- mend asking the questions so that the Left can actually begin to en- gage strategies within and around the languages of popular calcula- tion, the languages of practical consciousness, the discourse in which the man-in-the-pub says, "I'm for the war," or "That hasn't anything to do with us." We really need to shift him and his wife and his fam- ily from "Of course let's get at the 'Argies,'" at least to "This war is not our concern." I don't know that I could do it by saying, "Identify with the enemy, feel at one with them." I *have* to begin to talk the language in which popular calculation goes on, if I'm to appeal to any power- ful counternotions that don't send people marching off into the sun- set. . . . I can think of instances where the appeal to international solidarity does eventually overcome genuine differences. The Vietnam war, in the end, was such an example. (64–65)

The first paragraph, I think, is unassailable: writing off huge areas of po- litical life as the natural domain of the right is a recipe for the left's politi- cal irrelevance. But on the question of how to build an effective antiwar sentiment with regard to the Falklands, Hall becomes uncharacteristically diffuse. He relies on, and wrestles with, the premise that any appeal to the man-in-the-pub has to rest on the discourse of national identity and national interest, so that the options quickly become (a) convince the man and his family that this war isn't worth the trouble, or does not "concern" us, or (b) build international solidarity with the Argentines. Hall is right that the left, in opposing the Vietnam War, managed to build considerable solidarity with the Vietnamese victims of that war, and it is worth remarking that the American left worked the same terrain with regard to the victims of Reagan-funded death squads in Central America; but it is apparently such a "risky" strategy with regard to Argentina and the Falklands that Hall himself is not "recommending" it. He is merely suggesting we ask the questions that will allow the left to begin to engage strategies within and around various political languages—which sounds uncomfortably like a plan to think about a way to begin initiating the commencement of the prolegomenon to a theory of how to address the issue.

It does not help that whereas the war in Iraq is a tragedy, the war over the Falklands was a farce, staged by two leaders facing domestic unrest over economic issues and desperate for a timely diversion that would rally the people around their respective flags. As Hall remarked in "The Empire Strikes Back," "Rumour and speculation to the contrary, Mrs Thatcher did not invent the Falklands crisis. But she certainly now regrets that it was General Galtieri, not she, who thought of it first; for it is doing her government and its historic mission a power of good" (*Hard Road to Renewal*, 68–69). Because, in other words, the war was so clearly a diversionary tactic for both sides, it was easy for Hall—and everyone of like mind—to ridicule the casus belli altogether:

> As the country drifts deeper into recession, we seem to possess no other viable vocabulary in which to cast our sense of who the British people are and where they are going, except one drawn from the inventory of a lost imperial greatness. And now the country is going to war. Going to war for a scatter of islands eight thousand miles away, so integral a part of the British *Imperium*, so fixed in our hearts, that we have not managed to build a decent road across the place or to provide it with a continuous supply of power. (68)

It *was* ludicrous, no doubt about it—millions of Britons galvanized into identity by a war fought to retain possession of islands many of them were unaware of, or unable to find on a map, before March 1982. Suddenly, a chance to sing "Rule, Brittania" all over again, as if the Suez Crisis had never happened, as if Margaret Thatcher, combining the imagery of Queen Victoria and Winston Churchill, would restore Great Britain to world prominence by re-seizing a remote outpost in the South Atlantic. The idea was apparently so preposterous that Hall, despite having argued repeatedly that Thatcherism's project entailed the rearticulation of popular discourses to the right across the whole field of social significations, treated this instance of Thatcher's war of position as if it simply made no sense:

> The most powerful popular memory of all—the war, when we came to the rescue of oppressed people "under the heel of the dictator"; 1940, when "we stood alone" against enormous odds; and "1945"—Churchill's triumph, not the founding of the welfare state— has been totally colonized by the right.
>
> We have been invited to relive our last great moments of national greatness through the Falklands war. In the process, the legitimacy, the popularity and the justice of the one is transferred to the other. In this way, and to the astonishment of the left, Thatcherism has literally stolen the slogans of national self-determination and anti-fascism out of mouths. The sovereignty of people, the right of self-determination, the wickedness of dictators, the evil of military juntas, the torch of liberty, the rule of international law and the anti-fascist crusade: in a hideous but convenient ventriloquism, they have been run up the flagpole of the right. (72)

As a result, Hall writes, "we are up against the wall of a rampant and virulent gut patriotism. Once unleashed, it is an apparently unstoppable, populist mobilizer" (73). Note that Hall resorts to precisely the kind of language he eschews elsewhere: *colonized, stolen, ventriloquism, apparently unstoppable*. It is as if the left can struggle over the meaning of the "nation," but the right has no business adapting the language of antifascism and national self-determination. And it is as if Hall is willing to admit that Thatcherism has a rational basis when it comes to popular dissatisfaction with the welfare state but no plausible reason whatsoever to oppose Galtieri's opportunistic seizure of the islands: here, despite everything Hall has shown us about the operations of Thatcherite hegemony, we are in the realm of false national consciousness, where the sheeple are encouraged— if not hypnotized—into repeating the ancient verities:

Mrs T is simply our most-beloved Good Housekeeper. Children should be brought up as our parents brought us up. Mothers should stay at home. Tin-pot dictators should be stood up to. These are the grand truths which history and experience teach: what she called, to the Conservative Women's Conference on the eve of her election victory, the "tried and trusted values of commonsense." Better than "trendy theories"—and all that thinking. (71)

One does not have to support the Falklands War (I did not and do not) to believe that this is a serious mistake on Hall's part: to lump "tin-pot dictators should be stood up to" with "children should be brought up as our parents brought us up" and "mothers should stay at home" is *precisely* to leave the language of antifascism to the right. The question that should have been engaged here, and wasn't, was the question of *how* to stand up to Galtieri if not with a fleet and a flag. If indeed Argentina had quite a good claim to the Falklands, as it did and does, how should that claim have been pursued, other than by military occupation?

Hall was right to point out the stinking hypocrisy and selectiveness of Thatcher's appeal to antifascism:

> As the "war cabinet" drapes itself in the ensign of the Royal Navy, and the *Mail* remembers its past, who cares that the long-standing, well-documented obscenities of the Argentine regime against its people did not disturb Mrs Thatcher's sleep until the day before yesterday? Who minds that Argentina has so speedily become the only offending fascist military junta in Latin America, and that neighbouring Chile, where the roll-call of "the disappeared" is almost as long, is a friend of democracy? (72–73)

No one in the Thatcher government, surely, was about to propose a war of liberation for the Argentine people on the basis of Jacobo Timerman's 1981 memoir, *Prisoner without a Name, Cell without a Number.* On the contrary, "until a few weeks ago, the Argentinian generals were slipping in and out of quiet briefing rooms in Western military establishments and training schools around the globe," Hall notes. "Until yesterday, Mrs Thatcher's only concern about the international arms trade was how Britain could—to coin a phrase—'make a killing' in that lucrative market" (*Hard Road to Renewal,* 73).

But unfortunately for the left, be it the British left in 1982 or the American left in 2002–03, it avails little in the struggle for popular opinion to point out the hypocrisy and selectiveness of national leaders. Hall's (and the British left's) insistence on prior British complicity with the Galtieri junta had no more effect on British public opinion than did the American left's insistence on the fact that Donald Rumsfeld shook Saddam Hussein's hand and sold him a lifetime supply of weapons. Partly, I suspect, that is because there is a rich discourse of popular cynicism about international affairs, in which the man-in-the-pub and his family have long since inured themselves to the idea that the world is full of crazy and dangerous people who may be our "allies" one day, for some corrupt reason, and our "enemies" the next, for some other corrupt reason. But it is also because there *really was* a case to be made against Galtieri as against Saddam, whatever the nature of their previous engagements with the United Kingdom and the United States. Hall's neglect of that case—his refusal to address the question of whether it might not be appropriate for an internationalist left to oppose a fascist's military seizure of land, whatever the merits of his nation's claim to it—is a weakness in his argument against the war and a regrettable lacuna in his otherwise brilliant analysis of Thatcherism.

To give Hall his due, however, he knew something about the Falklands War that the Chomskians did not know about the aftermath of 9/11: that when one is trying to appeal to one's fellow citizens in the middle of an international political crisis, it is usually not a good idea to tell them they are the inhabitants of a leading terrorist state that has a centuries-old tradition of genocidal imperialism, from the settlement and colonization of the Americas through the 1857 Indian Rebellion, the 1916 Easter Rising, and the history of Rhodesia. "The culture of an old empire is an imperialist culture," Hall wrote toward the end of "The Empire Strikes Back"; "but that is not all it is, and these are not necessarily the only ideas in which to invent a future for British people. Imperialism lives on—but it is not printed in an English gene. In the struggle for ideas, the battle for hearts and minds which the right has been conducting with such considerable effect, bad ideas can only be displaced by better, more appropriate ones" (73). And bad ideas, one should add (though Hall clearly felt that it goes without saying), are more likely to be displaced by better, more appropriate ones if one is not opening the argument by haranguing one's fellow citizens with the long list of crimes committed in their names and their ancestors' names since European vessels first sailed west over the Atlantic.

Still, the question remains as to what those more appropriate ideas might be. For might it have been possible to convince the man in the pub (and his family) not that the Falklands were none of his concern but that the crisis be referred to the United Nations, Galtieri's seizure repudiated, and a peaceful, gradual transfer of sovereignty negotiated by legitimate means? Surely the primary reason ordinary Britons were led to feel possessive about the Falklands was that some tin-pot dictator issued them a deliberate provocation, a spit in the Atlantic eye. Take, as a useful contrast, the American handover of the Panama Canal—an artifact to which the United States had at least a plausible claim (more plausible, perhaps, than the British claim to the Falkland Islands), but which involved similarly difficult issues of national sovereignty, the legacy of imperialism, and international justice between the global north and the global south. Imagine that the Torrijos-Carter Treaties had never been signed, and that, instead, Manuel Noriega had seized control of the canal toward the end of Reagan's first term in office. Americans' emotional investment in the canal—which, at the time of the signing of Torrijos-Carter in September 1977, was confined to a small but vocal cadre of conservative cranks—would have flared, seemingly out of nowhere, and Reagan, who had opposed the transfer from the start, would have had a blank check for his crusades, not only in Panama but throughout the region. But because the transfer of power was managed in a legitimate and gradual way that strengthened international law and international institutions, when full Panamanian control over the canal became effective at noon on December 31, 1999, it barely registered in American consciousness—even the consciousness of the few remaining John Birch Society fanatics who had been willing to fight and die for the canal in 1977. It might have been worth arguing, in an English pub in 1982, that a thug like Galtieri shouldn't be allowed to get away with such a stunt but that England had no real interest in the Falklands anyway and should be encouraged to hand them over peacefully and resettle the inhabitants (who strongly desired to remain British subjects) on the condition that Argentina submit to international human-rights monitoring.[18]

I am not necessarily saying that this argument would have worked—either on the man in the pub or on the Argentine junta. I am merely suggesting that such an argument might reasonably have been part of what Hall called "the kind of long groundwork or preparation that is necessary" for the left to challenge the right in times of international conflict, so that the left "can actually begin to engage strategies within and around the languages of popular calculation, the languages of practical consciousness" with which people speak of "the issues of defence and foreign policy, war and peace." Instead of being astonished at the surge of seemingly farcical patriotism during times of war, and instead of consigning "tin-pot dictators should be stood up to" to the vocabulary of the reactionary, mothers-should-stay-at-home right, the left should find ways of negotiating the difficult terrain between tin-pot dictators and farcical neoimperialists: *all we are saying,* we might try saying, *is give international law and institutions a chance.* True, the slogan does not make for much of a countercultural anthem, and it is unlikely to rouse strong emotions; but as I suggest in chapter 3, the very thinness of the appeal to international law and institutions can be a virtue—especially when one is searching for arguments against war that won't send people marching off into the sunset.

THE END OF THATCHERISM

I do not want to propose that a fresh infusion of Stuart Hall's writing, 1978–88, can save us now. Nor do I even want to suggest that an updated and revised Stuart Hall package—Stuart Hall 2.0 for the U.S. market—is all the American intellectual left needs to download in order to get up and running. I do insist that the bulk of Hall's work on Thatcherism, particularly the bulk of his critiques of the "hard" and "fundamentalist" left, has been forgotten or ignored in the United States, even among cultural studies theorists (let alone leftists who disdain cultural studies), and that as a result, critical segments of the American intellectual left remain entranced by variants of "false consciousness" as a means of explaining why so few of the masses seem to be getting with the leftist program. But I do not think that the Stuart Hall of the 1970s and 1980s had all the answers we need today, cryogenically frozen for decades like Austin Powers. In this closing section, then, I call attention to matters about which Hall said very little or which cannot be easily translated from the United Kingdom to the United States—though I would be sorry if someone were to describe these as the "special American conditions" for cultural studies—and reflect briefly on Hall's legacy in British politics.

Dennis Dworkin's comprehensive history of postwar British cultural Marxism sets the stage for Thatcherism like so: "Internationally, the rise of Solidarity in Poland and the beginning of the end of existing socialism in Eastern Europe and the Soviet Union raised the issue of whether the democratic alternative was necessarily Marxist. The Iranian Revolution defied Marxist expectations of radical social transformation in the Third World. Rather than the driving revolutionary force being anticapitalism, it was religion, a social practice thought by Marxists to be residual" (*Cultural Marxism in Postwar Britain*, 247). Hall had a great deal to say about actually existing socialist states, and he had the intellectual honesty to raise the question of whether there could be a genuinely democratic socialism. But he said next to nothing about the Islamic Revolution. It is not surprising that Hall wrote so little about Islamism, perhaps, since it was not a front-burner issue in England or Western Europe in the 1980s; at the time, the name most often associated with terrorism was Abu Nidal rather than Osama bin Laden, and insofar as Islam was on the radar at all, it flew under the sign of British "multiculturalism," especially with regard to new immigrants from South Asia.

The fatwa issued by Ayatollah Khomeini against Salman Rushdie in 1989 changed the tenor of the discussion of religion and secularism in England, needless to say, and it raised the broader question (quite apart from its threat to a writer's life) as to whether Islamism would seek to enforce shari'a law even in secular states. (We now know enough to answer that question in the affirmative.) But in retrospect, the remarkable thing is not that Hall wrote so little about Islam and multiculturalism but that he wrote so little about religion *at all*.[19] It is difficult to translate Hall's program for a popular left, therefore, to a global political crisis in which one of the major players is a group of violent patriarchal theocrats; it is also difficult to translate Hall's program for a popular left to a country filled with fundamentalist Christians who make up the radical-right electoral "base" of one of two major parties. Hall's Gramscian analysis of Thatcherism, then, however supple and useful it may be for theorizing hegemony as a fluid, shifting ensemble of mobilizations, competing interests, and outright contradictions, cannot be applied directly to a United States whose right wing has been courting one band of religious fanatics at home while waging war against another band of religious fanatics abroad.

To say this, I hasten to add, is not to assume any moral "equivalency" between the Christian right and Islamism; the ideological affinities are clear enough, particularly with regard to the politics of sex and gender, but the Christian right has largely tended to eschew hijackings and suicide bombings in favor of more peaceful and legitimate tactics, creating institutions such as Focus on the Family and the 700 Club and grooming candidates for judicial appointments and key posts in the nation's regulatory agencies. (Their variously violent assaults on abortion clinics and abortion providers is a notable exception to the general rule.) Nevertheless, the point remains that any analysis of our current conjuncture must account for forces that were largely absent from, or overlooked in, Hall's accounts of Thatcherism. Likewise, but on the opposite front (namely, on the right wing of the Democratic Party), a thorough analysis of the Christian right—its desires, its sources, its "true consciousness"—would put to rest the delusional belief of many centrists and communitarians that the key to long-term Democratic electoral success lies in adopting a few of the Christian right's planks on the cultural front of the electoral platform, such as opposition to abortion and gay marriage.

More generally, a cultural studies account of the Reagan-Bush-Bush years—and the way in which the Reagan-Bush-Bush years set the terms for the Clinton interregnum as well—needs to foreground more emphatically the relation, the complex feedback loop, between domestic and international affairs. It will not do to read international affairs as a kind of false-consciousness-of-last resort explanation for domestic affairs; though "national pride" is considerably less tangible than real wages, safe schools, and health care, and therefore takes on a phantasmic appearance to leftists (myself included) who do not consider it sufficiently substantial as a ground for thought or action, it is every bit as important and volatile an element in the mix as race, class, gender, or any other social category one cares to name. If, as Hall insisted, we should ask what is true about any form of belief before asking what is false, then surely this stricture should apply to international relations as well as to matters of home and hearth.

After all, Reagan's popular appeal, like Thatcher's, lay partly in his image as someone who would "stand up to" the Soviet Union and call it an "evil empire" to its face—even if this also meant placing Pershing missiles a mere six minutes away from Moscow and potentially provoking another Cuban Missile Crisis; and that image of Reagan as unflappable Cold Warrior sustained the Republican Party even through the darkest hours of the recession of 1982 and the Iran-Contra scandal of 1986–87. Since 1945, American Democrats, like Hall's Labour Party rowing its pathetic little dinghy to the Falklands, have had no idea how to challenge the right for that image of national steadfastness (phantasmic as it is); as a result they have had to run to the right on communism (as did John F. Kennedy in 1960, successfully) or promise to hunt down terrorists and kill them, while stopping along the way for photo-ops of duck shoots (as did John F. Kerry in 2004, unsuccessfully).[20]

Meanwhile, the left, knowing that much of the right believes that war is the health of the state, is wont to understand international politics as the device by which the right clamps down on domestic dissent and distracts the great mass of the people from the economic misery into which it has plunged them—and this view has great merit; examples of war as domestic distraction-strategy are legion, and most are not as farcical as was the Falklands conflict. But this view of war is not the whole story, by any means. As a variant of the "false consciousness" theory, it assumes that war always dupes the masses, and it does not explain how certain unpopular wars *become* unpopular; just as important, it does not bother to delve into the rationales for war in order to distinguish just from unjust casus belli.[21]

For there are times—admittedly few, but critical nonetheless—when "national resolve" is appealed to *appropriately*, and Hall cedes the point (as would most people) with regard to World War II: his complaint is not that Churchill invoked (and thereby reinforced) the courage of the British people but that Thatcher deployed the same strategy for a ridiculous cause. But, of course, the appeal to national resolve in World War II was also international: no one single nation was threatened in that war, and the cause of the conflagration was not chimerical; we are not talking about the manufactured incidents of the U.S.S. *Maine* (the fraudulent justification for the Spanish-American War) or the Gulf of Tonkin (Vietnam). Fascism was a real and international threat in the 1930s and 1940s, and most leftists—including the premature antifascists who fought in the Abraham Lincoln Brigades—knew it.

Likewise, in the postwar period, communism promised an egalitarian utopia but posed a totalitarian and international threat—and was seen as such a threat by democratic leftists; indeed, the only leftists who managed to be utterly untroubled by Soviet and Chinese communism as standard-bearers for the international left were people who saw no problem identifying the left with tyranny and mass murder and who disdained bourgeois concerns like civil rights until they found themselves badly in need of some. One task for a democratic left, then, is to find the means to determine (and, just as important, the ways to cultivate the popular understanding of) when international aggression is and isn't appropriate—and when it is appropriate, what form it should take. "Aggression" here should not be understood as a euphemism for war: one may argue for the destruction of the al-Qaeda training camps and the capture of bin Laden in Afghanistan, for instance, while arguing only for containment (inspections, no-fly zones) of Saddam in Iraq. But "containment" is also a form of aggression;

it is aggression not in the service of imperialism, as the Manichean left would have it, but in the service of a form of international stability and security that does not coincide with the realists' cynical calculations of regional balances of power.

Stuart Hall was right to argue that the left needs to devise alternative discourses of things like "nation" and "law and order" rather than cede such important domains of public argument wholly to the right; he might have said the same, difficult as it may be to imagine, about international relations. The democratic left needs to find ways of popularizing the idea that long-term international (and, therefore, everyone's) security lies in international treaties, agreements, and institutions—ranging from the International Criminal Court to the United Nations to Human Rights Watch.[22] This idea does not seem to be terribly popular in left popular culture at the moment; it is far more wonky and far less sexy than antiglobalization protests and culture jamming. But if the Westphalian league of nations is ever to give way to a truly global vision of human affairs, this idea will have to be a prominent part of the left's intellectual apparatus.

And this, again, is why Kosovo was so important. For all the many faults of the Western powers—from their footdragging and indifference right through to their inaccurate high-altitude bombing—Kosovo represented a fledgling attempt, after the tragedy of Rwanda, to wage a war in order to strengthen international standards of conduct, realize a responsibility to protect vulnerable populations, and override national sovereignty in extraordinary circumstances. It was not an ideal test case for these principles, and, as I remark in chapter 3, the principles soon found themselves hijacked by liberal hawks and misapplied to Iraq. But the response of the Manichean left to Kosovo—searching for hidden pipelines, rallying around Milošević the Last Socialist, or denying Serbian atrocities outright—represented a complete failure to give any credence to these principles at all. Kosovo offered the left a chance to rethink war and international aggression, to develop a discourse of human rights, antifascism, and opposition to genocide in which concern over "ethnic cleansing" would override national self-determination in cases where national self-determination was predicated precisely on ethnic cleansing. One wing of the left took the opportunity and tried to articulate international principles that could challenge national sovereignty and create international structures that could override even the United States, the hegemon itself, in the service of the parliament of humankind (this, again, is why the American right so despises the United Nations and so distrusts the idea of an International Criminal Court); the other wing refused, and—as in its attacks on the democratic left's opposition to war in Iraq as "imperialism lite"— has begun to jettison internationalism tout court.

It is not hard, as Kenneth Roth's position paper demonstrated, to show that the war in Iraq does not meet the democratic left's standards for a proper response to a nation's challenge to international law and institutions ("War in Iraq"). Although George Bush went through the motions of appearing before the United Nations in September 2002 and making an internationalist case against Saddam's violations of U.N. resolutions, that does not mean that internationalism is tainted as a result; all Bush did was to argue—in his single convincing moment as a diplomat—that there were good grounds for resumption of U.N. weapons inspections. The second Security Council vote on Iraq, refusing to authorize war, made it crystal clear that the world heard Bush's U.N. speech as a rationale for inspections rather than for invasion, and a greater recognition of this fact would help the democratic left explain the difference between legitimate and illegitimate appeals to international institutions. Rather, the political problem posed by the Iraq war, for the purposes of this chapter, is that Tony Blair himself was so strong a supporter of it—and not only because Blair's government was rightly convinced that Kosovo was a war for international principles and institutions but also because Blair's government has some plausible links to Hall's work on Thatcherism.

I suggest in the preceding discussion that Hall can plausibly be credited with helping to bring about a rethinking of British national identity in the 1980s; but, arguably, Hall had as much influence on British electoral politics as on cultural politics. His influence was not, perhaps, as great as that of Anthony Giddens, inventor of the "Third Way," but it was not inconsiderable. As Chris Rojek has written, "his engagement with Thatcherism and analysis of the failures of the Left played a part in creating the intellectual and political climate that allowed New Labour to flourish" (*Stuart Hall*, 89). Hall was famously dismissive of New Labour, calling it "the Great Moving Nowhere Show" not long after Blair's election. But some of Hall's commentators have—rightly, in my opinion—seen that blanket dismissiveness as a betrayal of the spirit of Hall's own best work. In 2000, for instance, Joe Sim pointed out that the Blairite discourse of "law and order" differed significantly from that to which Hall had responded in the 1970s and 1980s:

It would be sociologically reductionist, politically naive and contrary to Hall's project to analyse Labour in power as simply a continuation of the Thatcher and Major governments. In the area of law and order the government has developed positions that previous Conservative administrations had either never espoused or to which they were vehemently opposed. The incorporation of the European Commission on Human Rights into U.K. law; the establishment of the inquiry into the racist murder of Stephen Lawrence; the proposals to change police disciplinary hearings; the references to domestic and racial violence in their flagship Crime and Disorder Act (CDA) and the shift away from the discourse of "Prison works" to a strategy of prevention, intervention and welfare all appear to signify that there is indeed (to paraphrase Michael Portillo) clear red water between Labour and their retributive predecessors. ("Against the Punitive Wind," 327–28)

On the international front, Chris Rojek writes, there is more clear red water:

Nobody who lived in Britain through the long night of the Thatcher-Major years can seriously doubt that New Labour better understands global civic responsibilities. . . . Its record on asylum seekers is equivocal and perhaps, on balance, discouraging. But this is also the government that detained General Pinochet for the contravention of human rights in Chile, much to the consternation of Margaret Thatcher, and expanded British responsibilities in protecting the global environment and international peacekeeping. (*Stuart Hall,* 155, 154)

As Adrian Hastings argued in response to Noam Chomsky, it would be a serious mistake to ignore or trivialize these forms of internationalism—not least because one wants to be able to criticize the Blair government for failing to live up to them in subsequent years. But once Blair cast his lot with Bush in Iraq, he threatened not only to bring down Labour but also to render incoherent the internationalist principles for which his early administration was to be lauded.

As the Iraq war began in March 2003, Angela McRobbie, writing in the online journal *openDemocracy,* did not fail to make the connection to Hall. In her essay "Tony Blair and the Marxists," McRobbie charged New Labour with forgetting its past, vilifying the left, and failing to connect with the vast majority of British people on Iraq. And she suggests, along the way, that Hall's work was central to the project that put Tony Blair in 10 Downing Street:

> It was by drawing on Stuart Hall's Gramscian account of Margaret Thatcher's rise to, and grip on, power that New Labour learnt how to govern. Stuart Hall has never been a Labour Party member (though I myself have been for twenty years) but his analysis of the Thatcher years had an extraordinary impact on those who at the time were in or near the Communist Party, and who were themselves gravitating towards Labour.
>
> The most prominent outlet for Stuart Hall's ideas was *Marxism Today*, the journal edited by Martin Jacques. This was the Eurocommunist-leaning, Communist Party magazine which prided itself on taking risks with left orthodoxies, guided by a belief that a failure to engage with the lives and desires of ordinary people was making the left more marginalised than ever.
>
> New Labour might today prefer to forget the role of *Marxism Today*, though it was in fact central to its modernisation project. Blair himself wrote for the magazine, and his key policy advisor Geoff Mulgan was a regular contributor.
>
> More important than either, Stuart Hall wrote many articles for the magazine—on how the success of the Tories was orchestrated, how they were able to forge a new "common sense" based around popular desires and aspirations, how they reached over the heads of the left middle classes to create a climate of "authoritarian populism" on issues like crime, which was appealing to those who felt abandoned by "old labour."
>
> All this offered those who were waiting in the wings (Blair, Peter Mandelson, Mulgan) a clear strategy. In a way this makes Stuart Hall the bad conscience of New Labour. Every time a minister talks about being tough on crime, or indeed reintroduces into the political vocabulary a word like "mugging" (which had been dropped precisely because of the way it had been used in the Thatcher years as an emotive, racialising term), it is possible to detect a kind of guilty discomfort at the way that modernisation (or what Hall then called "the great moving right show") is being enacted by New Labour.

One cannot legitimately charge Blair's hawkishness on Iraq to Hall's account, and to be sure, McRobbie lays the blame for this state of affairs squarely at the feet of Blair and New Labour rather than with Hall. But

I have no doubt that it has become possible, in the wake of Blair's contribution to the debacle in Iraq, for fundamentalist leftists to decide that if Hall's project on Thatcherism helped eventually to contribute to the election of Tony Blair, then the game was not worth the candle in the first place.

This would be a terrible conclusion for anyone on the left to reach, but it is quite easy to imagine such an argument. Indeed, the outlines of it were already visible in 2003, in Rojek's book on Hall.[23] On one hand, Rojek generally endorses the idea that Labour needed to divest itself of hoary Old Left orthodoxies, just as he argues that Hall's initial rejection of Labour in 1997 was too sweeping. Rojek also reminds us that the transitional figure for Labour was Neil Kinnock, despite his losses to Thatcher and Major in 1987 and 1992:

> In reality Blair owes an immense debt to Neil Kinnock, who led the Labour Party from between 1983 and 1992. It was Kinnock who took on the difficult job of expelling the far-left Militant Tendency from the party. In addition, after the third successive electoral defeat in 1987, Kinnock initiated a policy review that discarded most of the policies that were regarded as extreme by the electorate, notably the commitments to nationalize the banks and unilateral nuclear disarmament. More subtly, he softened Labour's opposition to Europe, a disastrous stance for a party with strong internationalist leanings to occupy. (209).

Lest Rojek sound like a champion of Blair and New Labour against Hall himself, however, I need to return to my first citation of his work, the passage in which he praises Blair's government for detaining Pinochet. The ellipsis in that passage omitted the following assessment of Blair's record:

> True, Pinochet was eventually released; and true the first Blair government expanded arms sales on dubious "ethical" grounds, and bombed Kosovo. Blair's second administration fell into line with American interests after the bombing of the World Trade Center in New York and the Pentagon in Washington by lending military and intelligence support to the war against the Taliban in Afghanistan. Blair's copy-book is far from unblotted. (154)

One does not have to strain to imagine where Rojek might stand on the war in Iraq, if he is willing to fault Tony Blair and the Labour Party for falling into line with most of the rest of the world in approving retaliation against the Taliban; indeed, later in the book, Rojek writes of "the Anglo-American blitzkrieg on the Taliban in Afghanistan" (191). In response to this—and in response to Rojek's condemnation of Blair's position on Kosovo—one can only suggest that some forms of antifascism, as well as some forms of opposition to international terrorism and regional ethnic cleansing, are worthy of support even if one finds oneself on the same side as the United States or the United Kingdom.

It should be unnecessary to add that the left need not always endorse war in order to oppose fascism and genocide; and it has become painfully apparent, thanks to the Bush-Cheney administration, that war is a particularly inadequate response to the rise of a global terrorist network. But if the left does not want to be astonished, time and again, when the right steals the slogans of antifascism from out of our mouths, then we need to demonstrate that our opposition to fascism is real and principled; and we need to base that opposition to fascism on a form of internationalism that will sometimes include the United States and the United Kingdom as key allies—and will allow us to criticize the governments of the United States and United Kingdom when, as in Iraq, they traduce the principles they claim to uphold.

WHAT IS THIS "CULTURAL" IN CULTURAL STUDIES?

OUTSIDE THE STILL-TINY world of academic cultural studies and communications departments, Hall's work on Thatcherism and the left is nearly invisible in the United States. *The Hard Road to Renewal* is out of print, and has been for some years now; and most of the anthologies that include Hall's essays tend not to include any of the material from *Hard Road* (remarkably, this is true even of the best anthology in the field, David Morley's and Kuan-Hsing Chen's *Stuart Hall: Critical Dialogues in Cultural Studies*). In my many conversations and correspondences with liberals, progressives, and leftists since the late 1980s, I have met only a small handful of people outside academe who are familiar with *Hard Road* or Hall's 1980s essays in *Marxism Today*. Moreover, within American academe, since the beginnings of the U.S. cultural studies "boom" in the late 1980s, two curious things have happened. One is that Hall's work in the late 1970s and early 1980s has not received as much attention as his brilliant late 1980s to early 1990s series of essays on race and diaspora (such as "Gramsci's Relevance for the Study of Race and Ethnicity," "New Ethnicities," and "What Is This 'Black' in Black Popular Culture?"); the other is that "cultural studies" as a whole (insofar as one can attempt to speak of "'cultural studies' as a whole") has been dismissed, either as a trivial enterprise that draws attention away from "real" political struggles or, even worse, as an academic cheering section for the corporate culture industry.

In this chapter, I revisit the debates over cultural politics and cultural studies as they took place in the United States in the 1990s, in order to try to explain why American left intellectuals remain so addicted to "false consciousness" theories of political behavior. And though I concentrate in part on commentators who got cultural studies entirely wrong, or who never had any significant sympathy with its intellectual project in the first place, I do not embark on a wagon-circling defense of the field. Something did indeed go awry with American cultural studies in the years before 9/11, and the people who helped to align the field with an uncritical populism in cultural and political matters are as much to blame for cultural studies' disconnection from public political debate as the people who argued that we need to turn away from uncritical populism and get back to the eternal leftish verities of how corporate and political elites dupe people into mis-identifying their real political interests.

The now-classic leftist broadside against cultural studies was issued by media theorist Robert McChesney, in a talk (later an essay) titled "Is There Any Hope for Cultural Studies?" which he delivered at the University of Illinois at Urbana–Champaign in late 1995. Perhaps to ensure that his auditors would not be left in suspense by the interrogative nature of his title, McChesney made it clear at the very outset that the answer was no:

> At some universities the very term cultural studies has become an ongoing punchline to a bad joke. It signifies half-assed research, self-congratulation, farcical pretension. At its worst, the proponents of this newfangled cultural studies are unable to defend their work, so they no longer try, merely claiming that their critics are hung up on out-moded notions like evidence, logic, science, and rationality.
>
> In my view there are two reasons for the decline of political radical-ism in cultural studies. First, this is the normal consequence of becom-ing institutionalized in the academy. As Russell Jacoby has pointed out, this has tended to undermine intellectual radicalism regardless of the discipline. The professionalization of cultural studies implicitly encourages depoliticization, which makes it far easier to get funding. For those who abhor radical politics or believe that radical politics must be secondary to institutional success, this depoliticization is a welcome turn of events, a sign of the field's maturity. Needless to say, institutionalization is especially damaging to cultural studies, in view of its explicitly populist origins and project.
>
> Second, the postmodern or poststructural turn in cultural stud-ies has had disastrous implications for its politics. I acknowledge that postmodernism has produced some keen insights. But it is too much like mainstream quantitative social science: each is well suited for spe-cific types of tasks, usually narrowly defined, but neither is especially useful for the "big picture." (3)

In response, I offer two observations and a brief overview. One: Mc-Chesney's complaint about the depoliticization of cultural studies was actually quite common at the time, especially among cultural studies theorists who were fond of celebrating "countercultural" movements—in other words, some of the very people McChesney ridicules in this essay. Their idea, and McChesney's, was that cultural studies will be defused and ruined once The Man co-opts it by way of his Academy, when cultural studies will find itself selling out for "funding" and "institutional success."[1] (Now that McChesney himself has experienced considerable institutional success as an academic theorist and media critic, one wonders whether he is inclined to revisit this aspect of Jacoby's argument.) Two: when Mc-Chesney (mis)uses the term "postmodernism," as the rest of his essay demonstrates, he means, above all, "identity politics," and he's very much against it. In the mid-1990s debates on the American left, this position places him squarely alongside Todd Gitlin, Michael Tomasky, and Richard Rorty who argued—ambivalently, in Rorty's case—that the left needs to eschew hifalutin' theories and PC identity politics in order to return to the fundamental issues of class and economic exploitation.[2] I point this out not to align McChesney with merely "liberal" intellectuals from whom he would surely recoil in horror but to indicate the differences between the pre-9/11 and post-9/11 terrain for American leftists. In the 1990s, the debates over identity politics and multiculturalism were narrowly nationalist debates (even when, or especially when, they did not acknowledge this), and, like cultural studies' theoretical overinvestment in the "national-popular," they proved difficult to adapt to the questions of defense and foreign policy, war and peace, that have shaped debate since 2001.

More importantly, McChesney's polemical characterization of cultural studies as "half-assed research, self-congratulation, farcical pretension" was echoed by Gitlin's critiques of the field throughout the period: from his claim in 1990 that "it is pure sloppiness to conclude that culture or pleasure is politics" ("Who Communicates with Whom," 191) to his complaint about the "antipolitical populism of cultural studies" in his 2006 book *The Intellectuals and the Flag*, Gitlin's disdain for cultural studies has matched that of any writer on the Chomskian left, and for (surprisingly) the same reason: namely, the conviction that cultural studies is at best a distraction from politics and at worst a lousy form of politics in which the celebration of consumerism substitutes for attention to social policy: "We like to argue about the political significance of movies and TV shows," Gitlin writes in *Letters to a Young Activist*, "not about the politics of pensions and living wages" (109). (Note, also, the slippage involved in Gitlin's dismissal of "culture *or pleasure*," as if culture consists entirely of leisure activities and the diversions of the "culture" section of the Sunday paper.) As Joel Pfister has pointed out in his 2006 book, *Critique for What?*

Cultural Studies, American Studies, Left Studies, Gitlin's formulation tendentiously ignores the fact that some arguments about movies and TV are, in fact, arguments about politics: "Many social and cultural critics—perhaps outside the undefined 'we' to which Gitlin refers—see the importance of examining a full range of contradictions, mystifications, and ideological concerns that make America tick. Their subjects of critique encompass living wages, pensions, movies, TV, and thankfully, much else" (271).[3]

The point remains, however, that the terms of this debate have survived well past their freshness date. And the result, so far, is that many American writers on the left are working with an impoverished and inadequate sense of the intellectual history of cultural studies, one that leaves them no way of understanding how that intellectual history might help them think about the present crisis. Paradoxically, critics like McChesney and Gitlin, who sought to combat what they saw as the political weakness of cultural studies, wound up contributing to the very problem they decried, thereby distorting or diminishing the American's left sense of what cultural studies is, what cultural studies was, and what cultural studies might yet be. In what follows, I'll try to explain how this happened.

CULTURE AND PLUTOCRACY

Cultural studies didn't get off the ground just because a group of British leftists found themselves repelled by Stalinism and the domestic fallout from the Suez crisis; it also had its intellectual origins in the conviction that orthodox Marxism offered manifestly inadequate analyses of culture, seeing it merely as a superstructural reflection of the base. Much of Raymond Williams's work, early and late, was devoted to unearthing the various meanings of "culture" since the late eighteenth century; and as Richard C. Lee has shown, the tradition interrogated and reinvigorated by Williams has roots that go back beyond F. R. Leavis and T. S. Eliot to the work of (among others) William Morris, Matthew Arnold, John Stuart Mill, Thomas Carlyle, and Edmund Burke.[4] Dismissing "cultural studies" wholesale, in other words, is not simply a matter of ridiculing a few breathless essays on Madonna or *Die Hard;* it entails, finally, writing off more than two centuries of work on the relations between culture and society, work written by reactionaries and radicals alike.

With regard to the postwar period, the focus of cultural studies understandably shifted to *mass* culture and the question of how mass culture advanced or impeded the forces of democracy. And whatever its wrong turns and excesses, British cultural studies is to be lauded for the central insight that the study of mass culture should take the actual lived experiences of ordinary people into account.[5] Doing so not only compels the cultural theorist to come to terms with where "the people" think they actually are rather than where the cultural theorist thinks they should be; it also repudiates the doctrinaire leftist position that because Joseph Goebbels and Leni Riefenstahl employed cutting-edge techniques of mass persuasion in the service of Nazism, all forms of mass culture therefore tend inevitably toward totalitarianism and mass political conformity.[6]

It is, without question, a serious political and theoretical mistake to overestimate the importance of popular culture and the power of its consumers (even if they are also, in some ways, its producers) and to strain to find world-historical political consequences in the film *Basic Instinct* or televised "reality" shows. But it is a still more egregious and lamentable mistake to ignore a vast terrain of popular culture and popular experience altogether, or to determine in advance (and in ignorance) that it can serve only reactionary ends, or to decide that certain cultural phenomena *might* be worth the attention of conscientious leftists—but only if they (the phenomena) have nothing to do with corporations. At the time McChesney penned his attack ("Is There Any Hope for Cultural Studies?"), cultural studies had more than its share of enthusiastic celebrants of the "active audience" thesis, it is true; they had already been repeatedly criticized *by other cultural studies theorists,* as when Tony Bennett complained about his colleagues' "sleuth-like searching for subversive practices just where you'd least expect to find them" ("Putting Policy in Cultural Studies," 32) or when Simon Frith wrote of "defending popular culture from the populists" ("Good, Bad, Indifferent," 101).[7] But it also contained plenty of people who understood that the struggle against the Reagan-Bush right could not be engaged exclusively on the terms of electoral politics, let alone defeated on the economic front by dragging out the charts and showing Americans that their real wages were falling while CEO wages were skyrocketing.

The truly appalling thing about the 1980s and 1990s, from the perspective of American liberal intellectuals, was that the rise of an academic left seemed to have no effect whatsoever on the Reagan-Bush ascendancy; gradually, over two decades, left perspectives became common (and sometimes de rigeur) in much of the humanities and social sciences, and yet New Right conservatism still remained hegemonic in the culture at large. The temptation became overwhelming, for some liberal journalists and intellectuals, to conclude that if the theorists of the academic left were not part of the solution, they were part of the problem. Perhaps, instead of simply trying and failing to provide some intellectual scaffolding for the resistance to the New Right, the academic left was somehow exacerbating the slide rightward, working as the New Right's secret enabler. The charge initially grew out of the scare over "political correctness" on American college campuses; "PC," as it has since become known, was criticized strenuously if not always carefully by writers across the liberal spectrum, from conservative liberals such as Jim Sleeper and Richard Bernstein to vital-center liberals like Arthur Schlesinger Jr. and Paul Berman to left-liberals like Gitlin and Tomasky.[8] Some of the work produced by this "liberal" consortium was remarkably overheated, even illiberal: Sleeper ridiculed the message on Robin D. G. Kelley's answering machine, thereby advancing the cause of social justice in ways yet untallied; Berman managed to keep a straight face as he associated campus PC with Stalinism; and Schlesinger decided the time had come to teach black people an important lesson, declaring that "the West needs no lectures on the superior virtue of those 'sun people' who sustained slavery until Western imperialism abolished it" (*Disuniting of America*, 76).[9]

It was not until 1997, however, when Richard Rorty published *Achieving Our Country*, that the indictment of the academic left's secret collusion with the New Right was delivered in so many words. "Leftists in the academy," Rorty charged, "have permitted cultural politics to supplant real politics, and have collaborated with the Right in making cultural issues central to public debate. They are spending energy which should be directed at proposing new laws on discussing topics as remote from the country's needs as were [Henry] Adams' musings on the Virgin and the Dynamo" (14–15). The reason I call Rorty an "ambivalent" participant in this debate, however, is that even as he distinguished the "cultural left" from the "reformist left" and argued that the latter has been the agent of social justice while the former either gets in the way or actively undoes the work of the latter, he added, later in the book, that "the American academy has done as much to overcome sadism during the past thirty years as it did to overcome selfishness in the previous seventy. Encouraging students to be what mocking neoconservatives call 'politically correct' has made our country a far better place. American leftist academics have a lot to be proud of. Their conservative critics, who have no remedies to propose either for American sadism or for American selfishness, have a great deal to be ashamed of" (82).

It is a remarkable thing, surely, that these two passages can coexist in the same book. Let it not be said that Rorty never sought to heighten the contradictions! But there is a good reason for his ambivalence: "it is as if the American Left could not handle more than one initiative at a time," Rorty notes, "as if it either had to ignore stigma in order to concentrate on money, or vice versa" (83). Since Rorty follows this observation with the admonition that the cultural left will "have to talk much more about money, *even at the cost of* talking less about stigma" (91; my emphasis), it seems fair to conclude that Rorty offers in *Achieving Our Country* a fair assessment of how intellectuals like himself could not help but think of the relation between cultural politics and public policymaking as a zero-sum game.

Into the mid-decade breach leaped Nancy Fraser, whose socialist-feminist theory of social justice sought to distinguish between "the politics of recognition" and "the politics of redistribution" in order to give each form of politics its due: instead of casting the former as a distraction from or drag on the latter, Fraser insisted that the politics of recognition were a politics in their own right and that leftists would do best to attend both to money and to stigma—which is, after all, another word for dehumanization. In her 1997 book, *Justice Interruptus,* Fraser wrote:

> Far from occupying two airtight separate spheres, economic injustice and cultural injustice are usually interimbricated so as to reinforce each other dialectically. Cultural norms that are unfairly biased against some are institutionalized in the state and the economy; meanwhile, economic disadvantage impedes equal participation in the making of culture, in public spheres and in everyday life. The result is often a vicious circle of cultural and economic subordination. (14–15)

However, Fraser made the fateful mistake of suggesting that "we may posit an ideal-typical mode of collectivity that fits the recognition model of justice" and proposing, as an example of this mode, "the conception of a despised sexuality" (18). While acknowledging that homophobia has economic consequences, Fraser characterized these as epiphenomena of injustices that were, at root, failures of recognition:

> Their sexuality thus disparaged, homosexuals are subject to shaming, harassment, discrimination, and violence, while being denied legal rights and equal protections—*all fundamentally denials of recognition.*

To be sure, gays and lesbians also suffer serious economic injustices; they can be summarily dismissed from paid work and are denied family-based social-welfare benefits. But far from being rooted directly in the economic structure, these derive instead from an unjust cultural-valuational structure. (18; emphasis added)

Fraser's argument is that homophobia is not intrinsic to capitalism, but the unfortunate implication is that homophobia is merely cultural; accordingly, Judith Butler replied to Fraser (and to an unnamed cohort of "orthodox" and "conservative" leftists) in a now-famous essay titled "Merely Cultural," charging that Fraser

> reproduces the division that locates certain oppressions as part of political economy and relegates others to the exclusively cultural sphere. Positing a spectrum that spans political economy and culture, she situates lesbian and gay struggles at the cultural end of this political spectrum. Homophobia, she argues, has no roots in political economy, because homosexuals occupy no distinctive position in the division of labor, are distributed throughout the class structure, and do not constitute an exploited class. "[T]he injustice they suffer is quintessentially a matter of recognition" (17–18), she claims, thus construing lesbian and gay struggles as merely matters of cultural recognition, rather than acknowledging them as struggles either for equality throughout the political economic sphere or for an end to material oppression. (270–71)

Fraser replied, in turn, that "misrecognition constitutes a fundamental injustice, whether accompanied by maldistribution or not" and that "injustices of misrecognition are fully as serious as distributive injustices" ("Heterosexism, Misrecognition, and Capitalism," 281); she observed that Butler "assumes that injustices of misrecognition must be immaterial and noneconomic" and insisted that "the material harms cited by Butler constitute paradigmatic cases of misrecognition" (282). Fraser suggests (rightly, I think) that Butler has underread—misrecognized, if you will— the term "misrecognition" in her framework.

But as far as most of the cultural/academic left was concerned, Fraser had made a fatal error in the course of her attempt to craft a judicious theoretical evenhandedness: while arguing that recognition politics should not be reduced to redistribution politics, she nevertheless implied that redistribution harms were prior to and determinative of recognition harms—that is, she consigned some conflicts to the "merely cultural" side of the ledger and set them at a discount unless and until they proved that they had material effects.[10] And if one wants to understand why Fraser's formulation was considered such a fatal error, it's necessary to remember just how volatile an intellectual contest Fraser was attempting to referee. For in the mid-1990s, once the anti-PC "liberal" backlashers like Bernstein and the class-first leftists like Tomasky had launched their fusillades against the cultural left, the battle lines were drawn, and the devotees of cultural politics were determined that no form of cultural politics would be left behind. In the pitched debate between the "cultural" and the "economic" left, even people who dared to suggest that there might, after all, be some qualitative difference between criticizing a popular film and passing a revision of the tax code found themselves cast as allies of the Liberal White Guys who allegedly wanted to throw the new black, feminist, and gay and lesbian social movements under the bus.[11]

In revisiting this impasse, we would seem to be far afield from the world of debate over Afghanistan and Iraq, but it is an important part of the prehistory of post-9/11 left debates in the United States for two reasons. First, because the impasse drew lines in the sand for much of the American intellectual left and helped to prevent post-9/11 alliances between writers who may have disagreed about multiculturalism but who might have found considerable common ground with regard to the invasion of Iraq; witness the curious phenomenon in which figures like Richard Rorty and Todd Gitlin became sworn enemies of the academic left not for their opposition to war in Iraq (since that would be odd) but for their positions on "cultural" politics almost a decade earlier, and the parallel phenomenon in which writers on the policy-oriented left, congregated around the *Nation, In These Times,* and the *American Prospect,* remain casually ignorant or dismissive of the past half-century of cultural studies. Second, because the impasse was framed as an implicitly nationalist question of how best to carve up the domestic pie in the United States—so much for recognition politics, and so much for redistribution, as if it were a matter of balancing the right mix of multiculturalism and progressive taxation. That is, what Eric Alterman called the "two lefts" debate was understood, by almost all participants therein, as an enterprise of balancing identity politics against the common good in and for the United States alone ("Making One and One Equal Two"). Rorty's forthright acknowledgment that he did not know what to think about immigration is one index of this: as he wrote in a footnote on Orlando Patterson's suggestion that the Mexican border be closed in order to protect American workers, "I suspect that the issue Patterson raised will be the most deeply divisive that the American Left will face in the twenty-first century. I wish that I had some good ideas about how the dilemma might be resolved, but I do not" (*Achieving Our Country*, 148–49).

Yet whatever the drawbacks to Fraser's recognition/redistribution formulation, the point remains that there needs to be *some* threshold for what counts as a "significant" form of politics, or all forms would be equally important—or equally trivial.[12] That is not to say that redistribution politics (or Rorty's "reformist left") is necessarily or by default more important than recognition politics. There are many trivial forms of financial, electoral, and regulatory politics; not every issue in civil procedure or zoning law is a constitutional matter. Conversely, there are many critical forms of recognition politics, and the struggles over abortion and gay rights are fundamental to American culture and society. It is only to say that patriarchy does not fall whenever a young female undergraduate decides to spell "womyn" with a y, and that Camille Paglia's complaints about the ethnic stereotyping of Italian-Americans in *The Sopranos* do nothing to improve the quality of people's lives. And it is to say that it is sometimes difficult beyond measure to try to measure the impact of recognition politics: some recognition harms may not affect the politics of redistribution for many years, or only in a circuitously indirect manner; and certainly no one who seeks social justice should be compelled to refrain from remarking recognition harms until the appropriate redistribution harms have been duly tabulated and recorded.

In my own life, for example, I do not see any point in arguing over whether my younger son is referred to as a "Down syndrome person," a "person with Down syndrome" or a "person with Down's syndrome"; I cringe when he is referred to as "retarded"; I would object strongly if he were labeled a "Mongoloid idiot"; and I would seek to remove from office any elected official who tried to repeal the Individuals with Disabilities Education Act or deny him Supplementary Security Income benefits under the Social Security Act. But I have no idea whether derogatory references to people with Down syndrome as "retarded" or "Mongoloid" will have any short-term or long-term effects on federal legislation concerning people with disabilities, and I do not see any need to wait for short-term or long-term redistributive effects before seeking to redress what I consider to be (unlike the difference-without-a-difference between "Down" and "Down's") nontrivial recognition harms. Such is my own sliding scale of recognition and redistribution with regard to that one issue.

But there is more at stake in this than my scales or the left's internecine squabbles from decades past. The question of what constitutes "politics," and how to theorize culture in relation to politics, is central to the history of cultural studies, and the centrality of that question helps explain why Gramsci became so important to Stuart Hall's work and to the development of the field as a whole from the late 1970s onward. As Hall wrote in "Gramsci's Relevance for the Study of Race and Ethnicity":

> The effect [of Gramsci's work] is to multiply and proliferate the various fronts of politics, and to differentiate the different kinds of social antagonisms. The different fronts of struggle are the various sites of political and social antagonism and constitute the objects of modern politics, when it is understood in the form of a "war of position." The traditional emphases, in which differentiated types of struggle, for example, around schooling, cultural or sexual politics, institutions of civil society like the family, traditional social organizations, ethnic and cultural institutions and the like, are *all* subordinated and reduced to an industrial struggle, condensed around the workplace, and a simple choice between trade union and insurrectionary or parliamentary forms of politics, is here systemically challenged and decisively overthrown. The impact on the very conception of politics itself is little short of electrifying. (430)

For Hall, in other words, Gramsci offered a way of thinking about the "new social movements" of the 1960s and their aftermath without construing them as a zero-sum game—and yet, on the American "reformist left" in the 1990s, this is precisely how the new social movements were seen: not as electrifying the conception of politics but as enervating it. And in the United States, Hall's work, unfortunately, was enlisted squarely on the "cultural" side of the "two lefts" (for is not cultural studies itself inevitably and exclusively "cultural"?)—both by Hall's supporters, who saw Hall's position on Gramscian "wars of position" as a useful tool with which to wage a war of position against the reformist left, and by Hall's detractors on the American reformist left, many of whom were unaware of his writings on electoral politics and social policy in *Marxism Today*.

There were, then, two distinct vortices into which "cultural studies" fell during the period of its ostensible American "boom" in the 1990s. One was the "two lefts" vortex just described; the other was a theoretical dispute that, at the time, was confined mainly to communications theorists and media activists. This was the dispute between "political economy" and "cultural studies" in communications departments: on one side, "political economy" advocates insisted that the media are owned by corporations and that corporations work inevitably to increase profit margins, deliver audiences to advertisers, and undermine democracy; on the other side, "cultural studies" advocates insisted that audiences are active participants in the creation of cultural meanings, regardless of whether the cultural products to which these audiences respond were created by vast corporate media conglomerates. Then the first group claimed that the second group had unaccountably ignored the fact that the media are owned by corporations, and the second group replied that the first group had failed to attend to the fact that audiences are active participants in the creation of cultural meanings. This predictable, neck-wearying tennis match went on for many years, in precisely this form; in fact, the Robert McChesney essay I cite at the outset of this chapter is a response, in part, to an important essay by Lawrence Grossberg titled "Cultural Studies vs. Political Economy: Is Anyone Else Bored with this Debate?" The fact that Grossberg's essay was half of a contentious debate in *Critical Studies in Mass Communication* with Nicholas Garnham ("Political Economy and Cultural Studies"), and was met with such a vitriolic response from McChesney, strongly suggests that in the mid-1990s, the response to Grossberg's titular question was *no, not yet, not by a long shot. Let's go around one more time!*[13]

Dispiritingly repetitive though the arguments were, they broached important questions. Just as the "two lefts" debate asked in what sense "culture" was political and how best to think about the possible relations between cultural change and political change, the debate between political economy and cultural studies asked how much it mattered, in the end, who owned the means of mental production—and, on the other side, whether it was worth examining what mass audiences did with the products of the culture industries. And if the hard-core adherents of political economy could reasonably be faulted for some old-fashioned Marxist reductionism, believing that the meaning of a cultural artifact is limited (or, at an extreme, entirely defined) by the conditions of its production, the hard-core cultural studies theorists could reasonably be faulted for some newfangled varieties of wishful thinking, in which, thanks to the wonders of Active Audiences, even the most banal or ephemeral cultural artifacts were shown to be important bearers of meaning in the war of position against all bad things. But the idea of academic leftists watching TV and movies or listening to popular music in order to understand and to try to influence the culture is not nearly as ludicrous as it was made out to be. Before it made a few critical missteps, which I describe in a moment, cultural studies offered a model of "impure" politics that eschewed the political and theoretical avant-gardism of the Frankfurt School, refusing the high-modernist gesture of valuing only those forms of art that are (allegedly) untainted by the market—a gesture, as I've noted, that is ubiquitous in the British and American "alternative" music scene.

Thus, for example, in the "Hip, and the Long Front of Color" chapter of his 1989 book *No Respect* (65–101), Andrew Ross argued that the racial fantasies and yearnings of Jack Kerouac's fiction may be embarrassing enough, and that rhythm and blues were a considerably more "corrupt" and "commercial" form of music than bebop, but that the cross-racial identifications enabled by those cultural forms, however far from the cross-racial ideal they might be, surely helped draw any number of white teenagers to Freedom Rides and the cause of civil rights. Similar arguments can be found in Dick Hebdige's *Subculture;* Paul Gilroy's *Black Atlantic;* and Simon Frith's *Performing Rites:* the analysis of postwar popular music, from R&B to reggae to punk, has attracted left critics precisely because the conjuncture of race, youth, integration, and national identity is every bit as rich in the field of popular music as it is in the legal sequelae to *Brown v. Board of Education.*[14]

Cultural change does not always happen from the bottom up, as post-Marxists have rightly insisted: in the United States, for instance, the 1967 Supreme Court decision of *Loving v. Virginia,* striking down state bans on interracial marriage, came at a time when over 70 percent of Americans—and an even more formidable majority of Americans living in the South—opposed what they called "miscegenation." Within a decade, however, the issue had largely dropped from the cultural radar, and within a generation, two-thirds of American adults saw no problem with interracial marriage.[15] The struggle for gay and lesbian rights, by contrast, seems to have percolated up from the grassroots and is more easily tracked by means of "cultural" politics than by way of the legislative or judicial process. The appeal of cultural studies to American left intellectuals, then, seemed to be that it would expand and electrify (to use Hall's term) the left's sense of the "political," allowing it to try to account for the perplexing fact that as the country's political culture moved steadily to the right, the country's *popular* culture became significantly more feminist, more multicultural, and more queer than it had been back in the good old Eisenhower days when the top individual tax rate stood at 91 percent.

So what went wrong with cultural studies?

COUNTERCULTURAL ANALYSIS AND ACADEMIC SUBCULTURE

The 1980s witnessed an extraordinary profusion of serious academic books on degraded popular cultural forms: the romance novel, the soap opera, the slasher film, and, of course, the most degraded form of them all, pornography. In each case, the argument was made that the close analysis of these forms was important not because the forms themselves were as aesthetically satisfying as *The Tempest* or as intellectually complex as *Paradise Lost* but because they offered representations of the world, however phantasmic, that attracted millions of people; therefore, so the argument went, it was only reasonable to try to discover and come to terms with the thoughts and impressions of the people who devoted significant portions of their lives to romances or soaps or slash films—or even porn. Following the publication of Stuart Hall's groundbreaking "Encoding/Decoding" essay and David Morley's *Nationwide Audience* in the United Kingdom, and Tania Modleski's *Loving with a Vengeance* and Janice Radway's *Reading the Romance* in the United States, many cultural studies theorists embarked on a kind of mass-media "ethnography" in which they sought the opinions of soap fans, romance readers, and TV viewers in order to try to understand how mass-cultural phenomena were actually "consumed" and understood by mass-cultural audiences.[16]

It is difficult to overstate the amount of derision with which this project met, inside academe and out. When senior (male) scholars weren't sputtering over what they considered books that should have been published as articles in *High Times,* mainstream (mostly male) journalists were guffawing at the idea that things like soap operas and romances merited a moment's thought.[17] That derision helped reinforce cultural studies theorists' initial point—namely, that certain mass cultural forms, and their audiences, are widely considered utterly unworthy of serious attention. But, unfortunately, it also confirmed cultural studies theorists' convictions that they were doing something Deeply Important, something that would shake academe and mainstream journalism and culture to their very foundations. The problem with those convictions of the theorist's importance, in turn, is part of the larger problem of studying mass culture from a left perspective that looks especially for moments of dissidence or subversion: for if there's one thing mass culture produces aplenty, it's moments of "dissidence" and "subversion" that are nothing but. And just as skateboarding and "slash" fanzines aren't really a threat to global capitalism in the end, so, too, the academic study of skate punks and "slash" fans doesn't really amount to much of a challenge to the established order—save for the established order in a handful of academic disciplines whose established order changes once or twice a decade anyway.

In the United States, this line of criticism of cultural studies is most readily associated with the work of Thomas Frank: in the *Baffler* magazine and in his second book, *One Market under God,* Frank has wittily skewered cultural studies for being an unwitting adjunct to the entertainment industry, celebrating the amazing consumer-empowering potential of commercial culture. Frank's criticism is not always accurate and not always very well informed: he ascribes Tyler Cowen's *In Praise of Commercial Culture* to "cult studs," even though Cowen, a libertarian economist, has no connection whatsoever to the cultural studies tradition.[18] And Frank's aspirations have more in common with cultural studies than he acknowledges: *One Market under God* describes the rise of a New Economy "market populism" in which, in Frank's words, "making the world safe for billionaires has been as much a cultural and political operation as an economic one" (15). The echo of Stuart Hall in the phrase "market populism" would be unmistakable (if only for its suggestion that populism is being mobilized against the people for whom it presumes to speak) save for the fact that when he coined the term, Frank did not know he was echoing Stuart Hall. Nevertheless, Frank's criticisms of American cultural studies were not without merit. He had many of the symptoms right: an inattention to business culture, an overinvestment in "hipness" (both its own and that of others), and a sometimes stupefying insularity and theoretical density. Frank had the symptoms right—but the diagnosis wrong. American cultural studies was not inattentive to the problems of critical populism, and it did not simply celebrate the joys of consumerism; but it did adopt some of the bad habits of the American "countercultural" left—bad habits that one can find, interestingly enough, in Frank's work as well.

Though Joseph Heath and Andrew Potter open *Nation of Rebels* by claiming that "our greatest intellectual debt is to Thomas Frank, who is to be credited with having first thematized the 'countercultural idea' and

who demonstrated the role that it played in promoting 'hip' or 'rebel' consumerism" (ix), their account of the countercultural left actually offers a
rebuke to one important feature of Frank's work. That account argues that
the "counterculture" continually finds itself "co-opted" by the dominant
culture, to its unending dismay; and the reason for this dynamic, according to Heath and Potter, is not that evil corporations go looking around
for "dissident" subcultures to infiltrate, incorporate, and destroy but that
countercultural thinking itself starts from a fatally incoherent premise. In
postwar countercultural critiques of mass society, the enemy is inevitably
conformity—embodied by the organization man, the man in the grey flan-
nel suit, the people in the ticky-tacky houses that all look just the same,
the well-respected man about town doing the best things so conservatively. Rebellion against conformity, then, is construed as a challenge to
the entire structure of corporate capitalism, which allegedly would prefer
to mass-produce us all just as it mass-produces cheeseburgers, Levis, and
Top 40 songs.

Strangely, however, it always turns out that rebellion against conformity, whenever it becomes attractive enough to a critical mass of people,
fails to challenge the logic of the market, instead producing new niche
markets for everything from organic food to extreme sports. And it turns
out this way because capitalism has no necessary investment in conformity; market diversity, from the seller's point of view, is just as good if
not better. By the same token, a counterculture that urges its members
to break away from social mores and march to a different drummer is a
counterculture that winds up subscribing to one of mainstream America's
most cherished *topoi:* that individuals need to rebel against "society" in order to discover and express themselves. Although Frank was right to note
the rise of "hip consumerism," therefore, it was something of a mistake to
characterize it as corporate America's "conquest of cool." "Cool" was always already marketable, and the assumptions of the counterculture were
always as American as McDonald's apple pie. To write, as Frank does in
What's the Matter with Kansas? that "counterculture has been taken up by
Madison Avenue and is today the advertising industry's stock-in-trade, the
nonstop revolution that moves cereal and cigarettes by the carload" (121)
is thus to endorse the counterculture's understanding of itself: revolutionary in the 1960s and then ruined by corporate cooptation thereafter.

American cultural studies' mode of "subcultural" analysis too often
made precisely the same mistake: the problem was not that it looked for
subversion in all the wrong places but that it did not have a sufficiently

rigorous set of political criteria for what kind of "subversion" might actually matter to the world and what kind of "subversion" was just American business as usual. This is not a question of distinguishing recognition politics from redistribution politics, but it does require the theorist to establish a threshold below which "subversive" cultural politics are deemed too trivial to warrant attention. It is a question, instead, of avoiding the trap of uncritically championing every form of ordinary *détournement* in which consumers engage.[19] One of the curious byroads taken by American cultural studies in the 1990s, for example, involved hauling out Michel de Certeau's *Practice of Everyday Life* and using it as a handy "four legs bad, two legs good" formula for assessing cultural politics: "tactics" were good and usually employed by powerless people in the streets; "strategies" were bad and usually employed by The Man in his corporate or political office.[20] The corollary of this position was that *all* popular "tactics" were good: whenever people refused to go along with what The Man told them to do, they were hailed for their counterhegemonic potential. Work like de Certeau's, when combined with a heady infatuation with countercultures and the American left's long-standing hostility to electoral politics, led American cultural studies to lose the necessary connection between cultural politics and social policy; cultural studies dealt with the "tactics" employed by ordinary people, and social policy was for wonks and reformist leftists and other "strategists." And though Stuart Hall was ritually cited throughout the decade, his work was nevertheless honored in the breach time and again by people for whom "cultural studies" signified little more than the study of popular culture from some generally leftish-oppositional position.

The cultural studies model of the "intellectual as fan"—as someone who does ethnography from the point of view of the *ethnos*, and who is in some sense a fan of the groups she or he studies—has been roundly criticized, and rightly so.[21] But even here, cultural studies was broaching an unavoidable and indispensable question, a question that should be central to the project of any democratic left: namely, trying to understand why people think what they think and do what they do—trying to understand precisely why, for example, romance readers find themselves alienated from feminism, rather than assuming that the proliferation of romances is a sign of a backlash against feminism and that romance readers are seduced away from feminism by a crafty Romance Industry designed to keep them docile and subservient.[22] Moreover, by embarking on these ethnographies, cultural studies was trying to challenge the doctrinal assumption of "media effects" theorists that because company A produces image B with intent C, consumers soak in image B with effect C in accordance with company A's intent. Cultural studies may have wound up developing its own doctrinal populist assumption in response—namely, that mass cultural audiences are always active, and they always manage some countercultural-tactical way of evading The Man—but it is worth remembering, nonetheless, that the impulse behind cultural studies' experiments with ethnography was unimpeachable.

Finally, there is the strange and lamentable fact that cultural studies *itself* became something of an academic subculture in the United States. It was not "institutionalized" in the way so many people feared: it did not form very many new academic departments or centers, it did not sweep all humanities disciplines before it, it did not restructure the field of knowledge production. Nor, for that matter, was it stopped at the door by nervous administrators and told to depoliticize itself pronto if it wanted any funding. (This is yet another version of the countercultural myth, of course—the fear that cultural studies has "sold out" if it achieves too much popular or academic success.) But it did produce its very own celebrity mechanisms, gossip mills, and fashion accessories; and the love-hate relationship that developed in the 1990s between cultural studies and the popular-academic magazine *Lingua Franca* helped cement the field's image as the domain of Kool Kids and their counterhegemonic cultural practices. That image (which was, admittedly, the self-image of some "cult studs"), as much as anything, is what Thomas Frank was responding to in *One Market under God.*

AN EXPANSIVE POPULAR SYSTEM

My argument so far is that, in the 1990s, some frivolous work in cultural studies, combined with an indiscriminate backlash against cultural studies, led some American left intellectuals to toss out the Gramscian baby along with the slash-fanzine bathwater. But to demonstrate how that development bears on some of the American left's more recent failures, I have to return to the work of Thomas Frank and Robert McChesney.

For the problem with Frank's criticisms of cultural studies in *One Market under God* is not, ultimately, that they are underinformed or misaimed; more than enough of his criticisms hit their mark. Rather, the problem is that Frank's willingness to mock cultural studies' commitment to ethnography renders his book incoherent when it comes to the big picture: namely, the question of what to make of all the starry-eyed New Economy gurus and management-theory tomes Frank mocks in the course of his book. It is never clear, in Frank's account, whether the American public was swayed by the various apologias for downsizing and advertisements for dot-com wealth penned by people like Spencer Johnson (*Who Moved My Cheese?*) and James K. Glassman and Kevin Hassett (*Dow 36,000*) or whether the American public somehow sagely rejected the notion that getting fired is just like having your cheese moved to another location and that the Dow Jones would soon hit 36,000. Frank closes his book by robustly making the latter claim and invoking a Popular Front of "wit and everyday doubt":

> And in the streets and the union halls and the truck stops and the three-flats and the office blocks there remained all along a vocabulary of fact and knowing and memory, of wit and everyday doubt, a vernacular that could not be extinguished no matter how it was cursed for "cynicism," a dialect that the focus group could never quite reflect, the resilient language of democracy. (*One Market under God*, 358)

But there are two problems with this stirring passage. The first is that it comes out of nowhere; there is no evidence, on any page of the book, that Frank has spoken to anyone in the streets or the union halls or the truck stops or the three-flats or the office blocks, or that he has heard from their lips the resilient language of democracy. The second is that it directly contradicts a number of other passages in Frank's book in which "the people" are themselves the problem—"all through the nineties the public had seemed to shrink ever further from any actual embrace of democratic power" (44)—and are the problem precisely because they have been reading starry-eyed New Economy gurus and management-theory tomes:

> That America was able to endure the wrenching upward redistribution of wealth that it did in the nineties with only small, localized outbreaks of social unrest must be chalked up, at least in part, to the literature that explicitly sought to persuade the world of the goodness and justice of that redistribution. (180)

At least from Morley's *Nationwide Audience* onward, cultural studies has operated on the premise that if you're going to make claims about how cultural products and political programs actually work with real people, you need to find out something about how cultural products and political programs are actually working with real people. Otherwise, you run the risk of projecting onto the people your own hopes and desires for "democracy," and then, whenever these hopes and desires are defeated by real living people who think differently than you, declaring that it is time to dissolve the people and elect another.

Frank's *What's the Matter with Kansas?* is an improvement over *One Market under God* on this score, for in the later book Frank returns to his native Kansas in order to find out just what the local "movement conservatives" believe about their movement. It is also a delightful book, written with flair and passion, and offers a lively account of how American conservatives have defined the term "elite" so that it refers not to the country's political or economic elite but to what the Club for Growth's early-2004 anti-Howard Dean ad famously called that "tax-hiking, government-expanding, latte-drinking, sushi-eating, Volvo-driving, *New York Times*-reading, body-piercing, Hollywood-loving, left-wing freak show." *What's the Matter with Kansas?* has been faulted by political scientists for contrasting the populist heyday of the late nineteenth century with the hard-right present but skipping over the fact that Kansas hasn't sent a Democrat to the Senate since Roosevelt's landslide of 1936 (in which even favorite son Alf Landon failed to carry the state); and it has been castigated by conservatives, who for some reason object to Frank's characterization of them as "deranged." Last but not least, the book has been criticized by liberals and leftists who find its treatment of cultural politics too glib and shallow. I address this last criticism in some detail, because I believe it is true that Frank continues to see cultural politics as a smokescreen for the right's economic shenanigans; but I especially call attention to Frank's approach to American popular culture and media, which has not been sufficiently noted in the various commentaries on his work to date.

Early in the book, Frank makes it clear that he will treat cultural politics as a sham, because, on his account, this is the way the New Right itself works:

> Cultural anger is marshaled to achieve economic ends. And it is these economic achievements—not the forgettable skirmishes of the never-ending culture wars—that are the movement's greatest monuments. . . .

> Thus the primary contradiction of the backlash: it is a working-class movement that has done incalculable, historic harm to working-class people.
>
> The leaders of the backlash may talk Christ, but they walk corporate. Values may "matter most" to voters, but they always take a backseat to the needs of money once the elections are won. This is a basic earmark of the phenomenon, absolutely consistent across its decades-long history. Abortion is never halted. Affirmative action is never abolished. The culture industry is never forced to clean up its act. (5–6)

Frank is right, of course, that the "backlash" consists of a working-class movement that has done incalculable, historic harm to the economic interests of working-class people. But he is mistaken to think that the leaders of the backlash have overlooked the culture wars in the course of walking corporate. Throughout the book, Frank minimizes the damage that movement conservatives have done to abortion rights and affirmative action over the years;[23] it is especially worth remarking on the difference between Democratic and Republican presidential administrations when it comes to policies regarding family planning organizations overseas. Moreover, these "cultural" issues aren't just smokescreens for the repeal of the estate tax; millions of people actually believe in them on their merits. For many heartland conservatives, cultural anger may be marshaled to economic ends (as Frank claims), but they're really in it for the cultural anger.

About conservative rollbacks of abortion rights and affirmative action programs, then, Frank is either underinformed or dismissive. But here I focus on Frank's claim that "the culture industry is never forced to clean up its act." What might this mean, and why might it matter? It turns out that Frank agrees, in part, with the backlash: our culture *has* become coarse and vulgar, and the backlash theorists of the right have simply fingered the wrong culprit. For the "aggrieved 'Middle Americans,'" he writes, "the experience has been a bummer all around. All they have to show for their Republican loyalty are lower wages, more dangerous jobs, dirtier air, a new overlord class that comports itself like King Farouk—and, of course, a crap culture whose moral free fall continues without significant interference from the grandstanding Christers whom they send triumphantly back to Washington every couple of years" (136).

The idea is that somehow, the cultural right is *right* to take offense at America's commercial culture and wrong only to blame it on liberal elites rather than on corporations. For the corporations are ultimately the real culprits: "All the incentives point that way, as do the never-examined cultural requirements of modern capitalism. Why shouldn't our culture just get worse and worse, if making it worse will only cause the people who worsen it to grow wealthier and wealthier?" (249–50) Accordingly, Frank closes the book not with the resilient language of democracy being spoken in the streets and the union halls and the truck stops and the three-flats and the office blocks but with a caustic account of what the backlash hath wrought:

> Behold the political alignment that Kansas is pioneering for us all. The corporate world—for reasons having a great deal to do with its corporateness—blankets the nation with a cultural style designed to offend and to pretend-subvert: sassy teens in Skechers flout the Man; bigoted churchgoing moms don't tolerate their daughters' cool liberated friends; hipsters dressed in T-shirts reading "FCUK" snicker at the suits who just don't get it. It's meant to be offensive, and Kansas is duly offended. The state watches impotently as its culture, beamed in from the coasts, becomes coarser and more offensive by the year. Kansas aches for revenge. Kansas gloats when celebrities say stupid things; it cheers when movie stars go to jail. And when two female rock stars exchange a lascivious kiss on national TV, Kansas goes haywire. Kansas screams for the heads of the liberal elite. Kansas comes running to the polling place. And Kansas cuts those rock stars' taxes. (249)

This is a witty passage, no doubt—but it is also strikingly ill considered. Setting to one side the fact that the infamous Madonna-Britney kiss at the 2003 MTV Video Music Awards was not terribly "lascivious," look at Frank's remarkable insistence that this is all the doing of the "corporate world," and that the corporate world operates this way "for reasons having a great deal to do with its corporateness." As Ellen Willis did not fail to notice, this is reductionism with a vengeance: "Like many critics of capitalism, Frank makes the mistake of imagining that mass culture is a pure reflection of the corporate class that produces it" ("Escape from Freedom," 11). It is almost as if we are being asked to believe that the Madonna-Britney kiss was brought to you by Archer Daniels Midland.

Actually, in a *Salon* interview published not long after the book, Frank comes close to saying something very much like this—and it is no coincidence that he does so in the course of taking yet another swipe at what he considers the free-market foolishness of cultural studies. The interviewer is Andrew O'Hehir:

O'HEHIR: You have a whole critique of pop culture that is difficult to summarize, but let's talk more about your sympathy with the right-wing activists. When they bemoan how coarse and cheap pop culture has become, you almost seem to agree, or at least to feel that they have a certain kind of point.

FRANK: Well, look. I should say this: I started out as a punk rocker, and we try to deal with cultural dissent, genuinely shocking things, at the *Baffler*. But as I have written about many, many times, so much of the shockery that surrounds us is not genuine. There's no avant-garde about it. It's not the real thing, it's a watered-down capitalist projection. You've seen this argument before, "the commodification of dissent."

The argument I'm making is not that they're absolutely right to be disgusted by our culture—although when I'm away from the country and I come back and turn on MTV, I'm always like, "Holy shit!" I'm just trying to play up the flagrant contradiction. If you hate this stuff, talk about capitalism! Talk about the forces that do it! I'm focusing on the contradiction there, rather than accepting their argument about obscenity or whatever.

O'HEHIR: Right, so your real problem is with the kind of cultural-studies intellectual who believes that pop culture really is subversive.

FRANK: Yes, exactly. The cultural studies people read these products of capitalism at face value. They see fake rebellion as the real thing. To put it in very vulgar terms, that's the argument.

O'HEHIR: Madonna kissing Britney is somehow actually socially meaningful.

FRANK: Right, exactly. And the heartland people often see it that way also. I'm saying it's not that, it is as pure an expression of business rationality as is a McDonald's hamburger. (O'Hehir, "How the Democrats Lost the Heartland")

I needn't belabor the point that this is an exceptionally reductive way of understanding how popular culture works. But I can suggest that the "cultural studies people" are serving, in this exchange, as devices that enable Frank to avoid addressing the initial question as to just how much sympathy he has for the right's disgusted reaction to the coarseness and cheapness of American mass culture. Frank's "holy shit" response to MTV, for instance, calls out for further explanation: Who, upon returning to the United States from, say, Japan, Brazil, or Italy, would be particularly horrified by the amount of flesh on display in your average video?

I hope it is clear that the question before us is not whether popular culture is vulgar and coarse. Many elements of popular culture unquestionably are; and there is no question that many forms of vulgarity and coarseness sell very well. Rather, the question is whether one can ascribe the coarseness and vulgarity of the culture to its "corporateness." For what kind of cultural vulgarity are we talking about? Personally, I can't stand prime time television's endless parade of reality shows and crime dramas; some people object to the relentless reification and commercialization of every aspect of our affective lives; others inveigh against misogyny or sexual explicitness in rock and hip-hop; still others recoil in horror from what they believe is the liberal media's promotion of the "gay agenda." So is there a United Vulgarity Front in our culture, such that one can say, "if you hate this stuff, talk about capitalism! Talk about the forces that do it!" then claim that one is "focusing on the contradiction" rather than accepting conservatives' arguments about obscenity? For Frank, oddly, the answer is an emphatic yes. In one of the most tellingly incoherent passages in the book, Frank writes:

> So it is with Sam Brownback right down the line: a man of sterling public principle, he seems to take the side of corporate interests almost regardless of the issue at hand. This is true even when the corporate interests in question are industries whose products Brownback considers the source of all evil. Such, at least, was the case in 2003, when one of Brownback's Senate committees was called upon to consider the growing problem of monopoly ownership in radio since the industry's deregulation seven years previously. Brownback, of course, has made a career out of denouncing the culture industry for its vulgarity, its bad values, presumably for the damage it has done to America's soul. Taking this opportunity to rein it in should have been a no-brainer. After all, as the industry critic Robert McChesney points out, the link between media ownership, the drive for profit, and the media's insulting content should be obvious to anyone with ears to hear. "Vulgarity is linked to corporate control and highly concentrated, only semi-competitive markets," McChesney says. And for many conservatives, "the

radio fight was the moment of truth. If people are seriously concerned about vulgarity, this was their chance to prove it." (74–75)

It is notable that McChesney makes an appearance at this point in Frank's argument, and it is notable that the argument itself is so wrongheaded. For not only does it insist that vulgar corporations make vulgar culture; it ignores the obvious fact—obvious to anyone with ears to hear, that is— that radio, for most cultural conservatives, is not a site of vulgarity; for them, vulgarity issues from the MTV Video Music Awards and Janet Jackson's exposed breast at the Super Bowl halftime show, whereas radio gives them Rush Limbaugh, Sean Hannity, James Dobson, and Oliver North. If one knows what American radio actually sounds like, the idea that cultural conservatives would band together with left-wing media theorists to disrupt media consolidation and undo monopoly control of the radio airwaves is a form of wishful thinking that rivals anything proposed by the most jejune populists in American cultural studies.

And the reason it's notable that McChesney makes an appearance just here is that McChesney's work underwrites a great deal of Frank's understanding of American culture and media. In *One Market under God*, for instance, Frank excoriates Angela McRobbie for describing the market as an "expansive popular system"; the quote is adduced, as one might imagine, as proof positive that cultural studies theorists are chirpily (and unwittingly) working as the intellectual PR department for American big business. In this as in much else, Frank is following McChesney's line in "Is There Any Hope for Cultural Studies?"—except that McChesney's response to McRobbie is rather more visceral than Frank's:

> Perhaps the stupidity—and there is no better word for it—of some cultural studies is best shown by its stance toward the market. I have heard leading figures in cultural studies argue that the market is not the top-down authoritarian mechanism that political economists claim, where bosses force the masses to swallow whatever they are fed. To the contrary, they exult, the market is where the masses can contest with the bosses over economic matters; it is a fight without a predetermined outcome. One cultural studies scholar goes so far as to characterize the market as "an expansive popular system."
>
> Perhaps these are extreme examples, but almost nowhere in cultural studies do we see sustained criticism of the market today. How

it has fallen from Stuart Hall's brilliant 1979 conception of the market and its relation to class inequality!

What a grotesque and callous mischaracterization of the political economic critique of the market. All radical political economy recognizes that the market is based on competition and has formal voluntarism. Of course people receive value for their money, otherwise they would not spend it! I am not opposed to the market per se; there may be some creative ways to use it in a post-capitalist world. But it is absurd—even vile—when one considers the human toll generated by neoliberal free market policies around the world today—to extrapolate from this that the market is an "expansive popular system." (10–11)

McChesney praises the good old days of cultural studies, of Stuart Hall's brilliant 1979 conception of the market and its relation to class inequality, and contrasts these with the fallen era in which people like Angela McRobbie make the "grotesque," "callous," "vile," and "absurd" claim that the market is an expansive popular system. And McChesney cites, as his source for McRobbie's claim, Grossberg's "Cultural Studies vs. Political Economy: Is Anybody Else Bored with this Debate?" in which McRobbie appears in the final footnote, for a work in press.

It may seem a minor matter, but this is a regrettably misleading citation on Grossberg's part. McRobbie may indeed have used the phrase "expansive popular system," and Grossberg may indeed be endorsing her view.[24] But as a matter of fact, the phrase originally appears in a 1984 essay by one Stuart Hall—yes, he of the brilliant 1979 conception of the market—titled "The Culture Gap." And it appears in a passage that goes directly to the central premises of McChesney's and Frank's analyses of vulgar popular culture:

Consumer capitalism works by working the markets; but it cannot entirely determine what alternative uses people are able to make of the diversity of choices and the real advances in mass production which it also always brings. If "people's capitalism" did not liberate the people, it nevertheless "loosed" many individuals into a life somewhat less constrained, less puritanically regulated, less strictly imposed than it had been three or four decades before. Of course the market has not remained buoyant and expansive in this manner. But the contradictory capacity, for a time, of the system to pioneer expansion, to drive and develop new products and maximize new choices, while at the same time creaming off its profit margins, was seriously underestimated. Thus the left has never understood the capacity of the market to become identified in the minds of the mass of ordinary people, not as fair and decent and socially responsible (that it never was), but as an expansive popular system. (*Hard Road to Renewal,* 215)

Furthermore, in "The State–Socialism's Old Caretaker," Hall adds that those ordinary people have good, ordinary reasons to prefer markets to planned economies: "The most widespread *and basically correct* 'image' of actual existing socialism among ordinary working people is the drab lack of diversity, the omnipresence of planned sameness and the absence of choice and variety" (228; my emphasis). For Hall—as, indeed, for Marx—capitalism is to be understood dialectically: it can create staggering economic inequalities, and it can loosen the strictures of church, state, liege lord and clan, and it can do both in the same motion, as all that is solid melts into air. That is why, even as one decries the depredations of unchecked capital, it is worth attending to "the alternative uses people are able to make of the diversity of choices and the real advances in mass production which it also always brings"—instead of, say, decrying cultural "vulgarity" and ascribing it to corporations.

I've argued that Hall's work on ideology and hegemony was not fully engaged by the American intellectual left—not only that part of the left that takes its cues from Chomsky on foreign policy but also that part of the left that wound up dismissing cultural studies on the grounds that it amounted to a wing of the advertising industry. Under that heading, it is hard to find a clearer example of someone citing Hall reverently and ignoring his actual work than McChesney. And yet McChesney's and Frank's vituperative responses to McRobbie vividly make Hall's point: their wing of the left *still* does not understand the capacity of the market to become identified in the minds of ordinary people as an expansive popular system. For when it is so identified, anticorporate leftists will denounce the identification as false consciousness, induced by corporate media and abetted by foolish cultural studies theorists. That maneuver, in turn, does a great deal of useful cultural work, as I point out in a moment. For when it comes to devising theories to account for how ordinary people experience popular culture and how best to understand capitalism's contradictory capacities, Frank's and McChesney's work should be seen as the Great Leap Backward. Backward into a time when everyone on the left knew that the ruling classes controlled the means of mental production and offered the masses bread and circuses to keep them in line—*and* that, as Raymond Williams famously noted, the "masses" were always other people.

THE LEFT OFF THE HOOK

In all fairness to McChesney, I should acknowledge that his mid-1990s attack on cultural studies was, in part, a contribution to that distinguished academic genre, the Complaint about the Colleague down the Hall. For at the time, McChesney taught at the University of Wisconsin at Madison, where the reigning cultural studies impresario was John Fiske, whose cheery brand of critical populism had flooded much of the American cultural studies market by mid-decade. Late in his essay, McChesney writes:

> One prominent cultural studies scholar, for example, points to the "tiny" victories—such as, in the extreme example, when slaves committed suicide rather than go to work on the plantations—as the true liberation politics, demonstrating the slaves' "ultimate undefeatability." I suspect the slaveowners were willing to concede some "tiny" victories to their slaves as long as their system remained intact. Contrast this with the idea that true liberation politics might also be organizing to smash slavery—a "big" victory—so that people would not have to kill themselves to subvert the system. ("Is There Any Hope for Cultural Studies?" 14–15)

That prominent scholar is Fiske, and in the 2002 update of his essay, McChesney prefaces this citation of Fiske with the observation that Fiske is "trivializing politics beyond recognition" (88). Indeed he is, and one can see in Fiske's celebration of tiny victories the imprint of de Certeau's elevation of "tactics" over "strategies": "strategies," alas, involve organizing for big victories. Formulations like these littered the landscape of cultural studies in the 1990s, as dozens of clever people devoted their energies to showing that little victories could be found in the unlikeliest places— even if those victories turned out to be very little victories, and even if they turned out to be victories over reductive cultural theorists (*See! The audience really is active after all!*) rather than victories over forms of political oppression. Likewise, McChesney's more sustained critiques of media consolidation have great merit even though there is no simple one-to-one correspondence between corporate culture and something called "vulgarity." There is no sense, then, in which my critique of McChesney and Frank is a defense of mass-media conglomerates or a celebration of the amazing powers of ordinary people to eke out tiny victories that are somehow analogous to slaves committing suicide. The problem with McChesney's line of argument is not that it takes on the wrong targets in cultural studies or in American culture at large; the problem is that it takes on the right targets with the wrong tools.

As a result, it winds up offering manifestly inadequate analyses of culture all over again, just as emphatically as its forebears in the bad Old Left. Let us return now to McChesney's equation of "postmodernism" with "identity politics" and watch how it allows him to move from a denial that the left emphasizes class politics over everything else to an insistence that the left must emphasize class politics over everything else—in only one convoluted paragraph:

> Politically oriented postmodernists in cultural studies and elsewhere might recoil at what I have just stated. To them postmodernism offers a basic repudiation of old-fashioned out-of-date left analysis and politics and points the way to a new radical democratic future. In particular, traditional leftists have put too much emphasis on economics and class exploitation and not enough on culture, sexism, and racism. To replace traditional socialist politics, postmodernism offers identity politics, a series of loosely related social movements linked to the distinct interests of groups usually defined by ethnicity and/or sexuality, that have no clear overarching political vision. There is a great deal to criticize in traditional left politics and theory concerning racism, sexism, and much else, but in my view postmodernists are being disingenuous to leap from this to calling for a rejection of materialism and class-based politics in favor of identity-based politics. Even a rudimentary study of history also shows that the left invariably has been among the leaders in battles against racism and sexism, despite its shortcomings. Radicals are opposed to all forms of oppression and it is ludicrous to debate which of sexism, racism, "classism," or homophobia is most terrible, as if we were in some zero-sum game. Socialists have traditionally emphasized class— and continue to do so today—because the engine of a capitalist society is profit maximization and class struggle. Moreover, it is only through class politics that human liberation can truly be reached. (4–5)[25]

The contradiction is glaring, but it should not blind us to the incoherence of the claim that advocates of cultural politics called for a *rejection* of class-based politics (and did so "disingenuously"). No one who reads Judith Butler's "Merely Cultural" can plausibly claim that Butler's poststructuralism seeks to replace class politics with identity politics; rather, Butler objects that Fraser "locates certain oppressions as part of political economy and relegates others to the exclusively cultural sphere," thereby misreading the relation of homophobia to political economy.[26] And just as McChesney's brand of leftism is dismissive of (while paying lip service to) "loosely related social movements . . . that have no clear overarching political vision," it is dismissive of (while paying lip service to) cultural studies' history of attempting to understand how, in fact, ordinary people experience and participate in contemporary culture. It is easy enough, as I've admitted, to make fun of people like John Fiske championing the counterhegemonic potential of films like *Die Hard*. But it is sheer foolishness to write off the "active audience" thesis tout court, as if it were nothing more than a branch of the marketing industry.

In all of McChesney's critiques of the corporate media, nothing makes this clearer than his attitude toward the Internet. Responding to the glassy-eyed techno-utopianism of the dot.com boom of the late 1990s, McChesney devoted a good portion of his breakthrough book, *Rich Media, Poor Democracy*, to throwing cold water on the idea that the Internet has any potential to challenge the dominant media system in the United States. Of course, McChesney was writing before blogging technology became widely available, and even after blogs became common in 2001–02, they were dominated at first by conservatives and libertarians and glassy-eyed techno-utopians; it took another three or four years for liberal and progressive bloggers to become a substantial grassroots phenomenon. It would be absurd to fault McChesney for failing to account for the "active audience" that—through the work of private citizens, most of them working with nothing more than a laptop and an Internet connection—produced the liberal blogosphere in less than five years. (The group MoveOn.org, however, was established in 1998; but it is not surprising that McChesney ignores it, for to this day, MoveOn is breezily dismissed by some leftists as being even less substantial than checkbook activism.)

But it is worth noting that McChesney was absolutely convinced that there was no way for something like the liberal blogosphere to come into existence in the first place, because of what he called the commercial nature of the Internet; and it is worth noting that when McChesney wanted to dampen Internet enthusiasm, he sometimes, as in the following passage, tried to dampen it on the left. In response to Patrick Barkham's 1998 *Guardian* article, "Dissidents and Defiants Slipping through the Net," and its citation of the political uses to which Zapatistas and Indonesian student protesters, among others, had put the Internet, McChesney wrote:

> When the Internet is viewed in this manner, it is hard not to see it as constituting the basis for a genuine revolution in information dissemination with striking and world historical implications for politics. This is the Internet that has enthralled the Tofflers and Negropontes and Gilders—the utopian futurologists—for the past decade. And the strength of this vision is that it has an important element of truth.
>
> But this point should not be exaggerated. Having a website does not mean many people will know of its existence and therefore seek it out. We should not extrapolate from the experiences of a small community of activists to think that this will become the heart and soul of the Internet experience. It has not and it will not. (*Rich Media, Poor Democracy*, 176)

With those last three words, McChesney undertakes his own foray into futurology—an especially risky enterprise with regard to something as amorphous as the Internet. He then proceeds to argue that the commercial nature of the Internet will guarantee that political activism will be kept to the margins:

> Despite its much-ballyhooed "openness," to the extent that it becomes a viable mass medium, it will likely be dominated by the usual corporate suspects. Certainly a few new commercial content players will emerge, but the evidence suggests that the content of the digital communication world will appear quite similar to the content of the pre-digital commercial media world. (183)

Unsurprisingly, this is the line adopted by Herman and Chomsky as well, in their new (2002) introduction to *Manufacturing Consent: The Political Economy of the Mass Media:*

> The Internet is not an instrument of mass communication for those lacking brand names, an already existing large audience, and/or large resources. Only sizable commercial organizations have been able to

make large numbers aware of the existence of their Internet offerings. The privatization of the Internet's hardware, the rapid commercialization and concentration of Internet portals and servers and their integration into non-Internet conglomerates—the AOL-Time Warner merger was but a giant step in that direction—and the private and concentrated control of the new broadband technology, together threaten to limit any future prospects of the Internet as a democratic media vehicle. (xvi)

Let me be clear about what I am and am not saying about online media, because there are many ways to take this argument, and I want to head a few of them off at the pass if I can. My point is not that McChesney, like Herman and Chomsky, failed to see the blogosphere coming out of nowhere; my point is not that the blogosphere, by itself, can serve as a counterweight to all the many failures of American mass media and mainstream journalism; and my point is not that McChesney is wrong about the media. Quite the contrary: as McChesney writes in *The Problem of the Media,* "arguably the weakest feature of U.S. professional journalism has been its coverage of the nation's role in the world, especially when military action is involved. . . . Most major U.S. wars over the past century have been sold to the public on dubious claims if not outright lies, yet professional journalism has generally failed to warn the public" (74). My argument with McChesney, rather, is that this mode of cultural analysis, like the mode in which one declares that "vulgarity" is the product of corporations, proceeds from the belief that we know the meaning of a mass-cultural artifact or phenomenon once we have understood the "political economy" that has produced it. The vulgar aspects of our culture are vulgar because they are corporate; the detrimental aspects of the Internet will be detrimental because they are commercial—and they will seek to "limit" (according to the propaganda model of mass media) the prospects of the Internet as a "democratic media vehicle." In response to this reductive theory of media, cultural studies theorists are right to insist that we do not know the meaning of a mass-cultural artifact or phenomenon until we find out something about how people participate in it.

And the reason this point is worth making—even by someone who largely agrees with McChesney and Chomsky about the sorry state of American mass media—is that this is not simply a theoretical dispute between cultural studies scholars and left-leaning communications theorists. It is central to how the American left should think about democracy. For according to the McChesney-Frank thesis, corporate capitalism is ultimately the reason that the American left is so feeble a political force: the mass of ordinary people might agree with us—we suspect many of them already do—but they are thwarted, confused, and misled by the corporate media. In other words, this line of argument assumes the very thing it needs to explain: where Stuart Hall saw the rise of Thatcherism as a crisis *for the left*, something that shook (or should have shaken) leftist assumptions to the core, requiring left intellectuals to reexamine just where they'd gone wrong and why and how it was that the New Right could appeal to ordinary people we think should be our natural allies, Robert McChesney sees right-wing populism as an epiphenomenon of the corporate media, and Thomas Frank ascribes the phenomenon of working-class conservatism to "derangement," to a cultural backlash against vulgar corporate culture, and to a feckless Democratic Party that has forsaken economic egalitarianism under pressure from corporate lobbyists. This line of argument, in effect, lets the left off the hook altogether: avoiding the question of how the left can win the hearts and minds of the ordinary people in whose names *we* presume to speak, it reassures us that the left is right to speak in the names of the people even—or especially—if the people themselves don't see it that way.

There is no question that mass media can and do dupe people. But that does not mean that the "media dupe people" theory should stand in for sustained left analysis of how the winning of popular consent actually works in civil society; for when that theory becomes axiomatic, it degenerates into an all-purpose excuse for the left's many strategies of self-marginalization. Conversely, when the "active audience" theory becomes axiomatic, it degenerates into meaningless celebrations of "tiny victories" and countercultural "tactics" that have no bearing whatsoever on any imaginable "war of position." But the fact remains that millions of ordinary Americans know perfectly well that much of the American mass media failed the country during the Clinton impeachment, during the 2000 election, and (most spectacularly) during the buildup to war in Iraq. And the fact remains that thousands among those millions took matters into their own hands and created an online grassroots movement to counter the sorry state of the American commentariat, to try to swing the Democratic Party leftward, and to create cultural networks to the left of the Democrats that can develop nonelectoral forms of progressive politics. Although people can be and often are misled by mass media, many of them are not; both online and off, therefore, active audiences sometimes engage in meaningful political activity—and the left ignores the activity of active media audiences at its peril.

CULTURAL STUDIES AND GLOBAL CULTURE WARS

But do the 1990s culture-wars debates on the left have any bearing on the question of how to understand global conflict after 9/11? In some ways, obviously not: first, people who were antagonists in the culture wars found themselves allies (pro or con) with regard to war in Iraq. And the "cultural left" versus "reformist left" formation in the United States was a comparatively parochial affair, devoted almost exclusively to the question of how to think about American public policy and the claims of ethnic and sexual minorities in American culture. Finally, even the terms in which Nancy Fraser attempted to adjudicate the dispute don't map very well onto international relations: it is difficult to assess the merits and drawbacks of war in Iraq, for example, or the claims of a global "responsibility to protect" vulnerable populations from ethnic cleansing and genocide, in terms of the politics of recognition and the politics of redistribution—which suggests that the recognition/redistribution schema is better suited to a conception of politics *within* a state (or whatever entity is charged with managing the distribution and redistribution of goods and resources) than to a conception of politics *between* states. And yet, even though it was largely a parochially liberal-nationalist enterprise, the "two lefts" debate of the 1990s had fascinating and underrecognized implications for the American left's approach to international affairs.

For one thing, the question of how to think about multiculturalism is not—except, of course, for the most egregious American exceptionalists—specific to the United States: it has everything to do with multiculturalism in Europe, and, beyond that, the broader question of how to negotiate cultural and religious identities in a common society. For as Hall argued in an eloquent 1993 essay, there is no reason to conflate "common culture" with "common society" and every reason to maintain a clear conceptual and legal distinction between the two:

> It should not be necessary to look, walk, feel, think, speak exactly like a paid-up member of the buttoned-up, stiff-upper-lipped, fully corseted "free-born Englishman" *culturally* to be accorded either the informal courtesy and respect of civilized social intercourse or the rights of

> entitlement and citizenship. . . . Far from collapsing the complex ques-
> tions of cultural identity and issues of social and political rights, what
> we need now is *greater distance between them.* We need to be able to in-
> sist that rights of citizenship and the incommensurabilities of cultural
> difference are respected and that *the one is not made a condition of the*
> *other.* ("Culture, Community, Nation," 360–61)

The alternative, of course, is to predicate the rights of citizenship on the
denial or eradication of cultural difference and to argue that common social and political rights need to be based on cultural homogeneity. (In the
United States, Samuel Huntington's 2004 book *Who Are We?* is a notable
recent addition to this literature of ethnic nationalism.)

But just as it is not always possible in practice to separate recognition
harms from redistribution harms, it is not always possible in practice to
maintain a healthy distance between the complex questions of cultural
identity and issues of social and political rights—as we are reminded every time a controversy erupts around a ban on head scarves in French
public schools or the dismissal of a British schoolteacher for wearing the
full *niqab.* These controversies are not only matters of "tolerance" with regard to Muslim minorities in Western secular democratic states, as if that
were not volatile enough in and of itself; they pose exceptionally difficult
questions about what kinds of "incommensurable cultural difference" do
and do not make claims on a state's common social foundations. (In the
United States, the state will not intervene if a group worships Moloch or
eschews modern technology; it will if a group practices polygamy or denies life-saving medical care to its children.) Such complexities are not
well served by the rantings of nativists who fear that multiculturalism is
a smokescreen for the Islamist plan to subjugate the globe to shari'a law;
nor are they well addressed by left-relativists who insist that any concern about the fate of women, gays, and lesbians in theocratic societies is
"imperialist."

And for another thing, the culture wars are not confined to debates
about multiculturalism and liberal tolerance, incommensurable cultures
and common societies; at their broadest reach, they have everything to do
with 9/11 and with the rise of Islamist radicalism, and they point to the
deeply contradictory nature of capitalism's relation to religious and cultural fundamentalisms. As Ellen Willis well knew, the culture wars are a
global phenomenon; moreover, they cannot ultimately be referred to the
evils of neoliberalism. Willis writes:

Another left rationale for rejecting cultural politics is rooted in the historical connection of cultural movements to the marketplace. The rise of capitalism, which undermined the authority of the patriarchal family and church, put widespread cultural revolt in the realm of possibility. Wage labor allowed women and young people to find a means of support outside the home. Urbanization allowed people the freedom of social anonymity. The shift from production- to consumption-oriented capitalism and the spread of mass media encouraged cultural permissiveness, since the primary technique of marketing as well as the most salient attraction of mass art is their appeal to the desire for individual autonomy and specifically to erotic fantasy.

Accordingly, left cultural conservatives have argued that feminism and cultural radicalism, in weakening traditional institutions like the family, have merely contributed to the market's hegemony over all spheres of life. . . . This mindset puts a progressive political gloss on what is really a form of puritanism, offended by the fleshpots of the market, not just the profits. What it ignores, or denies—as Marx never did—is the paradoxical nature of capitalism. In destroying the old patriarchal order, in making all that was solid melt into air, in fomenting constant dynamism and change, capital made space for the revolutionary ideas that would challenge its own authority. In letting loose the genie of desire in the service of profit, consumer culture unleashes forces that can't reliably be controlled. ("Escape from Freedom," 17–18)

Willis's argument is of a piece with Hall's recognition that the postwar boom in Western capitalist states "'loosed' many individuals into a life somewhat less constrained, less puritanically regulated, less strictly imposed than it had been three or four decades before" (*Hard Road to Renewal*, 215)—and, on another plane, of a piece with the Tom Tomorrow cartoon in which Uncle Sam champions America's dissidents, feminists, GLBT activists, and atheists.

Moreover, it points to a larger problem with the anticapitalist critique: just as, on Moishe Postone's reading ("History and Helplessness"), the "anti-imperialist" left misapplies the Cold War paradigm to the post-Soviet world, failing to distinguish between left and right variants of anti-Americanism (or denying the distinction altogether) and failing to see that the left has no business expressing "solidarity" with figures like Milošević or Muqtada al-Sadr, the anticapitalist critique fails to entertain the idea that the left has no business signing on to a campaign against cultural "vulgarity" that appeals to cultural reactionaries at home or abroad. (Further down that road waits Dinesh D'Souza [*Enemy at Home*], ready and willing to argue that Islamists are right to recoil at Western cultural depravity.) In both cases, an inattention to—or ignorance of—the work of British cultural studies on the complexity of hegemony and the contradictions of capitalism leads the American (and British) left into manifestly inadequate and incoherent readings of the relation of culture to politics.

And to return, one last time with feeling, to the weeks and months after 9/11: it was partly an inattention to (or ignorance of) the work of British cultural studies on the challenge of how to operate in the court of public opinion in the middle of a Great Moving Right Show that led the Manichean left to try to acquaint Americans with the sordid history of American foreign policy in the most histrionic and hyperbolic fashion, proclaiming on the afternoon of the attacks that they may not amount to the horror of the al-Shifa bombing and then proclaiming at the outset of the war in Afghanistan that U.S. actions constituted a silent genocide. It was a mistake on the part of some members of the democratic left to reply to these Chomskian provocations by urging the American left to be more "patriotic"; the best response to such declarations, instead, was to point out that they lacked the merit of being true, as well as the merit of being persuasive. That is to say: it is sometimes the case that intellectuals on the left have the difficult task of uttering profoundly unpopular truths. To do otherwise, in such cases, is to give in to the contemptible focus-group-polling kind of logic that prevented John Kerry from uttering the words "Abu Ghraib" during the presidential campaign of 2004. But "al-Shifa was worse than 9/11" and "Afghanistan constitutes a silent genocide" are not the same kind of utterance as "the United States has set up a network of detention-and-torture camps that defy international law." The latter is a simple statement of fact, to which millions of people on the left, inside the United States and outside, have rallied in outrage; the first two are judgment calls that betray highly questionable political judgment.

So why does the Manichean left in the United States say such things? Perhaps, as I try to suggest throughout this book, it is because that left operates as if it is living inside the Matrix, surrounded by people who *should* be on their side—and probably are, if only the benighted people themselves knew it—but are trapped helplessly inside a system so powerful as to induce mass delusions that the deluded will defend to the death. But this hypothesis has a couple of corollaries. One is that the Matrix thesis does important cultural work: it reassures the Manichean left that the task of winning popular consent for its arguments is a mug's game, rigged against them by a corporate media that will never allow The People to realize their true interests. "Consent" in mass culture is *manufactured*, not won, and it is manufactured by media and political elites. Consequently (and this is another corollary to the Matrix hypothesis), this wing of the left does not so much as try to appeal to the unconverted; on the contrary, they speak to provoke the outrage and disbelief of the unconverted.

For when Chomsky replies to the unconverted, it is to point out to them the extent to which they demonstrate the depravity of the prevailing moral and intellectual culture. And then, when, in response, the unconverted recoil, their recoiling confirms the vanguard Manichean left's faith in the essential rightness of its beliefs. At this point (and it is stunning how common this trope is; it appears even in McChesney's "Is There Any Hope for Cultural Studies?") the Manichean left trots out the analogy to slavery, likening itself to the abolitionist left that spoke profoundly unpopular truths to power and knew that it would be fully vindicated many years hence. Thus Ed Herman paints the "cruise missile left" as equivocators on slavery and casts himself as an antebellum freedom fighter:

> One can readily imagine the Cooper, Gitlin, Walzer, Bérubé, and Hitchens equivalents of the 1850s explaining to the abolitionists that they must tone down their message and alter or even drop their anti-racist and anti-slavery message given the "political realities" and public sentiment. But then, as now, a genuine left focuses on the struggle against basic exploitative and unjust policies and structures—it does not give up its radical educational and organizing role in order to win transitory victories and gain access and approval from the mainstream. ("Cruise Missile Left: Aligning with Power")

This analogy between defenders of slavery and advocates of the overthrow of the Taliban is ludicrous on its face, especially because it enables Herman to camouflage his indifference to the plight of Afghan women in the language of antiracism. But this move, too, does important cultural work: it not only enables the Manichean left to indulge in the classic Huckleberry Finn scenario—that is, the retrospective fantasy that if *they'd* been around in the antebellum United States, *they'd* have done the right thing, even if they believed that it entailed their eternal damnation—but also allows the Manicheans to avoid the obvious alternative: namely, that they would very likely have been, in the late 1850s, the kind of "radicals" who would argue that the election of 1860 is unimportant and that the so-called struggle to preserve the so-called Union is really just a campaign to expand federal power over the states and prepare the way for the United States to compete with the European powers in the global imperialism sweepstakes.

The Matrix theory of mass media is diametrically opposed to the project Stuart Hall and other British cultural studies theorists set out for themselves a generation ago—the project of understanding how a historic bloc works to win popular consent in modern democracies, by means of the mass media and other key institutions in civil society. It is also, crucially, a handy self-exculpatory device for the left's many failures in the public sphere—because those "failures," it turns out, are really signs of the left's refusal to bend with the political winds and tailor its message for the "mainstream." As I suggest throughout this book, this determination to snatch an ultimately self-confirming victory from the jaws of political defeat will be familiar enough to anyone who has followed the alternative music scene or the history of the postwar counterculture: the only thing that gives pause to countercultural revolutionaries, after all, is the sinking feeling that *too many people* are coming around to their side. For vanguardism in politics as for vanguardism in (un)popular culture, nothing fails like success, and nothing succeeds like failure.

Since the 1980s, both in academe and among the general reading public, "cultural studies" in the United States has become all but synonymous with the study of popular culture. Stuart Hall's weary response to this development speaks for itself: "I don't have words to describe that; I really cannot read another cultural studies analysis of Madonna or *The Sopranos*" (McCabe, "Interview with Hall," 29). Along the way, many people in the discipline lost sight of the "and society" part of the "culture and society" tradition and carried on as if competing with rock critics and film reviewers for commentary on hot new releases was, in and of itself, a form of politics (while defending the enterprise from anyone who would care to call it merely *cultural* politics). About that much, Robert McChesney and Thomas Frank are right. But their response has been to dismiss not only cultural studies' commitment to cultural analysis but also cultural studies' warnings about the dangers of theoretical reductionism. The result has been that politically reductive habits of thinking on the left have gone unchallenged, and left media theorists continue to operate as if the contemporary political landscape in the United States can be accounted for by the fact that the mass media are owned by large corporations. But time and again over the course of its history, from the invasion of Hungary to the rise of Thatcherism to the debates over multiculturalism and nationalism, cultural studies has aimed precisely to counter both reductionism and vanguardism on the left and to devise accounts of culture and society whose complexity does justice to the complexity of the actual workings of culture and society.

Can cultural studies revive that legacy today? Absolutely: it's never too late for antireductionist, antivanguardist ways of thinking. The antireductionism of cultural studies can serve as a useful corrective to the Manichean left's positions on foreign policy and to its blame-the-corporate-media-Matrix position in domestic and global affairs. But I hope also that the antivanguardism of cultural studies can help clear the way for a democratic American left that is undeceived about the darkest aspects of American history and American foreign policy—and that, in contrast to the countercultural left, is willing to construe popular consent *as* popular consent (rather than as propaganda); to understand popular success *as* popular success (rather than as failure); and to work through the apparatus of the state and the institutions of civil society for popular consent and success. Call it a particularly audacious kind of hope—a hope that requires both an optimism of the will and an optimism of the intellect.

CONCLUSION EQUALITY AND FREEDOM

ELLEN WILLIS'S INTELLECTUAL inspirations were not those of Stuart Hall. Where Hall looked back to Gramsci, Raymond Williams, E. P. Thompson, and C. L. R. James, Willis blended a feminist "cultural radicalism" with the Reichian conviction that political oppression has its origins in sexual repression. And Ellen Willis's background is not that of Stuart Hall: Willis grew up in Queens, New York, the daughter of a New York City police officer, and got her start writing rock criticism for the *New Yorker*; Hall was born in Kingston, Jamaica, almost ten years earlier and took a Rhodes Scholarship to Oxford. But however circuitous their journeys, they often wound up in the same place.

I rely on Hall and Willis at critical moments throughout this book, and I stake a great deal on the claim that the left they inhabit is distinct from and in many ways opposed to the left I designate as Manichean. But if I'm going to advocate an optimism of the will and an optimism of the intellect, I have to acknowledge that neither Willis nor Hall offers me a model of good cheer. Hall's 2007 interview with Colin McCabe is shot through with disappointment and disillusionment, as it closes with the grim determination that "we have to take hope where we can get it" (42). And, according to Stanley Aronowitz, Willis found hope to be in short supply:

> She was depressed by her perception that, however much she was "admired," her ideas had been effectively excluded from the public conversation, that few of her generation or the next had taken up her attempts to link freedom and equality, to raise the most fundamental questions of human relations. I cannot avoid the conclusion that, despite her incredible talents and achievements, at the deepest level she died of despair. ("Free Woman")

Aronowitz's account is especially moving, not only because he was Willis's husband (obviously enough) but also because he seems to be right on the merits: Willis was indeed "admired," but even her most brilliant work did not shape public conversation, and in academic circles she never received anything like the attention she deserved.

Willis's despair and Hall's discouragement are not merely personal matters. Disappointment and disillusionment seem endemic to left intellectuals, and why not? Certainly the radical egalitarians who lived through the tumult of 1968 only to see Reagan, Kohl, and Thatcher ride the backlash to power in the next dozen years had every reason to feel betrayed by their own fondest hopes. Nor is this a purely generational phenomenon: though I was but six years old in May 1968, I look at Israel and Palestine, or India and Pakistan, or global climate change and the mass extinction of species, or dwindling supplies of oil and (beyond that) fresh water, and I wonder where, precisely, we are to find hope so that we can take it where we get it. One does not want to believe that one is living in the era of Peak Hope, and that from here it will be available only in dwindling supplies, that it's all downhill from here for us as a species. Resisting that belief, for left intellectuals, means resisting some very familiar modes of leftist discouragement and despair, modes to which all too many leftists have become habituated since the 1960s.

I think there is only one viable way of resisting that belief, one way to imagine a left that manages to pull us, collectively, back from the brink. Those wings of the left that think globally as a matter of course—the fair-trade left and the ecological-sustainability left—must work in concert with the wing of the left that seeks to shore up international institutions and global human rights. As I acknowledge in chapter 3, the commitment to human rights and supranational legal structures seems too thin and wonky to some activists, less substantial and immediate than providing impoverished humans and endangered ecosystems with the necessities for sustenance. But without a viable international legal framework for realizing the global left's fondest hopes, international agreements about resources, carbon emissions, and fair trade are simply unworkable. Human life on the planet will slowly succumb to a series of tragedies of the commons combined with fierce and escalating conflicts over identity, ethnicity, nationality—and, of course, resources.

Unless, that is, humans devise a strong, reliable, international framework that can override the policies of rogue nations, including—when it behaves like a rogue nation—the United States itself. I think it might even be possible to argue that such a framework would be in the long-term interests of Americans as well, insofar as it would serve as a device for mediating international conflict long after the American empire has dissipated—for surely the American empire, like its predecessors, will eventually pass from the Earth. The United States had the good sense, after the devastation of World War II, to try to create such an institution; but that institution, the United Nations, is deeply structurally flawed—and, of course, its composition is based on the power arrangements that obtained in the aftermath of that war. Still, it is possible to appeal, even in the heart of the empire, to the millions of Americans who believe that the world is not well governed by empires. And in that sense I agree completely with Chomsky: if the choice is one between world domination and survival, I would prefer survival. What I have in mind is a robust international framework that makes possible fair trade and equitable economic development—and forbids violations of women's human rights while hauling Bush and Cheney into the Hague for trial as war criminals. For although much of the left tends to prefer movement politics to electoral politics, changes in the base—the global base—require changes in the superstructure as well.

But lest this sound *too* superstructural, as if all would be well if only Human Rights Watch ran the world, I turn to Ellen Willis one last time, as a reminder that her form of "cultural radicalism" understood that thinking globally was a matter of thinking culturally:

> The cultural radical impulse is rooted in the core elements of the democratic ideal: equality and freedom. There is a clear logic in the progression from affirming that all men are created equal, with the right to choose their government, enjoy freedom of speech and religion, and pursue happiness, to demanding that these rights apply to racial minorities, women, homosexuals, young people, atheists and other groups in one way or another denied them; that the challenge to oppressive authority extend beyond government to institutions like the corporation, the family, and the church; that the pursuit of happiness include freedom from sexual restrictions dictated by patriarchal religious norms; that free speech include explicitly sexual and anti-religious speech. Such demands, however, challenge not only deep structures of social privilege and subordination but our very definition of morality. All of us living in Judeo-Christian or Islamic cultures have imbibed from infancy a conception of sexuality—and desire more generally—as dangerous and destructive unless strictly controlled, of repression and self-sacrifice as indispensable virtues. Movements that

encourage us to fulfill our desires are bound to arouse conflicting emotions, to intensify people's yearnings for freedom and pleasure, but also their anxiety and guilt about such primal rebellion. An outpouring of social experiment and innovation liberates creative energies, but also rage—at oppression, at losses of status and privilege, at the sources of anxiety and confusion. Cultural radical demands immediately question and disrupt existing social institutions, yet building democratic alternatives is a long-term affair: this leaves painful gaps in which men and women don't know how to behave with each other, in which marriage can no longer provide a stable environment for children but it's not clear what to do instead. Is it really surprising that cultural revolution should cause conflict?

To argue that this conflict has no political significance is to say that democratic values have none—never mind the blood and passion expended by democrats and their enemies. ("Escape from Freedom," 10)

Willis is arguing here with Thomas Frank—and, with what must have been a profound sense of discouragement and weariness, with all the leftists whose economic-majoritarian arguments she'd addressed between 1980 and 1998, only to find them cheering for Frank's book in 2004 as if it were the bold new analysis of what ails the U.S. left.

But, importantly, Willis offers here and throughout her work a standard for the democratic left that applies to every inhabited spot on the globe. Like Hall, Willis knew that the right had successfully coopted the left's language of freedom and had rearticulated it to a program that is both culturally and economically anti-egalitarian—and that purchased its anti-egalitarianism by ridiculing the very notion of the common good. And yet in response to the right's hegemonic project, the Manichean left set about reinventing the same old triangular wheel that didn't work the first eighty times it hit the road: dismissing "freedom" as a bourgeois mystification, aligning it with free-market neoliberalism, and chortling over its invocation by hypocritical and opportunistic conservatives. The result has been a reactionary wing of the left that has largely abandoned the idea of opposing tyranny and genocide and taken the disaster in Iraq as license for giving up on the idea of creating and sustaining international institutions for freedom, equality, and justice. But what good is a left that opposes tyranny and genocide *only under certain circumstances*? Would anyone on the left think for a moment of defending—or just remaining neutral with regard to—some forms of mass starvation or ecological devastation?

The Bush-Cheney administration did the American democratic left the favor of reminding us why we are right to cherish freedom of speech, freedom of religion, freedom of assembly, the freedom of the press, the freedom to petition the government for the redress of grievances, and the freedom of the people to be secure in their persons, houses, papers, and effects against unreasonable searches and seizures; and why we are right to append to these essential freedoms the third and fourth of Franklin D. Roosevelt's famous four—the freedom from want and the freedom from fear. For those are freedoms that go well beyond the demand that rich and poor alike should have freedom of expression; their realization would require changes in the global order so radical that even some radicals might be willing to speak approvingly of them. As well they might: after 9/11, after Guantánamo, after Iraq, the left must take back the language and the project of human freedom from the right, and they must explain—both to the people on the right who, out of fear or hatred, support detention-and-torture camps and to fellow leftists who are, as Hall put it, scornful of civil liberties until they find themselves badly in need of some—how freedom of speech, freedom of religion, freedom from want, and freedom from fear are legitimate aspirations anywhere on Earth.

That then is my hope: for a democratic-socialist, internationalist left that seeks not to smash the state and crush capitalism but to pursue human equality and realize the four freedoms. It would not be a fully "socialist" left in the sense that it would not institute central economic planning; it would be aggressively redistributionist, and it would harbor no illusions about "free" markets. It would insist that food, shelter, education, and medical care are human rights and, as such, must not be contingent on anyone's ability to pay for them; it would put workers in control of factories and companies; and it would recognize, as well, that some industries—the financial sector most especially—cannot be trusted to regulate themselves. It would therefore establish an egalitarian, closely monitored and regulated market that fosters innovations and promotes policies that bring food, clean water, housing, schooling, and medicine to all, as well as establishing forms of political democracy that extend to every person born: male and female, straight and gay. This would be something of a disappointment to those radicals whose utopian longings lead them to cry, "be realistic, demand the impossible"; but it would be so radically different from the world we now inhabit that it might actually engage the radical imagination. For just after the Manichean left objects that my democratic-socialist internationalist left is the result of impoverished thinking, confined by narrow bounds of the thinkable, a capitalism with a human face and a denial of emancipatory horizons and desires, it will insist that such a left is *unrealistic*. To which the only sensible reply of a democratic-socialist internationalist left can be: very well then, let us be unrealistic. Let us make such a world possible.

NOTES

INTRODUCTION

1. See also the critique of Western intellectuals who cast the defense of Rushdie as a form of Western ethnocentrism in Brenkman, "Extreme Criticism."

2. For Cheney's relation to Mylroie, see Bergen, "Armchair Provocateur":

> Mylroie became enamored of her theory that Saddam was the master mind of a vast anti-U.S. terrorist conspiracy in the face of virtually all evidence and expert opinion to the contrary. In what amounts to the discovery of a unified field theory of terrorism, Mylroie believes that Saddam was not only behind the '93 Trade Center attack, but also every anti-American terrorist incident of the past decade, from the bombings of U.S. embassies in Kenya and Tanzania to the leveling of the federal building in Oklahoma City to September 11 itself. She is, in short, a crackpot, which would not be significant if she were merely advising say, Lyndon LaRouche. But her neocon friends who went on to run the war in Iraq believed her theories, bringing her on as a consultant at the Pentagon, and they seem to continue to entertain her eccentric belief that Saddam is the fount of the entire shadow war against America. . . . Around the second anniversary of 9/11, Vice President Dick Cheney continued to echo Mylroie's utterances when he told NBC's Tim Russert that Iraq was "the geographic base of the terrorists who have had us under assault for many years, but most especially on 9/11," a demonstrably false theory that Mylroie has been vigorously touting since this past summer.

For a stringent critique of Bush's signing statements, see Savage, *Takeover;* for the administration's faux news reports and payoffs to journalists, see Pear, "U.S. Videos, for TV News, Come under Scrutiny"; Toppo, "Education Dept. Paid Commentator to Promote Law"; and Goodnough, "U.S. Paid 10 Journalists for Anti-Castro Reports." The best sustained reporting on the corruption of the Department of Justice has been the work of blogger Joshua Micah Marshall of Talking Points Memo. In 2008, that work was recognized by the prestigious George Polk Award for Legal Reporting:

[Marshall's] sites, www.talkingpointsmemo.com and www.tpmMuck-raker.com, led the news media in coverage of the politically motivated dismissals of U.S. attorneys across the country. Noting a similarity between firings in Arkansas and California, Marshall and his staff (with his staff reporter-bloggers Paul Kiel and Justin Rood) connected the dots and found a pattern of federal prosecutors being forced from office for failing to do the Bush Administration's bidding. Marshall's tenacious investigative reporting sparked interest by the traditional news media and led to the resignation of Attorney General Alberto Gonzales. (George Polk Awards in Journalism)

CHAPTER ONE

1. The essay was actually published on December 26, 2004, not February 2005, and its purpose was not to warn Europe's Muslims to end their "ideology of contestation" if they wanted to avoid Marxism's fate of irrelevance. Rather, it argued (rightly) that the most significant dissent from liberal European orthodoxy now comes from Islam rather than Marxism, and it speculated whether this dissent will take "radical" or "pragmatic" form—noting, as well, that many European Marxists eschewed revolution in favor of electoral politics. Smith writes, in relevant part:

> The question is whether Islam in Europe will follow the same path that Communism did here, shedding its revolutionary extremism, electing mayors and legislators and assimilating itself into normal democratic political life. As with Marxism in the 1960's, Islam in Europe has its radical fringe and its pragmatic mainstream. The latter is much the broader, intent on expanding Muslims' political power in French society. It has consciously mimicked many of the tactics of the left, including organizing summer camps where urban young people learn the tenets of the movement. ("Europe's Muslims May Be Headed Where the Marxists Went Before")

2. I need hardly add that if one were to play the whimsical guilt-by-association game with Brennan that Brennan plays with Guinier, one could counterargue that the left should not have any business sympathizing with the people who were so outraged by Waco that they killed 168 people and wounded 800 others in Oklahoma City two years later.

3. The exchange between Professor McIntyre and myself can be found in the comments to Bérubé, "Re-entry," http://www.michaelberube.com/index.php/weblog/comments/993/.

4. Galloway chose to "glorify" Hezbollah and Sheikh Hassan Nasrallah

specifically to protest a recently enacted antiterrorism law in the United Kingdom. According to BBC News, "the bill was introduced after 7 July bomb attacks in London, and Prime Minister Tony Blair said the new law would allow action to be taken against people glorifying those attacks" ("New Terror Law Comes into Force"). Nonetheless, Galloway's choice of sympathies is par for the far-left course in the United Kingdom. For the boycott of Israeli academics, see Baker, "The Boycott of Israeli Academic Institutions"; Jaschik, "British Professors Seek to Cut Ties to Israeli Scholars"; and Jaschik, "British Union Abandons Boycott."

5. The transcript of the exchange is available on Horowitz's website, *Front-Page Magazine*, under the title "The Left Revealed."

6. For her Ahmadinejad worship, see Furuhashi, "Persian Chavez," and Furuhashi, "Ahmadinejad in the Arab Streets." The Srebrenica Research Group's website is http://www.srebrenica-report.com/; for an antidote, see Balkan Witness, at http://www.glypx.com/BalkanWitness/. On Darfur, see Furuhashi, "'Save Darfur': Evangelicals and Establishment Jews," and Furuhashi, "Who Wants Peace in Darfur?"

7. For Bush's "you've covered your ass" remark, see Suskind, *The One Percent Doctrine*, 2. For a critique of 9/11 conspiracy theory as offered by the film *Loose Change*, see Monbiot, "A 9/11 Conspiracy Virus Is Sweeping the World," and the follow-up, "9/11 Fantasists Pose a Mortal Danger."

CHAPTER TWO

1. For example, Finkelstein, "'Fraternally Yours, Chris': Hitchens as Model Apostate":

> A rite of passage for apostates peculiar to U.S. political culture is bashing Noam Chomsky. It's the political equivalent of a bar mitzvah, a ritual signaling that one has "grown up"—i.e., grown out of one's "childish" past. It's hard to pick up an article or book by ex-radicals—Gitlin's *Letters to a Young Activist,* Paul Berman's *Terror and Liberalism*—that doesn't include a hysterical attack on him. Behind this venom there's also a transparent psychological factor at play. Chomsky mirrors their idealistic past as well as sordid present, an obstinate reminder that they once had principles but no longer do, that they sold out but he didn't.

2. For such a critique of Foucault, see Windschuttle, *Killing of History*; for Chomsky, see Collier and Horowitz, *The Anti-Chomsky Reader*. Most notoriously, for Said, see Weiner, "'My Beautiful Old House' and Other Fabrications"; for a sense of Weiner's methodology, see Offman, "Said Critic Blasts Back at Hitchens":

> Christopher Hitchens told Salon Books that he believes that it is

Weiner's article that is disingenuous, if not negligent. "It doesn't deserve to be called a hatchet job because it is so inept," he said. . . . Hitchens also emphasizes that by neglecting to incorporate the material in Said's memoir—which comes out on Sept. 24—Weiner displays his invidious intentions. "If you're going to produce a long piece that says that somebody has totally fabricated their past, and you know that their memoir is about to come out, you have two courses of action. One is that I'd better publish this as soon as possible and spoil the publication of the book—or try to. The other is that I'd better hold up until I get ahold of the copy and check it against what I've got." Charles Lane, editor of the *New Republic,* confirms rumors that his magazine was offered Weiner's essay before *Commentary.* Lane says that Weiner had refused to "look at the galley of Said's memoir and take it into account. Discussions broke off at that point." Weiner then brought the story to *Commentary.*

3. Before his work on the Balkans, Chomsky's critics on the democratic left focused on his response to the aftermath of the Vietnam War—specifically, his convoluted attempt to assess (though some would simply say "minimize") the atrocities of the Khmer Rouge and the killing fields of Cambodia (Chomsky and Herman, "Distortions at Fourth Hand"). This essay has been the source of much controversy, as have Chomsky's subsequent defenses of the essay. I venture only one remark about it here. It seems to me to stop far short of apologetics for Pol Pot (the most incendiary charge against the essay), but it certainly does attempt to cast doubt on the reports of Cambodian refugees and to suggest that reports of genocidal mass murder in Cambodia are the work of a Western propaganda machine that overlooked U.S. bombing in Cambodia but now sees an opportunity for scoring political points against a declared enemy. This passage in particular seems to me every bit as problematic as its most severe critics claim:

> Nor is there any discussion in the *Times* of the "case of the missing bloodbath," although forecasts of a holocaust were urged by the U.S. leadership, official experts and the mass media over the entire course of the war in justifying our continued military presence. On the other hand, protests by some former anti-war individuals against alleged human rights violations in Vietnam are given generous coverage. This choice of subject may be the only basis on which U.S.—as opposed to Soviet—dissidents can get serious attention in the mass media today. (789)

The quotation marks around "case of the missing bloodbath" suggest not only that there has been no bloodbath in Cambodia but that the phrase is not the work of Chomsky and Herman; and the reference to "alleged human rights violations in Vietnam" (as well as the insinuation that people who bring such things to light are "former" antiwar individuals who now seek serious attention in the mass media) is unworthy of any leftist.

For their part, Chomsky and Herman have responded vigorously to critiques of their work on genocide in Cambodia, both in the two-volume *Political Economy of Human Rights* (Chomsky and Herman) and in *Manufacturing Consent* (Herman and Chomsky), where they write that critics of their work "provide an intriguing expression of what, in other contexts, is described as the totalitarian mentality: it is not enough to denounce official enemies; it is also necessary to guard with vigilance the right to lie in the service of power" (282). It remains unclear to this day, however, how many people who called attention to the Cambodian genocide were lying in the service of power.

4. "When asked if someone put a gun to his head and told him to vote for either Gore or Bush, which would he choose, Nader answered without hesitation: 'Bush'" (Heinrichs, "All Bulworth, No Rhythm"). See also Nader's 2004 interview with Patrick Buchanan in *American Conservative*, "Ralph Nader: Conservatively Speaking." On abortion, Nader states: "I believe in choice. I don't think government should tell women to have children or not to have children. I am also against feticide. If doctors think it is a fetus, that should be banned. It is a medical decision." I doubt that it is possible to pack more incoherence into forty words.

5. Chomsky's citation of the *American Prospect* is especially sloppy—perhaps necessarily so, since the magazine consistently opposed the Iraq war on principle and refused to credit the Bush administration's rationale for it. Chomsky seems to focus here on the phrase "trigger a democratic revolution across the Arab world," as if *American Prospect* itself believed this to be the real reason for the war. The Michael Steinberger essay from which this phrase is taken, however, is actually a critique of Colin Powell, and it concludes:

> On the most critical issue confronting the United States, the rise of Islamic fundamentalist terrorism, Powell helped Bush implement a course of action conceived by the neocons. What he didn't do—because he couldn't—was propose a different course of action that might have led to the same goal of political reform in the Arab world but that wouldn't have involved waging an unpopular war *on a trumped-up pretext,* a war that has extracted an enormous cost in American lives and American prestige. ("Misoverestimated"; emphasis added)

It is difficult to assess Chomsky's attempt to construe this essay as an example of "criticism praising the nobility of [Bush's] vision but warning that it may be beyond our means" unless one understands the "I alone have escaped to tell thee" trope.

6. Chomsky implies that the United States blocked a U.N. inquiry into the *consequences* of the al-Shifa bombing. The 1999 Human Rights Watch report on the Sudan makes clear, however, that the blocked inspection concerned the

rationale for the bombing and surely would have (rightly) embarrassed U.S. intelligence:

> The Sudanese war and famine were overtaken on August 20 by the bombing without warning by the United States of a privately-owned pharmaceutical plant in Khartoum on August 20. The attack was in response to the August 7 terrorist bombing of two U.S. embassies in Africa that killed hundreds and injured thousands. The United States alleged that Osama bin Laden masterminded these attacks and had an interest in the factory; bin Laden, a financier of "Afghan Arabs" and other Islamist militants, lived in Khartoum until 1996. He had been stripped of his Saudi citizenship earlier. The United States claimed the factory contained a precursor to deadly nerve gas and was linked to Iraq, but would not accept a U.N. chemical weapons inspection of the bombing site after the attack. (76)

7. Possibly, the Chomskian left will dispute, even now, that the human toll of 9/11 exceeds that of the al-Shifa bombing. But it is worth attending carefully to the logic Chomsky employs in his assessment of the consequences of the al-Shifa bombing, because if we were to apply that logic to 9/11 (that is, assigning to al-Qaeda's attack all the many consequences of 9/11), then we would actually wind up blaming bin Laden for the U.S. invasion of Iraq and for all the destruction and devastation that followed. Chomsky's method of tallying cumulative consequences, in other words, involves a slippery and malleable principle.

8. Unlike Chomsky, the 1999 Human Rights Watch report on the Sudan takes stock of bombings other than that of al-Shifa, noting that "the Sudan government bombed its own civilian population in the south, east, and in the Nuba Mountains. Among numerous such bombings was the March 1998 bombing of a hospital in Yei, southern Sudan, killing seven and wounding others; the hospital was bombed again in September, killing one. In the first few months of 1998, fourteen relief sites in southern Sudan were bombed by the government." The Casey-Chomsky exchange has been taken down from the *ZNet* website but is available through the Internet Archive (colloquially known as the "Wayback Machine"), at http://www.archive.org/index.php.

9. Earlier in the interview, Brzezinski explicitly claims that American aid to the mujahadeen preceded (and attempted to provoke) the Soviet invasion:

> *Question:* The former director of the CIA, Robert Gates, stated in his memoirs [*From the Shadows*] that American intelligence services began to aid the *Mujahadeen* in Afghanistan 6 months before the Soviet intervention. In this period you were the national security adviser to President [Jimmy] Carter. You therefore played a role in this affair. Is that correct?

Brzezinski: Yes. According to the official version of history, CIA aid to the *Mujahadeen* began during 1980, that is to say, after the Soviet army invaded Afghanistan, 24 Dec 1979. But the reality, secretly guarded until now, is completely otherwise. Indeed, it was July 3, 1979 that President Carter signed the first directive for secret aid to the opponents of the pro-Soviet regime in Kabul. And that very day, I wrote a note to the president in which I explained to him that in my opinion this aid was going to induce a Soviet military intervention.

Question: Despite this risk, you were an advocate of this covert action. But perhaps you yourself desired this Soviet entry into war and looked to provoke it?

Brzezinski: It isn't quite that. We didn't push the Russians to intervene, but we knowingly increased the probability that they would. (273)

10. There remained, however, the question of whether the Soviet Union would stop in Afghanistan or proceed to Pakistan—just as, a decade later, the United States and its allies faced the question of whether Saddam's invasion of Kuwait was a prelude to an invasion of Saudi Arabia. Interestingly, Alexander Cockburn, who strongly opposed the war in Afghanistan in 2001, did not have quite as much concern for the Afghan people during the Soviet invasion. In his January 21, 1980, "Press Clips" column for the *Village Voice,* Cockburn wrote:

> We all have to go one day, but pray God let it not be over Afghanistan. An unspeakable country filled with unspeakable people, sheepshaggers and smugglers, who have furnished in their leisure hours some of the worst arts and crafts ever to penetrate the occidental world. I yield to none in my sympathy to those prostrate beneath the Russian jackboot, but if ever a country deserved rape it's Afghanistan. Nothing but mountains filled with barbarous ethnics with views as medieval as their muskets, and unspeakably cruel too.

11. Simon Jenkins is not a specialist in the region, but he is a distinguished journalist and former political editor of the *Economist;* elsewhere in these notes, I cite the book he co-wrote in 1983 (Hastings and Jenkins, *The Battle for the Falklands*). The essay from which Chomsky quotes here is an opinion piece published on September 14, 2001 ("America Should Not Squander Its Sympathy"), and not (say) a scholarly study of the history of Afghanistan since the 1970s. In this 1,400-word op-ed, Jenkins is rightly "appalled by the hawkishness of pundits, politicians and commentators" and sensibly insists that "the pursuit of justice should be the essence of the strategy, building on the unprecedented sympathy shown to America throughout the region." But Jenkins's essay has its questionable moments as well, which Chomsky does not question. Notably, the paragraph

that contains the passage quoted by Chomsky manages to suggest that the Soviets never received the credit they deserved for fighting Islamist radicals in Afghanistan: "The Russians spent a decade trying to flush them from the Afghan mountains and were condemned by the West for their troubles. That conflict destroyed a moderate regime and created a fanatical one, from groups recklessly financed by the Americans." Additionally (and altogether tangentially), Jenkins floats an argument that Chomsky would repeat often in the ensuing months: "Britain did not declare war on America or Ireland for harbouring IRA [Irish Republican Army] killers" even though "they caused more deaths, proportionate to population, than were lost in Manhattan." I offer, in response, two readings of this argument: one, it deploys a juvenile debating technique in order to obscure the question at hand ("if harboring terrorists is the issue, what about IRA sympathizers in Boston?") and, two, it misrecognizes the relationship between the Taliban and al-Qaeda, for which there is no analogy whatsoever with the United States and the IRA . Worse still, Jenkins's remark manages to whitewash the history of the British response to Irish radicals. As I argue later in this chapter, Chomsky's account of the IRA is far from coherent, and it is possible that he takes his cue in this regard from opinion pieces like Jenkins's.

12. For a more in-depth analysis of bin Laden's array of motivations, and of the reasons behind U.S. support of Saudi Arabia, see Feher's brilliant essay, "Robert Fisk's Newspapers."

13. Bin Laden's 1998 fatwa does prominently mention the U.S. "occupation" of "the lands of Islam in the holiest of places, the Arabian Peninsula," and insists:

> If the Americans' aims behind these wars are religious and economic, the aim is also to serve the Jews' petty state and divert attention from its occupation of Jerusalem and murder of Muslims there. The best proof of this is their eagerness to destroy Iraq, the strongest neighboring Arab state, and their endeavor to fragment all the states of the region such as Iraq, Saudi Arabia, Egypt, and Sudan into paper statelets and through their disunion and weakness to guarantee Israel's survival and the continuation of the brutal crusade occupation of the Peninsula.

14. Likewise, I do not know what to make of Chomsky's invocation of the IRA in his Radio B92 interview. There, recall, he says that "Europe has suffered murderous destruction, but from internal wars, meanwhile conquering much of the world with extreme brutality. It has not been under attack by its victims outside, with rare exceptions (the IRA in England, for example)." Presumably Chomsky thinks of Ireland as being external to Europe. However, that does not help explain why he believes that the British response to the IRA was "to consider realistically the background concerns and grievances, and try to remedy them."

Notably, when the interview was cleaned up and reproduced in *9–11*, the reference to Ireland was deleted from this passage (12).

15. The paragraphs that follow the announcement of the U.S. demand to interrupt aid convoys, for example, read as follows:

> But Foreign Minister [Abdul] Sattar said today that Pakistan would continue "to exchange views with the government of Afghanistan in a spirit of friendship and fraternity."
>
> He dwelled at length on Pakistan's warm relations with the "Islamic Emirate of Afghanistan," the formal name adopted by the Taliban.
>
> The foreign minister chose that friendly tone despite a warning from the Taliban, issued through its embassy in Islamabad, that "the possibility of a massive attack by our holy warriors cannot be ruled out if any neighboring country offers its ground or air bases to U.S. forces."
>
> The Pakistani ambivalence posed a clear problem to the Bush administration: how to mount the large-scale military operation that many believe would be necessary to hunt down an elusive enemy—Mr. bin Laden and his followers constantly move around Afghanistan's deserts and mountains—without a secure land base in the region. . . .
>
> Another deep problem is this: might winning the cooperation of Pakistan lead to the destabilization of the country, which detonated a nuclear bomb in 1998, and its possible takeover by the very radicals the United States is trying to suppress or eliminate? (Burns, "Pakistan Antiterror Support")

Chomsky does not discuss any of these aspects of the article, from the "friendly tone" in Pakistani-Afghan communications to the problems posed by Islamist radicals in Pakistan; he is thereby enabled to suggest that the United States is simply planning to starve millions of Afghans absent any other consideration.

16. Too many, indeed, to cite in a note. Schell's "Letter from Ground Zero: Seven Million at Risk" is representative, both for its attention to the humanitarian crisis and for its insistence that mainstream U.S. media were not paying sufficient attention to the humanitarian crisis.

17. As Gitlin and Cooper became piñatas for the Manichean left, their work was strategically misread by people like Ed Herman. In his attack on the "Cruise Missile Leftists," for example, Herman writes that "the CMLs are very cagey in discussing the Israel-Palestine conflict. They regularly say that 'peace in Israel and Palestine' is desirable and that the United States should help bring it about. But none of them point out that for decades the United States has given unconditional support to Israel's occupation and long-term ethnic cleansing." Apparently Herman missed the passage in Gitlin's "Blaming America First" that reads, "A reasoned, vigorous examination of U.S. policies, including collusion in the Israeli

occupation, sanctions against Iraq, and support of corrupt regimes in Saudi Arabia and Egypt, is badly needed. So is critical scrutiny of the administration's actions in Afghanistan and American unilateralism on many fronts." For a still more strenuous defense of liberal nationalism, see Kazin, "A Patriotic Left."

18. My initial response to Herman's "Cruise Missile Left" essay is "Real Problems on the Real Left."

CHAPTER THREE

1. As a result, I wrote "Nation and Narration" in January 2002; it was published three months later. I had not written anything on 9/11 or Afghanistan up to that point, sifting slowly through my trepidations about the war and my abreactions to the vitriol on leftist listservs.

2. For a gripping account of the failures of Operation Anaconda, see Hersh, *Chain of Command*, 134–43. For first-hand accounts of American operations in Afghanistan, which largely fault the United States not for intervening but for doing so ineffectively (precisely because the Bush administration was fixated on Iraq), especially with regard to the U.S. failure to capture bin Laden at Tora Bora, see Schroen, *First In,* and Berntsen, *Jawbreaker.*

3. Having blamed "Blaming America First" for its appeal to national sentiment, however, I should add that the leftists who attacked Gitlin's essay made a point of overlooking its points of agreement with positions usually associated with writers to Gitlin's left. Gitlin does not fail to note, for instance, U.S. support for the mujahedeen:

> Of the perils of American ignorance, of our fantasy life of pure and
> unappreciated goodness, much can be said. The failures of intelligence
> that made September 11 possible include not only security oversights,
> but a vast combination of stupefaction and arrogance—not least the
> all-or-nothing thinking that armed the Islamic jihad in Afghanistan in
> order to fight our own jihad against Soviet Communism—and a willful
> ignorance that not so long ago permitted half the citizens of a flabby,
> self-satisfied democracy to vote for a man unembarrassed by his lack of
> acquaintanceship with the world.

4. I develop this claim briefly in Bérubé, "Richard Rorty and the Politics of Modesty."

5. The critical question here was whether international institutions would be weakened if the United States treated the attacks of September 11 as acts of war and pursued al-Qaeda as a military enemy. Again, I acknowledge that reasonable people may disagree as to the legal status of the attacks and the attackers. But I note that no one, not even Chomsky himself, has suggested that the United States would have failed to obtain U.N. Security Council authorization for a

counterattack. The fact that the Bush administration did not request such autho-rization, I believe, is evidence not of the weakness of the case but of the American right's desire to weaken international institutions—a desire they realized more fully in 2003 by flatly ignoring the Security Council's refusal to authorize the invasion of Iraq.

6. See Chomsky, *The New Military Humanism;* Chomsky, *A New Generation Draws the Line;* and Johnstone, *Fool's Crusade.* For a devastating rebuttal to Herman, see Weinberg, "Z Magazine Supports Genocide"; the reply is devastating not only for its demolition of Herman's argument but also for the fact that its author opposed the Kosovo war. As Weinberg notes in comments, "I opposed U.S. military intervention in the Balkans. But that opposition cannot be predicated on genocide denial or bogus moral equivalism or (worse) simply flipping reality on its head and portraying the Serbs as the victims and Bosnian Muslims as the aggressors."

7. For the website of the Srebrenica Research Group, see http://www.srebrenica-report.com/; for Srebrenica Group Members and Mission, see http://www.srebrenica-report.com/people.htm.

8. In late 2005 a controversy erupted over an interview between Chomsky and Emma Brockes in the *Guardian,* over the question of whether Chomsky had explicitly supported Srebrenica denial (Chomsky, "Greatest Intellectual?"). Indeed, the headline of the story ran, "Q: Do You Regret Supporting Those Who Say the Srebrenica Massacre Was Exaggerated? A: My Only Regret Is That I Didn't Do It Strongly Enough." In its November 17 "correction and clarification" of the interview, the *Guardian* noted, "The headline used on the interview, about which Prof Chomsky also complained, added to the misleading impression given by the treatment of the word massacre. . . . No question in that form was put to Prof Chomsky" ("Corrections and Clarifications: *The Guardian* and Noam Chomsky"). The *Guardian* took the Brockes interview off their website. (However, the "correction and clarification" went on to say that "neither Prof Chomsky nor Ms Johnstone have ever denied the fact of the massacre," and this is profoundly misleading with regard to Johnstone.) The original interview, published on October 31, 2005, is still available online at http://www.chomsky.info/onchomsky/20051031.htm under the title "The Greatest Intellectual?" The relevant passage reads as follows (Johnstone's name is misprinted as "Diane" throughout):

> As some see it, one ill-judged choice of cause was the accusation made by Living Marxism magazine that during the Bosnian war, shots used by ITN [Independent Television News] of a Serb-run detention camp were faked. The magazine folded after ITN sued, but the controversy flared up again in 2003 when a journalist called Diane Johnstone made similar allegations in a Swedish magazine, *Ordfront,* taking issue with

the official number of victims of the Srebrenica massacre. (She said they were exaggerated.) In the ensuing outcry, Chomsky lent his name to a letter praising Johnstone's "outstanding work." Does he regret signing it?

"No," he says indignantly. "It is outstanding. My only regret is that I didn't do it strongly enough. It may be wrong; but it is very careful and outstanding work."

How, I wonder, can journalism be wrong and still outstanding?

"Look," says Chomsky, "there was a hysterical fanaticism about Bosnia in western culture which was very much like a passionate religious conviction. It was like old-fashioned Stalinism: if you depart a couple of millimetres from the party line, you're a traitor, you're destroyed. It's totally irrational. And Diane Johnstone, whether you like it or not, has done serious, honest work. And in the case of *Living Marxism*, for a big corporation to put a small newspaper out of business because they think something they reported was false, is outrageous."

They didn't "think" it was false; it was proven to be so in a court of law.

But Chomsky insists that "*LM* was probably correct" and that, in any case, it is irrelevant. "It had nothing to do with whether *LM* or Diane Johnstone were right or wrong." It is a question, he says, of freedom of speech. "And if they were wrong, sure; but don't just scream well, if you say you're in favour of that you're in favour of putting Jews in gas chambers."

Suffice it to say that Chomsky does not go out of his way to distinguish his position on the Balkans from that of Johnstone. About Chomsky's belief that if you fail to toe the line on Bosnia, "you're a traitor, you're destroyed," one can only wonder how the many American opponents of the Kosovo war managed to escape the wrath of the hysterical Bosnia fanatics and their passionate quasi-religious convictions.

9. The report, originally commissioned by the Dutch government in 1996, held inadequate Dutch and U.N. peacekeeping efforts responsible for the massacre at Srebrenica; upon the release of the report, the government of Dutch Prime Minister Wim Kok stepped down. It is worth noting, though Chomsky does not do so, that the report offers a painstakingly detailed rebuttal of the kind of claims made by Diana Johnstone and Ed Herman.

10. The reader was one Ray Amberg, and his exchange with Chomsky is preserved on the archives of the Google group alt.fan.noam-chomsky at http://groups.google.com/group/ alt.fan.noam-chomsky/msg/5799d10331fd4df6?hl=en&lr=&ie=UTF-8&rnum=6.

11. "Nato's Invasion of Kosovo and Apologetics for State Violence." The exchange has disappeared from *ZNet* but is available in cached form

through the Internet Archive, 23 Jan. 2009, at http://web.archive.org/
web/20070702162217/ http://blogs.zmag.org/node/2562.

12. Again, this "explanation" dodges the question of why U.S. policy in the
Balkans took the form it did between 1989 and the onset of the Kosovo war.
More to the point, it engages in an extremely selective quotation and interpreta-
tion of this passage from Talbott's foreword to Norris's *Collision Course:*

> For Western powers, the Kosovo crisis was fueled by frustration with
> Milošević and the legitimate fear that instability and conflict might
> spread further in the region. The evolving political aims of the Alliance
> and the changing nature of the transatlantic community also played a
> role. In that vein, it is useful to more broadly consider how NATO and
> Yugoslavia came to be locked in conflict. . . .
>
> As nations throughout the region sought to reform their economies,
> mitigate ethnic tensions, and broaden civil society, Belgrade seemed
> to delight in continually moving in the opposite direction. It is small
> wonder NATO and Yugoslavia ended up on a collision course. It was
> Yugoslavia's resistance to the broader trends of political and economic
> reform—not the plight of the Kosovar Albanians—that best explains
> NATO's war. Milošević had been a burr in the side of the transatlantic
> community for so long that the United States felt that he would only
> respond to military pressure. Slobodan Milošević's repeated transgres-
> sions ran directly counter to the vision of a Europe "whole and free,"
> and challenged the very value of NATO's continued existence.
>
> Many outsiders accuse western countries of selective intervention
> in Kosovo—fighting on a hair-trigger in the Balkans while avoiding
> the Sudans and Rwandas of the world. This was hardly the case. Only
> a decade of death, destruction, and Milošević brinkmanship pushed
> NATO to act when the Rambouillet talks collapsed. Most of the leaders
> of NATO's major powers were proponents of "third way" politics and
> headed socially progressive, economically centrist governments. None
> of these men were particularly hawkish, and Milošević did not allow
> them the political breathing room to look past his abuses.
>
> Through predatory opportunism, Milošević had repeatedly exploited
> the weakest instincts of European and North American powers alike.
> Time and again, he had preserved his political power because nations
> mightier than his own lacked the political resolve to bring him to heel.
> His record was ultimately one of ruin, particularly for the Serbs, as Yu-
> goslavia dwindled into a smaller and smaller state verging on collapse. It
> was precisely because Milošević had become so adroit at outmaneuver-
> ing the west that NATO came to view the ever-escalating use of force as
> its only option. Nobody should be surprised that Milošević eventually

goaded the sleeping giant out of repose. NATO went to war in Kosovo because its political and diplomatic leaders had enough of Milošević and saw his actions disrupting plans to bring a wider stable of nations into the transatlantic community. Kosovo would only offer western leaders more humiliation and frustration if they did not forcefully respond. U.S. Secretary of State Madeleine Albright's view of Milošević was probably best revealed when she said that, at a certain stage at Rambouillet, it was evident that Milošević was "jerking us around." In early June of 1999, German Minister Joschka Fischer rather angrily responded to those who questioned NATO's motives. Fischer observed that he had originally resisted military action, but that his views had changed, "step by step, from mass murder to mass murder."

Chomsky reads the second paragraph above as evidence that Milošević was being chastised for not caving in to neoliberalism—and ignores everything else, from Milošević's refusal to "mitigate ethnic tensions and broaden civil society" to the European community's exasperation at mass murder after mass murder.

13. For a representative (if pedestrian) example, see Model, *Lying for Empire: How to Commit War Crimes with a Straight Face.*

14. Thankfully, many such books have already been written. For example, Sells, *The Bridge Betrayed: Religion and Genocide in Bosnia;* Glenny, *The Balkans: Nationalism, War and the Great Powers, 1804–1999;* Silber and Little, *Yugoslavia: Death of a Nation;* Rohde, *Endgame: The Betrayal and Fall of Srebrenica, Europe's Worst Massacre Since World War II;* Honig and Both, *Srebrenica: Record of a War Crime;* Rieff, *Slaughterhouse: Bosnia and the Failure of the West;* Judah, *Kosovo: War and Revenge;* Simms, *Unfinest Hour: Britain and the Destruction of Bosnia;* Sudetic, *Blood and Vengeance: One Family's Story of the War in Bosnia;* Maass, *Love Thy Neighbor: A Story of War;* and Malcolm, *Kosovo: A Short History.*

15. For example, Gourevitch, *We Wish to Inform You That Tomorrow We Will Be Killed with Our Families: Stories from Rwanda;* Falk, *Human Rights Horizons: The Pursuit of Justice in a Globalizing World;* Power, *"A Problem from Hell": America and the Age of Genocide;* Mills and Brunner, *The New Killing Fields: Massacre and the Politics of Intervention.*

16. Tape of November 12, 2002. See also Brown, "'Bin Laden Tape' Tested for Authenticity." Other translations offer "despicable role in" or "unjust support of" in place of "ignoble contribution to."

17. The literature on R2P is already too vast for summary here, but for general introductions to and discussions of the principle, see Daalder, *Beyond Preemption: Force and Legitimacy in a Changing World;* Hoffman and Weiss, *Sword and Salve: Confronting New Wars and Humanitarian Crises;* Thakur, *The United Nations, Peace and Security: From Collective Security to the Responsibility to Protect;*

and Weiss, *Military-Civilian Interactions: Humanitarian Crises and the Responsibility to Protect.*

18. The 2003 State of the Union address was the speech in which Bush made the case for war (insisting, of course, that "we seek peace" and "strive for peace") by claiming that "the British government has learned that Saddam Hussein recently sought significant quantities of uranium from Africa" and "our intelligence sources tell us that he has attempted to purchase high-strength aluminum tubes suitable for nuclear weapons production."

19. For Glaspie's July 25, 1990, assurance that "we have no opinion on the Arab-Arab conflicts, like your border disagreement with Kuwait," see "Excerpts from Iraqi Transcript of Meeting with U.S. Envoy." The invasion of Kuwait took place on August 2. For the official acknowledgment of munitions sales to Iraq, see "Iraq: U.S. Military Items Exported or Transferred to Iraq in the 1980s."

20. The Manichean left assumed that the history of U.S. support for Iraq would serve, in and of itself, as an argument against war. But the contrary argument could be (and was) made that the history of U.S. support for Iraq offered a substantial reason for the overthrow of Saddam, on the grounds that the United States would be righting a grievous wrong and atoning for its sorry past. The argument looks absurd after the actual U.S. invasion in 2003; it looks positively obscene after the revelations of Abu Ghraib in 2004. (Nor was it ever clear why the overthrow of Saddam should be entrusted to Americans.) But prior to the war, its most passionate and eloquent exponent was Christopher Hitchens, who wrote, in one of his final columns for the *Nation:*

> Sooner or later the Saddam Hussein regime *will* fall, either of its own weight or from the physical and mental collapse of its leader or from endogenous or exogenous pressure. On that day one will want to be able to look the Iraqi and Kurdish peoples in the eye and say that we thought seriously about their interests and appreciated that, because of previous interventions that were actually in Saddam's favor, we owed them a debt. It's this dimension that seems to me lacking in the current antiwar critique. ("Appointment in Samarra?")

Hitchens resigned from the *Nation* two weeks later and repeated the argument often in the ensuing months.

21. The PNAC letter, calling on President Clinton to embrace regime change in Iraq as official U.S. policy, is archived at http://www.informationclearinghouse.info/article5527.htm.

22. The blogger known as "Digby," of the blog "Hullabaloo" (http://digbysblog.blogspot.com), first drew my attention to Matthews's and Liddy's effusions. From the May 1, 2003 edition of *Countdown with Keith Olbermann:*

Matthews: We're proud of our president. Americans love having a guy as president, a guy who has a little swagger, who's physical, who's not a complicated guy like [former President Bill] Clinton or even like [former Democratic presidential candidates Michael] Dukakis or [Walter] Mondale, all those guys, [George] McGovern. They want a guy who's president. Women like a guy who's president. Check it out. The women like this war. I think we like having a hero as our president. It's simple. ("Mission Accomplished")

And from the May 7 edition of his own show, *Hardball:*

Matthews: What do you make of this broadside against the USS *Abraham Lincoln* and its chief visitor last week?
  Liddy: Well, I—in the first place, I think it's envy. I mean, after all, Al Gore had to go get some woman to tell him how to be a man. And here comes George Bush. You know, he's in his flight suit, he's striding across the deck, and he's wearing his parachute harness, you know—and I've worn those because I parachute—and it makes the best of his manly characteristic. You go run those—run that stuff again of him walking across there with the parachute. He has just won every woman's vote in the United States of America. You know, all those women who say size doesn't count—they're all liars. Check that out. I hope the Democrats keep ratting on him and all of this stuff so that they keep showing that tape.

23. This was not revealed until April 2008, however, when the *New York Times* ran a front-page story on the issue:

To the public these men are members of a familiar fraternity, presented tens of thousands of times on television and radio as "military analysts" whose long service has equipped them to give authoritative and unfettered judgments about the most pressing issues of the post-Sept. 11 world. Hidden behind that appearance of objectivity, though, is a Pentagon information apparatus that has used those analysts in a campaign to generate favorable news coverage of the administration's wartime performance, an examination by *The New York Times* has found. (Barstow, "Behind TV Analysts, Pentagon's Hidden Hand")

Tellingly, the *Times* report generated much discussion in the liberal blogosphere—and no reaction whatsoever among television networks. Certainly, I would be remiss if I did not acknowledge that this Pentagon disinformation apparatus and its treatment by U.S. media (including both the exposé by the *Times* and the deafening silence that followed) conforms quite nicely to the Chomskian model of mass media—especially what Chomsky and Herman call filter number three, "the reliance of the media on information provided by government, business, and 'experts' funded and approved by these primary sources and agents of power" (Herman and Chomsky, *Manufacturing Consent,* 2).

24. On Kosovo, see Friedman, "Stop the Music"; on Iraq, see Friedman, *The Charlie Rose Show.* The *Charlie Rose* clip was unearthed by blogger Duncan Black, also known as "Atrios" ("Deep Thoughts from Thomas Friedman").

25. The best contemporaneous critique of the *Post's* lurch to the right was that of Gitlin, "The Pro-War *Post.*"

26. The *New Republic* refrained from saying explicitly that the anthrax had been produced in Iraq, but in October 2001 the assumption was so widespread the magazine did not need to make it explicit. For example, the *Wall Street Journal* editorial of October 15, "The Anthrax Source: Is Iraq Unleashing Biological Weapons on America?" despite its interrogative title, claims definitively that "the leading supplier suspect has to be Iraq" and concludes "the government has to do everything possible to destroy the anthrax threat at its state sponsored source."

On July 22, 2004, Cohen penned a mea culpa of sorts, "Our Forgotten Panic," in which he wrote:

> Anthrax played a role in my decision to support the Bush administration's desire to take out Saddam Hussein. I linked him to anthrax, which I linked to Sept. 11. I was not going to stand by and simply wait for another attack—more attacks. I was going to go to the source, Hussein, and get him before he could get us. As time went on, I became more and more questioning, but I had a hard time backing down from my initial whoop and holler for war. . . . You could say we lacked judgment. Maybe. I would say we lacked leadership.

In response, Duncan Black, who has long argued that the anthrax scare was central to the hysteria that led the United States into Iraq (and has been forgotten by those who insist that George Bush "kept us safe" after 9/11), wrote, "Yes, we did. We lacked leadership from people in leadership positions like *Richard Cohen*" ("Failure of Leadership").

27. See also Berman, "Why Germany Isn't Convinced," and Berman, "Liberal Hawks Reconsider the Iraq War."

28. A still more pugnacious version of this move can be found in Beinart's *The Good Fight,* which apologizes for its author's support for the Iraq war but insists that al-Qaeda and Islamism are the contemporary counterparts to the Soviet Union. This analogy is wildly inaccurate in its overestimation of al-Qaeda—and, more to the point, serves the larger Bush-Cheney agenda of constituting Islamism as a deadly global enemy that requires, in response, a number of extraordinary warlike measures at home and abroad.

29. Berman has strongly denied having made such an analogy. On March

23, 2006, he wrote to Kevin Drum of the *Washington Monthly* blog, "Political Animal," and insisted that Packer's version of events is "fiction":

> George is a wonderful writer and a terrific journalist, not to mention a brave and intrepid one. *The Assassins' Gate* seems to me, apart from a few passages, truly a superb book. But George is also a novelist, and I can only say that the person who composed that paragraph about me and Prague and the bar was George Packer the novelist. Those particular lines in *The Assassins' Gate* are fiction. The paragraph contributes to the magnificent color and drama of his book. But he has invented that conversation.
>
> I didn't respond to your post back in December because, well, many silly things are said in public, and life is short, and some disputes are too picayune to pursue. I hoped that George's remark about me and Prague would simply go away. Maybe I hoped (excuse me for this) that no one was reading your blog. Big mistake! The story about me having made a preposterous comparison between Baghdad and Prague circulated, and has gone on doing so, until the *Los Angeles Times* got hold of it a few weeks ago and ran an op-ed saying that I had compared Baghdad to the Prague Spring of 1968—which shows how, over time, rumors grow ever more ridiculous.
>
> I am glumly aware that I will never be able to prove that George has invented this story. There was liquor at that bar, but there was no tape recorder, unless the agents of Homeland Security turn out to have been bugging the place. I will never be able to prove absolutely that what I am said to have said is something I could not possibly have said. George himself has made clear that he is going to go to his final hour swearing to the peerless accuracy of his barroom recollections. (Drum, "A Letter from Paul Berman.")

30. The term "Very Serious People," as well as the term "Dirty Fucking Hippies" and the term "Villagers," are coinages made famous by Duncan Black of "Eschaton." Very Serious People are people who were too wise and (of course) serious to give the antiwar position a reasonable hearing in 2002–03; "Dirty Fucking Hippies" encapsulates Black's theory that the mainstream punditocracy remains stuck in the iconography of the late 1960s, and specifically in the iconography that sees the New Left and the counterculture as the forces that repelled Middle America and drove the silent majority to vote for Nixon, and therefore sees every contemporary challenge to official Washington in those terms; and "the Village" and "Villagers" are Black's shorthand for the insularity and parochialism of the Beltway social circle and the conventional wisdom it produces.

31. Berman, too, provides the Manicheans with a great deal of good red meat on this score. In addition to *Terror and Liberalism,* see Berman's *Power and the Idealists;* for a powerful reply to *Terror and Liberalism,* see Buruma, "Revolution from Above."

32. Benjamin DeMott, writing in *First of the Month* ("With Friends Like These") in 2005, also deserves mention as one of Makiya's strongest supporters on the left. For instance, DeMott offered a scathing account of Edward Said's attempt to persuade Victor Navasky that the *Nation* should not publish an excerpt from Makiya's *Cruelty and Silence*. For a fine profile of Makiya long after the Iraq war had gone sour, see McKelvey, "Interventionism's Last Hold-Out." Unfortunately, as McKelvey notes, "Beinart, Berman, and Packer refused my requests for an interview." Five years after the invasion, Makiya contributed to *Slate's* "How Did I Get Iraq Wrong?" forum with a short, eloquent essay that began, "I know that I got many things wrong in the run-up to the 2003 war, but, in spite of everything, I still do not know how to regret wanting to knock down the walls of the great concentration camp that was Saddam Hussein's Iraq."

33. David Glenn calls attention to this aspect of Packer's work in his profile of Packer, "Unfinished Wars."

34. A slightly different version of the talk, "Todd Gitlin Responds," is printed in *Dissent*.

35. Much of the liberal left—or, at least, whatever segments of the left are not averse to taking advice from well-informed military officers—drew on the remarks of General Anthony Zinni, a sampling of which can be found in Eric Alterman's December 1, 2003, column in the *Nation*, "Why Chickenhawks Matter":

> What makes this catastrophe all the more infuriating is how predictable it was—except, of course, by those blinded by ideology and unwilling to listen to more experienced voices. If only the Administration had not turned a deaf ear when those former military men not under "color" contract to the networks spoke candidly about the proposed war. None did so with greater force or credibility than Maj. Gen. Anthony Zinni, who headed the U.S. Central Command from 1997 to 2000 and was later George W. Bush's special envoy to the Israeli/Palestinian negotiations.
>
> Just over a year ago, Zinni gave talks, one to the Middle East Institute in Washington, in which he predicted many problems now facing U.S. occupation authorities. Among Zinni's warnings....
>
> Is this a liberation? What comes next? "If it's short with minimal destruction, there will be the initial euphoria of change. It's always what comes next that is tough. I went in with the first troops that went into Somalia. We were greeted as heroes on the street.... [After] about a month ... a group of prominent Somalis ... wanted to talk to me. I met with them. The first question out of their mouths was that we'd been there a month, hadn't started a jobs program, and when were we going to fix the economy? Well, I didn't know it was my Marine unit's responsibility to do that. Expectations grow rapidly.... It's not whether you're

greeted in the streets as a hero; it's whether you're still greeted as a hero when you come back a year from now."

Is Iraq likely to become a democracy? "If we think there is a fast solution to changing the governance of Iraq, then we don't understand history, the nature of the country, the divisions, or the underneath suppressed passions that could rise up. . . . If you think it's going to be easy to impose a government or install one from the outside, I think that you're further sadly mistaken."

What are (were) the alternatives? "If I were to give you my priority of things that can change for the better in this region, it is first and foremost the Middle East peace process and getting it back on track. Second, it is insuring that Iran's reformation or moderation continues on track and trying to help and support the people who are trying to make that change in the best way we can. . . . The third is to make sure those countries to which we have now committed ourselves to change, like Afghanistan and those in Central Asia, we invest what we need to in the way of resources there to make that change happen. Fourth is to patch up these relationships that have become strained, and fifth is to reconnect to the people. We are talking past each other. . . . We have based this in things that are tough to compromise on, like religion and politics, and we need to reconnect in a different way.

"I would take those priorities before this one [deposing Saddam]. My personal view, and this is just personal, is that I think this isn't number one. It's maybe six or seven, and the affordability line may be drawn around five."

36. For example, Weisberg writes:

You can hardly read too much into Ned Lamont's defeat of Joe Lieberman in Connecticut's Aug. 8 primary. This is a signal event that will have a huge and lasting negative impact on the Democratic Party. The result suggests that instead of capitalizing on the massive failures of the Bush administration, Democrats are poised to re-enact a version of the Vietnam-era drama that helped them lose five out six presidential elections between 1968 and the end of the Cold War. . . .

Whether Democrats can avoid playing their Vietnam video to the end depends on their ability to project military and diplomatic toughness in place of the elitism and anti-war purity represented in 2004 by Howard Dean and now by Ned Lamont. ("Dead with Ned")

Calling Lamont's supporters "a pack of crazed, ignorant ideological cannibals," Chait wrote:

I can't quite root for Lieberman to lose his primary. What's holding me back is that the anti-Lieberman campaign has come to stand for much more than Lieberman's sins. It's a test of strength for the new breed of left-wing activists who are flexing their muscles within the party. These are exactly the sorts of fanatics who tore the party apart in the late 1960s and early 1970s. They think in simple slogans and refuse to tolerate any ideological dissent. Moreover, since their anti-Lieberman jihad is seen as stemming from his pro-war stance, the practical effect of toppling Lieberman would be to intimidate other hawkish Democrats and encourage more primary challengers against them. ("Don't Let the Left Defeat Lieberman")

The judgment of history has not been kind to these *New Republic / Slate* liberals—and the judgment of history wasn't long in coming, either.

37. Hari's review is something of a quarrel with former comrades, since Hari himself initially supported the war on humanitarian grounds. In the United Kingdom, a number of Euston Manifesto drafters and signatories responded to Hari's essay; Cohen himself called it "the most deceitful piece to be written about [my book] in any journal in any country" ("Taking Issue"). Responding to Hari's description of his "retraction," Norman Geras, the distinguished Marxist theorist and Euston co-founder, wrote:

> Johann speaks about "recantation" on the part of some on the pro-war left, including me; and he speaks of others who haven't recanted. It might seem to be making rather much of an innocent word if I say in response: the hell with that. I changed my mind about the Iraq war, in the way I explained here. I said that had I been able to foresee the scale of death and social breakdown the war was to bring I would not have supported it. I stand by this change of mind. But I am not *ashamed* that I supported the war; because the reasons why I did were compelling moral reasons, not disgraceful ones—reasons very much of the kind I believe Johann himself held at the time, reasons to do, precisely, with "solidarity with suffering strangers." When I recant on that is when I'll be ashamed of myself. ("Johann—Saved")

Geras's change of mind on Iraq—whether one wants to call it a "retraction" or a "recantation" appeared on his blog on October 15, 2006. (Geras mistakenly attributed the term "recantation" to Hari in place of "retraction," thereby making rather much of an innocent word that Hari did not use.) Then, Geras had written:

> Had I been able to foresee, in January and February 2003, that the war would have the results it has actually had in the numbers of Iraqis killed and the numbers now daily dying, with the country (more than three years down the line) on the very threshold of civil war if not already across that threshold, I would not have felt able to support the war and

I would not have supported it. Measured, in other words, against the hopes of what it might lead to and the likelihoods as I assessed them, the war has failed. Had I foreseen a failure of this magnitude, I would have withheld my support. Even then, I would not have been able to bring myself to oppose the war. As I have said two or three times before, nothing on earth could have induced me to march or otherwise campaign for a course of action that would have saved the Baathist regime. But I would have stood aside. ("Failure in Iraq")

38. Hitchens reportedly uttered the line during a June 2003 debate on the war, as cited in Hunter-Tilney, "The Preacher: Christopher Hitchens":

At the debate a few hours earlier, he lost his temper when someone asked about the country band the Dixie Chicks and the flak they copped for criticising George W. Bush's Iraq policy.

"Each day they dig up dead bodies in personal death camps run by a Caligula dictator," Hitchens shouted, "and I'm being asked to worry about these fucking fat slags—do me a favour!" The debate broke up soon after.

39. In mid-2006, Scott McLemee weighed in with a judicious critical assessment of the manifesto, "Euston. . . . We Have a Problem." McLemee noted that Gitlin had not signed the document:

His book *The Intellectuals and the Flag*, published earlier this year by Columbia University Press, defends the idea of left-wing American patriotism with a frank interest "in the necessary task of defeating the jihadist enemy."

This would seem to put him in the Eustonian camp, yet he did not endorse the manifesto. Why not? I contacted him by e-mail to ask. "I recognize a shoddy piece of intellectual patchwork when I see one," Gitlin responded.

He cites a passage referring to the overthrow of Saddam Hussein as "a liberation of the Iraqi people." A fine thing, to be sure. The sight of a humiliated dictator is good for the soul. "But the resulting carnage is scarcely worthy of the term 'liberation,'" Gitlin told me. "I'm leery of the euphemism."

40. For one of the most tangled and oblique mea culpa reassessments of Iraq, see Ignatieff, "Getting Iraq Wrong," an essay that consists largely of a string of Deep Thoughts: "I've learned that good judgment in politics looks different from good judgment in intellectual life. Among intellectuals, judgment is about generalizing and interpreting particular facts as instances of some big idea. In politics, everything is what it is and not another thing. Specifics matter more than

generalities. Theory gets in the way." Furthermore, "a sense of reality is not just a sense of the world as it is, but as it might be" (28). And so forth, for 2,500 words.

41. In *The Lesser Evil: Political Ethics in an Age of Terror*, Ignatieff did, however, let arguments about WMD and terrorism persuade him to adopt a host of positions consonant with Bush's War on Terror, including the legitimacy of preemptive war and coercive interrogation. For a properly skeptical review of the lesser-evilism proposed, see Steel, "Fight Fire with Fire."

CHAPTER FOUR

1. The final chapter of Williams's *Culture and Society* makes this quite clear, arguing that "the crucial distinguishing element in English life since the Industrial Revolution is . . . between alternative ideas of the nature of social relationship" (325) and "the struggle for democracy is a struggle for the recognition of equality of being, or it is nothing" (337). For Williams, understanding the emergence of the terms *industry, democracy, class, art,* and *culture* in the late eighteenth century, in other words, has everything to do with the struggle for democracy in the second half of the twentieth century.

2. I suspect this chapter requires a Stuart Hall Critic's Prolegomenon just as chapter 2 required a Chomsky Critic's Prolegomenon—though for rather different reasons. First, Hall's commitment to "conjunctural" analysis requires a high degree of historical specificity; one might say that cultural studies never steps in the same conjunctural river twice, which is why it is impossible simply to transpose Hall's work on Thatcherism to American politics after 9/11. Second, Hall did not work alone; though this chapter treats his work—and especially his work in *Marxism Today*—as the writing of a single individual, the individual who wrote that work did so in a cultural and institutional context that prized and enabled collective work. *Policing the Crisis* was, of course, jointly authored by five people, but even single-authored works coming out of the Birmingham Centre were incubated, so to speak, by the group. As Hall remarks in a 2007 interview, "The Centre was completely taken over by the idea of collectives. We worked as a collective, we wrote as a collective, we wrote each other's books and articles and that has never gone away" (McCabe, "Interview with Hall," 27).

3. Hall took great care, however, to hold Laclau and Mouffe's *Hegemony and Socialist Strategy* at arm's distance, insisting that he preferred Laclau's *Politics and Ideology.* In an important 1986 interview, Hall suggests that their position is *too* discursive and constitutes a kind of "reductionism upward" in which the proposition that social practices are *like* language is elided with the proposition that social practices are *nothing but* languages and, therefore, "there is no reason why anything is or isn't potentially articulable with anything." "I've gone a very long way along the route of rethinking practices as functioning discursively—i.e., like languages," Hall said:

That metaphor has been, I think, enormously generative for me and has powerfully influenced my thinking. If I had to put my finger on the one thing which constitutes the theoretical revolution of our time, I think it lies in that metaphor—it's gone in a thousand different directions but it has also reorganized our theoretical universe. It is not only the discovery of the importance of the discursive, and the utility of a particular kind of analysis; it is also the metaphorically generated capacity to reconceptualize other kinds of practices as operating, in some important ways, like a language. . . .

The question is, can one, does one, follow that argument to the point that there is nothing to practice but its discursive aspect? I think that's what their recent book [*Hegemony and Socialist Strategy*] does. It is a sustained philosophical effort, really, to conceptualize *all* practices as nothing but discourses, and all historical agents as discursively constituted subjectivities. . . .

I would put it polemically in the following form: the last book thinks that the world, social practice, is language, whereas I want to say that the social operates *like* a language. . . . I think that that often becomes its own kind of reductionism. I would say that the fully discursive position is a reductionism upward, rather than a reductionism downward, as economism was. What seems to happen is that, in the reaction against a crude materialism, the metaphor of x operates like y is reduced to $x = y$. (Grossberg, "On Postmodernism and Articulation: An Interview with Stuart Hall")

4. Alternatively, the right can simply try to redefine the slogan "power to the people," as in conservative pundit Laura Ingraham's 2007 book, titled simply *Power to the People*.

5. The best book on Goldwater conservatism and its legacy is surely Perlstein's *Before the Storm*.

6. *Marxism Today* occupied a distinctive cultural position on the British Left: at its best it was a gadfly, querying calcified Marxist orthodoxies and engaging energetically with popular culture; at its worst, according to its detractors, it encouraged a kind of "designer socialism" for the theoretically and culturally hip (Pfister, *Critique for What?*, 157–63):

In celebration of its thirtieth anniversary in 1987 *Marxism Today* published comments on the magazine by Left luminaries—assessments that testify to the magazine's openness to sometimes barbed criticism. Several writers pointed both to the trendy London-centered politics that the magazine represented and to its class profile. "*MT* to me," quipped author Michael Ignatieff, "is like an extremely bright, cheerful little rodent, with bright-rimmed glasses and bow tie, leaping off a sinking ship."

Journalist Ann Leslie proposed retitling the magazine *Socialism for the Thinking Yuppie*. (163)

Marxism Today may have tried to make socialism "fashionable," but as this chapter demonstrates, it remains impossible to dismiss Hall's contributions to the magazine as cavalierly as this. And Ignatieff's little quip now calls to mind the image of Ignatieff himself—and the sinking ship of liberal Iraq hawks.

7. The influence of Nicos Poulantzas is most evident here in the sentence, "This has its critical reference to 'class' as a determining level of analysis; but it does *not* translate whole classes directly on to the political-ideological stage as unified historical actors." Hall was fond of quoting Poulantzas's rejection of the "number plate" theory of ideology (first articulated in his 1973 book *Political Power and Social Classes*), according to which unified, monolithic classes march through history with their ideologies imprinted like number plates on their backs. For example, see Hall, "The Toad in the Garden," 42; Hall, "The Problem of Ideology," 41; and Hall, "Race, Articulation, and Societies Structured in Dominance," 49.

8. The extent of the rebuke to Althusser becomes clearer when the full context of the "functionalist" claim is considered. Discussing Thatcherism's successes in civil society, Hall insists that this "is precisely where the Althusserian formulation runs into difficulties":

> Althusser would argue that these ⌊i.e., institutions ranging from think tanks to the popular press⌋ are all ideological *state* apparatuses— regardless of what he considered the purely formal question of whether they belonged to the state or not. They are "state" by virtue of their function—the function, ascribed to the state, of sustaining the "reproduction of the social relations of production" in and through ideology. What is striking about Thatcherism is precisely its capacity to enter into struggle and win space *in civil society itself;* to use the trenches and fortifications of civil society as the means of forging a considerable ideological and intellectual *authority* outside the realm of the state proper and, indeed, *before*—as a necessary condition to—taking formal power *in* the state, as part of an internal contestation against key elements within the power bloc. . . .
>
> Is this merely a quibble? I think not. Despite the apparent similarities of phrasing (due in part to the fact that both Althusser's and my thinking on this point has been influenced by and reflects Gramsci), two fundamentally different processes are being described. The first (Althusser's "Ideological State Apparatuses" essay) is the use of existing apparatuses to reproduce the already given ruling ideology; the second (mine) is the struggle and contestation for the space in which to construct an ideological hegemony. The fact is that a position of ideological authority

and leadership—of intellectual and moral ascendancy—constructed by harnessing the lines of force and opinion in the apparently "free space" of civil society has a remarkable durability, depth, and staying power *because* the adhesion it wins among the people is not coerced, as it might be if the state were directly involved, but appears to be produced freely and spontaneously as the popular consent to power. The differences therefore touch what I regard as the key issue—the problem of explaining the popular consent to Thatcherism. ("Toad in the Garden," 47–48)

9. Althusser famously distinguishes between science and ideology in "Ideology and Ideological State Apparatuses: Notes toward an Investigation."

10. The essay is "The Battle for Socialist Ideas in the 1980s," in *Hard Road to Renewal*, 177–95. Timothy Brennan makes a similar argument against countercultural left-anarchism in "The Organizational Imaginary," *Wars of Position*, 147–69, and though I find much of Brennan's work in that book wrongheaded, I find myself in agreement with Brennan's argument that the "culturalist" left is insufficiently attentive to organized politics and to the power of the state.

11. Dennis Dworkin offers a rich and detailed account of this tradition, and its importance for the history of cultural studies, in *Cultural Marxism in Postwar Britain*, 10–44.

12. For a considerably more detailed and comprehensive account of this problem, see Walzer, *Spheres of Justice*.

13. I critique this aspect of Berman's book in my essay "Fighting Liberals," 272.

14. The immediate context of Brenkman's capsule history of Western Marxism is his account of why it has come to pass that a thinker like Carl Schmitt "has become a point of reference for leftist thinkers" such as Giorgio Agamben (65).

15. I do not want to suggest, even for a moment, that Stuart Hall accomplished this on his own; here is where the collective nature of the work of the Centre for Contemporary Cultural Studies needs most acutely to be acknowledged. For example, see the groundbreaking, collectively authored volume, *The Empire Strikes Back: Race and Racism in 70s Britain*. But even taking the collective nature of the work of the Birmingham Centre into account, I want also to point to Paul Gilroy's *There Ain't No Black in the Union Jack*. Perhaps no one associated with Birmingham, with the possible exception of Hall, did as much to contest the "Condition of England" tradition in British cultural studies—and to argue not only against reactionary, nativist flag-waving on the right but also against too parochial an investment in the Gramscian "national-popular" on the left. For a

brief discussion of Gilroy's importance to antinationalist debate in the United Kingdom, see Carrington, "Decentreing the Centre: Cultural Studies in Britain and Its Legacy," esp. pp. 279–85. I do, however, want to suggest that the work of Hall, Gilroy, and others helped to start the long process that led to (among other things) the formation of the Parekh Commission (on which Hall served) by Home Secretary Jack Straw in 1998, and the release of the Parekh Report (*The Future of Multi-Ethnic Britain*) two years later.

16. This is not to say that Mrs. Thatcher's attacks on the NHS were wholly ineffective. Joe Sim notes, for example, that cuts to the Health and Safety Executive had immediate and drastic consequences: "Between 1981 and 1985, 739 workers were killed on building sites. According to the Health and Safety Executive [HSE], 517, or 70 per cent, of those lives could have been saved if minimum safety standards had been observed" (Sim, "Against the Punitive Wind," 325). In this respect, one might say that Thatcher offered British workers a return to a Victorian era of traditional values and lethal working conditions.

17. Though Kristol dutifully claimed that the Clinton health care plan would "destroy the present breadth and quality of the American health care system," he also insisted that it would "relegitimize middle-class dependence for 'security' on government spending and regulation" and "revive the reputation of . . . the Democrats . . . as the generous protector of middle-class interests" (Kristol, memorandum of December 3, 1993, "Memorandum to Republican Leaders: Defeating President Clinton's Health Care Proposal," Project for the Republican Future, Washington, D.C., quoted in Skocpol, *Boomerang,* 145). Obviously, if the latter is true, the former cannot be: a plan that destroyed the breadth and quality of American health care would not, after all, relegitimate the welfare state and revive the Democrats' reputation as its defenders. I am therefore left to conclude that Kristol was much more worried about the possible success of health care reform—even the tepid, inadequate Clinton version—than its possible failure.

18. For a judicious and comprehensive overview of the grounds for Argentine and British claims to sovereignty in the Falklands, see Hastings and Jenkins, *The Battle for the Falklands,* 1–44.

19. As with his acknowledgment that *The Hard Road to Renewal* underemphasized matters of war and peace, Hall is the first to admit that his work has not dealt adequately with religion. In the *Critical Quarterly* interview, for instance, he asks of 9/11:

> Where did it come from? Maoism? Marxism? The revolutionary proletariat? The revolutionized peasantry? No, it comes from fucking religion—which we forgot about. We thought—and sociology told us—that secularisation is an unstoppable process. All our notions of modernity and of progress are harnessed to secularisation, the secular. I must say, I never quite liked secularisation in that sense. I've always

understood that religion came from very profound roots. I'm not religious myself, but I'm not a militant humanist, a militant atheist. . . . But in terms of our intellectual work, we just didn't give it a second thought. (McCabe, "Interview with Hall," 38)

20. Matthew Yglesias makes a similar point—though at greater length and in greater detail—in his 2008 book *Heads in the Sand*. However, he does so in such a way as to strengthen the Kosovo-Iraq connection; as Samantha Power points out, "Yglesias wrongly implies that support for one war inevitably entailed support for the other; he also unfortunately lends credence to the surprisingly prevalent fiction that Bush invaded Iraq for humanitarian purposes" ("The Democrats and National Security"). In 2008, Barack Obama broke with the long tradition of Democrats' rhetorical incompetence on foreign policy, largely by vowing to restore America's standing in the world—with the clear implication that he would repudiate the Bush-Cheney stand on torture, indefinite detention, unilateralism, and preemptive war.

21. The question of how unpopular wars become unpopular has to do chiefly with collective retrospective judgments—the gradual realization by a majority of Americans, say, that war in Vietnam is not central to U.S. national security and, in fact, is killing thousands of Americans and hundreds of thousands of Vietnamese, or the gradual realization that Iraq did not possess weapons of mass destruction and that the overthrow of Saddam may not have been worth the lives of thousands of Americans and hundreds of thousands of Iraqis. The "manufacturing consent" thesis can account for how it is that mass media can whip up a war frenzy, but it is not as deft at explaining how people reassess war once the frenzy dies down.

The question of whether a war is just or unjust, by contrast, is a question chiefly about prospective judgments, requiring proponents of war to offer rationales for their belief that armed conflict is a justifiable alternative to diplomacy, containment, economic sanctions, or any other means of conducting international relations. A general population that assessed war in those terms—as opposed to the retrospective assessment that relies on a calculus of budgets and body bags—would be a general population familiar with the contours of "just war theory," and it is worth entertaining the proposition that a democratic U.S. left should desire (and work toward) a world in which ordinary people in malls and barbershops can cite the work of Michael Walzer as a matter of routine. (See the following note for more about war and its popular justifications.)

22. During the 2004 presidential campaign, John Kerry was roundly mocked by the right—and by President Bush—for suggesting, during the first presidential debate, that U.S. actions should pass a "global test" for international legitimation. Two days after the debate, in a speech to the National Association of Home Builders, Bush described Kerry's remark as follows:

In the debate—in the debate, Senator Kerry also said something revealing when he laid out the Kerry doctrine. He said—he said that America
has to pass a global test before we can use American troops to defend
ourselves.

Audience: Booo!

The President: That's what he said. (Laughter.) Think about this, Senator Kerry's approach to foreign policy would give foreign governments
veto power over our national security decisions. I have a different view.
(Applause.) When our country is in danger, the President's job is not to
take an international poll. The President's job is to defend America. I'll
continue to work every day with our friends and allies for the sake of
freedom and peace. But our national security decisions will be made in
the Oval Office, not in foreign capitals. (Bush, "President's Remarks to
the National Association of Home Builders")

But what Kerry had actually said in the debate was this:

The President always has the right and always has had the right for preemptive strike. That was a great doctrine throughout the Cold War, and
it was always one of the things we argued about with respect to arms
control. No President, through all of American history, has ever ceded,
and nor would I, the right to preempt in any way necessary to protect
the United States of America. But if and when you do it, Jim, you've got
to do it in a way that passes the test, that passes the global test, where
your countrymen, your people understand fully why you're doing what
you're doing and you can prove to the world that you did it for legitimate reasons.

Here we have our own Secretary of State who's had to apologize to
the world for the presentation he made to the United Nations. I mean,
we can remember when President Kennedy, in the Cuban missile crisis,
sent his Secretary of State to Paris to meet with de Gaulle, and in the
middle of the discussion to tell them about the missiles in Cuba, he
said, here, let me show you the photos. And de Gaulle waved them off,
and said, "No, no, no, no. The word of the President of the United States
is good enough for me." How many leaders in the world today would
respond to us as a result of what we've done in that way?

So what is at test here is the credibility of the United States of America and how we lead the world. (Bush and Kerry, *Presidential Debate*)

This exchange, perhaps, might offer the democratic left one way of advising the
Manichean left on how to distinguish between American laundry detergents.
Here, Tide insists that when the United States takes action, it should do so in a
way that passes a global test, where your countrymen, your people understand

fully why you're doing what you're doing and you can prove to the world that you did it for legitimate reasons; Ivory Snow mocks the idea as "taking an international poll."

23. It bears noting that Rojek's study of Hall is quite strange in many respects, and often openly hostile to a great deal of Hall's work. Rojek opens the book by charging that "the secondary literature on Hall is a product of the Birmingham diaspora: the students and associates he worked with during his years in the Birmingham Centre for Contemporary Cultural Studies. This is the first full-length study to appear outside of the circle," then claiming that the Birmingham "circle" has maintained "a healthy degree of protectionism around Hall and the contemporary meaning of the Centre." Immediately after ascribing to Hall's students and associates "a depressingly defensive reaction that boiled down to the presupposition that if you weren't there (in the 1960s and 1970s) you can't know what it was like," Rojek suddenly becomes defensive: "I have no doubt that much of what I say will be challenged, especially by Birmingham alumni, for this book is no *hommage à Hall,* but an attempt to critically interrogate his ideas and evaluate his cultural and political influence. To write critically about Hall is to enter the lion's den" (*Stuart Hall,* ix–x). Rojek then proceeds, in a forty-seven-page introduction to Hall's work, to fault Hall for eclecticism, "slippage," and "anti-essentialism" (the last of which, according to Rojek, accounts for the first two). I am not a member of the Birmingham circle myself, and have met Hall on only one occasion, but I find this critique unfathomably bizarre; it is as if one were to say that Hall would be more valuable as a thinker if only he returned to essentialism and became more single-minded. I am also mystified by passages like "Hall is still recognizably a man of the Left. However, his political allegiance is now primarily devoted to what might be called emancipatory politics" (5), because I do not understand the conflict between being a man of the left and practicing an emancipatory politics, and I am completely flummoxed by Rojek's account of the British New Left: "In Communist Russia, Hungary, Poland, and the Palestine Liberation Organization, a radical intelligentsia engaged in direct political activity with a coherent programme based in part on organized violence and a disciplined party organization. There is no real equivalent in English intellectual life" (27). Rojek, notably, says this as if it's a bad thing.

For a withering critique of Rojek's study, see Schwarz, "Review of Rojek, *Stuart Hall.*" Rojek replied to Schwarz in turn in "On a Rant by a Little Musketeer." With regard to his point about the British New Left, Rojek writes:

> I shall not respond to *every* barb and provocation made by Schwarz. Often, his criticism is so intemperate that I see no reason to dignify it. Consider: in answer to my criticism that despite championing Gramsci's ideal of the organic intellectual, the Birmingham School failed to produce an effective interventionist political intelligentsia in the manner of

the Palestine Liberation Organization, or the party political cadres of the old Soviet power bloc, Schwarz (p. 183) accuses me of criticizing the New Left for not employing "organized violence." As an unprejudiced reading of my book can verify, the point being made there is not that the New Left / Birmingham School failed to emulate the terrorist tactics of certain organizations, but rather that the political influence of "Birmingham" was more limited, opaque and questionable. (490)

But what seems most remarkable to me is Rojek's insistence that the proper measure of one's realization of Gramsci's ideal of the organic intellectual is the production of an effective interventionist political intelligentsia in the manner of the Palestine Liberation Organization or the party political cadres of the old Soviet power bloc.

Many thanks to Ben Carrington of the University of Texas–Austin for calling my attention to Schwarz's review and Rojek's reply.

CHAPTER FIVE

1. As I noted at the time, this fear was palpable throughout the 1990 Illinois conference itself; many of the participants worried that the conference marked the beginning of a process in which cultural studies would be institutionalized, Americanized, and deradicalized (Bérubé, "Pop Goes the Academy: Cult Studs Fight the Power").

2. I refer, of course, to the following books: Gitlin, *The Twilight of Common Dreams*; Rorty, *Achieving Our Country*; and Tomasky, *Left for Dead*.

3. Though Pfister, in all fairness, adds that "Gitlin's critique is a heated response to an American cultural studies that was beginning to resemble a more theoreticist version of Bowling Green's American Popular Culture Association" (271). About that growing resemblance, as I argue here, Gitlin turned out (unfortunately) to be right.

4. For a discussion of *Culture and Society*'s extended response to T. S. Eliot's *Notes Toward the Definition of Culture*, see Lee, *Life and Times of Cultural Studies*, 19–34.

5. The question of whether mass culture advances or impedes the forces of democracy was broached from the very outset, in Richard Hoggart's *The Uses of Literacy* and the concluding chapter of Williams's *Culture and Society*. In "The Emergence of Cultural Studies and the Crisis of the Humanities," a retrospective essay published in 1990, Stuart Hall wrote, "for me, cultural studies really begins with the debate about the nature of social and cultural change in postwar Britain. An attempt to address the manifest break-up of traditional culture, especially traditional class cultures, it set about registering the impact of the new forms of affluence and consumer society on the very hierarchical and pyramidal structure of

British society" (12). As for its wrong turns and excesses: by my lights, it was too susceptible to the romanticization of young working class men, as in otherwise wonderful studies such as Paul Willis's *Learning to Labor* and Dick Hebdige's *Subculture,* and in the 1970s, it invested far too heavily in Althusser. E. P. Thompson's *The Poverty of Theory* therefore seems to me an overreaction to the Althusserian moment, but not altogether unjustified—as "The Toad in the Garden" acknowledges, even though it opens by dismissing Thompson's dismissal. For a gripping account of Hall's and Thompson's responses to the Althusserian moment, culminating in the December 1979 debate among Hall, Thompson, and Richard Johnson, see Dworkin, *Cultural Marxism in Prewar Britain,* 219–45.

6. What I am calling the "doctrinaire leftist position" on mass culture grows out of the thought of the Frankfurt School, from Horkheimer and Adorno's *The Dialectic of Enlightenment.* As I explain later in this chapter, this mistaken equation of mass culture with conformity with totalitarianism is central to Heath and Potter's argument in *Nation of Rebels* against countercultural leftism. In the cultural studies tradition, the refusal to treat capitalist mass culture as a conformity-enforcing enterprise was marked most dramatically by the "New Times" thesis, advanced by Stuart Hall and Martin Jacques, that "Britain and other advanced capitalist societies are increasingly characterised by diversity, differentiation and fragmentation, rather than homogeneity, standardization and the economies and organizations of scale which characterized modern mass society" (Introduction to *New Times,* 11).

7. Other classic critiques of populism in cultural studies include Frow, *Cultural Studies and Cultural Value;* Grossberg, *It's a Sin;* McGuigan, *Cultural Populism;* Morris, "Banality in Cultural Studies"; and, alphabetically last but chronologically first out of the box, Williamson, "The Problems of Being Popular," from way back in 1985.

8. Sleeper, *Liberal Racism: How Fixating on Race Subverts the American Dream;* Bernstein, *Dictatorship of Virtue: How the Battle over Multiculturalism Is Reshaping Our Schools, Our Country, and Our Lives;* Schlesinger, *The Disuniting of America: Reflections on a Multicultural Society;* Berman, *Debating P.C.: The Controversy over Political Correctness on College Campuses;* Gitlin, *The Twilight of Common Dreams;* Tomasky, *Left for Dead: The Life, Death, and Possible Resurrection of Progressive Politics in America.*

9. Berman's analogy between PC and Stalinism can be found in his introduction to *Debating PC:* "Dwight Macdonald defined 1930s fellow-traveling as the fog that arose when the warm ocean currents of American liberalism encountered the Soviet iceberg. Political correctness in the 1990s is a related syndrome. It is the fog that arises from American liberalism's encounter with the iceberg of French cynicism" (24). For Sleeper's complaint about Kelley's answering machine, see *Liberal Racism,* 19; see also Lott, "After Identity, Politics."

10. Some aspects of the Butler/Fraser exchange are too complex to be

summarized in two paragraphs and a footnote, and some readers may wonder why I award Fraser the palm on the basis of the brief synopsis I offer here. Two moments in Fraser's reply seem decisive. Fraser observes that Butler "conflates 'the economic' with 'the material'":

> Butler assumes that my normative distinction between redistribution and recognition rests on an ontological distinction between the material and the cultural. She therefore assumes that to deconstruct the latter distinction is to pull the rug out from under the former. In fact, however, this assumption does not hold. As I noted earlier, injustices of misrecognition are, from my perspective, just as material as injustices of maldistribution. ("Heterosexism, Misrecognition, and Capitalism," 286)

This argument underwrites Fraser's insistence that homophobia is not hard-wired into the structure of capitalism and is therefore not *fundamentally* a matter of redistribution:

> Homosexuals are more often constructed as a group whose very existence is an abomination, much like the Nazi construction of Jews; they should have no "place" in society at all. No wonder, then, that the principal opponents of gay and lesbian rights today are not multinational corporations, but religious and cultural conservatives, whose obsession is status, not profits. In fact, some multinationals—notably American Airlines, Apple Computer, and Disney—have elicited the wrath of such conservatives by instituting gay-friendly policies, such as domestic partnership benefits. (285)

I do not want to suggest that Fraser's recognition/redistribution framework is entirely unproblematic; her solution to it, notably, seems simply implausible: "The scenario that best finesses the redistribution-recognition dilemma is socialism in the economy plus deconstruction in the culture. But for this scenario to be psychologically and politically feasible requires that all people be weaned from their attachment to current cultural constructions of their interests and identities" (*Justice Interruptus*, 31). All we need to do is to wean all people from their attachments: one feared that Fraser was proposing something difficult.

11. For more recent versions of this debate, see Lisa Duggan's discussion of Fraser in *The Twilight of Equality?* 81–84, where she charges that Fraser "tends to entrench the split she describes in ways that implicitly recreate the hierarchy she eschews" insofar as "her spectrum is loaded with a distortion that truncates the force and range of queer politics" (82). For a free-swinging critique of the Gitlin-Rorty left, see Lott, *The Disappearing Liberal Intellectual*; for a free-swinging critique of the academic/cultural left, see Michaels, *The Trouble with Diversity*.

12. I return to this point below, in my discussion of Robert McChesney's critique of John Fiske; my aim here is to find a way of endorsing McChesney's

impatience with Fiske's celebration of "tiny" victories without reproducing McChesney's reductive class-first, culture-last polemic.

13. The way Grossberg's reply anticipates the Butler/Fraser dispute is startling, and the fact that his argument did not carry the day is depressing. Grossberg writes:

> No one in cultural studies denies the economic realities of racism or sexism, although they are likely to think that such inequalities cannot be directly mapped by or onto class relations. . . . Thus, while I do agree with Garnham (along with a number of key figures in cultural studies like Meaghan Morris) that too much work in cultural studies fails to take economics seriously enough, I am also convinced that political economy—at least this version of it—fails to take culture seriously enough. And ironically, I think it also fails to take capitalism seriously enough. ("Cultural Studies vs. Political Economy," 78)

For a more recent response to the debate, see Peck, "Why We Shouldn't Be Bored with the Political Economy versus Cultural Studies Debate."

14. For example, the closing chapter of Frith's *Performing Rites* includes this resounding note of longing for a world in which identities are dissolved into a form of social movement:

> In taking pleasure from black or gay or female music I don't thus identify as black or gay or female (I don't actually experience these sounds as "black music" or "gay music" or "women's voices") but, rather, participate in imagined forms of democracy and desire, imagined forms of the social and the sexual. And what makes music special in this familiar cultural process is that musical identity is both fantastic—idealizing not just oneself but also the social world one inhabits—and real: it is enacted in activity. Music making and music listening, that is to say, are bodily matters; they involve what one might call *social movements*. (274)

Frith then proceeds to quote Gilroy celebrating music in markedly Habermasian terms: "This reciprocal relationship serves as a strategy and an ideal communicative situation even when the original makers of the music and its eventual consumers are separated in space and time or divided by the technologies of sound production and the commodity form which their art has sought to resist" (275, quoting Gilroy, "Sounds Authentic: Black Music, Ethnicity, and the Challenge of a 'Changing' Same," 127).

15. I discuss this cultural shift in the final chapter of *What's Liberal about the Liberal Arts?*, in which I note that one year after *Loving v. Virginia*, "Captain Kirk kissed Lieutenant Uhura on *Star Trek* and got the show banned throughout the South—though *Star Trek* fans will note that the kiss took place during a sequence in which neither Kirk nor Uhura were acting under their own power, and cultural

critics like me might add that in a weird way, television's first representation of an interracial kiss took place in science fiction, which displaced it into the twenty-third century" (274). In numerical terms, the shift looks like this: "In 1968—the year after the U.S. Supreme Court struck down anti-miscegenation laws in *Loving v. Virginia*—Gallup reported that only 20% of Americans approved of interracial marriage while 72% disapproved. It wasn't until 1991, 23 years later, that for the first time more Americans (48%) approved than disapproved (42%) of such marriages" (GLAAD, *In Focus: Public Opinion and Polls*).

16. In addition to Radway and Modleski, notable feminist forays into some of the seamiest areas of popular culture include Clover, *Men, Women, and Chain Saws*; Williams, *Hard Core*; and Kipnis, *Bound and Gagged*.

17. For instance, William Kerrigan, a Miltonist who was once an emphatic exponent of Lacanian psychoanalysis but said an emphatic goodbye to all that at some point in the 1980s, complained:

> While I was reading difficult books, the new cream-bowl theorists, content with handbook-deep knowledge, went into serious professionalism, jerry-building "programs" and "concentrations" onto the traditional structure of academic majors, setting up "institutes" to secure their unearned self-importance, arranging conferences and starting journals. . . . People got tenure for writing about the imperialist fantasies of Marvel Comics or the gender rules in Harlequin Romances—ideas that might have made decent articles for *High Times* but, driven by theory, got seriously out of hand. ("Falls of Academe," 160)

Kerrigan offered no evidence that he was actually acquainted with Radway's work.

18. I point out this strange maneuver in Bérubé, "Idolatries of the Marketplace."

19. In the three decades since the publication of Hebdige's remarkable *Subculture*, cultural studies theorists have sometimes elided "subcultural analysis" with the kind of "countercultural" thinking that Heath and Potter critique. For the record, then, it's worth noting that Hebdige himself distinguished between subculture and counterculture on the grounds that the former was more politically elusive and indeterminate than the latter:

> The term "counter culture" refers to that amalgam of "alternative" middle class youth cultures—the hippies, the flower children, the yippies—which grew out of the 60s, and came to prominence during the period 1967–70. As Hall *et al.* (1976a) have noted, the counter culture can be distinguished from the subcultures we have been studying by the explicitly political and ideological forms of its opposition to the dominant culture (political action, coherent philosophies, manifestoes, etc.), by its

> elaboration of 'alternative' institutions (Underground Press, communes, co-operatives, "un-careers" etc.), its "stretching" of the transitional stage beyond the teens, and its blurring of the distinctions, so rigorously maintained in subculture, between work, home, family, school and leisure. Whereas opposition in subculture is, as we have seen, displaced into symbolic forms of resistance, the revolt of middle-class youth tends to be more articulate, more confident, more directly expressed and is, therefore, as far as we are concerned, more easily "read." (148, n.6)

Accordingly, counterculture has a greater chance of becoming mainstream culture, and falling prey to the contortions and convolutions described by Heath and Potter. (The "1976a" citation to Hall et al. is to Hall and Jefferson, *Resistance through Rituals*.)

20. The most visible and enthusiastic exponent of de Certeau was, of course, Fiske, *Understanding Popular Culture*, and Fiske, *Reading the Popular*. For an early (and bracing) critique of Fiskeism, see McGuigan, *Cultural Populism*. In more recent years, the most visible and enthusiastic populist in the field has undoubtedly been Henry Jenkins; for example, Jenkins, *The Wow Climax: Tracing the Emotional Impact of Popular Culture*; Jenkins, *Fans, Bloggers, and Gamers: Media Consumers in a Digital Age*; and, from back in the day, the book that launched his career as a scholar and fan of fandom, Jenkins, *Textual Poachers: Television Fans and Participatory Culture*. To give some credit where credit is due: at least Jenkins takes the blogosphere seriously as a cultural phenomenon, rather than writing it off at the outset as Chomsky, Herman, and McChesney have done.

21. In *NASA/Trek*, Constance Penley insists that "the fans taught me . . . that there is no better critic than a fan. No one knows the object better than a fan and no one is more critical. The fan stance toward the object could even be described as the original tough-love approach" (3). It is an appropriate gesture, but the tough-love part of the principle is honored more often in the breach than in the observance in Penley's own work on slash fandom; the danger of appearing to be the snooty college professor talking down to the ordinary fan-folk is just too great.

22. Accordingly, Radway opens *Reading the Romance* by taking issue with Ann Douglas's argument that romances are to be understood precisely as evidence of anti-feminist backlash:

> Because literary critics tend to move immediately from textual interpretation to sociological explanation, they conclude easily that changes in textual features or generic popularity must be the simple and direct result of ideological shifts in the surrounding culture. Thus because she detects a more overtly misogynist message at the heart of the genre, Ann Douglas can argue in her widely quoted article, "Soft-Porn Culture," that the coincidence of the romance's increasing popularity with

the rise of the women's movement must point to a new and developing backlash against feminism. (*Reading the Romance*, 19)

23. See Gurin et al., *Defending Diversity*. For a general (and scrupulously fair) overview of the history of affirmative action in the United States, see Anderson, *The Pursuit of Fairness*. Ellen Willis makes this point eloquently in "Escape from Freedom."

24. This is not to imply that Grossberg himself is unaware that the phrase is Hall's. That would defy belief, since Grossberg is justly considered to be Hall's leading exponent in U.S. cultural studies, and he certainly knows the Hall oeuvre backward and forward.

25. This passage survives largely unchanged in the 2002 version of the essay, which deletes only the sentence "'To replace traditional socialist politics, postmodernism offers identity politics, a series of loosely related social movements linked to the distinct interests of groups usually defined by ethnicity and/or sexuality, that have no clear overarching political vision." Apparently, between the years 1995 and 2002 McChesney became apprised of the fact that postmodernism and identity politics weren't the same thing. For the 2002 version of McChesney's essay, see Warren and Vavrus, *American Cultural Studies*, 76–93.

26. Butler does not merely charge Fraser with having located queer politics on the wrong side of the recognition/redistribution divide; Butler also challenges the recognition/redistribution distinction itself. At one point in "Merely Cultural," Butler asks, "is it possible to distinguish, even analytically, between a lack of cultural recognition and material oppression, when the very definition of legal 'personhood' is rigorously circumscribed by cultural norms that are indissociable from their material effects?" (273). Butler leaves the answer implicit in the question ("no," in a word), but the question presumes precisely what Fraser denies—namely, that a deconstruction of the material/cultural distinction pulls the rug out from under the normative distinction between redistribution and recognition. In other words, Butler's question assumes that material harms are necessarily economic in nature. Be that as it may, there is no sense in which Butler's critique of Fraser gives up on class politics altogether. This is an argument about how to conceive the relation between the material and the cultural, not, *pace* McChesney, an argument about how (as he puts it) to jettison "materialism and class-based politics in favor of identity-based politics."

WORKS CITED

Abdou, Nyier. "Scylla and Charybdis: Denis Halliday Navigates Dangerous Waters between a Cruel System and a Brutal Regime." *Al-Ahram Weekly* 618 (26 Dec. 2002–1 Jan. 2003). At http://weekly.ahram.org.eg/2002/618/sc6.htm (accessed 23 Jan. 2009).

Ackerman, Seth. "Afghan Famine On and Off the Screen: Aid Workers Mostly Quoted When U.S. Likes Their Message." *Extra! (Fairness and Accuracy in Reporting),* May/June 2002. At http://www.fair.org/index.php?page=1104 (accessed 11 Jan. 2008).

Adelman, Ken. "Cakewalk in Iraq." *Washington Post,* 13 Feb. 2002: A27.

Afary, Janet, and Kevin B. Anderson. *Foucault and the Iranian Revolution: Gender and the Seductions of Islamism.* Chicago: University of Chicago Press, 2005.

"After Fear." Editorial. *New Republic,* 29 Oct. 2001: 9.

Agamben, Giorgio. *Homo Sacer: Sovereign Power and Bare Life.* Stanford: Stanford University Press, 1998.

Ahmed, Samina. "The United States and Terrorism in Southwest Asia: September 11 and Beyond." *International Security,* 26.3 (2001–02): 79–93.

Albert, Michael. "Raise Your Voice but Keep Your Head Down." *ZNet,* 5 Feb. 2005. At http://www.kersplebedeb.com/mystuff/s11/churchill_albert.html (accessed 8 Aug. 2006).

Ali, Tariq, ed. *Masters of the Universe? NATO's Balkan Crusade.* London: Verso, 2000.

Alterman, Eric. "Making One and One Equal Two." *Nation,* 25 May 1998: 10.
———. "Why Chickenhawks Matter." *Nation,* 1 Dec. 2003: 10. At http://www.thenation. com/doc/20031201/alterman (accessed 23 Jan. 2009).

Althusser, Louis. "Ideology and Ideological State Apparatuses: Notes toward an Investigation." In *Lenin and Philosophy,* trans. Ben Brewster, 127–86. London: Verso, 1971.

Anderson, Amanda. "Cryptonormativism and Double Gestures: The Politics of Poststructuralism." *Cultural Critique* 21 (1992): 63–95.

Anderson, Perry. "Force and Consent." *New Left Review* 17 (Sept./Oct. 2002): 5–30. At http://newleftreview.org/A2407 (accessed 24 Jan. 2009).

Anderson, Terry H. *The Pursuit of Fairness: A History of Affirmative Action.* New York: Oxford University Press, 2004.

"The Anthrax Source: Is Iraq Unleashing Biological Weapons on America?" Editorial. *Wall Street Journal,* 15 Oct. 2001. At http://www.opinionjournal.com/editorial/ feature.html?id=95001324 (accessed 23 Jan. 2009).

Aronowitz, Stanley. "A Free Woman." Obituaries for Ellen Willis. *First of the Month,* Jun. 2007. At http://www.firstofthemonth.org/archives/2007/06/a_free_woman_wh.html (accessed 25 Jan. 2009).

Astill, James. "Strike One." *Guardian,* 2 Oct. 2001. At http://www.guardian.co.uk/g2/story/0,3604,561557,00.html (accessed 20 Dec. 2007).

Baker, Mona. "The Boycott of Israeli Academic Institutions." At http://www.monabaker.com/ontheboycott.htm (accessed 17 Nov. 2007).

Balkan Witness. At http://www.glypx.com/BalkanWitness/.

Barkham, Patrick. "Dissidents and Defiants Slipping through the Net." *Guardian,* 4 Dec. 1998.

Barsky, Robert F. *The Chomsky Effect: A Radical Works beyond the Ivory Tower.* Cambridge: MIT Press, 2007.

Barstow, David. "Behind TV Analysts, Pentagon's Hidden Hand." *New York Times,* 20 Apr. 2008: 1. At http://www.nytimes.com/2008/04/20/washington/ 20generals.html (accessed 11 Jul. 2008).

Beinart, Peter. *The Good Fight: Why Liberals—and Only Liberals—Can Win the War on Terror and Make America Great Again.* New York: HarperCollins, 2006.

Bennett, Tony. "Putting Policy in Cultural Studies." In *Cultural Studies,* ed. Larry Grossberg, Cary Nelson, and Paula Treichler, 23–37. New York: Routledge, 1992.

Bergen, Peter. "Armchair Provocateur." *Washington Monthly* (December 2003). At http://www. washingtonmonthly.com/features/2003/0312.bergen.html (accessed 12 Jan. 2008).

Berman, Paul, ed. *Debating P.C.: The Controversy over Political Correctness on College Campuses.* New York: Dell, 1992.

———. "Liberal Hawks Reconsider the Iraq War." *Slate,* 12 Jan. 2004. At http://www.slate.com/id/2093620/entry/ 2093798/ (accessed 31 Dec. 2007).

———. *Power and the Idealists: The Passion of Joschka Fischer and Its Aftermath.* New York: Soft Skull, 2005.

———. *A Tale of Two Utopias: The Political Journey of the Generation of 1968.* New York: Norton, 1997.

———. *Terror and Liberalism.* New York: Norton, 2003.

————. "Why Germany Isn't Convinced." *Slate,* 14 Feb. 2003. At http://www.slate.com/id/2078560/ (accessed 31 Dec. 2007).

————. "Will the Opposition Lead?" *New York Times,* 15 Apr. 2004: A27.

Bernstein, Richard. *Dictatorship of Virtue: How the Battle over Multiculturalism Is Reshaping Our Schools, Our Country, and Our Lives.* New York: Knopf, 1994.

Berntsen, Gary. *Jawbreaker: The Attack on Bin Laden and Al Qaeda: A Personal Account by the CIA's Key Field Commander.* New York: Crown, 2005.

Bérubé, Michael. "Fighting Liberals." Review of Paul Berman, *Terror and Liberalism.* In *Rhetorical Occasions: Essays on Humans and the Humanities,* 267–74. Chapel Hill: University of North Carolina Press, 2006.

————. "Idolatries of the Marketplace." Review of Thomas Frank, *One Market under God. Common Review* 1.1 (2001): 51–57.

————. "Nation and Narration." *Context: A Forum for Literary Arts and Culture* 10 (2002): 15–17. At http://www.dalkeyarchive.com/article/show/33 (accessed 23 Jan. 2009).

————. "Peace Puzzle: Why the Left Can't Get Iraq Right." *Boston Globe,* 15 Sept. 2002: E1–E2. At http://www.boston.com/news/packages/iraq/globe_stories/ 091502_bush.htm (accessed 22 Jan. 2009).

————. "Pop Goes the Academy: Cult Studs Fight the Power." In *Public Access: Literary Theory and American Cultural Politics,* 137–60. London: Verso, 1994.

————. "Real Problems on the Real Left," *ZNet,* 9 Dec. 2002. At http://www.zmag.org/content/showarticle.cfm?ItemID=2721 (accessed 27 Jun. 2007).

————. "Re-entry." Blog post. 17 Jul. 2006. At http://www.michaelberube.com/index.php/ weblog/comments/993/.

————. "Richard Rorty and the Politics of Modesty." *Common Review* 6.3 (2008): 25–33.

————. *What's Liberal about the Liberal Arts? Classroom Politics and "Bias" in Higher Education.* New York: Norton, 2006.

Bin Laden, Osama. "Al-Qaeda's *Fatwa* of February 23, 1998." *PBS Online NewsHour.* At http://www.pbs.org/newshour/terrorism/international/fatwa_1998.html (accessed 19 Dec. 2007).

Black, Duncan ("Atrios"). "Deep Thoughts from Thomas Friedman." *Eschaton,* 27 May 2007. At http://www.eschatonblog.com/2007_05_27_archive.html #6516378771035319906 (accessed 20 Jul. 2008).

————. "Failure of Leadership." *Eschaton,* 23 Jul. 2004. At http://atrios. blogspot.com/2004_07_ 18_archive.html#1090594046213205O7 (accessed 14 Jan. 2008).

Bogert, Carroll. "Letter to the Editor." *Salon,* 22 Jan. 2002. At http://dir.salon.com/story/people/letters/ 2002/01/22/chomsky/index.html (accessed 13 Jun. 2007).

Brenkman, John. *The Cultural Contradictions of Democracy: Political Thought Since September 11.* Princeton: Princeton University Press, 2007.

————. "Extreme Criticism." *Critical Inquiry* 26.1 (1999): 109–27.

Brennan, Timothy. *Wars of Position: The Cultural Politics of Left and Right*. New York: Columbia University Press, 2006.

Brown, Matt. "'Bin Laden Tape' Tested for Authenticity." *ABC* (Australia), 13 Nov. 2002. At http://www.abc.net.au/pm/stories/s726118.htm (accessed 23 Jan. 2009).

Brzezinski, Zbigniew. Interview in *Le Nouvel Observateur* (Paris), January 15 and 21, 1998: 76. Reprinted in *The Middle East and Islamic World Reader*, ed. Marvin E. Gettleman and Stuart Schaar. New York: Grove, 2003.

Buchanan, Patrick. "Ralph Nader: Conservatively Speaking." Interview with Ralph Nader. *American Conservative*, 21 Jun. 2004. At http://www.amconmag.com/2004_06_21/cover.html (accessed 2 Oct. 2006).

Burke, Jason. *Al-Qaeda: The True Story of Radical Islam*. London: I. B. Tauris, 2004.

Burns, John F. "Pakistan Antiterror Support Avoids Vow of Military Aid." *New York Times*, 16 Sept. 2001: 5.

Buruma, Ian. "Revolution from Above." *New York Review of Books*, 1 May 2003. At http://www.nybooks.com/articles/16211 (accessed 31 Jul. 2008).

Bush, George W. "President's Remarks to the National Association of Home Builders." Columbus, Ohio, 2 Oct. 2004. At http://web.archive.org/web/20080306175026/ http://www.whitehouse.gov/news/releases/2004/10/20041002-7.html (accessed 25 Jan. 2009).

————. 2003 State of the Union Address. 28 Jan. 2003. At http://www.cnn.com/2003/ALLPOLITICS/01/28/sotu.transcript/ (accessed 24 Jan. 2009).

Bush, George, and John Kerry. *Presidential Debate*. 30 Sept. 2004. Commission on Presidential Debates. At http://www.debates.org/pages/trans2004a.html (accessed 25 Jan. 2009).

Butler, Judith. "Merely Cultural." *Social Text* 52/53 (1997): 265–77.

————. *Precarious Life: The Powers of Mourning and Violence*. London: Verso, 2004.

Butler, Judith, Ernesto Laclau, and Slavoj Žižek. *Contingency, Hegemony, Universality: Contemporary Dialogues on the Left*. London: Verso, 2000.

Carrington, Ben. "Decentreing the Centre: Cultural Studies in Britain and Its Legacy." In *A Companion to Cultural Studies*, ed. Toby Miller, 275–97. Oxford: Blackwell, 2001.

Carter, Shan, Jonathan Corum, Amanda Cox, Farhana Hossain, and G. V. Xaquin. "The Shifts in the Map: The Areas That Voted More Democratic or Republican Than in 2004." *New York Times*, 11 Nov. 2008. At http://graphics8.nytimes.com/packages/flash/ politics/20081104_ELECTION_RECAP/electionChange2.swf (accessed 21 Jan. 2009).

Casey, Leo. "Let Us Not Inherit This Ill Wind: A Rejoinder to Chomsky's 'Reply to Casey' on Issues Emanating from the September 11 Mass Murders." *ZNet*.

At http://web.archive.org/web/20071103122746/http://www.zmag.org/casey2.htm (accessed 22 Jan. 2009).

———. "The Unbearable Whiteness of Chomsky's Arguments: Psychological Projection and the Erasure of African Victims in Chomsky's 'Reply' to Hitchens." *ZNet*, 2 Oct. 2001. At http://web.archive.org/web/20071110023213/http://www.zmag.org/casey.htm (accessed 22 Jan. 2009).

Centre for Contemporary Cultural Studies. *The Empire Strikes Back: Race and Racism in 70s Britain*. London: Routledge, 1982.

Chait, Jonathan. "Don't Let the Left Defeat Lieberman." *Los Angeles Times*, 7 May 2006. At http://articles.latimes.com/2006/may/07/opinion/oe-chait7 (accessed 23 Jan. 2009).

Chomsky, Noam. *Failed States: The Abuse of Power and the Assault on Democracy*. New York: Metropolitan, 2006.

———. "The Greatest Intellectual? Interview with Emma Brockes." *Guardian*, 31 Oct. 2005. At http://www.chomsky.info/onchomsky/20051031.htm (accessed 23 Jan. 2009).

———. *Hegemony or Survival: America's Quest for Global Dominance*. New York: Metropolitan, 2003. ("Afterword," 2004.)

———. Interview. *Independent* (London), 4 Dec. 2003. *BNet*. At http://findarticles.com/p/articles/mi_qn4158/is_20031204/ai_n12728839 (accessed 28 Jun. 2007).

———. "Kosovo Book Review." Exchange with Ray Amberg. At http://groups.google.com/group/alt.fan.noam-chomsky/msg/5799d10331fd4df6?hl=en&lr=&ie=UTF-8&rnum=6 (accessed 19 May 2009).

———. Letter to the Editor. *Salon*, 29 Jan. 2002. At http://dir.salon.com/story/people/letters/2002/01/29/chomsky/index.html (accessed 13 Jun. 2007).

———. "NATO's Invasion of Kosovo and Apologetics for State Violence." *Noam Chomsky ZBlog*, 6 Jan. 2007. At http://web.archive.org/web/20070702162217/http://blogs.zmag.org/node/2562 (accessed 19 May 2009).

———. *A New Generation Draws the Line: Kosovo, East Timor and the Standards of the West*. London: Verso, 2001.

———. *The New Military Humanism: Lessons from Kosovo*. Monroe, Maine: Common Courage, 1999.

———. "The New War against Terror." 18 Oct. 2001. At http://www.chomsky-info/talks/20011018.htm (accessed 19 May 2009).

———. *9–11*. New York: Seven Stories, 2001.

———. "On the Bombings." *ZNet*, 11 Sept. 2001. At http://www.zmag.org/chomnote.htm (accessed 3 Jan. 2008).

———. "On the NATO Bombing of Yugoslavia." Interview with Danilo Mandic. 25 Apr. 2006. At http://www.chomsky.info/interviews/20060425.htm (accessed 23 Jan. 2009).

————. Radio B92 (Belgrade). Interview with Svetlana Vukovic and Svetlana Lukic. *ZNet,* 18 Sept. 2001. At http://www.zmag.org/chomb92.htm (accessed 22 Jul. 2007).

————. "Reply to Casey.'" *ZNet,* 3 Oct. 2001. At http://web.archive.org/web/20071110023219/http://www.zmag.org/chomreply.htm (accessed 22 Jan. 2009).

————. "Reply to Hitchens." *Nation,* 1 Oct. 2001. At http://www.thenation.com/doc/20011015/chomsky20011001 (accessed 18 Jun. 2007).

————. "The War in Afghanistan." *ZNet,* 1 Feb. 2002. At http://www.chomsky.info/articles/20020201.htm (accessed 8 Jul. 2007).

————. "What a Fair Trial for Saddam Would Entail." *Toronto Star,* 25 Jan. 2004. At http://www.chomsky.info/articles/20040125.htm (accessed 14 Jul. 2007).

Chomsky, Noam, and Edward S. Herman. *After the Cataclysm.* Vol. 2 of *Political Economy of Human Rights.* Boston: South End, 1979.

————. "Distortions at Fourth Hand." *Nation* 25 Jun. 1977: 789–94.

————. *The Washington Connection and Third World Fascism.* Vol. 1 of *Political Economy of Human Rights.* Boston: South End, 1979.

Churchill, Ward. "Some People Push Back: On the Justice of Roosting Chickens." At http://www.kersplebedeb.com/mystuff/s11/churchill.html (accessed 14 Jul. 2008).

Clarke, Richard. *Against All Enemies: Inside America's War on Terror.* New York: Free Press, 2004.

Clover, Carol. *Men, Women, and Chain Saws: Gender in the Modern Horror Film.* Princeton: Princeton University Press, 1993.

Club for Growth. Advertisement. YouTube. At http://www.youtube.com/watch?v=K4-vEwD_7Hk (accessed 26 Jan. 2009)

Cocco, Marie. "Bush's 9/11 Myths Endanger U.S." *Newsday,* 23 Mar. 2004. Republished at *Common Dreams.* At http://www.commondreams.org/views04/0323-02.htm (accessed 7 Jan. 2008).

Cockburn, Alexander. "Press Clips." *Village Voice,* 21 Jan. 1980.

Cohen, Nick. "Taking Issue: Nick Cohen Disagrees with Johann Hari." *Dissent,* Fall 2007. At http://www.dissentmagazine.org/article/?article=944 (accessed 23 Jan. 2009).

————. *What's Left? How Liberals Lost Their Way.* London: Fourth Estate, 2007.

Cohen, Richard. " . . . And Now to Iraq." *Washington Post,* 30 Nov. 2001: A41.

————. "Our Forgotten Panic." *Washington Post,* 22 Jul. 2004: A21. At http://www.washingtonpost.com/wp-dyn/articles/A4328-2004Jul21.html (accessed 23 Jan. 2009).

————. "A Winning Hand for Powell." *Washington Post,* 6 Feb. 2003: A37.

Cohen, Steven, William Eimicke, and Jessica Horan. "Catastrophe and the Public Service: A Case Study of the Government Response to the Destruction of the World Trade Center." *Public Administration Review* 62.1 (2002): 24–32.

Coll, Steven. *Ghost Wars: The Secret History of the CIA, Afghanistan, and Bin Laden, from the Soviet Invasion to September 10, 2001.* New York: Penguin, 2004.

Collier, Peter, and David Horowitz, eds. *The Anti-Chomsky Reader.* San Francisco: Encounter Books, 2004.

Cooper, Marc. "Liberals Stuck in Scold Mode." *Los Angeles Times,* 14 Oct. 2001. At http://www.commondreams.org/views01/1014-02.htm (accessed 1 Jan. 2008).

"Corrections and Clarifications: *The Guardian* and Noam Chomsky." *Guardian,* 17 Nov. 2005. At http://www.guardian.co.uk/corrections/story/0,3604, 1644017,00.html (accessed 23 Jan. 2009).

Coulter, Ann. "This Is War." *National Review Online,* 13 Sept. 2001. At http://www.nationalreview.com/coulter/coulter.shtml (accessed 24 Jan. 2009).

———. *Treason: Liberal Treachery from the Cold War to the War on Terrorism.* New York: Crown Forum, 2003.

Cowen, Tyler. *In Praise of Commercial Culture.* Cambridge: Harvard University Press, 1998.

Daalder, Ivo, ed. *Beyond Preemption: Force and Legitimacy in a Changing World.* Washington, D.C.: Brookings Institution, 2007.

Danner, Mark. *The Secret Way to War: The Downing Street Memo and the Iraq War's Buried History.* New York: New York Review Books, 2006.

———. *Torture and Truth: America, Abu Ghraib, and the War on Terror.* New York: New York Review Books, 2004.

Daum, Werner. "Universalism and the West: An Agenda for Understanding." *Harvard International Review* 23.2 (Summer 2001): 19–23. At http://www.harvardir.org/articles/909/1/ (accessed 22 Jan. 2009).

Dayton Peace Accords. At http://www.state.gov/www/regions/eur/bosnia/bosagree.html (accessed 19 May 2009).

Dean, Howard. "Defending American Values—Protecting America's Interests." Speech delivered at Drake University. 17 Feb. 2003. At http://www.gwu.edu/~action/2004/dean/dean021703sp.html (accessed 23 Jan. 2009).

de Certeau, Michel. *The Practice of Everyday Life.* Trans. Steven Rendall. Berkeley: University of California Press, 1984.

DeMott, Benjamin. "With Friends Like These." *First of the Month,* July 2005. At http://www.firstofthemonth.org/archives/2005/07/with_friends_li.html (accessed 21 Jul. 2008).

Dickerson, John. "Bush's 'Bannergate' Shuffle." *Time,* 1 Nov. 2003. At http://www.time.com/time/columnist/dickerson/article/0,9565,536170,00.html (accessed 7 Jan. 2008).

Douglas, Ann. "Soft-Porn Culture." *New Republic,* 30 Aug. 1980: 25–29.

Drum, Kevin. "A Letter from Paul Berman." *Political Animal* (blog of *Washington*

Monthly), 23 Mar. 2006. At http://www2.washingtonmonthly.com/archives/individual/2006_03/008485.php (accessed 18 Aug. 2007).

D'Souza, Dinesh. *The Enemy at Home: The Cultural Left and Its Responsibility for 9/11.* New York: Doubleday, 2007.

Duggan, Lisa. *The Twilight of Equality? Neoliberalism, Cultural Politics, and the Attack on Democracy.* Boston: Beacon, 2003.

Dworkin, Dennis. *Cultural Marxism in Postwar Britain: History, the New Left, and the Origins of Cultural Studies.* Durham, N.C.: Duke University Press, 1997.

"Euston Manifesto." At http://eustonmanifesto.org/the-euston-manifesto/ (accessed 23 Jan. 2009).

"Excerpts from Iraqi Transcript of Meeting with U.S. Envoy." *New York Times,* 23 Sept. 1990: 19.

Falk, Richard. *Human Rights Horizons: The Pursuit of Justice in a Globalizing World.* New York: Routledge, 2000.

Fallows, James. "The Fifty-First State?" *Atlantic,* Nov. 2002: 53–64. At http://www.theatlantic.com/doc/200211/fallows (accessed 5 Jul. 2007).

Feher, Michael. "Robert Fisk's Newspapers." *Theory and Event* 5.4 (2001).

Finkelstein, Norman. "'Fraternally Yours, Chris': Hitchens as Model Apostate." *Counterpunch,* 10 Sept. 2003. At http://www.counterpunch.org/finkelstein09102003.html (accessed 15 Jul. 2008).

Fiske, John. *Reading the Popular.* New York: Routledge, 1989.

———. *Understanding Popular Culture.* New York: Routledge, 1989.

Frank, Thomas. *The Conquest of Cool: Business Culture, Counterculture, and the Rise of Hip Consumerism.* Chicago: University of Chicago Press, 1997.

———. *One Market under God: Extreme Capitalism, Market Populism, and the End of Economic Democracy.* New York: Doubleday, 2000.

———. *What's the Matter with Kansas? How Conservatives Won the Heart of America.* New York: Metropolitan, 2004.

Fraser, Nancy. "Heterosexism, Misrecognition, and Capitalism: A Response to Judith Butler." *Social Text* 52/53 (1997): 279–89.

———. *Justice Interruptus: Critical Reflections on the "Postsocialist" Condition.* New York: Routledge, 1997.

Friedman, Thomas. Guest, .*The Charlie Rose Show.* 30 May 2003. Excerpt on YouTube. At http://www.youtube.com/watch?v=HOF6ZeUvgXs (accessed 23 Jan. 2009).

———. "Stop the Music." *New York Times,* 23 Apr. 1999: A25.

Frith, Simon. "The Good, the Bad, and the Indifferent: Defending Popular Culture from the Populists." *diacritics* 21.4 (1991): 101–15.

———. *Performing Rites: On the Value of Popular Music.* Cambridge: Harvard University Press, 1996.

Frow, John. *Cultural Studies and Cultural Value.* London: Oxford University Press, 1995.

Furuhashi, Yoshie. "Ahmadinejad in the Arab Streets." *Critical Montages,* 28 Jun. 2006. At http://montages.blogspot.com/2006/06/ahmadinejad-in-arab-streets.html (accessed 7 Aug. 2006).

———. "Persian Chavez." *Critical Montages,* 20 Jun. 2006. At http://montages.blogspot.com/2006/06/persian-chavez.html (accessed 7 Aug. 2006).

———. "'Save Darfur': Evangelicals and Establishment Jews." *MRZine,* 28 Apr. 2006. At http://mrzine.monthlyreview. org/furuhashi280406.html (accessed 11 Jul. 2008).

———. "Who Wants Peace in Darfur?" *MRZine,* 30 Apr. 2006. At http://mrzine.monthlyreview.org/furuhashi300406.html (accessed 11 Jul. 2008).

Garnham, Nicholas. "Political Economy and Cultural Studies." *Critical Studies in Mass Communication* 12.1 (1995): 62–71.

The George Polk Awards in Journalism. Press Release Archives. 2007. At http://www.brooklyn.liu.edu/polk/press/2007.html (accessed 22 Jan. 2009).

Geras, Norman. "Failure in Iraq." *Normblog,* 15 Oct. 2006. At http://normblog.typepad.com/normblog/2006/10/failure_in_ iraq.html (accessed 23 Jan. 2009).

———. "Johann—Saved." *Normblog,* 27 Jul. 2007. At http://normblog.typepad.com/normblog/2007/07/johann_saved.html (accessed 23 Jan. 2009).

Gilroy, Paul. *The Black Atlantic: Modernity and Double Consciousness.* Cambridge: Harvard University Press, 1993.

———. "Sounds Authentic: Black Music, Ethnicity, and the Challenge of a 'Changing' Same." *Black Music Research Journal* 11:2 (1991): 111–36.

———. *There Ain't No Black in the Union Jack: The Cultural Politics of Race and Nation.* London: Routledge, 1987.

Gilroy, Paul, Lawrence Grossberg, and Angela McRobbie, eds. *Without Guarantees: In Honour of Stuart Hall.* London: Verso, 2000.

Gitlin, Todd. "Blaming America First." *Mother Jones,* January/February 2002. At http://www.motherjones.com/commentary/columns/2002/01/blaming-america-first (accessed 19 May 2009).

———. *The Intellectuals and the Flag.* New York: Columbia University Press, 2007.

———. *Letters to a Young Activist.* New York: Basic, 2003.

———. "The Ordinariness of American Feelings." *openDemocracy,* 11 Oct. 2001. At http://www.opendemocracy.net/conflict-us911/article_105.jsp (accessed 1 Jan. 2008).

———. "The Pro-War *Post.*" *American Prospect,* 1 Apr. 2003. At http://www.prospect.org/cs/articles? article=the_prowar_ipost/I (accessed 11 Jan. 2009).

———. "Todd Gitlin Responds." *Dissent* (Winter 2003). At http://dissentmagazine.org/article/?article=524 (accessed 13 Jan. 2008)

———. *The Twilight of Common Dreams: Why America Is Wracked by Culture Wars.* New York: Holt, 1995.

———. "The War Movement and the Antiwar Movement." *Talking Points Memo Café,* 18 Oct. 2005. At http://tpmcafe.talkingpointsmemo.com/2005/10/18/the_war_ movement_and_the_antiw/ (accessed 23 Jan. 2007).

———. "Who Communicates with Whom, in What Voice, and Why, about the Study of Mass Communication." *Critical Studies in Mass Communication* 7.2 (1990): 185–96.

GLAAD (Gay and Lesbian Alliance Against Defamation). *In Focus: Public Opinion and Polls.* Media Reference Guide. At http://www.glaad.org/media/guide/ infocus/polls.php (accessed 26 Jan. 2009).

Glassman, James K., and Kevin Hassett. *Dow 36,000: The New Strategy for Profiting from the Coming Rise in the Stock Market.* New York: Crown, 1999.

Glenn, David. "Unfinished Wars." *Columbia Journalism Review,* Sept/Oct. 2005. At http://cjrarchives.org/issues/2005/5/glenn.asp (accessed 8 Jul. 2007).

Glenny, Misha. *The Balkans: Nationalism, War and the Great Powers, 1804–1999.* New York: Viking, 2000.

Goldberg, Jonah. "Baghdad Delenda Est, Part Two: Get On with It." *National Review Online,* 23 Apr. 2002. At http://article.nationalreview.com/?q=YTFh ZGQ4Y2IyZmNlY2QyNDkwZTlkZjFkYjZiNWY0YzU=#more (accessed 3 Jul, 2007).

Goodnough, Abby. "U.S. Paid 10 Journalists for Anti-Castro Reports." *New York Times,* 9 Sept. 2006. At http://www.nytimes.com/2006/09/09/washington/09cuba.html?_r=1&oref=slogin (accessed 11 Jan. 2009).

"GOP Senator Labels Abused Prisoners 'Terrorists.'" *CNN.com,* 12 May 2004. At http://www.cnn.com/2004/ALLPOLITICS/05/11/inhofe.abuse/index.html (accessed 31 Dec. 2007).

Gordon, Joy. "Cool War: Economic Sanctions as a Weapon of Mass Destruction." *Harper's* (November 2002): 43–49.

Gore, Al. "Iraq and the War on Terrorism." Speech to the Commonwealth Club of Northern California. 23 Sept. 2002. At http://www.commonwealthclub. org/ archive/02/02-09 gore-speech.html (accessed 23 Jan. 2009).

Gourevitch, Philip. *We Wish to Inform You That Tomorrow We Will Be Killed with Our Families: Stories from Rwanda.* New York: Picador, 1998.

Greenwald, Glenn. "Only a Fool—or Possibly a Frenchman—Could Conclude Otherwise." *Unclaimed Territory,* 15 Nov. 2006. At http://glenngreenwald. blogspot.com/2006/11/only-fool-or-possibly-frenchman-could.html (accessed 23 Jan. 2009).

Grossberg, Lawrence. "Cultural Studies vs. Political Economy: Is Anyone Else Bored with This Debate?" *Critical Studies in Mass Communication* 12.1 (1995): 72–81.

———. *It's a Sin: Essays on Postmodernism, Politics and Culture.* Sydney: Power, 1988.

———. "On Postmodernism and Articulation: An Interview with Stuart Hall." In

Stuart Hall: Critical Dialogues in Cultural Studies, ed. David Morley and Kuan-Hsing Chen, 131–50. New York: Routledge, 1996.

Grossberg, Lawrence, Cary Nelson, and Paula Treichler. *Cultural Studies.* New York: Routledge, 1992.

Gurin, Patricia, Jeffrey S. Lehman, Earl Lewis, Eric L. Dey, Sylvia Hurtado, and Gerald Gurin. *Defending Diversity: Affirmative Action at the University of Michigan.* Ann Arbor: University of Michigan Press, 2004.

Hall, Stuart. "Culture, Community, Nation." *Cultural Studies* 7.3 (1993): 349–63.

———. "Drifting into a Law and Order Society." Cobdon Trust Human Rights Day Lecture. London: Cobden Trust, 1980.

———. "The Emergence of Cultural Studies and the Crisis of the Humanities." *October* 53 (1990): 11–23.

———. "Encoding/Decoding." In *Culture, Media, Language: Working Papers in Cultural Studies, 1972–1979,* ed. Stuart Hall, Dorothy Hobson, Andrew Love, and Paul Willis, 128–38. London: Unwin Hyman, 1980.

———. "Gramsci's Relevance for the Study of Race and Ethnicity." In *Stuart Hall: Critical Dialogues in Cultural Studies,* ed. David Morley and Kuan-Hsing Chen, 411–40. New York: Routledge, 1996.

———. "The Great Moving Nowhere Show." *Marxism Today* Nov.–Dec. 1998: 9–14.

———. *The Hard Road to Renewal: Thatcherism and the Crisis of the Left.* London: Verso, 1988.

———. "Marx's Notes on Method: A 'Reading' of the '1857 Introduction.'" *Working Papers in Cultural Studies* 6 (1975): 132–71.

———. "New Ethnicities." In *Stuart Hall: Critical Dialogues in Cultural Studies,* ed. David Morley and Kuan-Hsing Chen, 441–49. New York: Routledge, 1996.

———. "Notes on Deconstructing 'the Popular.'" In *People's History and Socialist Theory,* ed. Rachel Samuels, 227–40. London: Routledge and Kegan Paul, 1981.

———. "The Problem of Ideology: Marxism without Guarantees." In *Stuart Hall: Critical Dialogues in Cultural Studies,* ed. David Morley and Kuan-Hsing Chen, 25–46. New York: Routledge, 1996.

———. "Race, Articulation, and Societies Structured in Dominance." In *Black British Cultural Studies: A Reader,* ed. Houston A. Baker Jr., Manthia Diawara, and Ruth H. Lindeborg, 16–60. Chicago: University of Chicago Press, 1996.

———. "The Toad in the Garden: Thatcherism among the Theorists." In *Marxism and the Interpretation of Culture,* ed. Cary Nelson and Lawrence Grossberg, 35–73. Urbana: University of Illinois Press, 1988.

———. "What Is This 'Black' in Black Popular Culture?" In *Stuart Hall: Critical Dialogues in Cultural Studies,* ed. David Morley and Kuan-Hsing Chen, 465–75. New York: Routledge, 1996.

Hall, Stuart, and Martin Jacques. Introduction to *New Times: The Changing Face of Politics in the 1990s*, 11–20. London: Verso, 1989.

Hall, Stuart, and Tony Jefferson, eds. *Resistance through Rituals: Youth Subcultures in Post-War Britain*. London: Hutchinson, 1976.

Hall, Stuart, Chas Critcher, Tony Jefferson, John Clarke, and Brian Robert. *Policing the Crisis: "Mugging," the State, and Law and Order*. London: Macmillan, 1978.

Hall, Stuart, Chantal Mouffe, and Gary Younge. "The New World Disorder." *Soundings* 19 (Winter 2001–02): 9–22.

Hannity, Sean. *Deliver Us from Evil: Defeating Terrorism, Despotism, and Liberalism*. New York: William Morrow, 2004.

Hansen, Suzy. "Noam Chomsky." Interview. *Salon*, 16 Jan. 2002. At http://dir.salon.com/story/people/feature/2002/01/16/chomsky/ (accessed 13 Jun. 2007).

Hari, Johann. "Choosing Sides: On Nick Cohen's *What's Left?*" *Dissent* (summer 2007): 79–85. At http://www.dissentmagazine.org/article/?article=868 (accessed 19 May 2009).

Harpham, Geoffrey Galt. "Symbolic Terror." *Critical Inquiry* 28.2 (2002): 573–80.

Hastings, Adrian. "Not a Book about Kosovo." *Bosnia Report* 23–25 (2001). At http://www.bosnia.org.uk/bosrep/report_format.cfm?articleid=802&reportid=151 (accessed 23 Jan. 2009).

———. *SOS Bosnia*. London: Alliance to Defend Bosnia-Herzegovina, 1994.

Hastings, Max, and Simon Jenkins. *The Battle for the Falklands*. New York: Norton, 1983.

Heath, Joseph, and Andrew Potter. *Nation of Rebels: Why Counterculture Became Consumer Culture*. New York: Harper Business, 2004.

Hebdige, Dick. *Subculture: The Meaning of Style*. London: Routledge, 1979.

Heinrichs, Jay. "All Bulworth, No Rhythm." *Outside*, Oct. 2000. At http://outside.away.com/magazine/200008/200008 camp_nader1.html (accessed 2 Oct. 2006).

Herman, Edward S. "The Cruise Missile Left: Aligning with Power." *Z Magazine*, Nov. 2002. At http://web.archive.org/web/20080122130210/http://zmagsite.zmag.org/Nov2002/Herman1102.htm (accessed 22 Jan. 2009).

———. "The Cruise Missile Left, Part 2: The Anti-ANSWER Crusade," *Z Magazine*, April 2003. At http://musictravel.free.fr/political/politica137.htm (accessed 23 Jan. 2009).

———. "Much More Severe Problems on the Cruise Missile Left," *ZNet*, 9 Dec. 2002. At http://www.zmag.org/content/showarticle.cfm?ItemID=2722 (accessed 27 Jun. 2007).

Herman, Edward S., and Noam Chomsky. *Manufacturing Consent: The Political Economy of the Mass Media*. 2nd ed. New York: Pantheon, 2002.

Hersh, Seymour M. *Chain of Command: The Road from 9/11 to Abu Ghraib*. New York: HarperCollins, 2004.

Hitchens, Christopher. "Appointment in Samarra?" *Nation,* 30 Sept. 2002: 9. At http://www.thenation.com/doc/20020930/hitchens (accessed 27 Jan. 2008).

Hoffman, Peter J., and Thomas G. Weiss. *Sword and Salve: Confronting New Wars and Humanitarian Crises.* Lanham, Md.: Rowman and Littlefield, 2006.

Hoggart, Richard. *The Uses of Literacy.* London: Penguin, 1957.

Honig, Jan Willem, and Norbert Both, *Srebrenica: Record of a War Crime.* New York: Penguin, 1996.

Horkheimer, Max, and Theodor W. Adorno. *Dialectic of Enlightenment.* Trans. Edmund Jephcott. Stanford: Stanford University Press, 2002.

Horowitz, David. *Unholy Alliance: Radical Islam and the American Left.* Washington, D.C.: Regnery, 2004.

Horowitz, David, Daniel Lazare, and Michael Medved. "The Left Revealed." *FrontPage Magazine,* 4 Jul. 2005. Transcript of *Michael Medved Show* of 13 Dec. 2004. At http://www.frontpagemag.com/Articles/Read. aspx?GUID={87BFA507-74B3-4E81-A735-3F580FE7828B} (accessed 8 Aug. 2007).

Huband, Mark. "US Cruise Missile Attack May Have Upset a Shift at Heart of Sudan's Government." *Financial Times,* 8 Sept. 1998: 7.

Human Rights Watch World Report 1999: Events of December 1997–November 1998. New York: Human Rights Watch, 1998.

Hunter-Tilney, Ludovic. "The Preacher: Christopher Hitchens." *Financial Times,* 6 Jun. 2003. At http://search.ft.com/nonFtArticle?id=03060600390 (accessed 17 Jan. 2008).

Huntington, Samuel. *Who Are We? The Challenges to America's National Identity.* New York: Simon and Schuster, 2004.

Ignatieff, Michael. "Getting Iraq Wrong." *New York Times Magazine,* 5 Aug. 2007: 26–29.

———. *The Lesser Evil: Political Ethics in an Age of Terror.* Princeton: Princeton University Press, 2004.

Ingraham, Laura. *Power to the People.* Washington, D.C.: Regnery, 2007.

"Iraq: U.S. Military Items Exported or Transferred to Iraq in the 1980s." Letter Report of the U.S. General Accounting Office. 7 Feb. 1994. At http://www. fas.org/spp/starwars/gao/nsi94098.htm (accessed 9 Sept. 2007).

Jansen, Michael. "Denis Halliday: Iraq Sanctions Are Genocide." *Daily Star* (Lebanon), July 7, 2002. Reprinted by *CommonDreams.org.* At http://www. commondreams.org/views/070700-103.htm (accessed 23 Jan. 2009).

Jaschik, Scott. "British Professors Seek to Cut Ties to Israeli Scholars." *Inside Higher Ed,* 30 May 2006. At http://www.insidehighered.com/ news/2006/05/30/boycott (accessed 17 Nov. 2007).

———. "British Union Abandons Boycott." *Inside Higher Ed,* 27 May 2005. At http://insidehighered.com/news/2005/05/27/boycott (accessed 17 Nov. 2007).

Jenkins, Henry. *Fans, Bloggers, and Gamers: Media Consumers in a Digital Age.* New York: New York University Press, 2006.

————. *Textual Poachers: Television Fans and Participatory Culture.* New York: Routledge, 1992.

————. *The Wow Climax: Tracing the Emotional Impact of Popular Culture.* New York: New York University Press, 2006.

Jenkins, Simon. "America Should Not Squander Its Sympathy." *Times* (London), 14 Sept. 2001. *LexisNexis Academic* (Penn State Libraries). At http://www.lexisnexis.com.ezaccess.libraries.psu.edu/us/lnacademic/results/docview/docview.do?docLinkInd=true&risb=21_T5597582887&format=GNBFI&sort=RELEVANCE&startDocNo=1&resultsUrlKey=29_T5597582890&cisb=22_T5597582889&treeMax=true&treeWidth=0&csi=10939&docNo=2 (accessed 22 Jan. 2009).

Jensen, Robert. "Why Leftists Mistrust Liberals." *Counterpunch,* 27 Apr. 2006. At http://www.counterpunch.org/jensen04272006.html (accessed 24 Jun. 2007).

Jessop, Bob, Kevin Bonnett, Simon Bromley, and Tom Ling. "Authoritarian Populism, Two Nations, and Thatcherism." *New Left Review* 147 (1984): 33–60.

Johnson, Spencer. *Who Moved My Cheese? An Amazing Way to Deal with Change in Your Work and in Your Life.* New York: Putnam's, 1998.

Johnstone, Diana. *Fools' Crusade: Yugoslavia, NATO, and Western Delusions.* New York: Monthly Review, 2002.

Judah, Tim. *Kosovo: War and Revenge.* New Haven: Yale University Press, 2002.

"Kandahar 'No Go' for Aid Convoys." *BBC News,* 27 Dec. 2001. At http://news.bbc.co.uk/1/hi/world/south_asia/1730105.stm (accessed 26 Jun. 2007).

Kaufman, Marc. "Massive Food Delivery Averts Afghan Famine." *Washington Post,* 31 Dec. 2001: A1. At http://www.washingtonpost.com/ac2/wp-dyn/A42858-2001Dec30?launguage=printer (accessed 26 Jan. 2009).

Kazin, Michael. "A Patriotic Left." *Dissent* (Fall 2002): 41–44. At http://dissentmagazine.org/article/?article=560 (accessed 11 Jan. 2008).

Kelly, Michael. "Look Who's Playing Politics." *Washington Post,* 25 Sept. 2002: A27. Also available at the Jewish World Review website, http://www.jewishworldreview.com/michael/kelly092502.asp.

Kerrigan, William. "The Falls of Academe." In *Wild Orchids and Trotsky: Messages from American Universities,* ed. Mark Edmundson, 151–70. New York: Viking, 1993.

Kipnis, Laura. *Bound and Gagged: Pornography and the Politics of Fantasy in America.* New York: Grove, 1996.

Klein, Naomi. *No Logo: Taking Aim at the Brand Bullies.* New York: Picador, 2000.

————. *The Shock Doctrine: The Rise of Disaster Capitalism.* New York: Picador, 2008.

Kolhatkar, Sonali. "Superstars and Globalization: Interviewing Arundhati

Roy." *ZNet,* 31 Aug. 2004. At http://www.zmag.org/content/showarticle. cfm?ItemID=6136 (accessed 8 Aug. 2006).

Kushner, Tony, and Alisa Solomon, eds. *Wrestling with Zion: Progressive Jewish-American Responses to the Israeli-Palestine Conflict.* New York: Grove, 2003.

Laclau, Ernesto. *Politics and Ideology in Marxist Theory: Capitalism–Fascism–Populism.* London: Verso, 1977.

Laclau, Ernesto, and Chantal Mouffe. *Hegemony and Socialist Strategy: Towards a Radical Democratic Politics.* London: Verso, 1985.

Lee, Richard C. *Life and Times of Cultural Studies: The Politics and Transformation of the Structures of Knowledge.* Durham, N.C.: Duke University Press, 2003.

Lewis, Michael, and David Einhorn. "The End of the Financial World as We Know It." *New York Times,* 4 Jan. 2009: IV.9–10.

Lott, Eric. "After Identity, Politics: The Return of Universalism." *New Literary History* 31.4 (2000): 665–78.

———. *The Disappearing Liberal Intellectual.* New York: Basic, 2006.

Lowry, Rich. "Against Cruise Missiles." *National Review Online,* 12 Sept. 2001. At http://www.nationalreview.com/lowry/lowry091201.shtml (accessed 8 Feb. 2005).

Luttwak, Samuel. "Why Fascism Is the Wave of the Future." *London Review of Books,* 7 Apr. 1994: 3, 6.

Maass, Peter. *Love Thy Neighbor: A Story of War.* New York: Knopf, 1996.

Mahajan, Rahul. *Full Spectrum Dominance: U.S. Power in Iraq and Beyond.* New York: Seven Stories, 2003.

Makiya, Kanan. "How Did I Get Iraq Wrong?" *Slate,* 17 Mar. 2008. At http://www.slate.com/id/2186763/ (accessed 21 Jul. 2008).

Malcolm, Noel. *Kosovo: A Short History.* New York: New York University Press, 1998.

McCabe, Colin. "An Interview with Stuart Hall, December 2007." *Critical Quarterly* 50.1–2 (2008): 12–42.

McChesney, Robert. "Is There Any Hope for Cultural Studies?" *Monthly Review* 47.10 (1996): 1–18.

———. *The Problem of the Media: U.S. Communication Politics in the 21st Century.* New York: Monthly Review, 2004.

———. *Rich Media, Poor Democracy: Communication Politics in Dubious Times.* New York: New Press, 1999.

McGuigan, Jim. *Cultural Populism.* New York: Routledge, 1992.

McKelvey, Tara. "Interventionism's Last Hold-Out." *American Prospect,* 15 May 2007. At http://www.prospect.org/cs/articles?article=interventionisms_last_holdout (accessed 19 Dec. 2007).

McLemee, Scott. "Euston. . . . We Have a Problem." *Inside Higher Ed,* 24 May 2006. At http://www.insidehighered.com/views/2006/05/24/mclemee (accessed 23 Jan. 2009).

McRobbie, Angela. "Tony Blair and the Marxists," *openDemocracy*, 26 Mar. 2003. At http://www.opendemocracy.net/node/1093 (accessed 25 Jan. 2009).

Michaels, Walter Benn. *The Trouble with Diversity: How We Learned to Love Identity and Ignore Inequality*. New York: Metropolitan, 2006.

Military Commissions Act of 2006. At http://frwebgate.access.gpo.gov/cgi-bin/getdoc.cgi?dbname=109_cong_bills&docid=f:s3930enr.txt.pdf (accessed 19 May 2009).

Mills, Nicolaus, and Kira Brunner. *The New Killing Fields: Massacre and the Politics of Intervention*. New York: Basic, 2002.

"Mission Accomplished: A Look Back at the Media's Fawning Coverage of Bush's Premature Declaration of Victory in Iraq." *Media Matters*, 27 Apr. 2006. At http://mediamatters.org/items/200604270005 (accessed 23 Jan. 2009).

Model, David. *Lying for Empire: How to Commit War Crimes with a Straight Face*. Monroe, Maine: Common Courage, 2005.

Modleski, Tania. *Loving with a Vengeance: Mass-Produced Fantasies for Women*. New York: Methuen, 1984.

Monbiot, George. "A 9/11 Conspiracy Virus Is Sweeping the World, but It Has No Basis in Fact." *Guardian*, 6 Feb. 2007. At http://www.guardian.co.uk/commentisfree/2007/feb/06/comment.film (accessed 11 Jul. 2008).

———. "9/11 Fantasists Pose a Mortal Danger to Popular Oppositional Campaigns." *Guardian*, 20 Feb. 2007. At http://www.guardian.co.uk/commentisfree/story/0,,2017006,00.html (accessed 11 Jul. 2008).

Moore, Michael. *Dude, Where's My Country?* New York: Warner, 2003.

Morley, David. *The Nationwide Audience: Structure and Decoding*. London: British Film Institute, 1980.

Morley, David, and Kuan-Hsing Chen, eds. *Stuart Hall: Critical Dialogues in Cultural Studies*. New York: Routledge, 1996.

Morris, Meaghan. "Banality in Cultural Studies." In *Logics of Television: Essays in Cultural Criticism*, ed. Patricia Mellencamp, 14–43. London: British Film Institute, 1990.

Moten, Fred. "The New International of Decent Feelings." *Social Text* 20.3 (2002): 189–99.

Netherlands Institute for War Documentation. *Srebrenica, a "Safe" Area: Reconstruction, Background, Consequences and Analyses of the Fall of a Safe Area*. Amsterdam: NIOD, 2002. At http://srebrenica.brightside.nl/srebrenica.

"New Terror Law Comes into Force." *BBC News*, 13 Apr. 2006. At http://news.bbc.co.uk/1/hi/uk_politics/ 4905304.stm (accessed 31 Jul. 2006).

Norris, John. *Collision Course: NATO, Russia, and Kosovo*. Westport, Conn.: Greenwood, 2005.

Not in Our Name. "Statement of Conscience against War and Repression." At http://www.wagingpeace.org/articles/2002/09/00_not-in-our-name.htm (accessed 23 Jan. 2009).

"Notes from the Editors." *Monthly Review.* October 2007. At http://www.monthlyreview.org/nfte0907.htm (accessed 2 Jan. 2008).

Offman, Craig. "Said Critic Blasts Back at Hitchens." *Salon,* 10 Sept. 1999. At http://www.salon.com/books/log/1999/09/10/weiner/ (accessed 3 Jan. 2008).

O'Hehir, Andrew. "How the Democrats Lost the Heartland." Interview with Thomas Frank. *Salon,* 28 Jun. 2004. At http://dir.salon.com/story/books/int/2004/06/28/tomfranks (accessed 26 Jan. 2009).

O'Reilly, Bill. *Culture Warrior.* New York: Broadway, 2006.

Packer, George. *The Assassins' Gate: America in Iraq.* New York: Farrar Straus Giroux, 2005.

———. "The Liberal Quandary over Iraq." *New York Times Magazine,* 8 Dec. 2002: 104–07, 156. At http://query.nytimes.com/gst/fullpage.html?res=9403E5DF1F38F93BA35751C1A9649C8B63 (accessed 7 Jan. 2008).

Parekh Report. *The Future of Multi-Ethnic Britain.* London: Profile, 2000.

Pear, Robert. "U.S. Videos, for TV News, Come under Scrutiny." *New York Times,* 15 Mar. 2004: A1. At http://query.nytimes.com/gst/fullpage.html?res=9C07E2DF1631F936A25750C0A9629C8B63 (accessed 11 Jan. 2009).

Peck, Janice. "Why We Shouldn't Be Bored with the Political Economy versus Cultural Studies Debate." *Cultural Critique* 64 (2006): 92–126.

Penley, Constance. *NASA/Trek: Popular Science and Sex in America.* London: Verso, 1997.

Perkins, Dan [Tom Tomorrow]. "This Modern World." Cartoon of 22 Oct. 2001. At http://archive.salon.com/comics/tomo/2001/10/22/tomo/index.html (accessed 23 Jan. 2009).

Perlstein, Rick. *Before the Storm: Barry Goldwater and the Unmaking of the American Consensus.* New York: Hill and Wang, 2001.

Petras, James. *The Power of Israel in the United States.* Atlanta: Clarity, 2006.

Pfister, Joel. *Critique for What? Cultural Studies, American Studies, Left Studies.* Boulder: Paradigm, 2006.

Pollack, Kenneth M. *The Threatening Storm: The Case for Invading Iraq.* New York: Random House, 2002.

Postone, Moishe. "History and Helplessness: Mass Mobilization and Contemporary Forms of Anticapitalism." *Public Culture* 18.1 (2006): 93–110.

Poulantzas, Nicos. *Political Power and Social Classes.* London: Verso, 1973.

———. *State, Power, Socialism.* London: Verso, 1978.

Power, Samantha. "The Democrats and National Security." *New York Review of Books,* 14 Aug. 2008: 66, 68, 70–72. At http://www.nybooks.com/articles/21670 (accessed 25 Jan. 2009).

———. *"A Problem from Hell": America and the Age of Genocide.* New York: Harper Perennial, 2002.

Presidential Military Order of November 13, 2001. "Detention, Treatment, and

Trial of Certain Non-Citizens in the War against Terrorism." At http://www.fas.org/irp/offdocs/eo/mo-111301.htm (accessed 19 May 2009).

Project for the New American Century. Letter to President Clinton, 26 Jan. 1998. *Information Clearing House.* At http://www.informationclearinghouse.info/article5527.htm (accessed 23 Jan. 2009).

Proyect, Louis. "The Demonization and Death of Slobodan Milošević." *Swans Commentary,* 27 Mar. 2006. At http://www.swans.com/library/art12/lproy35.html (accessed 14 Jul. 2008).

Radway, Janice. *Reading the Romance: Women, Patriarchy, and Popular Literature.* 2nd ed. Chapel Hill: University of North Carolina Press, 1991.

Responsibility to Protect. "An Introduction to R2P." n.d. At http://www.responsibilitytoprotect.org/index.php/pages/2.

Rieff, David. *Slaughterhouse: Bosnia and the Failure of the West.* New York: Touchstone, 1996.

Robertson, Pat. Interview with Jerry Falwell. Transcript, 13 Sept 2001. *700 Club.* Available at http://www.commondreams.org/news2001/0917-03.htm (accessed 25 Jun. 2007).

Rohde, David. *Endgame: The Betrayal and Fall of Srebrenica, Europe's Worst Massacre Since World War II.* New York: Farrar Straus Giroux, 1997.

Rojek, Chris. "On a Rant by a Little Musketeer." *International Journal of Cultural Studies* 8.4 (2005): 486–503.

———. *Stuart Hall.* Cambridge, U.K.: Polity, 2003.

Rorty, Richard. *Achieving Our Country: Leftist Thought in Twentieth-Century America.* Cambridge: Harvard University Press, 1997.

Ross, Andrew. *No Respect: Intellectuals and Popular Culture.* London: Verso, 1989.

Roth, Kenneth. "Letter to Clinton Urges Sudan Factory Inspection." *Human Rights Watch,* 15 Sept. 1998. At http://web.archive.org/web/20080307022238/http://www.hrw.org/press98/sept/sudan915.htm (accessed 22 Jan. 2009).

———. "War in Iraq: Not a Humanitarian Intervention." *Human Rights Watch World Report 2004.* At http://www.hrw.org/wr2k4/3.htm (accessed 23 Jan. 2009).

Roy, Arundhati. "The Algebra of Infinite Justice." *Guardian,* 29 Sept. 2001. At http://www.guardian.co.uk/Archive/Article/0,4273,4266289,00.html (accessed 11 Jul. 2008).

———. "Tide? Or Ivory Snow? Public Power in the Age of Empire." *ZNet,* 24 Aug. 2004. At http://www.zmag.org/content/showarticle.cfm?ItemID=6087 (accessed 8 Aug. 2006).

Rozen, Laura. "Crying Wolf, or Doing Their Job?" *Salon,* 16 Nov. 2001. At http://dir.salon.com/story/news/feature/2001/11/16/aid/ (accessed 24 Jun. 2007).

Said, Edward. "Misinformation about Iraq." *Al-Ahram Weekly,* 28 Nov.–4 Dec.

2002. At http://weekly.ahram.org.eg/2002/614/op2.htm (accessed 23 Jan. 2009).

Savage, Charlie. *Takeover: The Return of the Imperial Presidency and the Subversion of American Democracy.* New York: Little, Brown, 2007.

Schell, Jonathan. "Letter from Ground Zero: Seven Million at Risk." *Nation,* 5 Nov. 2001: 8. At http://www.thenation.com/doc/20011105/schell (accessed 3 Jan. 2008).

Schlafly, Phyllis. "Cox Report Is a Real Whodunit." *Phyllis Schlafly Report,* July 1999. At http://www.eagleforum.org/psr/1999/july99/psrjuly99.html (accessed 29 Jun. 2007).

Schlesinger, Arthur M., Jr. *The Disuniting of America: Reflections on a Multicultural Society.* New York: Norton, 1992.

Schmemann, Serge. "What Would 'Victory' Mean?" *New York Times,* 16 Sept. 2001: IV.1.

Schroen, Gary. *First In: An Insider's Account of How the CIA Spearheaded the War on Terror in Afghanistan.* New York: Presidio, 2005.

Schwarz, Bill. "Review of Rojek, *Stuart Hall.*" *Cultural Studies* 19.2 (2005): 176–202.

Srebrenica Research Group. At http://www.srebrenica-report.com/. Also Srebrenica Group Members and Mission at http://www.srebrenica-report.com/people.htm.

Sells, Michael. *The Bridge Betrayed: Religion and Genocide in Bosnia.* Berkeley: University of California Press, 1998.

Silber, Laura, and Alan Little. *Yugoslavia: Death of a Nation.* New York: Penguin, 1996.

Sim, Joe. "Against the Punitive Wind: Stuart Hall, the State and the Lessons of the Great Moving Right Show." In *Without Guarantees: In Honour of Stuart Hall,* ed. Paul Gilroy, Lawrence Grossberg, and Angela McRobbie, 318–34. London: Verso, 2000.

Simms, Brendan. *Unfinest Hour: Britain and the Destruction of Bosnia.* London: Penguin, 2001.

Skocpol, Theda. *Boomerang: Clinton's Health Security Effort and the Turn against Government.* New York: Norton, 1997.

Sleeper, Jim. *Liberal Racism: How Fixating on Race Subverts the American Dream.* New York: Viking, 1997.

Smith, Craig S. "Europe's Muslims May Be Headed Where the Marxists Went Before." *New York Times,* 26 Dec. 2004: IV.1. At http://www.nytimes.com/2004/12/26/weekinreview/26smith.html?oref=login&pagewanted=all&position= (accessed 2 Jan. 2008).

Steel, Ronald. "Fight Fire with Fire." *New York Times Book Review,* 25 Jul. 2004: A13.

Steinberger, Michael. "Misoverestimated." *American Prospect,* 23 Mar. 2004. At http://www.prospect.org/cs/articles?article=misoverestimated_032304 (accessed 15 Jan. 2008).

Stephen, Andrew. Interview with Noam Chomsky. *New Statesman,* 19 Jun. 2006. At http://www.newstatesman.com/200606190028 (accessed 22 Jun. 2006).

Sudetic, Chuck. *Blood and Vengeance: One Family's Story of the War in Bosnia.* New York: Norton, 1998.

Suskind, Ron. *The One Percent Doctrine: Deep Inside America's Pursuit of Its Enemies Since 9/11.* New York: Simon and Schuster, 2006.

Talbott, Strobe. Foreword to John Norris, *Collision Course: NATO, Russia, and Kosovo.* Westport, Conn.: Greenwood, 2005.

Thakur, Ramesh. *The United Nations, Peace and Security: From Collective Security to the Responsibility to Protect.* Cambridge: Cambridge University Press, 2006.

Thompson, E. P. *The Making of the English Working Class.* New York: Vintage, 1963.

———. *The Poverty of Theory and Other Essays.* London: Merlin, 1978.

Timerman, Jacobo. *Prisoner without a Name, Cell without a Number.* New York: Knopf, 1981.

Tomasky, Michael. *Left for Dead: The Life, Death, and Possible Resurrection of Progressive Politics in America.* New York: Free Press, 1996.

Toppo, Greg. "Education Dept. Paid Commentator to Promote Law." *USA Today,* 7 Jan. 2005. At http://www.usatoday.com/news/washington/2005-01-06-williams-whitehouse_x.htm (accessed 11 Jan. 2009).

Tostensen, Arne, and Beate Bull. "Are Smart Sanctions Feasible?" *World Politics* 54.3 (2002): 373–403.

Walzer, Michael. *Spheres of Justice: A Defense of Pluralism and Equality.* New York: Basic, 1983.

Warren, Catherine A., and Mary Douglas Vavrus, eds. *American Cultural Studies.* Urbana: University of Illinois Press, 2002.

Watkins, Susan. "Vichy on the Tigris." *New Left Review* 28 (2004): 5–17.

Watson, Raymond. "Reclaiming the Muslim Empire." *Quadrant* 48.7 (2004). *BNet.* At http://findarticles.com/p/articles/mi_hb6459/is_7-8_48/ai_n29105638/pg_1?tag=artBody;c011 (accessed 23 Jan. 2009).

Weinberg, Bill. "Z Magazine Supports Genocide." *World War 4 Report,* 10 Jul. 2005. At http://ww4report.com/node/757 (accessed 22 Jun. 2006).

Weiner, Justin Reid. "'My Beautiful Old House' and Other Fabrications by Edward Said." *Commentary* 108 (Sept. 1999): 23–31.

Weiner, Tim. "Now, the Battle to Feed the Afghan Nation." *New York Times,* 16 Nov. 2001: A1, B6–B7.

Weisberg, Jacob. "Dead with Ned: Why Lamont's Victory Spells Democratic Disaster." *Slate,* 9 Aug. 2006. At http://www.slate.com/id/2147395/nav/tap1/ (accessed 23 May 2008).

Weiss, Thomas G. *Military-Civilian Interactions: Humanitarian Crises and the Responsibility to Protect*. Lanham, Md.: Rowman and Littlefield, 2005.

Wible, Scott. "On Chomsky's 9–11." *Politics and Culture* 4 (2002). At http://aspen. conncoll.edu/politicsandculture/page.cfm?key=195 (accessed 4 Aug. 2007).

Williams, Ian. "More Agitprop Than Reasoned Argument." *Bosnia Report* 17/18 (2000). At http://www.bosnia.org.uk/bosrep/julsept00/too.cfm (accessed 12 Jul. 2007).

Williams, Linda. *Hard Core: Power, Pleasure, and the "Frenzy of the Visible."* Berkeley: University of California Press, 1989.

Williams, Raymond. *Culture and Society: 1780–1950*. New York: Columbia University Press, 1983. (Originally published 1958.)

———. *The Long Revolution*. London: Penguin, 1961.

Williamson, Judith. "The Problems of Being Popular." *New Socialist*, Sept. 1986: 14–15.

Willis, Ellen. "Bringing the Holy War Home." *Nation*, 17 Dec. 2001. At http://www.thenation.com/doc/20011217/willis (accessed 22 Jan. 2009).

———. *Don't Think, Smile! Notes on a Decade of Denial*. Boston: Beacon, 1999.

———. "Escape from Freedom: What's the Matter with Tom Frank (and the Lefties Who Love Him)?" *Situations* 1.2 (2006): 5–20.

———. "Is There Still a Jewish Question? Why I'm an Anti-Anti-Zionist." In *Wrestling with Zion: Progressive Jewish-American Responses to the Israeli-Palestine Conflict*, ed. Tony Kushner and Alisa Solomon, 226–32. New York: Grove, 2003.

———. "Why I'm Not for Peace." *Radical Society* (April 2002): 13–19. At http://journalism.nyu.edu/faculty/files/willis01.pdf (accessed 25 Jan. 2009).

Willis, Paul. *Learning to Labor: How Working-Class Kids Get Working-Class Jobs*. New York: Columbia University Press, 1977.

Windschuttle, Keith. *The Killing of History: How Literary Critics and Social Theorists Are Murdering Our Past*. New York: Free Press, 1997.

Wright, Lawrence. *The Looming Tower: Al-Qaeda and the Road to 9/11*. New York: Knopf, 2006.

Yglesias, Matthew. *Heads in the Sand: How the Republicans Screw Up Foreign Policy and Foreign Policy Screws Up the Democrats*. Hoboken, N.J.: Wiley, 2008.

Zinn, Howard. *You Can't Be Neutral on a Moving Train: A Personal History of Our Times*. New York: Beacon, 2002. Documentary directed by Deb Ellis, Denis Mueller, 2004.

Žižek, Slavoj. *Did Somebody Say Totalitarianism? Five Interventions in the (Mis)use of a Notion*. London: Verso, 2001.

INDEX

9/11: al-Qaeda responsibility, 2; al-Shifa
bombing (1998) compared to, 48–54,
56–57, 245, 260n7; Bush-Cheney
administration's response, 2, 43, 54,
68, 70, 71, 74–75, 97, 101; Cheney
on, Dick, 255n2; Chomsky on, Noam,
43, 49, 54, 60, 70, 71–73, 74–75, 85,
88, 196; conspiracy theories of, 33;
as deserved, 88–89; Euro-American
unity following, 71–73; hard right's
response, 89–91; as international crime,
153–155; international support for
retaliation following, 100–101; Iraq
war as retaliation for, 43, 149; Jewish
responsibility for, alleged, 54; legal status
of attacks and attackers, 264n5; mining
of Nicaraguan harbors compared to, 70;
Muslim response, 155–156; Mylroie on,
Laurie, 255n2; NATO's response, 71–72;
"one percent doctrine" about, 5; police
work as response, 60–61, 154–155; as a
response to American policies, 15–16,
157–158; Saddam Hussein's connection
to, 5, 12, 33, 255n2; Schmemann on,
Serge, 69; Scholars for 9/11 Truth, 33;
victims of, 49; Willis on, Ellen, 157–158
9/11 Commission, 34
9-11 (Chomsky), 56–57, 73–74

Aaronovitch, David, 146
abolitionists, analogy to, 246–247
Abu Ghraib, 88, 245
Abu-Jamal, Mumia, 130

Abu Nidal, 199
academic left, 7, 14, 213–214, 217
Achieving Our Country (Rorty), 91, 99,
214–215, 217–218
ACLU (American Civil Liberties Union), 90
Act Now to Stop War and End Racism
(ANSWER), 34, 130–131, 140
active audience thesis, 220–221, 238, 241
Adelman, Kenneth, 133–134
Adorno, Theodor, 286n6
Afary, Janet, 2
Afghanistan: al-Qaeda training camps,
attacks on, 27; Albert on, Michael,
26–27, 82; Arab Afghans in, 64–65;
bombing of, potential deaths from,
26–27, 77, 82; cease-fires, 78; Chomsky
on, Noam, 43, 57, 64–65, 70–71,
75–81, 82, 263n15; CIA, 63–65, 260n9;
Cockburn on, Alexander, 261n10; food
convoys to, American interruption of
(2001), 43, 70–71, 75–81, 263n15; Iraq
war, diversion of funds and troops to,
102; mujahedeen, American support for,
63–65, 260n9, 264n3; nation-building
in, 101; Northern Alliance, cease fire
observed by, 78; Northern Alliance
as surrogates for Americans, 156;
Operation Anaconda, 98, 264n2; "silent
genocide" in, 76, 78–81, 100, 245; Soviet
invasion of, 7, 30, 63–64, 97; Taliban in
(*see* Taliban); Tora Bora, attack on, 98;
U. S. war in, 7, 11, 26–27, 97–101, 102,
154–155, 156–156

ABOUT THE AUTHOR

MICHAEL BÉRUBÉ is Paterno Family Professor in Literature at Penn State University. He is the editor of the NYU Press Cultural Front series, and author or editor of numerous books, including *Life As We Know It: A Father, a Family, and an Exceptional Child; What's Liberal about the Liberal Arts? Classroom Politics and "Bias" in Higher Education; Rhetorical Occasions: Essays on Humans and the Humanities;* and, from NYU Press, *The Employment of English: Theory, Jobs, and the Future of Literary Studies.*